ENCYCLOPEDIA OF
FISH

ENCYCLOPEDIA OF
FISH

Maurice and Robert Burton

Introduction by
Dr Gareth Nelson
Department of Ichthyology
American Museum of Natural History

octopus
in association with
Phoebus

Introduction

We think of a fish as an animal that lives in water, breathes with gills, and swims with fins—in contrast to a tetrapod (an amphibian, reptile, bird or mammal) which lives on land, breathes with lungs, and moves about with arms and legs. There are more than 20 000 different species of fishes alive today —as many different kinds of fishes as there are of amphibians, reptiles, birds and mammals combined. To a zoologist, however, fishes are backboned animals, or vertebrates, of two basic sorts: those with cartilaginous skeleton, without lungs, and with males having pelvic fins modified as claspers for reproductive purposes—the Chondrichthyes which include rays and sharks of which there are some 500 species alive today; and those

with a bony skeleton but with males lacking claspers—the Osteichthyes, the other fishes. The bony fishes are further subdivided into two sorts: those with fleshy fins that sometimes are modified as arms and legs, like the bichirs,—the Sarcopterygii; and the fishes with rayed fins—the Actinopterygii.

In fact, snakes, woodpeckers, squirrels and man are really only much modified bony fishes that during millions of years of evolution have become adapted to a life on land. Indications of the evolution can be seen in the embryonic development. In mammals such as man, gill-like structures form in the early embryo, which in its structural organisation is very similar to the embryos of bony fishes and of other backboned animals.

This encyclopedia, however, is about the fishes we know today: cartilaginous fishes— the rays and sharks; the fleshy finned fishes

such as the bichir; and the ray-finned fishes. This last group includes the fishes familiar to anyone—the angler, the commercial fisherman, the shopper in the market, or the aquarist. Ray-finned fishes are divided into three groups. The first of these includes sturgeons and paddlefishes (Chondrostei), which comprise about 24 species of the northern hemisphere freshwaters; the second includes the single species of bowfin and 7 species of gars of the North American freshwaters (Holostei); the third group (Teleosti) includes all of the others and of them it is said that where there is water there are fishes (and where there are fishes they can be caught). They are the dominant aquatic vertebrates and have been so since Jurassic times, beginning more than 120 million years ago. Where there is permanent water, there are almost always teleosts living

First published 1975 by
Octopus Books Limited
59 Grosvenor St, London W1

© 1968/69/70 BPC Publishing Ltd
© this compilation 1975 BPC Publishing Ltd

ISBN 0 7064 0393 2

This book is adapted from 'Purnell's Encyclopedia of Animal Life', published in the United States under the title of 'International Wild Life'. It has been produced by Phoebus Publishing Company in cooperation with Octopus Books Limited.

Distributed in USA by
Crescent Books

a division of Crown Publishers Inc.,
419 Park Avenue South
New York, N.Y. 10016

Produced by Mandarin Publishers Limited
22 Westlands Road, Quarry Bay, Hong Kong

Printed in Hong Kong

in it, whether it is warm or cold, shallow or deep, rich or poor in oxygen, light, or food resources. Some, such as a few of the eels, migrate overland and invade temporary freshwater habitats. Others spawn eggs which survive the seasonal drying of certain tropical areas, and hatch when the rains of the wet season come again to fill the small pools. There these fishes live the active phase of their life cycle, and die within the year. They are called annuals and some of the top minnows live in this way.

There are so many teleosts that they have been divided into four major groups; first, the bony tongues (Osteoglossomorpha), with over 100 species including the arapaimas, which occur mainly in the freshwaters of South America, Africa, India, southeast Asia and Australia, a geographical distribution suggesting that these areas once were united in one landmass, Gondwanaland; secondly, the eels (Elopomorpha), which are mainly marine fishes; their best known members are the true eels, of which there are several hundred species that abound parti-

cularly in coral-reef areas such as the Hawaiian Islands; thirdly, the herrings (Clupeomorpha, named after the herring, *Clupea*), number about 300 species; they are also mainly marine fishes such as sardines and anchovies. A few of them have supplied food to man, and those few are of great economic importance. Lastly, the fourth group, the Euteleostei, is the largest group of all and includes all the other bony fishes and has itself been divided into four groups. They include most of the fishes to be found in aquariums or nibbling at a hook—characins, catfish, cod and salmon among them.

Each fish species has a particular habitat which provides the conditions of life appropriate to its survival, such as mountain streams—for trouts, lakes—pikes, ocean beaches—flounders, or the high seas—tunas. Most species are restricted either to fresh or to saltwater and quickly die if transferred from one to the other. Freshwater fishes generally are very different in different continents; North America is characterised by its numerous minnows, South America by its characins, Eurasia by carp-like fish, Africa by cichlids and Australia by its stinging catfishes. Marine fishes tend to be

modified as a suctioncup-like device used to attach to larger fishes (sharks, tunas, sail-fishes) so as to hitch a ride. In gobies and lumpsuckers, the paired pelvic fins on the ventral surface are modified as suctioncup devices used to attach to rocks, usually in water swirling with strong currents. Angler-fishes have the front part of the dorsal fin on top of the head, but forward near the jaws, modified as a fishing pole and lure, which in the deep-sea species glows with its own light. Stonefishes, some catfishes and stingrays all have venom glands associated with fin spines which, when trodden on or handled by humans, can inflict fatal wounds. In the molly and guppy the anal fin of the male is modified for the transfer of sperm into the reproductive tract of the female—an act all the more remarkable for its splitsecond brevity. The skeletons of mammals are comparatively simple.

Man prides himself on his intelligence, but its significance is adaptive, enabling him to see himself and, hopefully, to survive in a world from which he might otherwise perish. As a feature of adaptation, his intelligence is neither better nor worse, biologically, than the successful adaptations of other living creatures. Of course, there are no fishes which are as perceptive as man; but in water, on the other hand, no man is a match even for an average fish.

The fishes most remarkable for their perception are, perhaps, the salmons, which are able to navigate thousands of miles through the open ocean, so as to return to spawn in the small upland streams where they hatched from eggs years before, and soon after drifted downstream to the ocean, where they grew into adulthood It is be-lieved that they use celestial navigation to achieve this feat. Also interesting in this respect are the electric eels of South America. These are generally nocturnal species, and many of them live in muddy rivers where eyes would be nearly useless. To know where they are and navigate, and even to com-municate among themselves, these fishes produce electric pulses—which provide them with, in effect, a built-in 'radar' system.

All fishes have a sensory system in their skin, still very poorly understood, called the lateral line. Modified lateral-line organs, for example, are the receivers of the 'radar' system of electric eels. Lateral-line organs are similar to those of the internal ear, which is the only part of the fish system retained by man and other tetrapods, but out of water, the fishes' system cannot function. It is said that man will never understand the fish because he cannot experience the world as the fish does, and the reason for this is that he lacks a lateral line. Perhaps so. But for man, the fish has a special fascination that begins early in life, and that prompts man to seek further understanding. May this book help you along your way.

more widely distributed, and the tropical marine fauna is similar throughout the world, although it is richest in the coral-reef areas of the Indo-Australian region.

Mankind has changed the native ranges of many freshwater species either by chang-ing the physical environment—cutting forests, draining swamps, damming rivers, or by introducing foreign species such as carp and goldfish (originally from Asia), rainbow trout (from western North Ameri-ca), or *Tilapia* (from Africa). The wisdom of introducing foreign species is questionable, for they are generally destructive to the native fish communities, though they may have some temporary appeal for sport or commercial fishermen. So far there have been very few freshwater fishes that have been exterminated, but the number will doubtless increase in the future unless the native fishes and their habitats are carefully

protected. Fortunately marine fishes are not easily introduced, and except for the effects of local pollution and the overfishing of certain species, the native communities of marine fishes have so far been relatively resistant to the destruction caused by man's increased interference.

Man may be tempted to think of fishes as undeveloped or primitive creatures, yet in certain ways modern fishes are more com-plex—even, some scientists consider, more evolutionarily advanced—than man. Their skeleton is generally more completely de-veloped, particularly the dermal skeleton —the jaws, the head bones, scales, finrays and spines. The fins of fishes have become modified for example, in ways other than turning them into the arms and legs of the lineage that invaded the land and became the tetrapods. In remoras or sharksuckers, part of the dorsal fin on top of the head is

Anchovy

The name of several out of nearly 100 species related to herrings. Members of the anchovy family are similar to herrings, except that they are mainly smaller, their maximum size being 8 in.

The anchovy familiar to Europeans is the small fish (*Engraulis encrasicolus*) that is canned or converted to anchovy paste. To Americans the anchovy is a very similar fish, of a different species, the northern anchovy (*Engraulis mordax*), ranging from British Columbia to Lower California, used in quantities as live-bait. A similar fish, called anchoveta (*Engraulis ringens*), represents for the Peruvians a sea-harvest that brought about an economic revolution. Anchovies elsewhere in the world are also fished commercially.

Vast shoals

Anchovies are most abundant in tropical seas but large numbers also live in the shallow parts of temperate seas, in bays and estuaries. Some species live even in brackish or fresh waters. They are one of the most numerous, if not the most numerous of marine fishes, the herring not excluded, and like the herring, they live in large shoals. Within the smaller shoals the large individuals tend to be below, the smaller individuals above, so light is allowed to filter through the whole shoal. This is probably important for shoaling behaviour. It has been noted in aquaria that a fish will swim towards another of similar size and appearance but of a different species, then sheer away when about a foot from it, as if it had discovered its mistake.

With larger shoals the formation is somewhat different. The anchovies separate out in sizes, and it is believed that the larger individuals drive away the smaller, which shoal on their own. This characteristic shoaling behaviour of the anchovy makes it especially valuable for canning—the catch does not need to be sorted out for size.

Plankton feeders

Like the herring, the anchovy is a plankton-feeder. But whereas herrings will select certain animals in the plankton, picking them up one at a time, the anchovy swims forward with its mouth open, taking in small plankton more or less indiscriminately.

The behaviour of the shoals is determined by the feeding method. If a shoal of anchovies swam straight forward those in front would capture the food, those in the rear would go hungry. Instead, the leading individuals turn to either side and return to the rear of the shoal. So each gets its turn to feed. One result of this is that the shoal assumes the shape of a tear-drop. When plankton is dense, however, the leading individuals fan out and the shoal assumes an oval shape, with its long axis at right angles to the line of advance.

The depth at which the shoals swim depends on the movements of plankton, which migrates to the surface by day and sinks down again at night.

△△ *Of the 7 million tons of fish harvested by Peru each year, much consists of these tiny fish whose maximum size is only 8 in. Anchovies are typified by a rounded snout and large jaw set far back.*
△ *Thousands of anchovies make a shoal which keeps together by hearing water rushing over their bodies. A well spread out shoal will suddenly contract into a writhing sphere of fish when threatened.*

Breeding

The shoals of adult European anchovies frequent the Bay of Biscay and the Mediterranean but migrate through the English Channel in spring to spawn. Their spawning ground was the Zuyder Zee, until this was reclaimed. Now it is the Elbe estuary. The eggs are oval and float at the surface, hatching 2—4 days after fertilisation.

Reaction to enemies

The main enemy is the tuna. The reaction of the anchovies to its presence is to clump. A shoal may be spread out, several hundreds across. At the approach of a tuna the shoal contracts to form a living, writhing sphere of thousands of fishes, a few feet across. Those with the least well developed shoaling instinct, which remain on the fringes of the frightened group, will be eaten by the tuna. Laboratory tests suggest that in any shoal there are a few individuals that panic less readily than the rest. In an alarm situation these 'stand their ground' and the rest congregate around them. The anchovies detect tuna by the sound of the larger fish moving through the water.

New industry

Most fisheries have a history stretching back into the distant past, but one important fishery is less than two decades old. The plankton-rich Humboldt Current supports multitudes of fish, mainly silvery anchovetas 3—6 in. long. These have been the food of sea-birds that rest on the islands off the coast, whose cliffs became covered with deep layers of guano. Thousands of tons of this rich fertiliser were gathered every year, such a rich harvest that the birds responsible were protected by government. Furthermore, great shoals of these small fishes were caught to supply the fish markets.

In the early 1950's it was argued that birds must digest 20 tons of anchovetas to produce 1 ton of guano. The same amount of fish could be machine-ground to produce 4 tons of fish-meal. Blended with soya-bean meal it could be exported for pig and poultry feed. As a result a new fishing industry sprang up. Since 1955 the populations of Peru's ports have been quadrupled by people moving in to work there, a fleet of 1,500 fishing boats is at work supplying 140 factories, and Peru exports annually fish products worth millions of dollars. To conserve this harvest a Marine Resources Institute has been established at Callao. The anchoveta has made Peru the world's leading fishing nation, but it is a fragile economy, for, as in 1972, changes in the ocean current system result in poor catches. Meanwhile, the sea-birds that once produced the guano eldorado are in poor shape, perhaps because so much of their food supply is being taken away from them.

class	**Pisces**
order	**Clupeiformes**
family	**Engraulidae**
genus & species	*Engraulis encrasicolus* *E. mordax.* *E. ringens* *and others*

Marine angelfish, **Holacanthus** *, living among the coral reefs of tropical seas, outstanding for its varied patterns and colours.*

Angelfish

The name 'angelfish' has been used commonly for two types of fishes. Both of these types are bony fishes, one of which is marine, the other freshwater. The latter has long been a favourite with aquarists who, perhaps to avoid confusion of names, developed the habit of using its scientific name, **Scalare** *(see page 188). Since not everyone followed their example, however, at least part of the confusion remains. There is another perplexing usage. Some scientists 'lump' the marine angelfishes into the butterfly fish family (see page 41), but the butterfly fish is only distantly related to them and belongs to an entirely separate family.*

There is little to choose between these angelfishes and butterfly fishes. Most are brilliantly coloured, mainly coral-reef dwelling fishes; the angelfishes, however, have a sharp spine on the lower edge of the gill-cover which is lacking in the butterfly fishes.

It hardly needs explaining that these vernacular names are prompted by the enlarged flap-like or wing-like fins.

Most angelfish are small, up to 8 in. long, but the marine ones reach 2 ft in length. The outline of the body, because of the well-developed fins, has much the shape of a flint arrowhead.

Colourful and curious

The marine angelfishes, and the similar butterfly fishes, which together number more than 150 species, live mainly in shallow seas and a few enter estuaries. They live in pairs or small groups at most, around reefs, rocks or corals.

They are inoffensive as adults, they are peaceable, they do not dash away as most fishes do when, for example, a skin diver intrudes into their living space. They move away but slowly, every now and then tilting the body to take a closer look at the newcomer.

The outstanding feature of these fishes is the wide range and the beauty of their colours and patterns. In many of them the young fishes have the same colours as the adults, but in others the differences are so great that it looks as if there are two different species involved. Their behaviour tends to be different also. Quite small —that is, up to a few inches long—they tend to be solitary, and individuals are usually found in the same places day after day, in each case near a shelter into which the fish darts when disturbed. The shelter may be under a rock bed or among seaweed. A tin can lying on the sea-bed will readily be used for shelter. In an aquarium the sub-adults will be aggressive towards each other, but one kept on its own readily becomes tame and learns to feed from the hand.

Probably the most beautiful of the angels is the rock beauty, coloured jet black in front and yellow in its rear half, its fins bright yellow with red spots. It has a strong sense of curiosity that makes it draw near to the underwater swimmer. The queen angelfish, when small, is largely dark brown to black with three bluish vertical bands on the sides of the body and a bluish band along the dorsal fin. Adult, it is mainly a startlingly bright yellow with irregular and diffuse patches of violet or red on various parts of the body. The French angel

is black with strongly contrasting bright yellow vertical bands and a yellow face (see illustration page 14).

Feeding

Angelfishes have small mouths armed with many small teeth and they use these when they browse on the algae and coral polyps or catch the small invertebrates on which they feed. In some species the snout is somewhat elongate, and may be inserted in cracks and crevices in rocks or coral to capture small animals for food.

In certain species of butterfly fishes, such as *Chelmon rostratus*, the snout is very long and tube-like with the small mouth at the end. This enables the fishes to probe even deeper into the crevices of coral rock for their food.

Parental care

Little is known of the breeding habits of marine angelfish, but they probably conform to the pattern of their better known relations in that they show quite close care of the eggs and fry.

Both fish clean a patch of flat rock, and the female lays her eggs on it, the male swimming close over them shedding sperm for fertilisation. The eggs are tended for 4–8 days by the parents, when the fry hatch, and sink to the bottom.

The parents guard them until they are sufficiently free-swimming to hide in crevices and weed. The fry are unlike the adults in that their bodies are long and slim. They do not not assume full adult shape before three or four months have passed.

Conspicuous colouring

All angelfishes and butterfly fishes are conspicuous. To the underwater swimmer

△ *Angelfish are strongly territorial and use their colours both to advertise possession of their territory and to warn off an intruder of their own species. One of these freshwater* **Scalare** *is displaying at the other with a sideways flick of its bright pectoral fins like flashing signals.*
▽ *These freshwater angelfish,* **Scalare***, are favourites with aquarists, being easy to care for and attractive to look at.*

their colours stand out and 'hit the eye'. Especially striking are the patterns of the imperial angelfish or blue angelfish, with their inscribed patterns of white and black curves and half circles on a rich blue and violet background, dazzling to the eye when seen at close quarters.

We are used to the idea of colours and colour-patterns serving as camouflage to hide an animal from its enemies or enable it, if a predatory animal, to steal close to its prey undetected. We are used also to conspicuous colours, especially combinations of yellow, black and red, serving as warning colours, the wearer of these colours being poisonous or bad-tasting or having a sting. The colours of angelfishes certainly fail to hide their wearer. Although one writer has described angelfishes as nestling among coral heads like hummingbirds among brilliant blossoms, most underwater swimmers agree you can see these fishes clearly at a distance. There is no indication that angelfishes are poisonous or unpalatable, or have a sting. They are eaten by the local peoples wherever they occur, although their skins are said to be tough.

Perhaps the comparison with hummingbirds is not so far-fetched as it appears at first sight. Conspicuous colours in birds are associated with displays, especially aggressive displays, as they are in lizards such as the anole and the same may be true of angelfishes. Experimentally, a mirror was placed in an aquarium with a French angelfish. The fish drew near, nibbled at its reflection in the mirror, then threw itself sideways and flicked its bright blue pectoral fins like flashing signals. This suggests that angelfishes are strongly territorial and use their colours both to advertise possession of a territory as well as to warn off an intruder of their own species.

There was at least one angelfish that escaped attention for a long time despite its colouring, a bright orange head with a glowing dark blue contrasting body. This, the pygmy angelfish, was wholly unknown until 1908, when one was brought up in the trawl off Bermuda from a depth of 540 ft. It was dead when it reached the surface and its carcase was committed to a jar of alcohol to preserve it. It became something of a mystery fish and it was not until 1951 that it was given a scientific name, when one scientist examining it realized it was a new species of angelfish. The next year a second specimen was taken from the stomach of a larger fish, a snapper, caught in 240 ft of water off Mexico. In 1959, this fish, believed to be so rare, was caught in fair numbers by a skin-diver off the Bahamas, in 40 ft of water.

◁ *Marine French angelfish,* Pomacanthus paru, *showing one of the bizarre shapes and patterns typical of these fish, which look quite different when they are seen either from the side or from the front view.*

class	**Pisces**
order	**Perciformes**
family	**Chaetodontidae**

Anglerfishes

There are more than 350 species of anglerfish, the Pediculati, but because of the distinct differences between them it is convenient to consider them as two groups: angler-fishes (225 + species) and deep-sea anglers (125 species). All have developed the characteristic habits of anglers: they keep still most of the time, using a rod and line to catch small fishes. The rod of the angler-fish is a modified spiny ray of the dorsal fin. Habitual immobility means little expenditure of energy, and less need for breathing. This is reflected in the small gills of anglerfishes with only a small gill-opening.

'Pediculati', the old name for anglerfishes, means 'small foot', referring to the elbowed pectoral fins used like feet to move over the seabed in short jumps. The pelvic fins are also somewhat foot-like but they are small, usually hidden on the undersurface in advance of the pectoral fins. Because of their squat shape, bottom-living habits and method of locomotion the angler-fishes have been given a variety of des-criptive vernacular names: goosefishes or monkfishes, frogfishes or fishing frogs (because of the wide mouth) and batfishes. One of the best-known is **Lophius piscatorius,** *up to 4 ft long with a large head, about 2½ ft across, and a wide mouth. Although the fish is so ugly the flesh is highly palatable and is widely used as fried fish.*

Camouflaged and immobile

Anglerfishes of one kind or another are found at all depths throughout tropical and temperate seas. Bottom-living for the most part, their bodies are ornamented with a variety of warts and irregularities, as well as small flaps of skin. These, with their usually drab colours arranged in a broken pattern, serve to camouflage the fish as it lies immobile among rocks and seaweed. The sargassum angler specializes more than most anglerfishes in camouflage. It lives exclusively among the weed of the Sargasso Sea, and uses its pectoral fins to grasp the weed, so that it is not easily shaken from its position.

Angling for food

The general method of feeding is to attract small fishes near the mouth with some form of lure. In the goosefishes or monkfishes this is a 'fishing rod' bearing a fleshy flap at its tip, which is waved slowly back and forth near the mouth. In others the rod lies hidden, folded back in a groove, or lying in a tube, and is periodically raised or pushed out and waved two or three times before being withdrawn. The lure at the end of the rod often is red and worm-like in shape. A small fish seeing it swims near and then suddenly disappears!

Breeding

Several deep-sea species of anglerfish show a peculiar relationship between male and

Anglerfish's body is camouflaged by flaps of skin resembling surrounding seaweeds.

female; the dwarf male, about ½in. long, attaches itself to the female (whose length is up to 45 in.) so securely that the two grow together, even sharing a blood system. The female is then, in effect, a self-fertilising hermaphrodite, the male being reduced to a mere sperm-producing organ.

Another outstanding feature of the breed-ing cycle of some anglerfishes is the size of the egg-masses. The female goosefish or monkfish lays eggs in a jelly-like mass, up to 40 ft long and 2 ft in width. This floats at the surface. The relatively large pear-shaped eggs are attached by the narrow end to a sheet of spawn, which floats at the surface, and may contain nearly 1½ million of them.

The larva, even before it leaves the egg, begins to develop black pigment. Seen from above the spawn appears as a dark patch in the water, the enclosed larvae looking like currants in a cake. One of these masses, seen by rowers in a boat off Scapa Flow, was mistaken for a sea-monster and the rowers pulled away from it for dear life! The larva is in an advanced stage when hatched and already has the beginnings of its fishing rod. Later, other spines develop on the back and branched fins grow down from the throat, so the larva looks very unusual.

The compleat angler

It.is an interesting pastime to list how many human inventions have been anticipated in the animal kingdom. Anglerfishes have used a rod and line (or a lure) long before man did. It is not surprising that both human and fish anglers should use similar methods because their aims are identical. But although attention is always drawn to this by writers on the subject, nobody seems to have commented on the other piece of apparatus the two have in common: the landing net. Both kinds of anglers play their fish but the anglerfish does not allow his quarry to take the bait. Instead, the lure is waved until a fish draws near, then it is lowered towards the mouth. As the victim closes in on it the rod and its lure is suddenly whipped away, the huge mouth is opened wide, water rushes into this capacious 'landing net' and the prey is sucked in, after which the mouth snaps shut. And it all takes place in a flash. Only when a fish is large, so that the tail protrudes

Small fishes attracted to the anglerfish's mouth by a lure are snapped up. (⅓ natural size.)

from the mouth after the first bite, can we see what has happened. The anglerfish's ability to snap up its prey like lightning is quite remarkable. One moment the small fish is there near its mouth, the next moment it is no longer there, and the speed with which the anglerfish moves its jaws is too fast for the human eye to follow.

The batfishes take their angling to even greater lengths. The whiskery batfish, of the Caribbean, for example, is covered with outgrowths of skin that look exactly like small seaweeds and polyps known as sea-fire, that coat rocks like so much moss. Small fishes are deceived to the point where they will swim near and try to nibble the flaps of skin. The final touch to this master-piece of deception lies in the batfish habit of gently rocking its body, making the flaps of skin sway from side to side, just as polyps and seaweed gently sway as the slow currents in the sea move back and forth. This is so much an ingrained habit that a batfish, removed from its surroundings and placed in an aquarium, will period-ically rock itself even although it is sur-rounded only by clear water and glass.

When the small fish, deceived in this way, swims near, out comes the rod with its lure, looking like a wriggling worm. With this the batfish 'plays' its quarry. It will dangle the lure in front of the fish then withdraw it to entice the little fish nearer. It will vary the wriggling of the lure, now waggling it in an agitated manner, now moving it slowly. Watching this one gets the impres-sion of a fish 'playing cat-and-mouse' with a smaller fish until—'snap'—and only the larger fish can be seen, motionless, and with a dead-pan expression.

class	**Pisces**		
order	**Lophiiformes**		
families	**Lophiidae** *anglerfishes*		
	Antennariidae *frogfishes*		
	Ogcocephalidae *batfishes*		

Arapaima

The arapaima, said to be one of the largest freshwater fishes, is rather like a pike. It has a long cylindrical body, with the unpaired fins set well back towards the tail, a small flattened head, and a jutting lower jaw. The fish is coloured green in front but the rear half of the body becomes increasingly reddish, the tail being crimson. In Brazil it is known as the pirarucu, pirá meaning fish and urucú being the name of a bush in Brazil bearing flaming red seeds from which is made the annato dye, used for colouring cheese and butter. In Peru it is known as paiche. It also occurs in Guyana, and probably in Venezuela and Colombia.

Freshwater fishes are generally smaller than marine fishes, and only a few of them attain giant size. The arapaima is one of the larger ones and is said to reach nearly 15 ft in length and 440 lb in weight, but usually it is 7—8 ft long. The family to which it belongs is characterised by stout, bony scales each containing canals that form a mosaic-like pattern. Rings on the scales indicate age. The arapaima matures at 4 to 5 years and can live 18 years or more.

The arapaima is placed in the family Osteoglossidae or bony tongues, fishes with a lineage that can be traced back over 100 million years. So the arapaima is a living fossil, and some of its more primitive features are the bony head, peculiar shape of the fins, lobe-like tail and the lung-like air-bladder.

△ A gigantic arapaima about to grab a tasty fish. The operculum which covers the gills has been raised so the gill arches are visible. The rings on the large scales indicate the fish's age. A lifespan of over 18 years is not unknown.

▷ The arapaima can grow to over 5 ft in length in 5 years from birth. Certain features, such as the head, the shape of the fins, the lobe-like tail and the lung-like swimbladder, indicate its primitiveness. Its family can be traced back over 100 million years.

Air breathing

The arapaima keeps to shallow water where it moves about lethargically, periodically rising to the surface to gulp air into the swim-bladder, which opens by a duct into the back of the throat, functioning as a lung. The swim-bladder is large and occupies the whole area above the gut. It is made of cellular, lung-like tissue, and it opens direct into the gullet. This system is probably aided by the arapaima's large human-like red blood corpuscles. (The blood also clots on exposure to air—another development in the direction of land-living.) This development of air breathing apparatus recalls that of lungfishes, and it is of interest that the Osteoglossidae have nearly the same distribution as the lungfishes (see map), and both provide evidence suggesting that all continents were once joined and have drifted apart (see amphisbaena for similar evidence for the theory of continental drift).

Omnivorous feeder

Though essentially a fish-eater, the arapaima seems ready to eat anything. The fish it preys upon include the hassar, lukamani, and baira, but examination of 5,000 stomachs revealed the remains of many other items, including water snails, freshwater shrimps, worms, vegetable matter, freshwater turtles, snakes, frogs, crabs, grasshoppers, pebbles, sand, mud, and even coal. The young fry feed on microplankton, later take general plankton, and as they increase in size they take plankton and small fishes. When the young have reached this last stage they stand a risk of being eaten by their parents. There is an interesting adaptation of the fourth gill-arch, which was once thought to help in breathing. In one of the five species in the family this has now been shown to be a filter, which strains small particles from the water passing across the gills. These are trapped in mucus which is then carried to the gullet and stomach. When the water-level is low, in the dry season, this food is important.

Breeding season

The breeding season lasts from December to May. Spawning takes place in shallow water, at depths of $2\frac{1}{2}-5$ ft. During April and May, when the rivers overflow and flood the low-lying land, the arapaima move into this shallow water, select sandy areas clear of vegetation and hollow out nests, digging with mouth, chin, and fins. These saucer-like nests are 20 in. across and up to 8 in. deep.

Normally there is little difference between male and female, but at the breeding season the female goes a chestnut shade, the male develops a black head and his tail turns a bright vermilion. Each female lays up to 180,000 eggs in several batches, each in its separate nest. The eggs, $\frac{1}{8}-\frac{1}{4}$ in. in diameter, hatch in 5 days. The larvae, $\frac{1}{2}$ in. long and black, swarm in a group over the male's head near the surface. So as he rises to gulp air the larvae swarming round his black head are made invisible. They also swarm round his head when disturbed, protected no doubt by this camouflage. The female, meanwhile, swims around father and offspring, ready to drive off intruders.

Enemies

It is caught and eaten in large numbers, its flesh being salted or dried. The aboriginal American Indians kill it with bow and arrow or trap it in the shallows. Jaguars also are said to catch arapaima.

Size in question

While its lineage and anatomy are in little doubt, the arapaima's size has been the subject of much speculation. Nearly every book on fishes, every dictionary and encyclopedia, tells us that the arapaima reaches 15 ft in length and a weight of 400 or even 600 lb. This, it seems, is a myth. The fish is extensively eaten and therefore must be very well known. The numbers caught annually are high, as indicated by the investigator who, wishing to catalogue the things the arapaima eats, examined 5,000 stomachs in a short while. Yet nobody has so far recorded, from actual measurements, one longer than 7 ft or a greater weight than 246 lb.

When we look into this we find that the naturalist Schomburgk, writing in 1836 about his visit to Guiana, stated that 'the natives' told him 'the fish reached 15 ft long and 400 lb weight'. Every writer since has repeated these figures, most of them being unaware that the evidence was hearsay. Other writers have aided and abetted by using such phrases as 'too long and wide to fit into a 15-ft canoe' or 'I estimate 300 to 400 lb because one fish filled up to busting point 181 Indians. . . .'

Since Schomburgk's day hundreds of thousands of arapaima have been caught and eaten, many thousands have been examined by scientists. Yet the largest recorded is still only 7 ft.

class	**Pisces**
order	**Osteoglossiformes**
family	**Osteoglossidae**
genus & species	*Arapaima gigas*

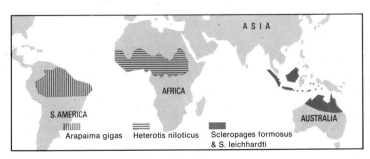

Distribution of the Osteoglossidae. Note the discontinuous distribution through South America, Africa, the Malay Archipelago and Australia.

Archerfish

Any of five species of fishes, which reach up to 1 ft in length, noted for obtaining insects by shooting them down with a stream of water drops. The first accurate account of this was written in 1765 by the Dutch governor of a hospital in Batavia (now Jakarta) the capital of Java. The governor decided to send a specimen to Europe, with his description, but by mistake he sent a long-nosed butterfly fish. Scientists studied the report and also the specimen and not surprisingly they could not see how this fish could spit water several feet. In any event, the butterfly fish lives in the sea, on coral reefs, where insects do not normally fly. Consequently, the story of the archerfish was disbelieved until 1902, when a Russian scientist obtained some specimens, kept them in an aquarium and verified their shooting abilities.

Distribution and habitat

Archerfishes extend from India through south-east Asia, the Malay Archipelago, and parts of Australia to the Philippines. Their habitat is mainly the brackish waters of mangrove belts, but they are also found far up freshwater streams.

Feeding habits

Their main food consists of small water animals swimming or floating near the surface, but when hungry, archerfishes shoot down insects crawling on leaves and stems of overhanging vegetation. A fully-grown adult is able to hit insects 6 ft above the surface of the water. Indeed, one fish has been seen to miss its target and the jet of water travel a measured 15 ft. If it misses with the first jet it will follow with several more in rapid succession. At the moment of shooting, the tip of the snout is just breaking water, the eyes being submerged. Water in the gill-chambers is driven into the mouth by a sudden powerful compression of the gill-covers. At the same time the tongue is pressed upwards, converting a groove in the roof of the mouth into a tube, which increases the speed of the outgoing stream.

Archerfishes begin to 'spit' when very young and only a few centimetres long, but the jets of water they produce do not travel much over 4 in. As they grow so their marksmanship improves and the length to which they spit increases.

Earl S Herald has described how, at Steinhart Aquarium, in the United States, one of the most popular exhibits was 150 archerfishes in a tank which were fed daily. The level of water in the tank was lowered and finely ground hamburger thrown against the exposed glass walls of the tank. The fishes would reconnoitre, then one bolder than the rest would leap out of the water to the distance of 1 ft in an endeavour to knock the food down. Eventually all the fishes would bombard it with drops of water and in 15 minutes about ⅓ lb of ground hamburger would be washed down from the glass.

Michael Tweedie has recalled visiting the Aquarium at Batavia in 1934 and leaning over the tank to watch the archerfishes. He received drops of water on the cheek, which stung sharply. Other observers have noted that the normal blinking of their eyelids stimulates an archerfish to shoot at them.

Breeding

The adults apparently spawn far from land, in the regions of coral rock or coral reef. The young return to the brackish water or even beyond, into the fresh water. They have the dark bars on the back, as in adults, and they also have 'light-flecks', yellow iridescent flecks on the back between the dark bars. At times the flecks shine so brightly they appear like tiny greenish fluorescent lights. It is suggested they may act as recognition marks between members of the species, helping them keep together in the muddy water.

Counteracting refraction

For 137 years disbelief and an air of mystery surrounded the activities of archerfishes. For a further 59 years there was a second mystery within the first: how does the archerfish with its eyes below water judge distance and take aim at targets in the air above? If a stick is dipped at an angle into water, it appears bent due to the bending of light rays as they pass from air into water. This is known as refraction. The archerfish will therefore see its food in a different position from the true one and yet it still manages to carry out very good sharpshooting. It was assumed that the archerfish in some way allowed for refraction. In 1961, however, the truth was realised, just by more careful observation of an archerfish feeding on insects. It swims forward until it is almost under its target, appears to take aim, then as it ejects the water jet, it jerks its body nearly to the vertical. In this position, just as a stick dipped straight into the water does not look bent, because refraction is reduced to a minimum, so the archerfish, looking straight up out of the water, sees the exact position of its insect target.

It has been noted that archerfishes sometimes miss their target. This is probably when, over-eager to take aim, they shoot their water drops before they have positioned themselves as nearly vertical as possible.

All the same, it is the general opinion that archerfishes are relatively intelligent. That their marksmanship improves with practice indicates learning ability.

Instinct or intelligence?

The idea that archerfishes are unusually intelligent seems to be based largely on the kind of eyes they possess. These are large and more highly organized than in most fish, and give binocular vision, that is, they are forward facing, with a large overlap of vision, thus enabling the fish to focus well and judge distances accurately. This is only one of the specializations. Others are the shape of the mouth and tongue and the mechanism for producing a jet of water, as well as the behavioural adaptations associated with them. When an animal has many adaptations to one end we assume these have been brought about by pressure of natural selection and are therefore necessary for its survival. The strange thing is that in spite of its elaborate equipment for shooting down insects, an archerfish does not use this as the main way of obtaining food. Indeed, it can get along quite well without using it. Archerfishes that live in the sea, for example, apparently never shoot insects down.

Perhaps even more odd is the way the fish will use its jet when quite unnecessary, and this seems to contradict the idea of unusual intelligence. Archerfishes will catch insects flying low over the water by leaping up and seizing them with the mouth. They have also been seen to aim their jet of water at insects already fallen on the surface, which they could easily have snapped up directly. They have been seen, in addition, to direct a jet at a small object, edible or inedible, lying on the bottom. The jet is not then visible but its trajectory can be appreciated by the sudden compression of the fish's gill-covers and the puff of sand or mud raised at the point of impact. Perhaps the archerfish instinctively 'shoots' at any interesting target and its intelligence is limited to improving its accuracy.

class	**Pisces**
order	**Perciformes**
family	**Toxotidae**
genus & species	*Toxotes jaculatrix*

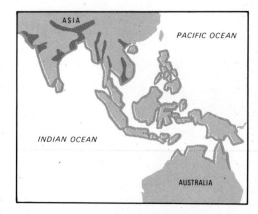

The tropical distribution of the archerfish. They prefer the brackish waters of the mangrove belts, but will live in the sea as well as entering the fresh water streams on the coast.

Archerfish shooting accurately aimed drops of water at a ladybird target. Water in the gill-chambers is ejected via a groove in the roof of the mouth by sudden compression of the gill-covers. Archerfish have been known to hit insects at a distance of 6 ft.▷

*Armoured catfishes **Corydoras aneus** members of the mailed catfish family Callichthyidae, resting on some pebbles using their pelvic fins as support. This family is identified by the clear arrangement of two rows of armour plates along the sides of the body. The 'whiskers' or barbels give catfishes their name.*

Armoured catfish

There are more than 50 species of armoured catfishes and all live in the streams of South America. They are small, the largest being less than 1 ft long, and they are remarkable for two things. One is their bony armour. The other is the method of fertilisation used in most of the species. They belong to three separate families, the first of which, with only five species, is known as the thorny catfishes. The second, known as the mailed catfishes, have a smooth armour of two rows of overlapping bony plates on each side of the body. The third family, which has no common name and is consequently spoken of as the Loricariid catfishes, has the whole body covered with overlapping scales. All have barbels, the 'whiskers' which give catfishes their name.

Talking habits

Mailed catfishes often travel overland for considerable distances, pulling themselves along with the strong spines on the breast or pectoral fins and using intestinal respiration, like that in the thorny catfishes. Both have a supplementary breathing system, in which air is swallowed and the oxygen from it taken up by a network of fine capillary blood vessels in the wall of the intestine. One species of thorny catfish is known to aquarists as the talking catfish because both in water and when taken out it may make a grunting sound which is caused by movements of the spines in the pectoral fins, amplified by the gas-filled swim-bladder acting as a resonator. Several other catfishes also make these sounds.

Carnivorous feeders

Mailed catfishes live in small groups in slow-flowing streams, rarely in standing water, and they feed on small animals, such as water fleas. The thorny catfishes are active mainly at twilight, when they grub on the

bottom for worms and insect larvae. Both feed on small pieces of carrion.

The Loricariid catfishes are bottom dwellers, mainly in mountain streams or swiftly flowing streams in the lowlands, and they have thick lips forming a sucker-like mouth by which they cling to stones and water plants. This serves two purposes: to maintain position against a strong current and, while doing so, to feed by scraping small algae from the surfaces of the stones and plants with their bilobed or spoon-shaped teeth.

Spawning with the mouth

Little is known about the breeding of the thorny catfishes, and although they have been kept in captivity by aquarists, none has been seen breeding. One of the mailed catfishes, known as the hassar, will spawn in captivity only when water is sprayed onto the surface of the water in the aquarium, simulating a tropical shower. There is some disagreement about which of two methods of mating is used by the mailed catfishes. Some observers say that the male grips the barbels of the female with his strong pectoral fins, so that the two lie with their underside apposed. In this position the male pours out his milt as the eggs are extruded, so fertilising them. The second method that has been described is the one in which the female takes the milt direct from the male into her mouth. There is a certain amount of ritual courtship beforehand in which the male nudges the female with his snout and then the two break off, swim over to the surface of a stone and clean it by removing the minute growths of weed and debris with their mouths. The nudging and the cleaning alternate so that by the time pairing takes place they are in a highly excited state and there are several clean surfaces. The purpose of the female sucking in the milt now becomes clear. She is able to swim the short distance over to one of the clean surfaces. There, the milt streams out across her gills to the exterior as she breathes and the current of water carries it over the eggs as she deposits them on the cleaned surface, where they adhere.

As many as 250 eggs may be laid at one spawning and there may be more than a dozen spawnings during the course of a week, with several spawning periods during the year. The young hatch in 5 to 8 days. Some mailed catfishes make bubble nests. They rise to the surface to take in air, then release it from the mouth, in the form of saliva bubbles, under a roof formed by an overhanging rock or the underside of a waterlily leaf. The eggs are then laid among the bubbles.

The courtship of the Loricariid catfishes is more elaborate. For several days the couple clean a spawning site, and then the female takes up position in the middle of this site ready to lay. The male positions himself parallel to her, with his underside towards her, stretches himself so that both tail and head point upwards, the whole body forming a curve. In this position he begins to extrude his milt while the female fans with her fins drawing a current of water from him to her, bringing the milt washing over the eggs, so fertilising them. The strength of the current is increased by the female breathing more strongly than usual, which means that she opens and closes her mouth more vigorously, drawing water in and driving it out across the gills. The total result is to create a current which travels from her mate to herself and forms a whirlpool over the place where the eggs are being laid, so that the eggs are bathed by a concentrated suspension of milt in water. After 9 to 12 days the eggs are ready to hatch. The male, who has meanwhile kept guard, frees the baby fishes from the eggs. He does this by alternately sucking up the spawn with his mouth and squirting it out and fanning it with his fins, until the membranes break and the babies can escape from the eggs.

Enemies

Nothing is known of the natural enemies of these fishes, but presumably they fall victim to the usual predatory fish and water birds. Mention of enemies, however, raises the point about heavy armouring, and recalls that one writer has spoken of the talking catfish as the 'touch-me-not fish'.

Elaborate armour

It is usually assumed that animals wearing some form of armour enjoy protection from enemies as a consequence. This is only half true. The real situation is that, as an animal evolves armour, either enemies find a new method of attacking them, or other enemies arise capable of dealing with the armour. It is the same in human warfare. As soon as warships became armour-clad, an armour-piercing shell was invented. Similarly the invention of the tank was quickly followed by the anti-tank gun. In the talking fish, the most heavily armoured animal in the world today, the armour and armament seem to be out of all proportion, as if evolution had run amok in this particular species. One writer has suggested that a larger fish attempting to eat it would receive a sensation of having bitten a chestnut burr. The first item in this elaborate armour is the very bony skull, which is continued backwards as a bony plate overlapping the backbone, almost to the base of the dorsal fin. This fish, like other catfishes, has no scales. Instead there is a row of bony plates along each side of the body, and each of these plates bears thorn-like spines. All the fins are armed with spines, as is usual in so many other fishes, but a special feature of the talking fish is the large size of the pectoral fins. Each is relatively long and strongly constructed, and armed with strongly toothed spines. It has been suggested that, should the talking fish clasp an enemy with one of these fins, holding it against the saw-like rows of spines on the plates covering the flank, the enemy would suffer severe lacerations. The trouble with this theory is that nobody seems to have seen the fish using its armament in this way.

The suggestion is in fact most improbable, and it is more likely that this is an instance in which a structure is evolved serving no very great purpose. The toothed spines on the fins, and the thorn-like spines on the plates of the flanks, may or may not have a value in protecting the fish. But when we look inside and see that the bones of the shoulder girdle are also toothed, we can say with certainty that this is something that just happened, and cannot conceivably have any defensive value for the fish.

class	**Pisces**		
order	**Siluriformes**		
families	**Doradidae** *thorny catfishes*		
	Callichthyidae *mailed catfishes*		
	Loricariidae		

◁ *Very rare striped sailback* **Panaque nigro-lineatus** *a Loricariid catfish, comes from Venezuela and Ecuador.*
▽ *Mailed catfishes out of water can pull themselves along on their pelvic fins breathing by swallowing air.*

Atlantic salmon

With a slim, streamlined body, the salmon is obviously built for speed, and this is confirmed by its long, leaping and powerful struggle when captured on rod and line. It is 40—50 in. long, exceptionally 60 in., with silver underside, flanks verging on green, and a silver-grey back. The flanks and back are covered with black spots. It is one of the family Salmonidae, which consists of only five genera, and perhaps two dozen species, including the familiar brown and rainbow trout. The salmon feeds in the sea and breeds in freshwater, a type of behaviour we call anadromous (from the Greek for running upwards). It is a matter of opinion whether the species was originally marine and took to migrating into rivers to spawn, or a freshwater fish that has taken to going down to the sea to feed. Most evidence is in favour of the former.

A thousand mile migration

Most of our knowledge of the habits of salmon concerns their stay in fresh water. Since this is part of the breeding migration, with no regular feeding, the details are given in the next section. What happens to salmon in the sea is still largely a closed book, although it has been a focus of interest for scientists for many years. Recent results from tagging experiments show that in fact most of the European and North American salmon travel to the Greenland region to feed. Some European fish are known to migrate to the Norwegian Sea. Since a salmon returns to spawn in the same river in which it was hatched, there has been a great deal of speculation and some research on how this is done. Some of the suggestions are: that the returning salmon is guided by currents, that it smells or tastes

the water from its parental river and so is led to the source, that it uses celestial navigation to guide it, or that it can detect the varying salinities or the oxygen content of the water. Possibly all these are used in varying degrees at different stages of the journey. The one thing we can be sure of is that, once the salmon has entered its ancestral river, it has the urge to go upstream no matter what the obstacles. So we have the famous leaps up waterfalls, 10 ft leaps being recorded. Where a river is dammed, as for an hydro-electric station, fish 'ladders' are often built, in the form of a series of steps, for the salmon to make their way upstream.

The upstream migrations from the sea may be in winter or early spring (spring fish) or summer to autumn (summer fish). When they run up-river, the salmon are in good condition, their flesh firm and red and the surface of the body silvery. There is much fat stored in the body but later, as a result of spawning, this is used up, the flesh becomes pale and watery, and the outside of the body loses its silvery appearance, becoming dark red. The skin of the back becomes thick and spongy, with the scales deeply embedded in it. Large black spots margined with white appear on the body, which is spotted and mottled with red and orange. This gives the 'red fish', which are males, the females being similarly coloured but darker, and known as 'black fish'. The males are further distinguished by the way the snout becomes longer and the lower jaw hooked.

Feeding habits

During their stay in the sea, the salmon spend much of their time in the upper layers, which may account for the infrequency with which they are caught in trawls. They probably come nearer the surface at night, following the plankton on its daily migration upwards, since they feed on various shrimp-like crustaceans. It is from the pigments in these, especially the

carotenoids, that the salmon's flesh derives its pink colour. In addition sand-eels, small herring and other fishes are taken. When in fresh water no regular feeding takes place, the salmon drawing on its reserve food store of fat.

Never safe from predators

Eels take the eggs, and many birds as well as perch, pike and trout feed on the young fish. Otters will take adults of quite considerable size. In the sea the main enemies are seals, porpoises and cormorants, perhaps also some of the larger predatory fishes.

From gravel stream to ocean deep

The Atlantic salmon breeds in the rivers of Europe, from Spain to the White Sea, off Iceland, the southern tip of Greenland, and North America, from Labrador to the New England coast.

The life-cycle begins in the shallows of a stream where the water is clean and there is a gravel bed. Spawning is from September to January, mainly in November and December. The ripe female digs a trough by lashing movements of her body and in this lays her eggs, the total numbers laid in a season being 800—900 for every pound of her weight. They are fertilised by the male in attendance on her, by shedding his milt over them, after which she covers the eggs with gravel and moves up-stream to repeat the process. The spawning ground is spoken of as a redd. The eggs are about 7 mm diameter. They hatch in 5—21 weeks, depending on the temperature.

The fry, when hatched, still carry a yolk-sac, are ½ in. long and are called alevins. They remain among the pebbles of the redd until the yolk-sac is absorbed, in 4—8 weeks from hatching, then leave for shallow water when 1—2 in. long. They are then called fingerlings. At the end of a year, when 3—4 in. long, the fingerlings become parr, and by the end of the second year they reach a length of 4½—8 in. At this stage

▽ *Mature male salmon in fine condition caught while returning to his ancestral breeding ground. By the time he reached the spawning ground the curved hook on the lower jaw would have become more elongated and grotesque.*

▷ *Salmon leaping up waterfall.*

Mature salmon return from the sea to spawn in the same river where they were hatched. No matter what obstacles are encountered they will struggle onwards, leaping determinedly up waterfalls, until they reach their ancestral birthplace.

the body is marked with ten or eleven dark bands, like thumb-marks, on each side of the body.

The time at which the various stages are reached varies with temperature and other factors, including latitude. The discrepancies become even more pronounced in later stages, as when the parr becomes more silvery and, as a smolt, is ready to go to sea. At this stage it is not easy to distinguish it from a trout. In southern England, for example, the smolt stage may be reached in a year, while in northern Scandinavia, it may take seven or eight years.

On reaching the sea, the salmon feeds for one to six years, before coming back to the same river to spawn. The returning salmon has been called a grilse, a name that has been given so many meanings that some authors have discarded it and prefer to speak of the returning salmon as a maiden, and then as a spawner when it reaches the spawning grounds. After spawning, the spent salmon, or kelt, drop down river tail-first, weakened by fasting and spawning, often attacked by disease. Many, especially the males, die on the way. Those that reach the sea, the mended kelts as they are called, soon recover and start to feed. They are now 'once spawned sea-fish'. Some may return to spawn a second time, although very few will go back a third time.

Fall in numbers

Eating the King of Fish, the Atlantic salmon, is a luxury. Catching it provides sport for the well-to-do and profit for the poacher. Ten years ago five million pounds of salmon were marketed. Even farther back in British history apprentices were rebelling at being given salmon to eat more than twice a week. Now it has disappeared completely from rivers where it was once plentiful, the result of pollution by factory effluents. Other rivers are being poisoned by pesticides washed out of farmlands, and this is happening over the whole range of the species. In fact, it has been suggested that the salmon may be doomed to extinction.

On the northern seaboard of Spain are many rivers where salmon can still be caught. Elsewhere in the Iberian Peninsula, which for centuries produced fantastic numbers of this fish, salmon are gone. In the 11th century they were the prerogative of noble families and abbeys. In 1258 they were protected by royal edict. In the 18th century up to 10,000 salmon were caught in Spain every day. By 1949 only 3,000 salmon a year were being caught. Under rigid protection this has increased to 7,000 in 1968, but the rivers where salmon have been lost are not being replenished by natural or artificial means. The causes of this tremendous fall

in the numbers of salmon are illegal fishing leading to over-fishing, the damming of rivers for irrigation and pollution by waste from factories.

The disappearance of the bulk of French salmon dates from the Revolution. Before, they were conserved by the monarchy, nobles and church, for their own ends, it is true, but they were conserved. Following the Revolution they were anybody's fish. Even later, when laws were made for their protection, illegal fishing with nets, poaching with tridents, damming of streams for mills and, later, hydro-electric schemes, as well as pollution, helped the decline of salmon resources. A law of 1865 required anyone building a dam to put in a salmon ladder, for the fish to migrate upstream. It did not, however, lay down that sufficient water should be allowed to flow down the ladder to allow the salmon up, so the law was honoured in the breach.

The situation in the Baltic is mixed. The salmon has suffered drastically in some countries, notably Poland. The fishery has actually improved in Norway, and in Sweden the use of hatcheries has so improved remaining stocks in the Baltic itself that one in four of salmon caught are from these hatcheries. Such declines as there are may be due to illegal fishing, damming of rivers, industrial pollution and the netting of salmon at sea, when young as well as mature fish are netted.

In England and Wales where the salmon was once king, few salmon rivers remain. Typical is the River Thames, which once teemed with 'fat and sweet salmons' ascending the river to 65 miles above London. It is now barren, for most of its length a sewer of industrial and human waste. Elsewhere the story is much the same.

Salmon was the first fish to be mentioned in the chronicles of North America. Now it is referred to as 'the American disaster' in the annals of fishing. The story is much the same as for Europe, perhaps more intensified: over-fishing, damming of rivers for mills, blockading of rivers for lumbering, pollution with sewage and industrial waste.

Two new factors cause even greater apprehension for the future. One result of the tagging of thousands of young and mature salmon is that the fishes are now being traced to their feeding grounds. These will certainly be in international waters, and there, as history shows, the chances of controlling over-fishing are slim. The second adverse factor is the cumulative pollution of all rivers, indeed all waters on the globe, with pesticides and other toxic residues.

Despite all that is now known we are still ignorant of many aspects of the salmon's biology, a better knowledge of which could help us prevent the disastrous demise of this useful food fish. The Atlantic Salmon Research Trust was set up in 1967 and if it can work quickly enough it may yet save the valuable and beautiful fish.

class	**Pisces**
order	**Salmoniformes**
family	**Salmonidae**
genus & species	***Salmo salar***

Barber fishes

The barber fishes constitute a group classified by behaviour rather than body form; many species, indeed families, have barber, or cleaner, fishes among them. Surfperch, wrasse and angelfish, as well as the young of some other species, have been recorded cleaning other fish.

The original barber fish was a pink or red fish (Anthias anthias) of Madeira and the Mediterranean, belonging to a family related to the Grouper and sea bass family. Later, Mexican fishermen working in the Gulf of California named a fish el barbero because it manicured or groomed other fishes. This is a butterfly fish (Heniochus nigrirostris), belonging to the family Chaetodontidae. The common names given to these fishes proved later to have a scientific significance

Early scepticism

William Beebe, American marine zoologist, while diving off Haiti, in 1928, saw several fishes of the wrasse family cleaning the bodies of parrotfishes. But it was not until some 20 years ago that scientists began to take the matter seriously, when a film was shown before an international audience. In this, one fish could be seen cleaning another by eating the skin parasites from its body, while other fishes queued up, taking their turn to be cleaned, like customers in a barber's shop.

Conrad Limbaugh, skin-diving off the coast of California, saw a walleye surfperch leave the shoal and swim over to a golden kelp perch half its size, hold its body rigid at an unnatural angle with its fins extended while the kelp surfperch picked at its skin for about 3 minutes. After this, the kelp surfperch darted back to the patch of kelp from which it had come and the surfperch rejoined the shoal. This led Limbaugh to make a serious study of what is now known to be a common and widespread phenomenon. Moreover, we now know that cleaner fishes as they are also called, are highly important in the economy of the sea.

Brilliantly coloured fish

The human barber calls attention to his shop by a sign, usually a coloured pole. Barber fishes usually advertise their presence by living near conspicuous coral heads, or a highly coloured sea anemone or sponge, which serves as their sign. Many cleaner fishes are themselves brightly coloured, with a striking pattern in garish colours, as if deliberately drawing attention to themselves. Even though belonging to unrelated families they tend to be coloured and patterned in a similar way.

Each cleaner has its station, at its particular place on the reef, where it gives a surprisingly complete cleaning service. Patches of dead skin, bacteria, fungus and the animal parasites known as fish-lice, are picked off by the barber fishes. The barbers go over the body carefully, entering the gill

Barber fish *Labroides* removing parasites from flagtailed surgeon fish.

Rock beauty cleaning blue surgeon fish

chambers and even the mouth to make a thorough job of it, while the fish being cleaned co-operates in every way possible. It will raise the gill-cover on one side of the body to let the small barber enter, and when that gill chamber is thoroughly spring-cleaned, the cleaner will swim over to the other side, the larger fish then raising the gill-cover on that side to let it in. Then the larger fish may open its mouth for the cleaner to enter. Large fishes which normally feed on smaller fishes will allow cleaner fishes to enter their mouths, and to depart unharmed.

The cleaner gets free meals and the fish being cleaned is protected from disease, and from having its body cluttered with parasites. Furthermore, the barber fish will clean wounds, by nibbling away the dead flesh around them, in what can be called a truly surgical operation.

Some fishes are cleaners only when young, the fish-lice and bits of skin being for them a kind of baby food. Confirmed cleaners that ply their trade throughout life usually have pointed snouts, often with tweezer-like teeth, with which they probe the crevices and grooves in their customers' bodies.

Fishes come from far and wide

Larger fishes may deliberately seek out the cleaner fishes and solicit their attentions. Deep sea fishes will come into shallow waters to be barbered, and fishes living in the open ocean make long journeys for this purpose. For example, the large ocean sunfish, with a hugh disc-like body weighing up to a ton, will lumber into inshore waters occasionally, where a whole team of small barber fishes quarters its body. Large sharks have been seen with a team at work on their skin, some of the small fishes even going into their mouths and coming out again unharmed.

The value of the services rendered by the cleaner fishes was strikingly shown by keeping some marine fishes in aquaria. When no cleaner fish was included in an aquarium, the others soon became infested with parasites. As soon as a cleaner was put in, it set to work on one of its patients while the others, as if they knew what was happening, queued up for treatment.

The degree to which many fish rely upon the barbers has been shown in the sea, too. Skin-divers have gone down and caught alive all the cleaner fishes around a reef, bringing them one by one to the surface and putting each in an aquarium, with a note of the place from which it was removed. As soon as all have been taken away, the shoals of other fishes, often numbering thousands, disappear, presumably in search of new barbers. When the cleaner fishes are put back the shoals return. The second time the removal of all the cleaner fish was tried there was no change in the population of the other fishes.

This cleaning relationship is more obvious in the warmer seas, because there the fishes are brightly coloured, whereas in temperate waters they are duller and tend to escape notice. Moreover, the cleaners in cooler seas are mobile, following their customers instead of taking up a fixed station.

Some years ago, the Americans began dumping old cars into the sea, off the coast of Florida, where the bottom is plain sand and the waters above it not very well populated with fishes. Wrecked ships lying on the sea-bed soon became populated with shoals of fishes, and it was thought this otherwise useless hardwear piled on the sea-bed might similarly encourage fishes to come and live there, for the benefit of sport fishermen. Since then, artificial reefs of large concrete blocks have been tried. Success is less due to the shelter so provided for sportfish, than to cleaner fishes coming to live in these artificial reefs.

The demon barber

Several plays have been written around the story of Sweeney Todd, the Demon Barber who is alleged to have lured customers into his shop to murder them. These Victorian melodramas could easily have been inspired by what is happening in the world of fishes. It has its Sweeney Todds, fishes that mimic the colours, patterns and habits of the cleaner fishes. When other fishes, needing the attentions of the manicurist, go to these false barbers, they are set upon and attacked instead of merely being groomed.

class	**Pisces** *Barber fishes are found in several orders and families*

The barracuda is one of the most feared and dangerous predatory fishes. Apparently they may be dangerous in one area and not in another.

Barracuda

Barracuda are pike-like fishes, not related to pike but having a similar long-bodied form, with a jutting lower jaw and a wicked-looking set of fangs. Fishermen, in handling even the dead fish, treat them with respect. There are more than 20 species, but most of them are harmless. The evil reputation of barracudas has perhaps been over-stated, and it is difficult to know what to believe. One eminent authority, speaking of the fear fishermen in the West Indies have for the barracuda, has referred to merciless struggles waged between man and barracuda in the shade of the mangroves. This is at variance with all that one hears from skindivers, as well as with what is said of the speedy attack by this fish. Nevertheless, there are a number of authentic records of attack, especially from the great barracuda, also called picuda, or becuna, the giant of the family, which ranges through tropical and subtropical waters the world over, and may reach a length of 8 ft or more. The northern barracuda, or sennet, of the western North Atlantic, reaches only 18 in., but the European barracuda, barracouta or spet, of the Mediterranean

and eastern Atlantic, may reach 3 ft. Other species are the Indian barracuda and Commerson's barracuda, both of the Indian Ocean, and the California barracuda.

Most voracious fish

More fearful to some people than even the shark, the larger barracudas are among the most voracious of predatory fishes. Long and torpedo-shaped, the barracudas swim swiftly and feed voraciously, especially on plankton-feeding fishes, charging through their shoals, attacking with snapping bites. It is said that when a pack of barracuda has eaten enough, it herds the rest of the shoal it is attacking into shallow water and keeps guard over it until ready for another meal.

Small or half-grown barracudas swim in shoals, the larger individuals are solitary. A solitary barracuda attacks swiftly, bites cleanly and does not repeat its attack (shoaling barracuda seldom attack people). It hunts by sight rather than smell, as sharks do, and advice given to bathers and divers reflects this. For example, murky water should be avoided because the fish, aware of every movement you make through its keen sight, may over-estimate your size, thereby over-estimating the danger you represent to it, and attack. A metallic object flashing in clear water looks to a barracuda

like a fish and stimulates attack. An underwater spear fisherman towing a fish may be in trouble also, and it is not unknown for a barracuda to snatch a captured fish from a skindiver's belt.

Virtually all the interest in this fish has been concentrated on its behaviour towards man, apart from its use for food. On two occasions American scientists have collected all reports of alleged attacks on human beings. It seems these amount to fewer than 40, making the barracuda less dangerous in aggregate than sharks. To a large extent the reputation of this fish is the result of what appears to be an insatiable curiosity. It will hang around a skin-diver, watching his movements and following him, generating in him a very uncomfortable feeling. There is evidence that a barracuda is most dangerous—some say only dangerous—when provoked. Even so, there are records of a person standing in no more than 1 ft of water having the flesh bitten from the lower leg, or the bone almost severed.

One feature of barracuda behaviour, for which there is as yet no explanation, is that the fish may be dangerous in one area and not in another. Barracuda in the Antilles, for example, should be avoided, but around Hawaii they seem to be harmless.

Barracuda spawn over deep water offshore in the Caribbean, ocean currents distributing the larvae and young.

Reputation prejudiced

All barracudas are regarded as good food-fishes, but there is some prejudice against the barracuda because its flesh is, on occasions, highly poisonous. This may be a seasonal danger, the flesh being poisonous at some times of the year and not at others, it may be due to the flesh being allowed to go slightly bad before being cooked, but it is also due to what is known as ciguatera, which is due to toxins, originating in toxic algae and diatoms, building up from plant-eating fish to predators, and concentrating. The toxin is the cause of sickness, and even death, in humans who eat the predator (for example the barracuda). In the Caribbean, some species of fish are safe to eat from only one side of an island.

Prejudice is not confined to the fish. Sir Hans Sloane, writing in 1707, maintained that barracudas were more fond of the flesh of dogs, horses and black men than that of white men. Père Labat, in 1742, carried this prejudiced statement further. He declared that, faced with a choice of a Frenchman and an Englishman, a barracuda would always choose the latter. He attributed this to the gross meat-eating habits of the Englishman, which produced a stronger 'exhalation' in the water, as compared with the more delicate exudations of a Frenchman, who is a daintier feeder.

class	**Pisces**
order	**Perciformes**
family	**Sphyraenidae**
genus & species	***Sphyraena barracuda*** great barracuda
	S. borealis northern barracuda
	S. sphyraena European barracuda others

△ *The skull of the great barracuda showing its wicked-looking set of fangs and the jutting lower jaw.*

▽ *School of barracuda swimming past coral of the Great Barrier Reef, Australia. Shoaling barracuda seldom attack people.*

Basking shark cruising near the surface in the coastal waters off Devon. As it moves through the sea large quantities of water enter its huge open mouth and pass across its gills, where the gill-rakers sieve plankton from the water for food.

Basking shark

The common basking shark is one of the largest of sharks, going to 40 ft or more in length. In spite of its large size and the frequency with which it is seen, and in spite of its being fished commercially in places, there are still many serious gaps in our knowledge of the basking shark's habits.

It is found in temperate seas throughout the world but is most common in the North Atlantic. There is only one well-known species but it is suspected there may be a second species in Australian seas.

The body may be bluish-grey to greyish-brown, sometimes almost black, but the underparts are whitish.

*Some of the outstanding features of this leviathan are its very minute teeth, its very large gill-slits that almost encircle the body behind the head and the curious rakers on the hoop-like gill arches, which filter plankton from the sea for food. Another point is worthy of mention: on a number of occasions the decomposing body of a basking shark has been washed ashore and has been mistaken for the carcase of the sea-serpent. In such instances the gill-rakers, exposed by the decomposition, have been interpreted as the mane of the sea-serpent. The famous monster of Stronsay, in the Orkneys, which was actually given a scientific name, **Halsydrus pontoppidiani**, is a case in point. Some of its vertebrae were salvaged, fortunately, and these proved beyond doubt that the so-called monster was a basking shark.*

Atlantic cruiser

With its huge mouth open, like a drag-net, the basking shark moves through the sea, large quantities of water entering its mouth and passing across the gills. The gill-rakers sieve minute plankton from the water and this is then swallowed as food.

A sluggish swimmer, this shark enters coastal waters in summer, singly, in twos or threes, or in shoals of 60 or more. It cruises slowly, at 2 knots, at the surface, with the prominent dorsal fin, and sometimes the upper lobe of the tail fin, showing above the surface.

Not until 1953 were clues obtained as to what happened to basking sharks in winter. Several of them caught in the North Sea at the beginning of winter were found to have shed their gill-rakers. The scientists who first examined these thought they were a new kind of basking shark, perhaps freaks.

It became clear they were normal basking sharks, and the assumption then was that the sharks shed their gill-rakers and cease to feed with the onset of winter. Gill-rakers are an essential feeding mechanism to the basking shark. In autumn the amount of plankton grows less. Therefore the sharks stop feeding, retire to the depths and probably hibernate.

Filter feeder

The plankton taken in by a basking shark is largely made up of minute shrimp-like copepods (especially *Calanus*), the eggs of other fishes and arrow-worms. In spring and summer these are abundant, but even so the basking shark has to work hard for a living. The shark needs the equivalent of a third of a horse-power to swim. This means taking in 663 calories merely to replace the energy used in swimming to collect the food. It has been estimated that an average-sized basking shark 22 ft long would filter from the sea about 1 500 cu yd of plankton, or 2½ lb of plankton an hour under the most favourable conditions for November when plankton supply has fallen for the winter. This would yield only 410 calories an hour. So in November a basking shark would be using up markedly more energy in feeding than it would be getting from its food.

Shark gives birth to babies

Little has been discovered about the life history. If they laid eggs, these would have been contained within a leathery capsule, like the well-known 'mermaid's purse' picked up commonly on the sea shore; when a female of one of the egg-laying sharks is cut open the unlaid eggs are commonly found in the oviducts. No such egg capsules have been found in any female basking sharks, nor any in the sea. It was therefore assumed that the young are born alive because this is the case with other sharks. There the matter would end but for a chance occurrence in 1923 off Norway. A female basking shark, at the moment of capture, gave birth to six young. Five of these escaped and swam away. The sixth was dead. It was 5 ft long and weighed 18 lb. These are the only baby basking sharks ever to have been seen.

Life style deduced

Although so often seen, basking sharks were hard to capture except by those who are experienced in the fishery. The scientist who wished to study this shark was not welcomed by the shark fishers who, in the brief season that baskers are inshore, could not waste a moment. All their time was taken with hauling in the huge carcasses and slitting them open to take out the liver, from which 'cod liver oil' was extracted. The rest of the carcase is thrown overboard, and any nosey-parker scientist wishing to dissect them received scant courtesy. Consequently, our knowledge of the habits of the species is largely built up on indirect knowledge derived from the few basking sharks washed ashore or obtained in some such way. Deduction from meagre facts must be used in a manner worthy of Sherlock Holmes.

For example, the facts and figures on feeding given above were largely derived

△△ *Head of young basking shark showing the gill-arches which support the gill-rakers. Its teeth are so small they don't show in the photo.*

△ *The battle between a shark crew and a 30-ft shark. Nearby another shark is dangerously close, but they are not usually vicious.*

from measuring the size of the shark's mouth, calculating the flow of water through at 2 knots, measuring the amount of plankton in a known quantity of sea-water, and so on. Known mathematical formulae are then applied, and the result we have quoted here.

Similar detective work has been used on the shark's life-history. To begin with, it has been found that the back-bones or vertebrae have growth-rings like those in a tree-trunk. Using these, it has been shown that most basking sharks examined by scientists fall into two age-groups: five-six and eight-nine years. Another piece of information obtained from studying the vertebrae is that the first few growth-rings are slightly different in character from the rest and are almost certainly laid down before birth. If this is correct then the gestation period — the time between conception and birth —

is longer in basking sharks than that known in almost any other animal: 2–3 years. The probability is that basking sharks do not come into inshore waters, where they can be caught, until sexually mature, at 3–5 years of age. Having mated it seems they disappear for 2 years — perhaps they go back to deep waters. It may be presumed they then have their babies, which remain in deep waters for the next 3–5 years, while the parents once more come into inshore waters, being now 8–9 years old.

class	**Pisces**
order	**Selachii**
family	**Cetorhinidae**
genus & species	***Cetorhinus maximus***

Basses

The bass has spiny fins, some of which can pierce human flesh, and there are spines on the gill-covers. The large mouth is equally well armed. It has, besides the usual teeth in the jaws, teeth on every surface of the mouth, even the tongue.

The bass is a uniform silver grey, with a slight tinge of pink at the bases of the fins. Its weight goes up to 20 lb. The original name was barse, which is Old English meaning bristly or spiny, but this, in the 15th century, was the name for what is now called the freshwater perch. The marine fish, now known as the bass, is silvery like a salmon, and like the salmon its flesh is slightly pink, although the two are not related. One result of this is a variety of local names: salmon-dace, sea-salmon and white salmon. The confusion of names has been made worse by the word bass being taken overseas by emigrants from Britain, so that it has been applied, with or without some qualifying word, to a number of spiny-finned marine or freshwater fishes. In North America, for example, there is a whole group of basses (of the sunfish family) including rock bass, largemouth black bass, spotted bass as well as the white bass and the striped bass (which are relatives of the European bass).

The common bass, or sea perch, extends from the waters of the Mediterranean to the British Isles.

Popular sport fish
Bass are very popular as sport fish and make good food. They come inshore in June and stay there until October, when they go out to sea. During this summer period the bass may even enter estuaries or go up the rivers, particularly on the south and west coasts of Britain where they are caught by bait towed behind a boat or by casting from the beach.

Crustacean feeders
Food consists largely of crustaceans, including prawns, shrimps and crabs, as well as small fishes.

Breeds from May to August
Spawning may take place in the sea or in brackish water, from May through until the end of August. In the sea the eggs, just over 1/25 in. diameter are just buoyant enough to float, but in freshwater they sink. They hatch in 6 days. The fry grow rapidly and by autumn are 4–6 in. long. They follow the adults in their migration out to sea.

A very mixed family
The common bass is quite ordinary but some of its close relatives are most unusual. One, known as the stone bass or wreckfish, lives in the Mediterranean and tropical Atlantic, sometimes wandering north to the south coast of England. It has the habit of swimming beside any wreckage or floating logs,

Largemouth black bass, **Micropterus salmoides,** *surface feeding.*

Common bass extend from the waters of the Mediterranean to the British Isles, becoming rare in the North Sea. Besides the usual teeth in the jaws it has teeth on every surface of the mouth, even the tongue.

planks, boxes and the like, as well as wrecks lying on the seabed. One trawler caught 5 tons of this fish from the vicinity of a wreck lying in 370 ft of water. Wreckfish may weigh up to 80 lb and measure 6 ft long. They are highly aggressive, often attacking and killing fishes larger than themselves.

The largemouth black bass belongs to another family, that of the freshwater sunfishes, but it has the belligerence of the wreckfish. When small it eats tadpoles, worms, snails and crayfish, but as it grows and its mouth widens it takes almost anything it can engulf, from frogs and water snakes to rats and birds swimming at the surface. After spawning, the female leaves the male to guard the eggs and, later, the fry. It is then most ferocious for the male will attack the largest enemies, except perhaps the otter, in defence of its offspring.

A relative of the European bass living off the tropical Atlantic coast of North America —the belted sandfish—is hermaphrodite, each individual being both male and female, This recalls the Nassau grouper or black sea bass of the same region. Most young are

females, but many of these, at the age of five years, turn into males, so eventually restoring the balance between the sexes.

Hermaphrodite

In the family Serranidae, to which the bass and its relatives belong, there is an almost complete series between the normal separation of the sexes and the condition known as inter-sexes. In between these two is hermaphroditism. A hermaphrodite is an organism in which both female and male reproductive organs are present. In complete hermaphroditism these organs are both fully functional and there are a few species of animals which are either known to be self-fertilising or are suspected of being so. The belted sandfish is suspected of being capable of self-fertilisation.

Hermaphroditism is normal for most plants and for most of the lower invertebrates, but is exceptional in the higher invertebrates, such as insects and spiders. It is rare in fishes, and in the rest of the vertebrates it is extremely rare and even then one sex predominates.

The term inter-sex is used for an animal that is either male or female to begin with and later changes to the other sex, as in the black sea bass. Sex change is more common among invertebrates and decreases up the animal scale. It may occur as a normal change, as in the black sea bass, but is usually abnormal in higher vertebrates. A well-known example is the hen that grows wattles, starts to crow and yet continues to lay the occasional egg.

class	**Pisces**	
order	**Perciformes**	
suborder	**Percoidei**	
family	**Serranidae**	
genera & species	***Epinephelus striatus*** *Nassau grouper* ***Dicentrarchus labrax*** *common bass* ***Polyprion americanum*** *stone bass*	
family	**Centrarchidae**	
genus & species	***Micropterus salmoides*** *largemouth black bass*	

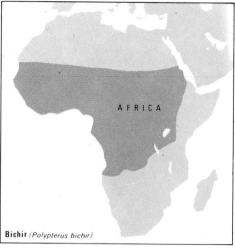

Bichir (*Polypterus bichir*)

◁ *This strange fish not only breathes air but also uses its front fins like legs to stalk its prey. It will even die if it cannot gulp air from the surface. To do this, the bichir swims slowly to the surface, takes a quick gulp, then rapidly swims down to the bottom.*

Bichir

A freshwater fish just over 2 ft long living in the Upper Nile, Lakes Rudolf and Chad, and their associated rivers. There are four other related species, all in tropical Africa. The bichir has a long body, small but broad head, and rounded tail, but its distinctive feature is a series of finlets along the back which may be raised or lowered. Each finlet is flag-like and consists of a single ray to which one or several fin-rays are attached. The pectoral fins, too, are peculiar. They are fan-like, almost as if stalked. The body is covered with an armour of hard rhombic scales, made of the hard protein, ganoin. Bichirs are fishes with many primitive features and in fact are surviving Palaeniscoids.

Air-breathing

The bichir lives hidden among the thickets of large water plants at the margins of rivers and lakes, from which it comes out at night, to feed. It has gills in addition to the lung-like swim-bladder, yet if denied air for even a short time it dies. To breathe air, a bichir swims slowly to the surface, takes a quick gulp, then quickly swims down to the bottom. In most fishes, even in those that gulp air, the swim-bladder is single. In the bichir it is paired, like the lungs of a land vertebrate, although the two parts are of unequal size.

A peculiar feature of its behaviour is its use of the pectoral fins almost as legs, as supports for the front part of the body. The fish may rest supporting itself on these fins, with the head raised, rather in the manner of a quadruped on land, such as a lizard. When hunting for food it behaves quite unlike other fishes. It prowls, moving forward slowly inch by inch, stopping, raising the head as if sniffing around, then moving forward again. Its unusual tubular nostrils, coupled with the small eyes, suggest that the sense of smell is used in finding food.

The almost cat-like prowl is seen, also, when a bichir is confronted with any new object. It moves forward much in the manner of a cat stalking a mouse, but its pectoral fins are fluttering and the finlets on its back are raised, all ready to swim backwards if need arise. When moving quickly, the finlets are laid back, the pectoral fins are pressed close to the body, and the bichir drives itself through the water with side-to-side eel-like movements of the body.

Predator of small animals

The food consists chiefly of small fishes, but small aquatic animals, mainly insect larvae and small worms, and small frogs are also taken.

Leaping courtship

Spawning takes place, usually in August and September, at the time of floods, when the rivers and lakes overflow to form marshes and swamps. The bichir moves out into these. Courtship begins with two bichir leaping out of the water, after which they chase each other, keeping close together. After a while the pursuit is broken off. There follows a brief rest which is ended by the male going over to the female and nudging her with his head or brushing her with his anal fin, which is said to be swollen and folded at the breeding season. Practically nothing is known of the spawning itself until the larval stage. The larvae are tiny miniatures of the adults but with external feathery gills, like those of newt larvae.

One of the missing links

The bichir has been described as one of the most interesting fishes for anatomical and evolutionary studies. To understand why, we need to go back nearly half a century. Then, anything that was fish-like and had fins was a fish, and this was true whether we were dealing with sharks, sturgeons or sticklebacks. Then came a change in outlook. Somebody put forward the idea that sharks were not fishes. That is, they were not true fishes, because they had a skeleton

of cartilage instead of bone. Now the habit grew of speaking of two groups of animals, the sharks, or cartilaginous fish, and the true or bony fishes.

However, this is a point about which anyone who is not an ichthyologist or a student of fishes can rest easy. To anyone but an ichthyologist the old idea of what can be regarded as a fish is still workable. Moreover, even to the specialist, the division between the cartilaginous fishes and the bony fishes is anything but definite. In between are various links, of which the bichir is one. Its skeleton is bony but has more than the usual amount of cartilage in it. Its intestine has a spiral valve, one of the hallmarks of a shark. It has spiracles, openings behind each eye like an extra gill, which are a feature of many cartilaginous fishes. In its anatomy, therefore, it shows a mixture of shark and true fish. Also in its lungs, the limb-like pectoral fins and in features of its behaviour, it indicates the line along which, in all probability, the dramatic step was taken by which a land-living amphibian, some form of primitive salamander or newt, arose from an air-breathing fish able to use its paired fins as limbs. This, of course, fits in with the bichir's habit of breeding in marshes where the water contains little oxygen and a fish that can breathe air is at an advantage. There are others in this noble company, among them the bowfin, sturgeon, lungfishes and the celebrated coelacanth. One or other among the ancestors of this distinguished company took the evolutionary line which led to the first amphibian, later the first reptile, and through it to the mammals and birds.

class	**Pisces**
order	**Cladista**
family	**Polypteridae**
genus & species	***Polypterus bichir**, others*

Black molly

*This is a black variety of a live-bearing tooth-carp of the family Poeciliidae. It occurs naturally in three out of the eight species of **Mollienisia**. It has been selectively bred by fish fanciers, and both the black variety and the naturally-coloured forms are favoured by aquarists. It is chosen here to represent the peculiarities of several species of **Mollienisia**. All 'mollies' are small, 2–5 in. long, live in Central American rivers, and are characterised by having a large rounded tail and a prominent dorsal fin. This, in the male, is extra large and sail-like. The biology of all species of **Mollienisia** is similar.*

Aggressive fin display

The most interesting feature of black mollies is their large dorsal fin like a sail, which is used in aggressive displays and in courtship. Rival males swim at each other with all fins expanded, but the fin display is more bluff than anything, the contest being bloodless. The male displaying most actively or with the larger 'sail' usually intimidates his rival. In courtship the male comes over to the female with all sails set and with fins quivering takes up position across her path. At the same time he displays colours which, though always present, are shown on these occasions only.

Food

The mollies are mainly vegetarian but also take small amounts of animal food, such as water fleas and mosquito larvae.

Eggs develop inside female

The mollies' reproductive life is full of unusual events. The male's anal fin is modified to form a gonopodium with which he puts sperm into the female's oviduct where the young develop and are subsequently born alive. Several weeks pass between fertilisation and birth, the length of time depending mainly on temperature. The young lie curled head to tail in the oviduct and are born one or two at a time.

Genetical peculiarities

There is a natural tendency in mollies towards the production of the black pigment, melanin, and occasionally all black 'sports' are produced. The aquarist takes advantage of this to breed black mollies. The black sports are obtained mainly from the sail-fin *Mollienisia latipinna*, less often from

Female black molly on the right of the picture is pursued by males. The male anal fin is modified to form a gonopodium with which he puts sperm into the female's oviduct. The anal fin of the female is fully developed. The large sail-like dorsal fin is used in aggressive and courtship displays.

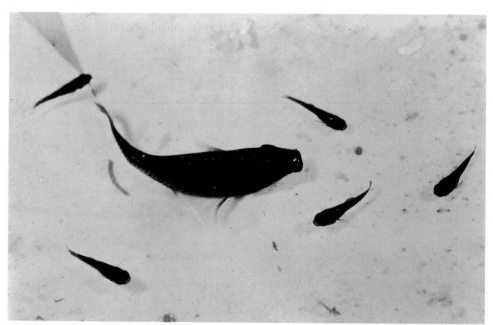

△ *Mother with young mollies, which developed curled head to tail in the female's oviduct. (Lifesize)*

▽ *Black mollies have been selectively bred by fish fanciers from several molly species.*

the sail-bearer *M. velifera* and occasionally from the wedge-face *M. sphenops*. When the young blacks are born they may be light or dark in colour. Most of them become light in a few weeks and only when about 1 in. long do they begin to show black spots. Six months from birth some will have become all black. Others may not become black for 2 years, and some never do. One strain, the 'permablack', however, is born black and remains so.

The black mollies themselves are attractive to the eye and so have become favourites of the dilettante aquarist. To the more discerning, they are even more attractive, for their genetical peculiarities. This is true of all the mollies. One is *M. formosa* living in the rivers of Texas and Mexico.

M. formosa is a natural hybrid resulting from a cross between *M. latipinna* and *M. sphenops*. The hybrid has characters intermediate between those of the two parents and this intermediate form is perpetuated in a quite unusual way. The hybrids are nearly all females, and they produce only female offspring. They cannot do so, however, unless a male *M. latipinna* or *M. sphenops* is present. Mating then occurs and presumably the sperms enter the ova but they are rejected, so that what the sperms have done is to set in motion all those things which normally result from the fertilisation of an ovum, while contributing nothing to the offspring.

So, when a *formosa* female mates with a *latipinna* male, all the progeny look like the mother in every respect. When a *formosa* female mates with a *sphenops* male all the progeny, again, look like the mother. In fact, the same is true if a *formosa* female mates with the male of any of the species of *Mollienisia*. Moreover, very rarely, perhaps once in every 10 000, a male *formosa* is born. Presumably it can mate, but so far there is no evidence as to whether it contributes anything to the offspring.

This extraordinary state of affairs can be tested merely by looking at populations of *formosa*. Mother and offspring look alike, behave alike, and have the same internal anatomy. That they are truly alike can be tested by transplanting tissues.

We are familiar now with the surgical operations of heart and kidney transplants, the early attempts at which were mainly unsuccessful. This was because the patients' bodies rejected the alien tissues. We can be fairly certain that a heart transplant would be wholly successful if performed between identical twins, because experiments have shown that other tissue grafts between identical twins are always successful. Many experiments have been carried out on mollies, transplanting fins, heart and spleen from daughter to mother and between the progeny of a single mother, and there is never any rejection.

class	**Pisces**
order	**Atheriniformes**
family	**Poeciliidae**
genus & species	***Mollienisia latipinna*** *sail-fin* ***M. formosa*** *Amazon molly* *others*

Blenny

The blennies, together with the related blenny-like fishes, are almost as numerous as the stars in the heavens. There are nearly a score of families and most of these contain numerous species of mainly small shallow water fishes living in tropical and temperate seas. They can readily be found on rocky shores when the tide is out, under stones or seaweed, especially in rock pools. They have elongated bodies, and are usually less than 6 in. long. The pelvic fins are placed far forward, in most are long, if only two-rayed, but in some are very small. The dorsal fin extends from the back of the head almost to the tail or is even continuous with it.

Portrait of the common blenny. Living in shallow waters blennies are vulnerable to many enemies. Independent movement of the eyes gives the blenny a good wide view, so it sees if danger threatens.

Research on fish behaviour

The casual naturalist searching the shore sees the blenny only as a small fish that darts across a rock pool, when a stone is lifted, and vanishes under another stone. The ease with which blennies can be found and caught has made them favourites for study in aquaria. This has shed light on their behaviour in relation to tides and on their social hierarchies.

As long ago as 1877, a Mr Ross of Topsham, in Devon, kept a shanny, a species of blenny, in a glass tank filled with sea water. He noticed the fish became restless as the time of high tide approached. When he put a large stone in the tank, with its top clear of water, the shanny would leave the water to lie on the rock when the time for low tide arrived. It would drop back into the water at high tide. Ross found, during the many months he had it, that the shanny always knew the state of the tide.

There are places, the Mediterranean being one, where the tides are feeble or non-existent. The blennies living there have no need for a biological clock, and it has been found by experiments similar to those made by Ross, but differing in that the blennies could not leave the water, that after a while the fishes behaved as if they were living in a tideless zone.

With such small fishes living on a rocky or stony bottom observation of their behaviour once the tide is in is almost impossible. It can, however, be pieced together by watching them in aquaria that approach as nearly as possible the natural state. From such studies it is clear that once they are covered with water by the returning tide they become fully active. One of their activities, naturally, is feeding, but much time is spent in chasing one another.

Each digs a shelter under a stone or rock, excavating the sand by wriggling its body. It may make several such shelters and it alternately comes out to feed and darts back to shelter. There is, however, no holding of territories with fixed boundaries which birds and other animals are known to do. A blenny moves about over what is called its home range. It has an individual distance and it grows uneasy should another blenny intrude within that distance. Then we see that one blenny will be dominant, another will be subordinate. Two coming near each other will show fight, butting with the head or biting, or merely raising their fins in a display of force. The dominant individual always prevails, the subordinate giving way and retreating.

Similarly, if a subordinate is in a shelter and a dominant enters the subordinate will leave it. The tables are reversed when a subordinate enters the shelter of a dominant. It is driven out. Blennies also have favourite resting places on rocks, and these are determined by this same kind of 'peck order', the boss blenny driving the others away.

The scale of dominance, which can be seen even in young blennies, is largely determined by size, and the more nearly two blennies are matched for size the more likely a fight is to develop. The most this amounts to is that one may bite the other, inflicting only superficial wounds. Something of this kind was demonstrated by two American scientists with blennies in an aquarium, that became tame enough to swim across for food. If a cupped hand was lowered into the water one of the blennies would come to rest in the hand. Soon it would be driven out by one of the others nibbling its tail. At times a continuous procession would result, each taking a turn to lie in the hand and then being driven out by the next.

In aquaria blennies are alert and they look intelligent. Several experimenters have shown that blennies can be readily taught, to come for food at certain places, even to take food off particular hooks, or to wait at other places to be fed. This is done by what is called reward and punishment, or, to use the terms preferred by scientists, 'positive and negative reinforcement'. One scientist showed that blennies could be trained to tell apart objects by their colours, brightness, shape and size, numbers and position. For example, they could be taught to tell the difference between such letters as U and E, W and L, and to recognize two or more letters in a group.

One feature of the behaviour which may contribute to the appearance of intelligence, if not to an actual intelligence, is the ability to move the eyes independently. Certainly this gives an air of watchfulness, but this may be no more than a normal requirement for fishes living in shallow water with many enemies.

Omnivorous eater

Little is known precisely about the food of blennies in the natural state. It is usually said that they are carnivorous or omnivorous. In aquaria they will eat bits of meat, worms and small crustaceans swimming near the surface. From this we can presume their diet is wide. A shanny in an aquarium will even browse acorn barnacles, crushing the strong shells with its teeth.

Male guards the eggs

Blennies usually lay eggs but at least one bears living young and is called the viviparous blenny. The eggs are oval or pear shaped, and are laid, as a rule, in empty mollusc shells, in crevices in rocks, in empty bottles lying on the bottom. One was even seen to lay eggs in a large hollow beef bone. They are attached to the inner surfaces of such objects and guarded by the male, rarely by both parents, who by movements of his tail keeps the water around the eggs moving to oxygenate them. Some of the blennies which live in the waters of the Caribbean actually lay their eggs inside sponges. The young fishes stay for a while inside the sponge, feeding on small plankton brought in by the currents of water drawn in by the sponge.

The viviparous blenny *Zoarces viviparus* is not a true blenny but is one of the blenny-

Male butterfly blenny guards eggs laid in a disused milk bottle. He moves his tail to keep the water round the eggs moving to oxygenate them.

Blenny peering out from its shelter. Each blenny digs a shelter, or often several, under a rock or stone, excavating sand by wriggling its body.

like fishes referred to in the introduction. Also known as the eelpout, it belongs to the family Zoarcidae, most of whose members are oviparous. The eggs hatch within the female's body about 3 weeks after fertilisation but the babies are not born until 4 months later. Each is 1½ in. long when born, and a single female 7–8 in. long may give birth to 20–40 at a time. The largest females may give birth to as many as 300 at a time.

The shanny can live as long as 4 years and other blennies probably have a similar life-span.

Vulnerable at low tide

Blennies are probably more vulnerable at low tide, and more especially when breeding, than when covered with water. Gulls may then take them, and so may rats scavenging

the shore. Nevertheless, it must be conceded that blennies are well camouflaged by their colours and the mottled patterns on the bodies. Some, like the shanny, are capable of changing colour according to their background.

Enlarged thyroid gland

Blennies, as we have seen, readily survive each period of ebb-tide sheltering under stones or seaweeds. Some carry this further and tend to leave the water for appreciable periods of time. It was some such tendency that caused the original invasion of land by fish ancestors that gave rise to the land vertebrates, including man.

It seems that this was not necessarily due to any impulse or urge to leave the sea to escape competition, the reason usually given, but the result of an enlarged gland.

Fishes, like the blennies, capable of an amphibious existence, have a large thyroid gland. Moreover, there is one blenny *Blennius ocellatus* that normally spends its whole life in water, breathing by gills, taking in oxygen dissolved in the water. When injected with an extract of thyroid it takes on an amphibious life and it has been found that it breathes air (atmospheric oxygen) for as much as 8 hours at a time.

class	**Pisces**
order	**Perciformes**
family	**Blenniidae**
genera	**Blennius, Hypsoblennius** *others*

▽ *Boss blenny on an empty crab case waiting to drive a small one away as soon as it comes out.*

▷ *A blenny exposed at low tide is vulnerable to gulls and rats scavenging on the shore. The body colours and mottled patterns give, however, quite effective camouflage.*

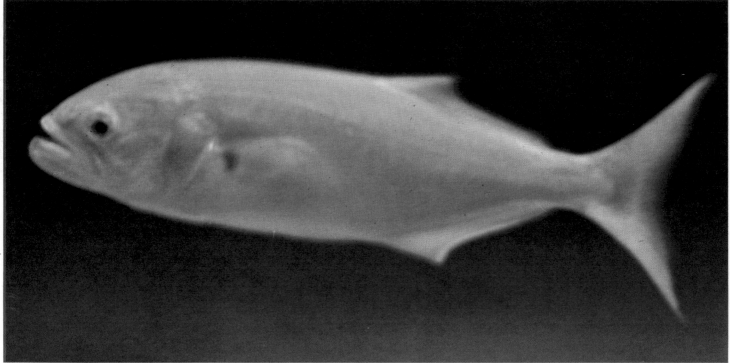

The swift-moving bluefish swims in large shoals and attacks other fishes with unparalleled ferocity. It is caught commercially and for sport.

Bluefish

The bluefish is remarkable for its voracity and has long been known as an ocean killer. There is a single species occupying a family to itself. The bluefish, bass-like and and about 4 ft long, lives in schools in tropical and subtropical waters, except for the central and eastern Pacific. Its range seems to be extending. Since 1945, for example, it has become familiar to the fishermen of Tuscany who believe it followed American ships there in the Second World War, and to whom it is known as the American fish. Bluish or greenish in colour with a black blotch at the base of each pectoral fin, it has a dorsal fin in two parts, the spinous portion in front being the smaller. In summer they may come into estuaries when seasonally abundant offshore.

Ferocious

Bluefish are swift-moving fish that appear suddenly in large shoals as much as 4—5 miles long and attack other fishes with almost unparalleled ferocity. Little is known of their migrations, except that they may travel considerable distances, but it is believed there may be regional races. Also they may winter in deep water, between perhaps 300—600 ft, as bluefish have been caught in trawls at these depths in winter.

Enormous appetite

Other fishes of all kinds are attacked, and off the Atlantic coast of North America menhaden *Brevortia tyrannus* especially are preyed upon. A feature of bluefish is that they behave like animated chopping machines, cutting fishes even as large as themselves to pieces and continuing to do so until satiated. The trail of a shoal is then marked by frag-

ments of fish and blood, often with dead fish having only a portion bitten away. It has been estimated that a thousand million bluefish may occur annually in the western Atlantic in summer. Allowing a ration of ten fish a day for each bluefish, this amounts to 1 200 000 000 000 fishes killed in a single season. These figures may be slightly exaggerated but they epitomize the habits of bluefish, which, even when only a fraction of an inch, are a menace to other fishes.

40 000 000 pounds caught annually

There are no known enemies other than man, who catches bluefish for its palatable flesh. Commercial fisheries in the United States account for 4 million pounds weight annually, and sports fishermen catch over ten times this amount.

Bluefish rising to fisherman's bait.

Life history studied in the laboratory

Spawning is in June to August, the eggs, 1¼ mm diameter, are probably laid well out to sea. These hatch 44—46 hours later, the newly-hatched fish being about $\frac{1}{10}$ in. long. At first, the jaws and gills are non-functional, the eyes are without pigment and there are no pectoral fins, the young fish being dependent on its yolk sac for a supply of food. At a year old it will have grown to 16 in.,

at 2 years to 20 in., at 3 years to 28 in., with weights of 1, 2 and 4 lb respectively. The record fish caught on a line weighed 24 lb 3 oz and measured 41 in. North African bluefish are said to reach 45 lb.

The most detailed account of the development of the eggs is that given by LP Salekhova, from study of bluefish taken in the Black Sea and kept in aquaria. The eggs were transparent and at 25 hours after fertilisation the chief organs had been formed in the embryo. At 37 hours the heart began to beat. After that the embryo turned from time to time during the remaining 7—9 hours before hatching.

Historical influence

In 1871 Spencer Fullerton Baird was invited to investigate a supposed decline in the New England commercial shore fisheries. Hook and line fishermen blamed trap fishermen, who in turned blamed the bluefish. Baird, in his report, recommended controls for trap-fishing but included a blistering attack on the iniquities of the bluefish. It was he who suggested the astronomical figures given above under food. Baird's Commission, the United States Commission for Fish and Fisheries, was still in being when he died, in 1887. He was still Fish Commissioner, with a permanent laboratory at Wood's Hole, on Cape Cod, the oldest marine laboratory in North America. Moreover, the US Fish and Wildlife Service, now a tremendous organisation, can trace its beginnings to Baird's Fish Commission and the bluefish!

class	**Pisces**
order	**Perciformes**
family	**Pomatomidae**
genus & species	***Pomatomus saltatrix***

A living fossil, the bowfin is the sole surviving member of a family which flourished 130 million years ago.

Bowfin

The bowfin, with many primitive features, is a living fossil whose ancestors abounded 130 million years ago. A single species now occupies a family and an order on its own. It is a freshwater fish found only in the lakes and streams of the eastern United States, although its ancestors were widely distributed over North America and Europe, where their fossils may be found. Normally about 2 ft in length, it may reach 3 ft. Long-bodied, pike-like, it has a long soft-rayed dorsal fin, a rounded tail and thin scales with an enamel-like covering of ganoine. The male has a dark spot circled with orange or yellow at the base of the tail fin. In the female it is either lacking or is merely a dark spot.

Air breathing fish

The bowfin, mudfish, or spotfin is quite a remarkable fish which can breathe air. It lives in still waters and sluggish streams, and can survive in water with little or no oxygen. As with several other primitive fishes the swimbladder of the bowfin has a spongy inner lining well supplied with blood-vessels and acts as a lung, the bowfin rising to the surface to gulp air. It can live out of water for as much as 24 hours. It is said to utter a bell-like note which is possibly due to exhaling before taking in more air. Another primitive feature, which is more pronounced in sharks, is the spiral valve in the intestine. There is only a vestige of this valve in the bowfin, but even that is unusual in the bony or true fishes, to which the bowfin belongs. Another feature characteristic of primitive bony fishes is the large bony gular plate on the underside of the head between the two lower jawbones. The bowfin swims by a motion of its dorsal fin.

Voracious feeders

The bowfin eats crustaceans, worms, frogs and fishes, as well as dead flesh. It is so voracious and takes such a wide variety of animal foods that where the fish is abundant it is considered destructive and steps are taken to eradicate it. In the southern United States it is used as food, smoked or dried and in fishballs and jambalaya. Fishing for bowfins is said to be exciting sport because they will snap at almost any bait, although frogs and minnows are most used. The bowfins' strong jaws, sharp teeth and predatory habits have earned them the names of freshwater dogfish and freshwater wolves.

Male nests and guards the young

Spawning takes place in May to June, when the male's dark spot with its ring of colour becomes more intense. The male selects a weedy area along the margin of a lake or stream. There he builds a circular nest among a clump of water plants. He is said to swim round and round pressing the vegetation down, much as a bird fashions a nest by pivoting in it. Several females lay their eggs in the nest and the male, after fertilising these by shedding his milt on them, guards the nest until the eggs hatch, which they do in 8—10 days. The eggs stick to the stems and leaves of the plants. The guardian male, by swimming round and round the nest, creates currents that aerate the eggs. He also guards the young until they are about 4 in. long, when his parental instinct wanes. Such parental care behaviour is obviously an advantage for a species living in sluggish and poorly oxygenated water. The young fishes have their own protective device in the form of cement organs at the end of the snout. With these they can cling to water plants when first hatched and until their rapid growth makes them large enough and strong enough to swim, when they leave the nest in a compact group with the male in attendance.

Link with the past

The bowfin is only one of many animals to have been called a 'living fossil'. This term was first used by Darwin for a tree, the ginkgo or maidenhair tree, which was worldwide in Mesozoic times 200 million years ago, when the giant reptiles roamed the earth, but was found by Europeans, in the 18th century, to be still surviving in China and Japan. It was about the same time, in the Mesozoic age, that large-mouthed predatory fishes first appeared. The family to which the bowfin belongs sprang from these and during the last 150 million years reached its zenith and then declined, the only species left being that now found in the eastern United States. Another species persisted in Europe until 50 million years ago and then died out. So this fish is a typical 'living fossil'; not a missing link but a link with the past. It has outlived its era and is the sole survivor from a past heyday.

Bowfin *(Amia calva)*

class	**Pisces**
order	**Protospondyli**
family	**Amiidae**
genus & species	*Amia calva*

Butterfish

The butterfish is an eel-like blenny living between tide-marks on the North Atlantic coasts, as far south as the English Channel in the east and Wood's Hole, USA, in the west. Alternative names for it are gunnel and nine-eyes, from the row of dark spots along the back. The butterfish, up to 6 in. long, is ribbon-shaped, with a low dorsal fin running the length of the back, a long low anal fin, a small tail and very small paired fins. The body, coloured yellowish-green with darker markings, is covered with very small scales. The snout is short, and the teeth are very small.

'Butterfish' refers to the slippery nature of the fish and the difficulty one has in holding it between the fingers. Another name is butter-eel. Since this is a characteristic of many fishes it is not surprising to find a New Zealand wrasse also called a butterfish, as well as two other unrelated species in coastal waters of the United States, all of which have slimy bodies.

Uncovered at low tide

The butterfish, like other blennies, is most commonly seen when the tide is out, sheltering under stones or seaweeds, or in rock crevices kept damp by overhanging seaweeds. When disturbed it darts rapidly through the water of a rock pool, or wriggles over the wet stones or seaweeds. It becomes more active when, at high tide, it is completely covered with water. And, as with other blennies (see page 35), butterfish living close inshore alternate active with resting periods, with the rise and fall of the tide.

Meat eaters

Little is known of feeding in the natural state but butterfish kept in aquaria take shreds of meat and small invertebrates of various kinds, suggesting a wide diet, mainly carnivorous.

Eggs rolled into a ball

Spawning is from December to March. The female lays her eggs in a mass, usually in a cavity in a rock or in an empty bivalve shell. The egg-mass's diameter is a little over 1 in. The female curves her body into a loop while laying, so rolling the egg-mass into a ball. Once the mass is laid the male coils himself round it and continues to protect the eggs in this way until they hatch. The usual explanation for this is that the eggs are sticky only when first laid, and the parent's action in rolling the body round the mass is to prevent them from becoming scattered. It is unusual for marine fishes to show this amount of parental care. It is even more rare for the female to take turns with the male, as the butterfish is reputed to do.

The eggs hatch more than a month after laying, the larvae being $\frac{2}{5}$ in. long. They drift out to sea and spend several months at depths of about 190 ft before returning to the shallow coastal waters.

Joint development

The protective membrane around each egg is so fragile that it is almost impossible to remove one from the mass without rupturing it. This is probably why such devotion is needed from the parents. If the eggs became separated, the chances of their surviving would be negligible. There may, nevertheless, be another need for their being kept together in a mass.

Experiments carried out on other species in which eggs are laid in masses suggest that each egg helps the development of the others. That is, they must keep together for the common good. In one experiment, some eggs from a mass were carefully separated one by one and put in separate aquaria. The remainder were left in an aquarium on their own, still tightly packed. All had similar water, air, and light. The separated eggs either failed to hatch or the larvae from them were deformed.

class	**Pisces**
order	**Perciformes**
family	**Pholidae**
genus & species	***Pholis gunnellus***

△ *The butterfish is a 6 in. eel-like blenny.* ▽ *The name refers to its very slippery skin.*

*The freshwater butterfly fish **Pantodon buchholzi** found in the waters of western Africa is one of the strangest of the so-called flying fishes. It spends most of its time swimming just under the surface and is capable of leaping out of the water for a distance of 6 or more feet.*

Butterfly fish

It is virtually impossible to speak about butterfly fishes without confusion since the name is commonly used for different kinds of unrelated fishes. The same can be said of angelfishes. Attention has already been drawn to this on page 12, where butterfly fishes have been described, together with their very close relatives, the marine angelfishes. Here we return to this subject in order to deal with a freshwater fish that has also been called a butterfly fish. At the same time this gives us the opportunity to contrast and compare

it with the marine fishes, inhabitants of coral reefs especially, which are also called butterfly fishes. For our description of the habits of marine butterfly fishes we must refer to page 12. But here on the next two pages we portray these fishes, belonging to the family Chaetodontidae, in a series of fascinating and beautiful photographs.

The one species of freshwater butterfly fish is sufficiently extraordinary to merit close attention on its own. Never more than 4 in. long, it lives in the rivers of tropical West Africa. Its head and body are boat-shaped, flattened above, bluntly rounded below. It is coloured grey-green to

brownish-silver, marked with spots and streaks. The large mouth is directed upwards, and the nostrils are tubular. Another remarkable feature is its fins. The pectoral fins are large and wing-like. Each pelvic fin has four very long filamentous rays not connected to each other, and the unpaired fins are large, transparent and supported by long rays.

For a long time the relationships of this fish, first discovered in 1876, have been in doubt, but it is now placed in a family on its own near that of the large South American fish, the arapaima. It has no relationship with the marine butterfly fishes of the family Chaetodontidae.

A fish that flies

This remarkable fish is reckoned to fly over the water, flapping its wings like a bat or a bird. The freshwater butterfly fish spends most of its time just below the surface of still or stagnant waters in the Congo and Niger basins, in the weedy backwaters and standing pools. But it is most renowned for its ability to leap out of water for distances up to 6 ft, its large pectoral fins being used, as are those of the true flying fishes, in gliding flight. It has also been credited with flapping these fins in true powered flight, as in bats and birds. By 1960, however, it had been generally agreed that this was not so.

Then came a remarkable sequel. PH Greenwood and KS Thomson investigated the anatomy of this fish. They found it had a most unusual shoulder girdle, the arrangement of bones to which the pectoral fins are attached. In fact, these two authors described it as unique among fishes. The bones were so thin that they had to be very careful not to damage them while dissecting them out. The whole of the shoulder girdle is broad and flattened to give support to a highly developed system of muscles, comparable with the large pectoral muscles that work the wings of birds. The two scientists also found that the fins could not be folded against the body, as is usual in fishes, but could be moved up and down. In brief, they concluded that, while it was still unproven whether or not the butterfly fish could make a powered flight, its shoulder girdle and muscles were such that it ought to be able to fly. The best that can be said is that the fish has been seen to beat its fins up and down when held in the hand. It has, however, been suggested that this is only used to give the butterfly fish a push-off from the water to become airborne.

Insect feeder

The food consists almost entirely of the small insects, such as flies, that fall on to the surface of the water.

Life history

Relatively little is known about the breeding, and such details as we have are from the few butterfly fishes that have bred in captivity. Numerous false matings have been seen, with the male riding on the back of the female, sometimes for hours at a time, holding her firmly with the long rays of the pelvic fins. Mating finally is effected by the two twisting their bodies together to bring the vents opposite each other. Fertilisation seems, however, not to be internal. As soon

▽ *The freshwater butterfly fish is not related to marine butterfly fishes of the tropical seas.*

▽▽ *Four-eyed butterfly fish, so-called because of the false 'eye' markings at its tail end.*

▽ *Vividly-striped marine butterfly fishes are deep-bodied and flattened from side to side*

as they are laid the eggs float to the surface, and in 3 days these hatch. The fry remain at the surface feeding on the tiniest of the insects, such as springtails and aphides, which fall on them.

Flying or gliding

The ability to make either gliding or powered flights through the air is rare among fishes, although to be able to leap from the water is common enough. For years, scientists have argued among themselves whether or not the flying fishes of the oceans beat their wings when airborne. At present, evidence suggests that they do not. Similarly, it may be some years before we can be sure whether the West African butterfly fishes beat their wings or not. There is, however, one group of freshwater fishes that do beat their fins to achieve true

flight through the air. These are the hatchet fishes of northern South America, found from the River Plate to Panama.

As so often happens, another confusion of names arises. We already have it over butterfly fishes, as we have seen. There are also two kinds of hatchet fishes. One is marine (see page 108) and the other is freshwater. Both are named for their shape, the body being flattened from side to side, so that it looks like the blade of a hatchet.

The freshwater hatchet fishes beat their pectoral fins rapidly when making a take-off run over the surface before becoming airborne, and they continue to beat their fins when airborne.

To make the confusion even more confounded, it may be mentioned that freshwater hatchet fishes do a butterfly-like dance

during their courtship. Fortunately we can note the scientific names and there can be no doubt as to the animal referred to. Each animal has a binomial name of genus and species, rather like the surname and christian name used to identify humans.

class	**Pisces**
order	**Osteoglossiformes**
family	**Pantodontidae**
genus	*Pantodon buchholzi*
& species	*freshwater butterfly fish*

▽▽ *Marine butterfly fishes* **Chaetodon** *live around coral reefs in shallow tropical seas.*

▽ *The butterfly fish* **Heniochus acuminatus** *lives in the warm seas around the Philippine Islands. It has a very deep body, most of the depth being due to a highly arched back.*

Cardinal fish

This is the name of many small fishes, usually red or with red in the pattern of the body, that live mainly on coral reefs in tropical seas. A few live in freshwater streams on tropical Pacific islands. All but a few deep-sea forms are shallow-water fishes, usually not more than 4 in. long. The largest are up to 8 in. long and these live in the brackish water of mangrove swamps.

There are great numbers of cardinal fishes, suggesting that they are the main-stay of many predatory fishes. They easily form associations with sedentary animals.

Shelter in a shell

The best-known are two species of 2 in. conchfish of the Caribbean, Florida and Bermuda. These shelter in the large molluscs *(Strombus)* known as conches, resting in the mantle cavity and coming out at night to feed on small crustaceans. Not every conch contains a fish and not every cardinal fish shelters in a conch. Some shelter in sponges, empty conch shells or empty bivalve shells, in fact in any convenient hollow object or cavity.

American scientists studying a Hawaiian species of cardinal fish collected over a thousand specimens from a small area of dead coral. This gives a picture of the conchfish hidden away in all manner of cavities and shelters on the sea-bed by day, and swarming out at night to feed. As it is, the fish is mainly seen when a conch is taken from the sea for food. As the mollusc lies on the bottom of the boat it opens its mantle cavity and out flops the cardinal fish.

Sea-urchin host

One cardinal fish *Siphamia versicolor* of the Nicobar Islands in the Indian Ocean, lives in association with a dark-red sea-urchin. When nothing is happening to disturb the peace, the urchin parts its long spines so that they form pyramid-like clusters, and between these the fish moves, cleaning the sea-urchin's skin. At the slightest alarm, even a shadow falling on the urchin, the spines are spread defensively and the fish shelters among them, usually head-downwards.

At night the fish comes out to feed, but if driven from its sea-urchin host it will swim to another. If this urchin is a different colour the fish will change colour to match that of its new host.

Mouth-breeding

The breeding habits of the cardinal fishes are simple. As the female lays her eggs, the male takes them into his mouth and there they remain until they hatch. Sometimes, the males alone hold the eggs, sometimes the females, and in other species both parents may share the duty. There are a few species in which the eggs are picked up by the male only when danger threatens. Some idea of what this mouth-breeding involves can be had from a comparison of two species. The female of one in Australian waters lays eggs $\frac{1}{5}$ in. in diameter

△ Cardinals are usually red in colour.
▽ Barred cardinal's striped body breaks its outline—quite an effective camouflage.

▷ A group of cardinal fish sheltering amongst sea urchin spines. They are found in the limpid waters of Australia's Great Barrier Reef.

and the male holds 150 in his mouth. In a Mediterranean species the eggs are $\frac{1}{50}$ in. in diameter and the male holds 22 000 in his mouth.

In this Mediterranean species the eggs are fertilised inside the female's body and there is a curious inversion in the copulation. The genital papilla of the female is long and she inserts it into the male's body to take the sperm for fertilising her eggs. This form of 'petticoat government' is completed by the male taking over the care of the eggs, as we have seen.

Death-like ruse

Little is known about the enemies of cardinal fishes. Consequently, it is possible to make only the generalization that they must be eaten by many small and medium-sized predatory fishes. This is supported by the behaviour of the brownspot cardinal fish. Animals at the mercy of others often use the tricks which used to be known as shamming dead or feigning injury, but which are now included under the comprehensive title of distraction displays. The 3 in. brownspot, so named from a dark spot above each of its breast fins, flops on one side and gives every appearance of being dead when one tries to catch it.

Elaborate light-organs

There are many animals and some plants which produce living light. In some there is an obvious advantage, as when the female

glowworm shines the light at the tip of her abdomen, so bringing the male to her side. In other instances it is hard to see what purpose is served, as with the fungus which grows inside hollow trees, glowing with a spectral light at certain times of the year.

Some bacteria are luminous, and they present much the same case as the fungus: it is hard to see what purpose is served by it. Coastal fishes that have light-organs are dependent on these bacteria for them, unlike deep-sea fishes which produce their own light. Several cardinal fishes have these light-organs. One of them *Apogon ellioti*, from southeast Asian seas, not only has a population of bacteria, but the gland in which this is located has a reflector. Moreover, the muscles below the gland are translucent and act as a lens. The result is that this small cardinal fish swims about at night with a lamp in its throat. The purpose of this elaborate light-organ is unknown.

More remarkable is the cardinal fish that has in its intestine three such lamps, each containing luminous bacteria and each with its reflector and lens. The absurd part of this story is that these lamps are directed towards the interior of the intestine.

class	**Pisces**
order	**Perciformes**
family	**Apogonidae**
genera	***Apogon***, *others*

Carp

Of the extensive carp family (Cyprinidae), this is the most widely distributed. Native of Japan, China and Central Asia, from Turkestan to the Black Sea and the Danube basin, it has been introduced into many European countries as well as the United States. It differs from other members of the family in its unusually long dorsal fin, with 17–22 branched rays, the strongly serrated third spine of the dorsal and anal fins, and in its four barbels, two at each corner of the slightly protrusible mouth. There are no teeth in the mouth, but there are throat-teeth. The colour of the wild form is olive to yellow-green on the back, greenish-yellow to bronze-yellow on the flanks, and underparts yellowish. The fins are grey-green to brown, sometimes slightly reddish.

Wild carp at home

Carp prefer shallow sunny waters with a muddy bottom and abundant water plants. They avoid clear, swift-flowing or cold waters. Wild carp are found in large rivers and, more commonly, in ponds. Their food is insect larvae, freshwater shrimps and other crustaceans, worms and snails, as well as some plant matter. The barbels, organs of touch, and the protrusible mouth are used for grubbing in the mud, much of which is swallowed and later ejected when the edible parts have been digested. In winter feeding ceases and the fish enter a resting period, a form of hibernation. In May to June carp move into shallow water to spawn, the eggs laid on the leaves of water plants. Each lays over 60 000 eggs/lb of her body-weight. The larvae hatch out in 2–3 days, the adults return to deeper water, while the young fishes remain in shallow water, near the bank. They become sexually mature in 3–4 years. Small carp will be eaten by almost any fish significantly larger than themselves, including larger carp.

Domesticated varieties

As with many other domesticated animals, carp are found in a number of varieties, of two main types: leather carp and mirror carp. The first is scaleless, the second has large scales in two rows on each side of the body. Both can throw back to the original carp form. The shape of the body varies, from relatively slender to deep-bodied with a humpback. Some fish culturists claim these vary with the food, sparse feeding producing the slender forms, abundant feeding giving rise to humpbacks.

How old is a carp

Carp have probably been domesticated for many centuries, and have been carried all over the world for ornamental ponds, or for food. Surprisingly, therefore, in view of the familiarity that should have resulted from this, there is a conflict of opinion on important points—for instance, their longevity and maximum weights. Above all, there are serious discrepancies about when carp were introduced into Europe.

△ *Cyprinid fishes, for instance roach, tench and some carp, often show red forms which breed true to type. Aquarists take advantage, with results like these Japanese **Hi-goi**, golden carps.*

Gesner, the 16th-century Swiss naturalist, mentioned a carp 150 years old. Carp in the lakes of Fontainebleau, France, have been credited with ages of up to 400 years. Bingley, writing in 1805, records a carp in the pond in the garden of Emmanuel College, Cambridge, England, that had been an inhabitant more than 70 years. Tate Regan, authority on fishes in Britain in the first half of this century, was of the opinion that under artificial conditions a carp may attain 50 years but that 15 years would probably be the maximum in the wild state.

Perhaps one reason for the excessive claims is their hardiness when removed from water. This is also the reason why the fish could be spread over such a wide area by man. Wrapped in damp moss or water plants, it can survive transport over long distances. If Pennant is to be believed, this remark has the force of under-statement. In his *British Zoology* he tells of a carp wrapped in moss, with only its mouth exposed, placed in a net and hung in a cellar. It was fed with bread and milk and lived over a fortnight. It is only fair to add that it was 'often plunged in water'.

Carp usually grow to about 15 lb in the United States but in Europe a fish of over 60 lb and a length of 40 in. has been recorded. Claims have been made for 400 lb carp. Frederick II of Prussia is said to have caught one of 76 lb and a 140 lb carp is said to have

△ *Clarissa, the largest carp caught in Great Britain, was taken from Redmere Pool by R Walker in 1952. She was about 15 years old and weighed 44 lb. She lived in an aquarium until 1972.*

△ *The mirror carp is identified by rows of large scales along its back and sides.*

▽ *Some think carp found in Britain today came from carp cultivated in monastery stewponds.*

been caught at Frankfurt on Oder. There are several records of carp around 25 lb in Britain, but there is one for 44 lb taken by R Walker in 1952.

Historical uncertainty

The introduced form of the common carp was known to the Greeks and Romans, and has long been kept in ponds in parts of Europe. We know it is today found widely over England, the southern parts of Wales and in southern Scotland. The question remains: when was it first introduced into Britain?

Writers on the subject seem to have been fairly unanimous that all our carp must be regarded as descendants of fishes cultivated by the monks for centuries in their stewponds. Certainly, carp are still to be found in many of the surviving stewponds adjacent to ruins of monasteries and priories. That on its own is very little help in finding the date when they were first put there. Other than this, information comes from documentary evidence or guesswork, or a mixture of the two.

Eric Taverner, in his *Freshwater Fishes of the British Isles* (1957), suggested that carp were brought here from France and the Low Countries in the 14th century. Richard Fitter, writing in 1959, invokes an entry in *The Boke of St Albans* for dating their introduction prior to 1486. Emma Phipson, in *The Animal-Lore of Shakespeare's Time* (1883), speaks of Leonard Mascall, a Sussex gentleman, who has had the credit for importing the carp into England about the year 1514. She also points out that in the Privy Purse Expenses of Elizabeth of York, 1502, mention is made of a reward paid for the present of a carp. Izaak Walton, in *The Compleat Angler*, opined that the date was around 1530. Dr Albert Günther, celebrated authority on fishes in the last half of the 19th century, fixed the date at 1614.

The latest pronouncement is by Günther Sterba, in his *Freshwater Fishes of the World* (1962), that the carp reached England in 1512, Denmark in 1560, Prussia 1585, St Petersburg (Leningrad) 1729, and North America (California) 1872.

The dissolution of the monasteries began in 1535. A plan of a Benedictine monastery of the 12th century shows the site of a fishpond. Accepting the dates quoted here the fishponds of religious houses in England must have been stocked for at least two centuries with fish other than carp. Two of our seven authorities give dates about or after the dissolution of the monasteries, and three give dates only slightly before that event.

It is a romantic idea that English monks could supply themselves with carp to be eaten on fast days. But the evidence seems to be in favour of some other fish, probably the perch.

class	**Pisces**
order	**Cypriniformes**
family	**Cyprinidae**
genus & species	***Cyprinus carpio***

47

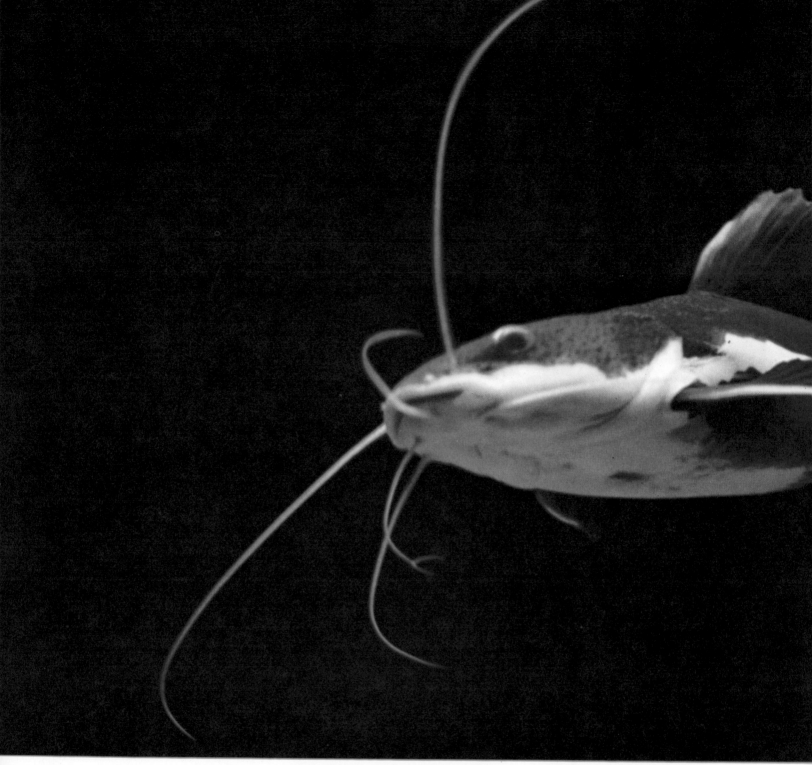

Catfish

The European catfish, or wels, grows to 9 ft or more in the rivers of central and eastern Europe and western Asia, and is the most famous of a large group called the naked catfishes. Its head is large and broad, the mouth has a wide gape and around it are three pairs of barbels or 'whiskers', the feature of all catfishes. In the wels the three pairs of barbels can be moved about and one pair is very long. The eyes are small. The body is stout, almost cylindrical in front, and flattened from side to side in the rear portion. The skin is slimy and has no scales. The fins, except for the long anal fin, are small. The colour is dark olive-green to bluish-black on the back, the flanks being paler with a reddish sheen, the belly whitish, the whole body being marked with spots and blotches.

The wels has many common names: silurus, the name given it by the Romans, glanis, sheatfish, or sheathfish, said to be from a fanciful resemblance to a sword scabbard, and waller. It has been introduced to a number of lakes in different parts of England.

Night hunter

The European catfish lives in rivers or deep lakes with plenty of water plants. It spends the day under overhanging banks or on the mud in deep water, foraging in the mud with its barbels in search of small invertebrates. At night it hunts, feeding voraciously on fish, crustaceans, and frogs. The larger ones take small water birds and mammals.

In May to June, the breeding season, the catfish moves into shallow water, where the female lays her eggs in a depression in the mud formed by lashing movements of her tail. A large female may lay 100 000 eggs, which are said to be guarded by the male. The fry are black and tadpole-shaped.

Legendary criminal

It would be surprising if a large fish, with hearty appetite, that lurks in dark places did not gather an evil reputation. The wels has been accused of swallowing lambs, even children. Gesner, in the 16th century, reports that a human head and a hand bearing gold rings were taken from the stomach of one of these large catfish.

Many strange habits

Although related, the various naked catfishes show remarkable diversity in form and habits. The banjo catfishes of South America may live in rivers and brackish

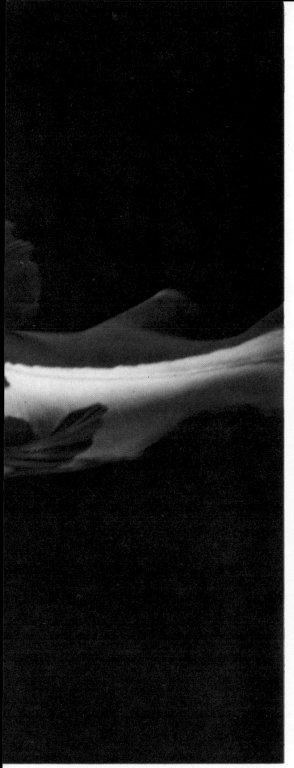

◁ *Most of the many different kinds of catfishes have three pairs of barbels round the mouth.*

△ *Glass catfish, like many catfishes, has no scales.*
▽ *The barbels are used to probe in mud for food.*

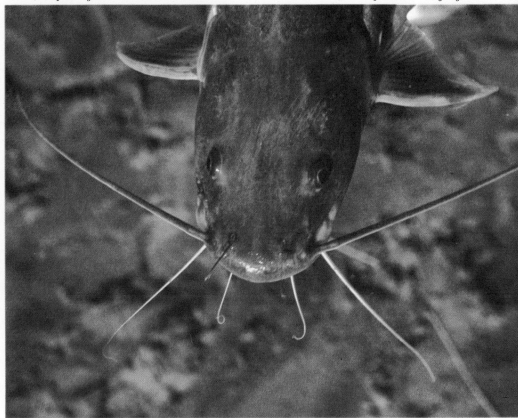

estuaries, some species in the sea. They are named for their flattened bodies with an unusually long tail. In one species *Aspredinichthys tibicen* the tail is three times the length of the body. In the breeding season, the females of this species grow a patch of spongy tentacles on the abdomen, and carry their eggs anchored to these.

Marine catfishes of the family Ariidae are mouth-breeders. That is, the male holds the eggs, which in some species are nearly 1 in. diameter, in his mouth, and when they hatch he continues to shelter the fry in the same way. For a month he must fast. Another name for these catfishes is crucifixion fish, because when the skull is cleaned, a fair representation of a crucifix is formed by the bones of the undersurface.

Another family of marine catfishes (Plotosidae) contains one of the most dangerous fishes of the coral reefs. The dorsal and the pectoral fins carry spines equipped with

poison glands. Merely to brush the skin against these spines can produce painful wounds.

Equally dangerous are the parasitic catfishes. Some of this family (Trichomycteridae) are free-living but many attach themselves to other fishes using the spines on the gill-covers to hook themselves on, piercing the skin and gorging themselves on the blood. Others insinuate themselves into the gill-cavities, eating the gills. The candiru *Vandellia cirrhosa* is prone to make its way into the urethra of a naked person entering the water, especially, so it seems, if water is passed. A surgical operation may be necessary to remove the fish. Men and women in the unsophisticated areas of Brazil wear a special guard of palm fibres to protect themselves when wading into rivers.

North America has the flathead (family Ictaluridae), a useful catfish reaching $5\frac{1}{2}$ ft long and 100 lb weight. The channel

catfish is a most valuable foodfish. There are, however, the madtoms, 5 in. or less, but with pectoral spines and poison glands.

Mad in another sense are the upside-down catfishes of tropical African rivers. From swimming normally these catfishes may suddenly turn and swim upside-down, for no obvious reason. When courting, the male and female upside-down catfishes swim at each other and collide head-on, repeating this at half-minute intervals.

class	**Pisces**
order	**Siluriformes**
family	**Siluridae**
genus & species	*Silurus glanis* European catfish others

Catshark

A shark of the family Scyliorhinidae which contains many species, distinguished by the picturesque patterns of stripes, bars and mottlings of so many of its members. One species, a South African skaamoog, is covered with markings that look like Egyptian hieroglyphics. The well-known dogfishes form part of the catshark family. It is better to deal with catsharks as a family, separately from the widespread and thoroughly well-known members, the dogfishes, if only because two of them are very interesting types of sharks usually wholly ignored in books on fishes. The first of these is the skaamoog or shy eye of South Africa, the second the swell sharks, which are widely distributed in the seas off the Pacific coast of America (from California to Chile), Japan, South Africa, Australia and New Zealand. The family also contains a number of species of deep-water sharks, *Apristurus*.

There is a related family of false catsharks, the Pseudotriakidae, which also live in deep water. One species lives in depths of 1 000—5 000 ft in the Atlantic, the other off Japan. These are up to 10 ft long, have an unusually long dorsal fin, but relatively few specimens have ever been seen.

Shy sharks and swell sharks

The catsharks have two dorsal fins and the upper lobe of the tail is horizontal, not uptilted in the usual shark fashion; there is no nictitating membrane (third eyelid) to the eye. This last feature may be linked with the unusual behaviour of the skaamoogs which, when caught, curl their tails over their heads, as if trying to hide their eyes, whence their alternative name 'shy sharks'.

The six species of swell sharks are better-known, especially the Californian species. They are small with broad bodies not more than 4 ft long, and live in shallow seas, especially in beds of kelp. They have large mouths with a formidable set of teeth, but their prey is small fishes, although they probably take carrion since they often find their way into lobster traps.

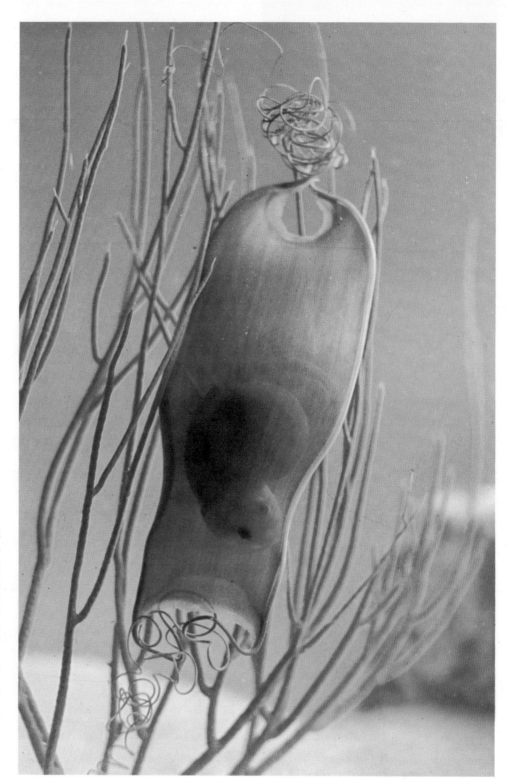

Catsharks and dogfishes
The best known of the catshark family are the dogfishes, dissected in biology classes all over the world. This catshark is much less well known but has the engaging habit of covering its eyes with its tail when caught, hence its common name: shy eye.

Holohalaelurus regani
skaamoog or shy eye

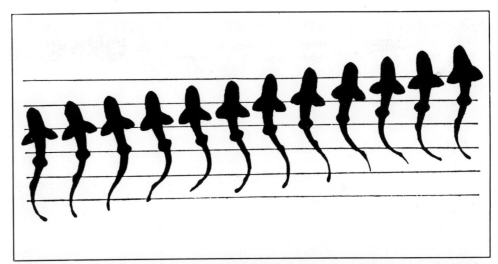

How a fish swims

▷ *Fins of fishes are generally used for stability and steering rather than for swimming. The force which most fishes use to move through the water comes from the blocks of muscles in the body and tail running down each side of the backbone. When a muscle block contracts it bends the body. As each block contracts after the one in front (while the one on the opposite side relaxes) waves transmit a backward momentum to the water which, by action and reaction, makes the fish move forward.*

◁ *The mermaid's purse is the egg case of certain sharks and skates. On the left an embryo swell shark, still attached to its yolk sac, can be seen developing inside the horny egg case. The entwining tendrils anchor the case until the young shark is ready to hatch (below right).*

Birth of a shark

All members of the family have similar breeding habits. Fertilisation is internal and the female lays eggs enclosed in rectangular, translucent horny cases with a long tendril at each corner. The tendrils become entangled with such things as the branches of soft corals (sea fans) and are anchored for the 8 months (in swell sharks) during which the embryo is developing, feeding on the large supply of yolk contained in the egg. At the end of this time the developing baby shark, which has been, during the later stages, rotating slowly and spasmodically within the horny case, breaks out at one end.

Stomach full of air

Swell sharks are named for their most distinctive feature. When hauled out of water they swell up to twice their normal diameter. This is due to their swallowing air, causing the stomach to swell like a balloon. When a swollen shark is thrown back into the water it is likely to float until it can discharge the air. The time taken to do this varies.

Some will deflate fairly quickly and then swim to the bottom. Others may take as long as 4 days, during which time they float.

Normally no shark leaves the water voluntarily and any intake will be of water, which would not put the fish at the same disadvantage as a stomach full of air. Presumably this is some form of defence mechanism, although how it helps is hard to see. Without stressing the analogy it is tempting to recall how general is the habit of inflating the body among toads. The two processes have probably arisen separately, and yet there is a further comparison to be made. The common frog of Europe will at times, when handled, go into a kind of catalepsy, holding its body rigid and somewhat flattened. Its limbs also are held rigid, with the forefeet over its eyes, rather as the shy-eye sharks cover the eyes with the tail.

class	**Selachii**
order	**Pleurotremata**
family	**Scyliorhinidae**
genera & species	***Cephaloscyllium uter*** *Californian swell shark*
	Holohalaelurus regani *shy eye*
	others

Living for the most part in total darkness, cave fishes have no need of eyes or body colouring. The pink colour of these cave fishes Anoptichthys jordani *is due to blood vessels showing through the skin. The remnants of eyes can be seen beneath the skin of the head.*

Cave fishes

There are 32 known species of fishes that spend their whole lives in underground caves or in artesian wells. Although they belong to unrelated orders and families they have many characters in common. All are small, the largest, the Kentucky blindfish, being 8 in. long, whereas most of them are 3½ in. or less. As they have little or no skin pigment, they are mainly pinkish in colour, due to the surface blood-vessels showing through the scaleless, or nearly scaleless, skin.

Most cave fishes are blind. The remnants of eyes are often hidden under the skin, but even in species with visible eyes, these are degenerate, serving only to distinguish light from darkness. The young of cave fishes often start with a perfect eye, which degenerates as they grow. In the Mexican cave fish the eyes of the adults differ according to where they are living. In isolated caves the fishes are totally blind. Those living in caves connected with a surface river have eyes that are almost perfect. All gradations between these two extremes, totally blind or perfect sight, are found in the 32 species according to the situation of the cave and how much light enters it.

Not all blind fishes are cave-dwellers. Many deep-sea fishes are blind, and so are some living among rocks on river beds or in swamps. Most cave fishes have their nearest relatives in normal freshwater fishes, but two species, one in Cuba, the other in Yucatan, are related to deep-sea blind fishes. A minnow-like cave fish in Dalmatia is washed to the surface during floods and then spawns in the surface waters.

Compensation for blindness

One of the advantages of this underground life is the absence of predators with abundance of food. Here life is certainly easy, if lacking in excitement. Among the animals living in caves, there are few fishes, the majority being numerous invertebrates, especially insects and crustaceans. Surprisingly, the only firm information we have on the cave fishes' feeding habits is that one species lives on insects washed into the cave and another feeds on bat droppings.

Few cave fishes have been well studied but it is known that there are marked differences in behaviour. The loss of sight is compensated by the development of the lateral line system which detects vibrations or changes of pressure in the water, or by an increase in the numbers of taste buds. Many cave fishes have a more sensitive lateral line, and this is extended on to the head in the form of sensory canals or rows of tiny sense-organs, which act as 'touch at a distance' organs. In other species, notably in a cave fish from Iraq, the lips and barbels are abundantly sprinkled with taste buds, as many as 400 per sq mm. Taste buds are normally found on the tongue. That the fishes have them on the outer skin means they are tasting their environment as a means of keeping in touch with their surroundings as well as finding food.

Different methods of feeling their way

The Iraq cave fish, with its taste buds, moves slowly when in still water, by alternating flicks of the tail followed by glides, at intervals varying from 1–10 seconds between flicks. In a current it swims with vigorous flicks of the tail. When obstacles are met the fish shows no evasive action except to turn gently away from them at the last moment. The Mexican cave fish, by contrast, using its touch-at-a-distance, is constantly swimming around, apparently aimlessly and vigorously, and seems to detect an obstacle

from a greater distance. It also responds readily to vibrations, such as a tap on the side of the rock basin, whereas the Iraq fish shows no visible response.

Various breeding methods

Breeding habits also differ. Some bear live young, after a gestation period of 3 months. In other species the female lays eggs and carries these in her gill chambers for 2 months. The Mexican cave fish has an elaborate courtship in which male and female make exaggerated movements of the mouth and gills. Presumably the turbulence this produces keeps each notified of where the other is. Then the pair suddenly swim side by side and mate, the fertilised eggs sinking to the bottom where they stick to the rock. In all species there is a long breeding season, and most breed all the year round.

Conserving energy

There has been much speculation as to why cave fishes should lose their eyes. It is easy to see that by taking refuge in underground waters they escape enemies and also are not bothered by competition for the available food. Yet although it is possible to speak of their food being abundant, it varies with the seasons and cave fishes must be able to fast for long periods. It has been suggested therefore that by not growing eye tissues, or allowing these to degenerate, cave fishes economise in energy. It is a strange thought, but not impossible.

class	**Pisces**
genera & species	**Typhlogarra widdowsoni** *Iraq cave fish*
	Anoptichthys jordani *Mexican cave fish*
	Caecobarbus geertsi *African cave fish* *others*

Characin

Outstanding characin relatives (for example, piranha page 161 and hatchet fish page 108) are treated separately. Here we deal with the family as a whole, which includes a large number of fishes of many shapes, sizes and habits, living in Central and South America and in tropical Africa. So numerous are the species that they are sometimes split into a dozen families, with up to 30 subfamilies. Many of them figure in the extensive business of providing aquarists with 'tropicals', and for this reason alone some attention must be given to the group as a whole.

Known to aquarists as characins, the family name, now Characidae, used to be Characinidae. So 'characin' has become, by usage, a common name. The majority look like minnows and carps, but have a small adipose fin between the dorsal fin and the tail. Some are vegetarians, others are omnivorous and a few are carnivores. The smallest is 1 in. long, the largest, 5 ft.

An interesting feature of characins as a family is that not only are they so numerous, but that some of them look so very like fishes belonging to other families. One looks and behaves like a trout, another looks like a herring, a third looks like a sucker of the family Catostomidae, another like a mullet, and so on. It is this that makes scientists studying them almost throw up their hands in despair. The best way to deal with them here is to describe a few of the more remarkable or the more familiar (to aquarists) individually.

The gorgeous technicolor of the cardinal tetra *Cheirodon axelrodi* which lives in forest pools in the upper Rio Negro in South America.

Eggs laid out of water

Most characins breed like any other freshwater fishes, laying their eggs among water plants and leaving the young to look after themselves. One South American species, known as the spraying characin *Copeina arnoldi* lays its eggs out of water. The pair jump out of water, their fins locked, to cling for about 10 seconds to a rock or a leaf. The female lays a dozen eggs in a jelly mass, which sticks to the rock or leaf, and the pair fall back into the water. They repeat this a number of times until a flat mass about 2 in. across has accumulated. When the spawning is completed the male visits the egg-mass every quarter of an hour, splashing water over it with his tail. Fortunately for him the eggs take only 3 days to hatch.

Characins are so numerous that they can afford to be reckless with their eggs and young, and many are eaten by the adults. The spraying characin's method of laying eggs out of water is something of a safeguard against this.

Heads up, tails up

A group of species, now transferred to a separate family, Anostomidae, is remarkable for the habit of swimming or feeding out of the horizontal. They are known as pencil fishes from their long slender bodies and pointed heads. Some swim with head down, others with the head up. Some are bottom-grubbers, swimming head down to feed on the mud or to scrape slime with their teeth from the backs of larger fishes.

X-ray fish

One characin that created quite a sensation when first introduced into aquaria has been called the water goldfinch but is better known as the X-ray fish. It was first discovered in 1907. Shortly after this the Aquarium was built at the London Zoo and the 1in. long X-ray fish enjoyed a brief period of fame. Its name refers to its transparent body in which the internal anatomy can be clearly seen.

Tetras

When the hobby of keeping tropical fishes in home aquaria first became popular many of the small characins were classified in the genus *Tetragonopterus*. This 15-letter word was soon abbreviated for trade purposes to tetra or even tet, and these shortened versions became omnibus terms covering all small characins. These small fishes are highly colourful and it was inevitable they should be known by their colours.

The rosy tetra is a small characin typically rose-coloured. The colour varies according to the angle of light but mainly it is yellow tinged with red and with black fins. Some were named after the place of origin, like the Buenos Aires tet, the silver Guiana tetra and the Rio tet, red tetra or flame fish. Others were named after their colour, so we have the yellow tetra, blue tetra, black tetra, platinum tetra and brass tetra.

One particularly colourful fish is the dawn tetra. It glows with a warm golden-coppery tint over which suffuses an iridescent red or orange. The fins are golden and the gillcovers flash blue-green. This description is no more adequate than a verbal description of a sunrise, with which the colours of the fish so easily compare, and more especially because black spots on the fish's body remind us of the black flecks of cloud over the dawn horizon.

To this engaging company can be added others with names like feather-fin, bloodfin, dragon fin, swordtail characin, glowlight tetra (very like the X-ray fish) and the head-and-tail-light fish. The last of these is an iridescent silvery-blue with glittering eyes at one end and what looks like a luminous red spot at the base of the tail. A similar motif is seen in the neon tetra with the iridescent blue-green line along the flank and below it, in the rear half of the body, a red band, the whole fish seeming to glow like a neon sign, when seen in an illuminated aquarium.

Popular hobby

Keeping goldfish in bowls was popular in the early years of this century but the cult of 'keeping tropicals' succeeded it and outstripped it. Aquarists form almost a secret brotherhood whose aims and ambitions are uncovered largely by accident, by the chance word which acts almost as a password. In due course one begins to realize how widespread they are, permeating society from top to bottom: the bishop, the eminent surgeon, the hall-porter, the bricklayer, all have their lighted and colourful aquaria in study, consulting room, back kitchen or cellar. And tetras are largely responsible for this. The story of the neon tetra will speak for all.

In 1936 a French banker received a consignment of small fishes from a collector in Brazil. He got in touch with William Innes, the American authority on aquarium fishes, and later sent him two pairs of 'the most beautiful of aquarium fishes', which were later named neon tetra. Innes has himself described how they 'made an instant hit: the universal acclaim with which they were greeted established history in our hobby'. A quantity of neon tetras was received in New York followed by a second consignment of 10 000, bought by an importer at an unheard-of price, the largest single deal in the history of the now extensive trade in aquarium fishes.

And this was only the beginning.

class	**Pisces**
order	**Cypriniformes**
family	**Characidae**
genera & species	*Copeina arnoldi* spraying characin *Paracheirodon innesi* neon tetra **Pristella riddlei** X-ray fish others

Cichlid

The 600 species of cichlid fishes, favourite 'tropicals' of the aquarist, live in rivers and lakes all over Africa, Madagascar and most of South and Central America north to Texas. There are also two species in southern India and Ceylon. Their bodies are flattened from side to side, as in the familiar scalare, the freshwater angelfish, shaped almost like a plate set on edge. In most the head is well developed, the jaws strong, and the lower jaw somewhat jutting. Their colours are attractive and their breeding habits of outstanding interest. This varies in small details from species to species, but for most of them it follows certain general lines.

Colourful courtship

With the onset of breeding conditions, cichlids' colours become heightened, especially in the male. At the same time there is a noticeable difference in behaviour. The male, at such a time, becomes far less sociable and lays claim to a part of the lake or river as his territory. Should another fish, especially one of his own species, swim into this, the breeding male immediately goes into display. His colours become more intense, his fins are fully erected, and the gill-covers are raised. He looks like a galleon going into action, with colours flying, sails set and guns run out.

If the intruder is another male, subsequent action will depend upon whether he is in breeding condition or not. If he is not, he turns and flees, and is chased to the boundary of the territory. But a male in an aggressive mood will return the display. Thereupon the two circle head to tail, each presenting a flank to the other, at the same time beating towards the other's flank with his tail. Very often it goes no farther than this, the fight being broken off by the intruder's flight. It may, however, end in the two contestants seizing each other by the mouth. In any case, the owner of the territory, almost invariably, is victorious. Having your feet on your own property gives a courage and a confidence which the trespasser invariably lacks. So it is with fishes.

Trial of strength

The first reaction of an occupying male, when a female fish of his species swims in, is the same as for an intruding male. He displays belligerently. Her behaviour is, however, different. She goes coy, in what has been called an attitude of symbolic inferiority. This does not always save her from attack, but instead of retaliating she accepts the blows, which gradually subside, as the male becomes aware of the presence of a potential mate. In some cichlids there are further preliminaries, the pair seizing each other by the mouth, tugging and twisting in an apparent trial of strength. This may be repeated several times. Usually it ends in a successful mating, although it may end fatally for one or the other.

The choice of partners is only the first stage in a courtship, during which the two

△ *A typical cichlid, the discusfish* **Symphysodon** *with flattened, plate-shaped body, bright colours, and a slightly jutting lower jaw. Cichlids are adept at guarding their own rigidly defined territories.*

fishes do their best to guard the boundaries of their territory, the male doing most of the displaying or fighting, the female assisting when necessary. Merely defending the territory is only a means to an end, and preparations for spawning go on actively. These include digging pits in the sand with the mouth, and cleaning an area for the reception of the spawn. The spawning site may also be the surface of a stone or, when the cichlids are in an aquarium, part of the glass. Whatever surface is chosen, the two fishes set about cleaning it scrupulously with their mouths.

Cleanliness important

When the eggs are laid and fertilised, both parents take part in their care. One of them takes up position over the surface on which they are laid, and, stationary, fans the eggs continuously with fins and tail. Every few minutes the parents change over. The fanning probably gives a higher supply of oxygen for efficient development of the eggs, but it may also prevent fungal spores settling and germinating on them. Cleanliness seems to underlie all the attentions given by the cichlids to their eggs. Any that are infertile are eaten, thus reducing the risk of an infection for the rest. At a later stage, too, the eggs are removed from the spawning site to one of the pits dug in the sand. This is done a few at a time, each parent taking the eggs in the mouth to the pit, and as each makes a journey the other stands on guard. Later, by the same laborious process, the eggs are transferred to another of the pits.

When the fry hatch, the parents keep close watch on them. Usually, and especially in the early stages, the fry keep well together, but any that stray are taken in the mouth by one of the parents and returned to the fold.

△ *Many cichlids hatch their eggs in their mouths, and later may take the young into their mouths.*

Invisible wall

The most spectacular aspect of cichlid behaviour is the way a male holding a territory will stop suddenly at its boundary as if bumping its nose against an invisible wall. Although it may swim towards it at speed, there will be the sudden stop at the boundary. Conversely, other fishes beyond the boundary recognize it in like manner and do not normally cross it.

There are two factors involved, both worthy of further consideration. First, the boundary is not only well defined and geometrically regular, but is readily recognized

by all concerned. Its position is established by constant fighting before spawning takes place, and it is maintained by the same display of force until the young are old enough to go off on their own. For all that, to appreciate how the other fishes as well as the holders of the territory recognize the boundaries, we have to imagine human properties without fences or hedges and ourselves knowing the boundaries by relatively few landmarks. The second factor is that, for the most part and for most of the time, all fishes in the neighbourhood seem to respect the boundary. Even when invisible, 'good fences make good neighbours'.

Territory rights displayed in tank

To give an example of this, some years ago in the Aquarium of the London Zoo a pair of black-banded cichlids had 200 babies in a tank 3 ft square and 4½ ft deep. The family occupied a territory at one end. In the same tank were 50 other cichlids, such as firemouths, Brazilians and others. The black-banded cichlids were slightly smaller than the others, yet they might have been enclosed in a glass box. None of the others attempted to enter their territory. Every now and then one of these outsiders would swim towards the well-defined but invisible wall and immediately one of the black-banded cichlids would dart across with fins up, colours temporarily intensified and gill-covers raised. Yet many visitors who looked at the tank saw nothing of this drama.

◁ *Cichlid couples share the job of patrolling their territory, the female assisting as necessary.*

class	**Pisces**
order	**Perciformes**
family	**Cichlidae**
genera & species	***Cichlasoma nigrofasciatum*** black-banded cichlid ***Geophagus brasiliensis*** Brazilian cichlid others

The cod is a voracious eater taking other fish and invertebrates. Even keys, a partridge and a book have been found in a cod's stomach.

Cod

The cod is perhaps the most valuable food fish in the world, after the herring. The cod family contains 150 species, of which a dozen are valuable food fishes, including the haddock, hake and pollack, which are dealt with separately (see pages 102, 104, 168).

The Atlantic cod is round-bodied, up to 211 lb in weight and 6 ft long, although those usually sold are 2½—25 lb. Its colour is olive-green to brown, the back and flanks marbled with spots, the belly silvery. There are 3 dorsal and 2 anal fins. The snout projects over the mouth and there is a whisker-like barbel on the throat.

Local populations

The distribution of cod is shown by the main fisheries: North Sea, Norway, Bear Island, Iceland, Greenland, Newfoundland and Labrador. The closely related Pacific cod lives in the north Pacific where, it has been predicted, there may some day be a large commercial fishery. Cod live on the continental shelf, at depths of 60—600 ft, although the bulk of the catch is taken in depths of 60 to 240 ft, on long lines, each carrying snoods bearing hooks. A single line may be 12 000 ft long. At times they can be caught as close as 50 yd off shore.

Within each area, such as the North Sea, Norway, Iceland and so on, the populations of cod are self-contained, but there are long migrations of several hundred miles by the larger fishes between the areas, for example

from Newfoundland to Greenland, Greenland to Iceland. Within each area there are feeding grounds and spawning grounds between which the cod move with the seasons. In autumn they come into the shallower inshore waters, but move temporarily into deeper water when feeding, and are then mainly bottom-feeders. In summer they feed farther out still, mainly on smaller fishes.

There is also a daily movement which is related to the intensity of light, similar to that found in a number of other shoaling fishes. Even at depths of 600 ft, the cod form compact shoals during the daylight hours, disperse at sunset and re-form at sunrise.

Indiscriminate eater

The main food of cod is other fishes, especially herring, mackerel and haddock, as well as sand eels. Squid are eaten in fair quantity and also bottom-living invertebrates such as shrimps, crabs, molluscs and worms. It is not surprising, therefore, to find that cod have strong sharply-pointed teeth, nor that their digestive juices dissolve seashells and the shells of crabs. But their voracity seems to know no bounds. Articles taken from stomachs of cod include a bunch of keys, a hare, a partridge, a black guillemot, a white turnip, a book bound in calf and a long piece of tallow candle!

Millions of eggs

There is no marked outward difference between the sexes, which become sexually mature at 4—5 years when 2—3 ft long. In the first 3 months of the year they move to the spawning grounds. This may take them across very deep water, for example

from Norway to Bear Island, or Iceland to Greenland.

The females shed their eggs and the males their milt into the sea, where fertilisation is random. A well-grown female lays 4—6 million eggs, $\frac{1}{20}$ in. diameter, which float to the surface. In 10—20 days these hatch and the larvae, $\frac{1}{4}$ in. long, remain in the surface plankton for the next 2½ months. At just over $\frac{3}{4}$ in. long they move down to the bottom, in depths of about 240 ft, to feed on small crustaceans, amphipods, isopods and small crabs. As they grow they move into deeper water. At the end of the year the young cod is 6 in. long, and 1 ft long a year later. Young cod of these sizes keep together in age groups, and are known as codling.

Only one need survive

Fishes that lay large numbers of eggs are beset by enemies and other natural hazards. Only one of the 4—6 million eggs laid by the female cod need survive to keep the population steady. Many eggs fail to be fertilised, and these and many of the fertilised eggs are eaten by other fishes as well as smaller predators in the plankton. All are at the mercy of winds and currents, large numbers being cast ashore or killed off by changes of temperature. Damage to the fry is similar, and when the young fishes go down to the bottom, other predatory fishes continue the slaughter.

Cod fry are among several species of fishes that take refuge under the umbrella and among the stinging tentacles of large blue jellyfishes. Even so, some brush against the tentacles and are paralysed and eaten by the jellyfish. Even those not lost by these accidents enjoy no more than a temporary immunity from attack by larger fishes.

Long history

Cod have been fished in quantity since the 16th century and in this century the annual catch has reached 3−400 million fish. As a source of revenue they have had an important bearing on the course of human history. At the beginning of the 16th century, Spanish, Basque, French and English fishermen were catching cod in the North Sea and North Atlantic. Many sailors fighting the Spanish Armada had learned seamanship in the cod ships. Already in 1536, however, Jacques Cartier had pushed across the North Atlantic, a 6-month journey in those days, to discover the islands of St Pierre and Miquelon, on the Grand Banks of Newfoundland. A century later there were 300 French ships fishing for cod off these islands, together with Spanish and Dutch fishermen.

England was slow to exploit these silver mines, as the seemingly inexhaustible supplies of cod off Newfoundland were called. Early in the 17th century, however, there came a two-pronged attack. Ships from Bristol and the Devon ports were making the long journey and returning with valuable cargoes of salted cod. By 1634 an estimated 18 680 English seamen were working the Newfoundland fishery. The colonists of New England had also discovered this source of wealth and by 1635, one generation after the colony was founded, 24 vessels were bringing back up to 300 000 cod a year, and the first export from Massachusetts was a cargo of cod.

Cod led the English and the French to Canada, to a long trail of strife, and when the United States was founded a title to the cod-fishing ground was included in the Act of Independence. The cod appears on bank notes, seals, coins and revenue stamps of the New England colonies, and a carved figure of a cod still occupies a place of honour in the Massachusetts State House. The fish left its mark on the history of the fishing grounds, in the form of open strife between crews of different nations.

Salted cod early became a standby for seamen, explorers and armies during the period when Europeans were spreading out into the new found continents. Nothing of the fish was wasted. Its skin yielded glue, its swimbladder furnished isinglass, its liver gave a high-grade oil. Even cods' tongues, originally cut out and strung on wires as a tally of the daily catch, were salted in barrels.

By 1770, cod liver oil was being used for poultices and as a medicament for the sick and aged. By 1820 it was being used against rickets, a disease linked with town life in the Industrial Revolution. It was considered useless by many medical men, and it was not until 1921 that the value of cod liver oil in the treatment of rickets was set beyond doubt.

class	**Pisces**
order	**Gadiformes**
family	**Gadidae**
genus & species	**Gadus morhua**

Engraving of fishermen fishing for cod from a dory or flat-bottomed boat off Newfoundland.

△*The fleet waiting. Codfishing boats at Henningsvaer, Lofoten Islands, Norway.*
▽*Cod drying in the sun. The skin yields glue, the swimbladder isinglass and its liver high grade oil.*

Conger

The conger is a stout-bodied marine eel, normally up to 4—5 ft long but may reach 9 ft or more and a weight of 100 lb. There is an unconfirmed weight for 1940 of 160 lb. The body is scaleless, brown to dark slate and the underside may be silvery. The colour varies according to the sea-bed; on a sandy bottom being more or less colourless, and dark on a gravel bottom or among rocks. The gill-openings are large and extend to the underside of the body. The mouth runs backwards to below the level of the eye and is armed with rows of sharp teeth, one row in the upper jaw being set so close together they form a cutting edge. The front pair of nostrils are tubular, each of the hind pair being opposite the centre of the front edge of the eye. The eyes are large, reminiscent of those of deep-sea fishes. The pectoral fins are fairly large, the pelvics are lacking. The dorsal fin begins from above the pectorals, is continuous along the back and runs into the anal fin.

Congers are often called conger-eels. This is unnecessary. The name is from the Latin congrus *meaning sea-eel.*

The conger lives off rocky coasts, in the north and south Atlantic, Mediterranean, Indian and Pacific Oceans, but is not found on the west coast of the Americas. It also lives in deeper water, down to 660 ft or more.

Congers are distinguished from freshwater eels by their complete lack of scales. Their powerful jaws have a formidable battery of teeth—and a vice-like grip. With jaws agape, they often lurk in rocky crevices waiting to slip out after their prey.

Graceful acrobat

The conger swims easily and gracefully. When cruising it is propelled largely by wave-like movements passing down the dorsal and anal fins, from the front backwards. At greater speeds the body moves in a serpentine, side-to-side undulation. Not uncommonly it turns on its side to swim by undulating movements of the body. When doing this at the surface it presents a series of humps rather like those of the legendary sea-serpent. It spends the day lying among rocks or in crevices, sometimes on its back, periodically yawning, an action probably connected with respiration rather than fatigue. Congers are given to somewhat lethargic 'acrobatics', remaining poised head-down, sometimes doing so at the surface with a third or more of the body sticking up vertically out of the water. Or they may contort the body into other odd postures, holding each position for a perceptible time.

No flesh refused

Congers are carnivorous, taking any animal food including carrion and even smaller congers. Crabs and lobsters are held in the mouth and battered against rocks before being swallowed. The voracity of congers can be judged by stories of men having fingers bitten off when sorting a catch in which a conger lies hidden, or having a finger seized when feeling in rock crevices and having to cut it off to avoid being held

and drowned when the tide came in. There is a story of a conger biting off the heel of a fisherman's sea-boot.

Thin-headed larvae

Like the freshwater eel the conger spawns once and then dies. The congers of European Atlantic waters spawn near the Sargasso Sea at depths of 10 200 ft in late summer. There is another spawning ground in the Mediterranean. Before spawning congers stop feeding, become almost black with very much enlarged eyes, especially in the male, and then look like deep-sea fishes. The female lays 3—8 million eggs, each $\frac{1}{10}$ in. diameter. These float in the intermediate layers of the ocean but occasionally reach the surface.

The first eel larva, of the freshwater eel, was found in 1777 and named *Leptocephalus* (thin-head) by the Italian naturalist Scopoli, under the impression that it was a new kind of fish. The first conger larva was found in 1763 by William Morris, of Holyhead, but was not described until 1788, when the German scientist Johann Gmelin named it *Leptocephalus morrisii*. And it was not until 1864 that it was recognized to be the larval stage of the conger. Even then, Albert Günther, distinguished ichthyologist, held that it was a kind of freak, a case of arrested development. In 1886, however, Yves Delage the French zoologist proved beyond doubt that *Leptocephalus morrisii* was a larval conger by watching a leptocephalus change into a young conger in an aquarium. Later in the 19th century the true nature of what are now called the leptocephali became more firmly established when the Italian naturalist Raffaele managed to keep eggs and larvae of five species of eel alive in aquaria.

The conger leptocephali lose their larval teeth, on reaching coastal waters after their journey across the Atlantic, and change into young eels. The body becomes rounded and

eel-like and its length drops from 5 to 3 in. Until they reach a length of 15 in. the young congers are a pale pink. After this they gradually take on the dark colour of the adult. When about 2 ft long they move down the continental shelf, and beyond, into water more than 600 ft deep, and spend most of their time on the bottom.

Eighty tons of eels

Dr Frank Buckland, in his *Curiosities of Natural History*, has recorded the observations made during January and February, 1855, by a surgeon who lived at St Leonards on the southeast coast of England: 'During the intense cold, some few miles out at sea, *thousands* of conger-eels were found floating on the surface of the water. They could progress readily in any direction, but could not descend, and consequently fell an easy prey, the boatmen catching them by means of hooks on the end of a long stick. In this manner no less than *eighty tons* were captured, of all sizes, some being as much as six feet long, and of a surprising circumference. The greater part of them were sent to London per rail. One of them I opened, and found the air-vessel (that is, swimbladder) distended with air to the utmost, so as to completely close the valvular opening. It was this, evidently, that buoyed them up.'

class	**Pisces**
order	**Anguilliformes**
family	**Congridae**
genus & species	***Conger conger***

Croaker

Croaker is the name given to 160 species of the family of North American fishes, remarkable for the noises they make. Some of them have been called drums or drumfishes. They usually have a rounded snout, two dorsal fins almost joining, the front part being spiny. Some have a number of small barbels under the chin. Most of them are used as food-fishes. One, known as the channel bass, is over 4 ft long with a weight of up to 83 lb although most of them are only a few pounds in weight.

The Atlantic croaker is well known from Massachusetts to Argentina. These are fairly ordinary carnivorous fishes laying small eggs which, since each contains an oil globule, float at the surface.

Submarine choristers

By far the most spectacular feature of these fishes is the way in which their noises are used like bird song. They are not the only fishes to do this, but as a family they are outstanding in their performances. The sounds are made in most instances by the vibration of muscles with the swimbladder acting as resonator. Sometimes the muscles are attached directly to the surface of the swimbladder, in other species the muscles are attached to the body wall. In all the use is similar: by contraction and relaxation, at a rate of about 24 contractions a second, the muscle is made to vibrate almost like the strings of a guitar. The sounds have been variously described as drumming, humming, purring, whistling, creaking, croaking, hissing, snorting, even a 'melodious vocal effort'. In some the sounds are relatively feeble, but the loudest of the croakers has been heard by a person, 6 ft above the surface of the sea on the deck of a boat, while the fish was calling from a depth of nearly 60 ft. In Malaya fishermen locate the fish by their sounds.

Fishes not deaf

It used to be argued that fishes are unable to hear, just as it used to be supposed they made no sounds. Fishes in which the swimbladder is not directly connected to the bones of the inner ear can respond to frequencies between 13 and 2 000—3 000 cycles per second. Where there is a connection they can respond to frequencies between 16 and 10 000 cps. The noises they make are well within these ranges, but are mainly low notes.

The sounds are put to many uses in different species of fishes: to enable members of a shoal to keep in touch, possibly as an echo-sounder for depth, for breeding and as an expression of emotions. Illustrating the last of these we have the experience in a public aquarium in the United States. Visitors could, by pressing a button, hear yellowfin and spotfin croakers 'talking' in one of the tanks. All went well until the fishes had settled in and felt at home, when they ceased being loquacious—and visitors had to be content with a recording.

Dawn and dusk choruses

The evidence for the other uses is equally scanty and this study is as yet in its infancy. As to members of a shoal keeping in touch, we have observations of the kind recorded for croakers living in the seas around Japan. These are known to assemble in large schools of up to a million and synchronize their drumming. In many species of croakers the volume of sound given out increases as the breeding season approaches, reaches a peak during it, and dies out afterwards. In a few species the sounds begin in the evening, reaching a high pitch towards midnight then sharply dying away. It has been shown by close observation that some species have a dawn chorus, others have both dawn and dusk choruses. In some species only the males 'croak', in others both sexes do so. All this is so like what is found in birds that it seems reasonable the croakers are using their 'guitars' for the same purposes.

Some croakers lack a swimbladder and, as if not wishing to be outdone by their relatives, they make a small amount of sound by grinding their teeth.

There was a time when we thought of the dark depths as being noiseless and talked of 'The Silent Sea'. With the development of underwater listening devices, this notion has been blown skyhigh. In addition to the croakers and the many other fishes now known to break the underwater silence, it has been discovered that whales, dolphins and porpoises are always chattering to each other or using sounds to test the depth of water beneath them, or to locate food. Even lowly shrimps and prawns add to the submarine cacophony.

There are other sounds to add to the confusion. A submarine in the First World War followed a supposed enemy submarine, only to find it was picking up the heartbeat of a large whale! In the Second World War, with more sophisticated listening devices, submarines, picking up the sounds of croakers and other fishes, suspected enemy craft were in the neighbourhood. Later they used the sound barrage to mask their own noises.

The sirens unmasked

Modern naval personnel were not the first to be deceived. It has been suggested that the song of the Sirens, the subject of the Greek myth, may have been nothing more than the 'voices' of the meagre or weakfish, which is common in the Mediterranean. This is a member of the croaker family which ranges from southern Australia to South Africa and the Mediterranean. Occasional individuals, up to 6 ft or more long, appear from time to time off the coasts of the British Isles.

Yellowfin croakers. Apart from their extraordinary capacity for sound output, croakers are fairly ordinary carnivorous fishes with almost-touching twin dorsal fins.

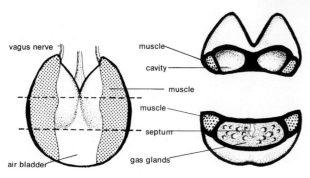

◁ *The sound mechanics of a croaker's swimbladder, with the cutaway sections' plan views at far left. At a very rapid rate—about 24 contractions per second—the muscle surrounding the bladder cavities vibrates with much the same effect as the strings of a guitar, with the bladder cavities amplifying the sound.*

vagus nerve
muscle
cavity
muscle
muscle
septum
air bladder
gas glands

class	**Pisces**
order	**Perciformes**
family	**Sciaenidae**
genera & species	***Micropogon undulatus*** Atlantic croaker
	Roncador stearnsi spotfin croaker
	Argyrosomus regius meagre
	Umbrina roncador yellowfin croaker
	others

Damselfish

Most damselfishes, or demoiselles, live in shallow tropical waters, especially around coral reefs. Many are brightly coloured, as shown by their names, such as the orange-coloured garibaldi and the blue chromis, and some, such as the sergeant major, are spotted or striped. The majority are less than 6 in. long. The body is deep, somewhat flattened from side-to-side with prominent dorsal fins, the front one of which is spinous.

Quarrelsome fishes

Many damselfishes live near coral reefs, hovering close to the coral heads, perhaps several hundred at a time. When disturbed they dart with one accord into the crevices among the corals. Damselfishes living in temperate seas, the garibaldi of the Bay of California, for example, live over the kelp beds or on rocky coasts, places offering shelter equivalent to that of coral reefs. Many others tend to take up station near large anemones and this has led in several cases to either a loose or a close symbiosis between the fish and the anemone. This reaches an extreme in the often quoted association between the giant anemone and the small clownfish.

A peculiarity of the family is that some species use their pectoral fins almost like oars. They are brought forward almost edgewise and pulled back more or less broadside on.

Damselfishes are often aggressive, with a strong territorial sense. Some live in pairs once they mature and are aggressive towards others of their kind using their particular shelters or going anywhere near them. Their aggressiveness is expressed largely by clicking noises made with teeth lining the throat, the pharyngeal teeth. In fact, these small attractive fishes seem more deserving to be called amazons than damsels. As is usual in fishes, the strong territorial instinct is linked with a marked degree of parental care.

Carnivorous eaters

The feeding habits of damselfishes are not well known. They seem to be carnivorous, feeding mainly on smaller fishes, even the weaker ones of their own kind, especially if there are not enough places in which the small ones may hide.

Prolific breeders

Breeding in the spotted damselfish of the Indo-Pacific has been studied by Dr J Garnaud. He kept these in the Aquarium at Monaco and found that each pair spawned in the early morning, as often as three times a month, and at each spawning the female laid 20−25 thousand eggs. These are sticky and are laid in small clusters, on rocks or other firm surfaces. The male guards the eggs until they hatch 4−5 days later.

The garibaldi, another damselfish studied, spawns at depths of 4−42 ft. Before spawning, the male cleans an area of rock around a clump of red seaweed, and on this the

△ *Clown fish sport among the tentacles of anemones growing on a coral reef.*
▽ *Garibaldi, the charmingly-named **Hypsypops rubicunda**. This youngster will later lose his blue spots and become a brilliant orange.*

▷ *Dangerous landlord: this anemone has become used to the attentions of these two clown fish. It takes time for a clown fish to be 'accepted' by an anemone—and until this happens the fish is literally dicing with death.*

female lays her eggs. The young garibaldi is orange-red with blue blotches which begin to disappear when the fishes reach a length of about $2\frac{1}{2}$ in. and are completely gone by the time they are adult.

Sheltered by giant anemone

The best known damselfish is the clown anemone fish which shelters among the tentacles of a giant anemone which can reach up to 4 ft across. There are other damselfishes that have this habit but the clown fish is the one most often quoted. It may leave the anemone to swim around but at first alarm dashes back to take refuge among the tentacles. It is claimed that when the fish darts back to the shelter of the anemone's tentacles any fish pursuing it will be caught and held by the tentacles, the clown fish receiving fragments from the anemone's meal.

Years ago it was supposed that the stinging cells were brought into action the moment anything touched them. Then it

was realized that they were more selective. They are not discharged if, for example, any kind of plant material touches them. Now we know that the slime on the scales of a clown fish inhibits the stinging cells. But this is not the end of the story.

When a giant anemone and its clown fish are placed in an aquarium the fish seems to recognise the anemone and quickly swims towards it. Then it circles the anemone, getting nearer and nearer to it until it is close enough to nibble its body. It does this several times then it swims over the tentacles and eventually touches one or two of them. Having done this it immediately races away. Later it returns and again touches the tentacles. This is repeated several times, and each time the tentacles of the anemone can be seen sticking to the fish, showing that the stinging cells have been discharged at it. Finally the fish swims deeper into the tentacles, which no longer cling to it. The fish and the anemone were becoming used to each other's company. It seems as if the

anemone must get to know its own particular damselfish, perhaps becoming immunised, as it were.

By contrast, if a clown fish living with one anemone is removed and placed with another anemone it is stung and killed. But a pair of clown fishes may raise a family among the tentacles, the father guarding the offspring until they are old enough to go out and find their own anemones. What we do not know is how the acquaintance between a damselfish and an anemone is struck in the first place.

class	**Pisces**
order	**Perciformes**
family	**Pomacentridae**
genera & species	***Abudefduf saxatilis*** sergeant major ***Amphiprion percula*** clown fish ***Chromis cyanea*** blue chromis ***Hypsypops rubicunda*** garibaldi others

Blue demoiselles **Chromis caerulea** *swarm past a coral reef in the Seychelles, Indian Ocean. Damselfish or demoiselles are found in shallow tropical waters around the world, especially near coral reefs.*

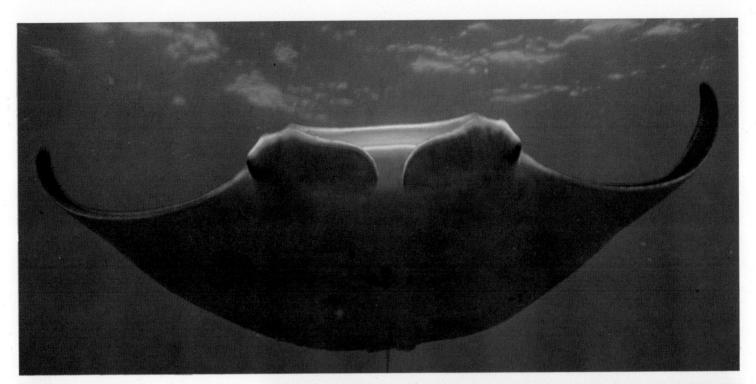

Devil ray

Less than a score of species of devil rays, or devil fish, are known. They are related to skates, rays and sharks and like them have a cartilaginous skeleton. The largest is the manta ray, or greater devil fish, 22 ft across and weighing up to 3 500 lb or more. Cornel Lumière, French skin-diver, referred to a maximum size of 60 ft across and 5 000 lb weight. The smallest is the pygmy Australian devil ray, only 2 ft across. 'Manta' is Spanish for blanket and refers to the widespread shape of the pectoral fins. As in other rays, the body is flattened from above downwards, the pectoral fins are large and triangular. The tail is long and slender and may have a small poison spine. In the related stingrays the spine is large. Many devil fish lack the spine entirely. The mouth is large and at the front of the head whereas in most sharks, skates and rays it is underneath. At each corner of the mouth and directed forwards is a large 'horn' formed from a part of the pectoral fins.

*Dr Bernard Heuvelmans, in his book **Monstres marins**, tells how a South American scholar, Enrique Onffroy de Thoron, on seeing in 1866 a large devil ray from a ship, jumped to the conclusion that it was a living **Chirotherium**, a giant amphibian whose fossil remains had been found in 1833 in Thuringia.*

Bat-like fish

Devil rays live in tropical and subtropical seas. Unlike other rays and skates which live mainly on the seabed, they spend most of their time swimming at or near the surface. They swim with graceful flapping movements of the enormous pectoral fins, as if

flying through the water. The devil ray resembles an enormous bat, and has been called sea bat. Usually solitary or in pairs, devil ray sometimes form small schools. Normally their movements appear slow and somewhat lazy. At times a devil ray will swim slowly at the surface or turn complete somersaults in the water, while at others it will leap high into the air, landing with a tremendous impact.

Large fish, small food

When feeding, a devil ray uses its 'horns' like scoops to fan food towards the enormous mouth as it cruises through water

Top: Head-on approach of a 14ft manta, with its 'horns' folded crossways. Bottom: A skin-diver hitches a ride on an impassive manta.

rich in plankton. Its food includes small crustaceans, young or very small fishes and other members of the plankton, very much as in the other leviathans, the whale shark and basking shark. There is a special lattice-work covering the gills which keeps the food in the mouth until it can be swallowed. Without this the gills would be fatally clogged.

Large young

Devil rays bear their young alive. Mating is

carried out by the two partners coming together, their undersides facing, the female curving her pectoral fins upwards to embrace those of the male. The male has a pair of organs, known as claspers, which are in fact intromittent organs used alternately to convey the sperms into the female's oviduct. Usually there is only one young at birth but it is well-developed and large. One female 15 ft across contained an embryo 5 ft across which weighed 20 lb.

Gentle giant

Old beliefs among pearl-divers include the notion that these flattened giants would cover them with their vast wings and, holding them, would devour them. A devil ray's teeth are very small and flattened, and the giant manta has teeth in the lower jaw only. It was also a belief among seamen that a devil ray could seize an anchor and tow a vessel away.

Probably three things, over and above their large size, have added colour to such notions. One is that a manta can be dangerous, inadvertently, by smashing or capsizing a small boat with a blow of its pectoral fin, especially if it lands on the boat following a leap. Secondly, a harpooned manta will tow a fair-sized vessel, and it can take enormous punishment from harpoon, lance and gunshot before succumbing.

A third thing must be the tremendous noise it makes on returning to water after

a leap. JR Norman, in his *History of Fishes,* quotes a Mr Holder for an account of a jumping devil ray: 'There came out of the darkness, near at hand, a rushing swishing noise; then a clap as of thunder, which seemed to go roaring and reverberating over the reef, like the discharge of a cannon'

Because of their large size it has not been possible to study closely the habits of devil rays. Nevertheless, with the advent of skin-diving enough has been gleaned to confirm what was already suspected by scientists half a century ago, that devil rays are not as black as they are painted. They seem to have excellent sight and an overwhelming sense of curiosity, and skin-divers tell of giant mantas swimming elegantly to within 6 ft to examine them.

Cornel Lumiere has described devil rays as no more dangerous to the skin-diver than a litter of puppies.

A shoal of smoothtail mantas in the Gulf of California.

class	**Selachii**
order	**Batoidei**
family	**Mobulidae**
genera & species	***Manta birostris*** ***Mobula diabolis*** *others*

*Greater spotted dogfish **Scyliorhinus stellaris** showing mouth and nostrils on the underside of the head. A dogfish will nose its way over the bottom of the seabed seeking food, such as worms, hermit crabs, and prawns, by smell and not by sight.*

Dogfish

For tens, if not hundreds, of thousands of people who have passed through biology classes, the dogfish will always be associated with a repulsive object on the laboratory bench reeking of the eye-stinging preservative, formalin. Yet dogfish do live, and as live animals are far less unsavoury.

*Although we speak of 'the dogfish' the name is applied to several species. The one commonly dissected by students in Britain is the lesser spotted dogfish, formerly known as **Scyllium canicula**, now named **Scyliorhinus caniculus**. Students in North America will have dissected the spiny dogfish **Squalus acanthias**, or **S. suckleyi** if at schools or universities near the Pacific coast. The last two belong to the family Squalidae and are therefore true, if small, sharks, whereas the lesser spotted dogfish, believe it or not, is a catshark, family Scyliorhinidae.*

There are other dogfishes and, surprisingly, one of them, the alligator dogfish or bramble shark, feeds on spiny dogfish.

Very common in west European and Mediterranean waters, the lesser spotted dogfish, or rough hound, is slender, brownish with many small dark spots above and whitish below, and up to 3½ ft long. The greater spotted dogfish, or nurse hound, is similar except that its spots are larger and it may reach 5 ft long. Both are used to train budding doctors and biologists, but the first is used most. In true

sharks there are two triangular dorsal fins, the first being the largest and set in the middle of the back. These fins in dogfish are equal in size and are sited close together and well back.

The pectoral and pelvic fins are of moderate size, the mouth is on the underside of the head, as are the nostrils and there are the usual five gill slits on each side behind the head, not hidden under a gill cover, as in bony fishes. The skin is rough, which is best appreciated by passing the hand from the rear forward over a dogfish body. The roughness is due to the denticles set in the skin.

Chases prey by smell

Dogfish are frequently the fisherman's curse. The lesser spotted dogfish normally keeps somewhere near the bottom and at times is present in enormous numbers, getting in herring trawls or taking the bait of line fishermen, thus robbing them of a better catch. Sometimes a trawl will come up with as many as 400 dogfish—useless to the trawlermen. Their normal feeding has been described by Dr Douglas P Wilson, who watched them in aquaria of the Plymouth Laboratory. A dogfish will nose its way over the bottom seeking food by smell. Its nostrils are on the underside of the head. When it comes to some food it stops, backs if neces-

Section of dogfish skin showing small scales or denticles. These are each like a small sharp tooth, made up of a pulp cavity enclosed in dentine with an enamel layer to the outside.

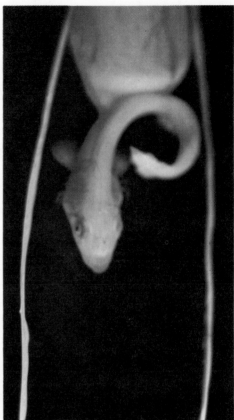

Mermaid's purse—the home of a developing dogfish. The fertilised egg is laid inside an oblong, horny case. As the female lays pairs of eggs she moves around seaweeds so the long tendrils attach the case.

Dogfish embryo, 3—4 months old, in artificial case. It is nourished from the large yolksac.

sary, and picks it up. The eyes are not used in hunting, and a dogfish hunting another fish will follow its trail, swimming along the same course, following every bend and turn, even passing its prey without seeing it should it double back.

Fish forms only a small proportion of its food, the bulk being worms, sea-cucumbers, prawns, shrimps, hermit crabs and some whelks, cuttle, squid and octopus.

Born in a purse

Its breeding season is November—July, and during this time one-third of all the females will be carrying embryos. In mating, the male coils his body around the female, passing sperms into the female oviducts with his claspers. These are rigid parts of the pelvic fins, so named because it used to be thought they were used for holding the female. The eggs begin to develop in the oviduct and later are laid, each inside an oblong horny case, sometimes called a mermaid's purse. They are laid in any month of the year, but chiefly in spring and summer. At each corner of the egg-case, or egg-purse as it is often called, is a long tendril. As she lays pairs of eggs, the female moves around seaweeds so the tendrils wrap round them. Inside the capsule the baby dogfish is nourished from a large yolksac, and 6 months after laying it bursts out of the capsule, a miniature of its parents, but 3 in. long. Lesser spotted dogfish may live 8 years.

The spiny spurdog

The spur dogfish has a somewhat stouter body than the lesser spotted, is slate-coloured above, with small white spots on the flanks and whitish on the underside. There is a prominent spine at the front of each of the dorsal fins and the lines on these

tell the age of the fish. Spurdogs, or spiny dogfish as they are also called, may live 30 years. They are cosmopolitan in temperate seas, living from shallow water to 3 600 ft. In the summer they make long northward migrations, up to 1 200 miles, in large schools. They eat much the same things as the lesser spotted dogfish but mainly fish, taking other creatures only by chance. The females come inshore to give birth to 3—11 live young, each 11 in. long. The males follow soon after from deeper water, and mating takes place during February and March, the babies being born 22 months later.

Used as sandpaper

Dogfish are put to many uses. The best known is as a subject for dissection in biology classes where 100 000 are used each year in North America and Britain. Formerly an oil was extracted from them in North America, used for machinery, for lamps and for dressing leather. Fishmeal from dogfish mixed with Peruvian guano gave a fertilizer. Their skin was used as a sandpaper in cabinet-making. Nowadays their flesh makes food, marketed in Britain as rock eel or flake, especially as fried fish, and extensively eaten in Japan. In North America, as grayfish, its use for human consumption is increasing.

Some idea of their numbers is given by the following figures. A school 1 000 strong has been known to follow herring shoals. Long-line fishermen have taken 1 000 in a night. As many as 3 500 have been taken in one trawl. Off the coast of Massachusetts 27 million are caught per year. Britain, Germany, France and Portugal landed 10 000 tons in 1964. But the catches are going down.

Disliked by fishermen

Despite the uses to which dogfish are put, sea-going fishermen would have no regrets if they became extinct. Dogfish have been described as the most hated fish. Some British trawlermen do not hesitate to scrub the decks with the rough skin of the dogfish while the live fish is still inside it.

Albert C Jensen of the New York Conservation Department, Bureau of Marine Fishes, writing in *Sea Frontiers* for 1967, tells how in 1904 several schemes were put forward by fishermen to rid their world of dogfish. One plan was to tie coloured streamers, bells or jingling chains on hundreds of dogfish and then to put them back into the sea to frighten away the rest. Dynamiting the schools of dogfish was suggested. Surrounding them with nets, catching some and inoculating them with virulent diseases which they would pass on to their fellows when put back into the sea, were two other suggestions, imaginative but, fortunately for the dogfish, impracticable.

Ironically, on the eastern side of the Atlantic, fears are being expressed that the main grounds supplying 'rock eel or flake' are being overfished. The principal losers, if the decline is not stopped, would be the fish-and-chip shops in the south of England.

class	Selachii
order	Pleurotremata
families	Scyliorhinidae *catsharks*
	Squalidae *spur dogfishes*

Dolphin fish

It is always confusing to have two animals known by the same name but belonging to very different families, especially when they live in the same areas. Nowhere is this more true than in the case of the dolphin, a mammal, and the dolphin, a fish. The mammal has first claim to the name since it has been known from Greek and Roman times. When the name was first given to the fish is unknown. It was almost certainly given by ocean-going seamen, and probably arose from the similar shape and jumping habits of both animals.

There are only two species of dolphin fish, in a family of their own. The better-known of the two is up to 5 ft long with a maximum weight of 67 lb. The male has a squarish head, the female's being more rounded, but both are heavier in the front half of the body, which tapers away to end in a forked tail (a female is shown in the illustration below). The dorsal fin runs almost the length of the back. The dolphin is a beautiful blue in life, which is lost in death, but the dying fish is said to undergo spectacular changes of colour.

The second species, the pompano dolphin, has a maximum length of 2½ ft and is seldom more than 1 ft long. The two species are not easy to tell apart, when the specimens being examined are of similar size, except by counting the number of rays in the dorsal fin. The pompano dolphin has 48–55, the commoner species has 55–65.

Chasing the flying-fish

Dolphin fish live in tropical seas, singly or in schools. They swim fast, reaching speeds of up to 37 mph. Such speeds are necessary to catch flying-fishes, which are an important item in their diet. N B Marshall speaks in his *Life of Fishes* of dolphins having such a lust for flying-fishes that they will often hurl themselves out of the water in pursuit of their gliding prey. At other times a dolphin will swim underneath as the flying-fish is airborne, ready to snap it up as it re-enters the sea. Flying-fishes are, however, not the only prey. More than 30 species of fish belonging to 19 families have been taken from the stomachs of dolphins.

A short life

Most probably dolphins fall prey to larger predatory fishes, particularly when young. Practically nothing is known of the early stages of their life history except that growth is very rapid. Dolphins kept in the Marine Studios in Florida had to be fed three times a day, indicating that they were living at a fast rate, rapidly using up energy and needing a large quantity of food to replace it. Part of this energy is taken up in rapid growth. The 52 captive dolphins were at most 18 in. long and 1½ lb weight when put into the aquarium. One was measured and weighed 4½ months later. It was 45 in. long and 25 lb weight. Three months later two more were found to be 50 in. long and up to 37 lb weight. It is suspected that the life span is probably short, perhaps 3 years only.

Studies have been made on many fishes to find the ratio between the surface area of the gills (a measure of how much oxygen the fish can take in) and the weight of the body. Highest on the list is the menhaden with the figure of 1 773 (sq mm of gill per gram of body weight). Second is the mackerel with 1 158, third is the mullet with 954 and fourth is the dolphin with 710. All four are fast-growing fishes, and it may well prove to be that they are all relatively short-lived.

Differing behaviour in the young

While the smaller pompano dolphin and the common dolphin fish are so alike that one needs to count fin rays to tell one from the other, there is one way in which the very young fish differ markedly in behaviour. Earl S Herald, noted American ichthyologist, tells of a strange encounter. He saw many small fishes swimming under the night lights of a ship lying off the Philippines. He netted some, examined them under the microscope and found they were very young pompano dolphins. Herald, on pursuing the subject, found that very few young of the commoner dolphin fish came to the lights anywhere around the Philippines, but could be seen swimming in the same places by day. Apparently it is the same in the Atlantic.

class	**Pisces**
order	**Perciformes**
family	**Coryphaenidae**
genus & species	***Coryphaena hippurus*** ***C. equiselis*** pompano dolphin

The dolphin fish lives in tropical seas, singly or in schools, swimming very fast—often reaching 37 mph, so it can catch flying fishes, which are an important item in its diet.

Dragonet

The dragonet is a fish with a remarkable courtship. The male is so different from the female that the two were once thought to belong to different species, the gemmeous dragonet and the sordid dragonet—the second being the female. In Mediaeval English a dragonet was a baby dragon. The name, which was not applied to the fish until the 18th century, was probably suggested by the appearance of the male.

Dragonets, 4½—12 in. long, live on the seabed in tropical and temperate areas. They are scaleless, and have a flattish belly and a rounded back. The head is oblong and flattened, with large eyes set close together on top of it. The mouth can be pushed outwards, and has large lips at the end of the snout. The pelvic fins are widely separated and are well forward on the throat. The pectoral fins are large and have 2—3 free rays which are organs of touch. The long dorsal and anal fins are larger in the male than the female, and the front part of the male's dorsal fin has a very long leading spine.

Built-in suction pump

These fishes are not built for speed, and they spend their time close to the seabed. With their large pectoral fins they can, however, dart forward suddenly. Otherwise their movements are leisurely, skimming just over the bottom, resting at frequent intervals with the head slightly raised. Bottom-living fishes are at a disadvantage in their breathing, compared with those that swim freely. A fish always briskly on the move need only open its mouth for water to flow in and across the gills. Bottom-livers need something more. Dragonets have only a small opening to the gills and the gill cavity and its associated bones and muscles are so constructed that water is forced through by a bellows action of the gill covers. The fish merely opens its mouth and the suction pump of the gill chamber does the rest.

They feed on small crustaceans, molluscs and worms on the sea floor and, despite the position of the eyes high on the head, pay little attention to anything that swims.

A clutch of floating eggs

The breeding season is from February to June or even later, and spawning takes place close inshore. The eggs are small, less than 1/30 in. diameter, and marked with a honeycomb pattern. Soon after they are laid the eggs float to the surface. They hatch in about a fortnight and the young fishes remain near the surface, going down to the bottom during the following winter.

Undoubtedly it was the bright colours and the striking fins of these fishes, especially those of the male, that led to their being called 'baby dragons'. It is unusual to find in fishes such a marked difference between the sexes. Because the dragonets spawn inshore where there is a good deal of dis-

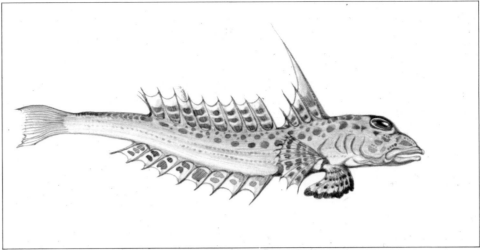

△ Colourful display of young male dragonet gives a good idea of how it got its name. Females are so drab by contrast that they were once thought to be a separate species.

▽ Pair of dragonets. The dragonet spends much of its time on the bottom of the sea, using its large pectorals for sudden bursts of speed.

turbance of the water from the wash and the surf, something is needed to ensure that sperms and ova keep together long enough for fertilisation to take place. Otherwise, if they shed them at random as most fishes do they might quickly become separated and the ova remain unfertilised.

Little dragons

The male dragonet is yellow to brown on the back and orange on the flanks and underside, the whole tinged with red, with azure blue spots and stripes. His pelvic fins are dark blue and his eyes blue-green. The female is brown with a white underside and looks even more sombre by contrast with the male when, excited and with his colours heightened and intensified, he dashes about before her with his colourful fins fully spread. Normally his dorsal fin is laid back along the body, but now it is fully erect. The male then pulls faces at her, pointing his mouth downwards while protruding his upper lip. This seems to be the final step that wins her acceptance.

Once the female has accepted him he places his pelvic fin under hers and together they swim steeply upwards towards the surface. As they near the surface their position changes slightly so that the anal fins of the partners lie side-by-side forming a gutter

into which ova and sperm are shed. This keeps them together long enough for the eggs to be fertilised.

Females live longer

The age of a fish can be told in many ways, by the growth rings, similar to those of trees, on the earbones (otoliths) or on the vertebrae or other bones. In the dragonet the most reliable method is to look for the growth rings in certain bones of the shoulder girdle, known as the second radials. From these we know that the males grow quickly but live for not more than 5 years; the females grow more slowly, do not reach as large a size as the males—8 in. maximum against 12 in. for a male—but live up to 7 years.

Moreover, males die after they have bred once. Some males breed when 3 years old, others at 4 or 5 years, but in all instances they only breed once in a lifetime.

class	**Pisces**
order	**Perciformes**
family	**Callionymidae**
genus & species	***Callionymus lyra***

Eagle ray

These lozenge-shaped rays have large wing-like fins with a long thin tail trailing behind. Unlike skates and the other rays the pectoral fins do not extend to the snout but leave the head clear. The result is that the head and snout, and the overhanging brows to the eyes, are somewhat like the head of an eagle. Eagle rays are grey, brown or black, usually whitish on the underside, but young ones may be striped or spotted. As with all skates and rays, the mouth and gill-openings are on the undersurface. The tail is armed with a poison spine. The skin has only sparse denticles, lacking altogether in some species.

The family Myliobatidae includes also the bat rays and cow-nosed rays. The first of these are named for their bat-like appearance when swimming. The second are named for the fleshy fold below each eye which together give the impression of the fish having a split upper lip on a blunt snout, the resemblance to a cow's muzzle being somewhat fanciful. The larger species of eagle rays may be 15 ft long with a weight of 800 lb.

Eagle rays live in warm seas but some occasionally wander into temperate seas. The common eagle ray is sometimes caught off the British Isles.

Outsize flying fish

Although the shape of eagle rays suggests they are bottom-living fishes, they spend much of their time swimming gracefully and rapidly, with ballet-like up-and-down movements of the pectoral fins. Had they not received their name before skin-diving became popular, there would have been the suspicion that it referred to their strong but elegant flying underwater. Sometimes eagle rays will swim near the surface and occasionally break surface to skim for a short distance through the air just above the waves. In some parts of the sea they are found in small numbers. Elsewhere there may be thousands.

Shellfish-crushing teeth

The teeth are flattened and arranged on the jaws in a regular mosaic pattern. The pattern differs from one species to another. In the common eagle ray both upper and lower jaws have a central row of hexagonal bars with rows of smaller hexagonal plates on either side. In other species there may be more and members of the genus *Aetobatus* have only one row of broad bar-like teeth. Whatever the pattern, the teeth are powerful crushing organs, the main food of eagle rays being shellfish such as clams, oysters, crabs, and lobsters. They also eat marine worms, sea-pens, sea snails and fishes. An eagle ray can create havoc on an oyster bed.

Small males

Females of the Californian bat ray are larger than males. They reach a weight of 140 lb, sometimes as much as 209 lb, but the males seldom more than 25 lb. The number of young at birth increases with the weight of the female, from 6 in a young female to 12 in one fully grown. There is one brood a year. The baby eagle ray weighs 1 lb at birth and it leaves the mother tail first, its sting being soft and flexible but quickly hardening on exposure to water.

The sting in the tail

Little is known of eagle ray enemies but in any case the fish can defend itself with thrusts of its poison spine. It does this shortly after birth, the baby ray being able to stab forwards, by thrashing its whip-like tail over its back, but it can also stab to left or to right. As it grows, the tail becomes less flexible, and the adult can only stab forwards with this stiffened weapon.

Enlarged tooth

An eagle ray lashing at its enemies with its tail is defending itself almost literally tooth-and-nail, for the poison spine in its tail is little more than an enlarged tooth.

There was a time, less than 50 years ago, when sharks and their relatives, the skates and rays, were classed as Pisces, with all the other fishes. Then came a separation into two classes, the Selachii (sometimes called Chondrichthyes), or cartilaginous fishes, and the Pisces (or Osteichthyes), the bony or true fishes. The main difference between the two is in the skeleton, whether it is made of cartilage (that is gristle) or bone. But an almost equally important difference is in the scales. The scales of sharks are usually called denticles, or little teeth. Each denticle has a pulp cavity, complete with blood-vessels and nerves, which is surrounded by dentine over which is a layer of enamel. It is in fact a tooth although its enamel differs somewhat from the enamel of our teeth and is referred to as vitrodentine. All the same, if you took a piece of shark's denticle and showed it to your dentist he would almost certainly say it was a piece of somebody's tooth.

So a shark's skin can be said to be literally bristling with teeth, and they differ from the scales of true or bony fishes in that they do not grow with the fish. Instead, new denticles are added between those already there. Eagle rays, like stingrays (page 213), have few denticles, but some of those on the tail have joined together and become very large, to form a dagger-like super-tooth with saw-edges and a groove down which poison can flow. If damaged, the spine can be replaced. Sometimes a new spine will grow out from the base of the old one, not waiting for it to be shed. The ray is then doubly armed.

class	**Selachii**
order	**Hypotremata**
family	**Myliobatidae**
genera & species	***Myliobatis aquila*** *common eagle ray* ***M. californicus*** *others*

▷ *Submarine silhouette: a graceful eagle ray glides between the camera and the sunlit surface. Despite their bottom-living shape, eagle rays like to swim near the surface.*

Eel

Eels are remarkable for the vast distances they travel in migration. There are 16 species of freshwater eel, all of which spend their adult lives in rivers, ponds and lakes but migrate to the sea to spawn, and from this they never return.

The European (also in North Africa) and American freshwater eels are identical except for the number of their vertebrae, 110—119 in the former, 103—111 in the latter. The body is elongated, females growing up to 5 ft long, males to 20 in. There are no pelvic fins and the pectorals are small. The dorsal fin starts well forward and continues to the end of the body where it joins the long anal fin. The gills are enclosed in a pouch and the opening from the gill-chamber on each side is small. The skin is thick and slimy, with very small scales embedded in it.

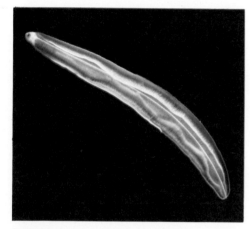

Leaf-thin larva: an eel leptocephalus.

Breathing through their skin

Eels are most active at night. They spend the day under stones or in rock crevices, but may sometimes be seen swimming at the surface in broad daylight or even out of water, lying on a bank, apparently basking in hot sunshine. They are, however, at a disadvantage at such times because of their manner of breathing. An eel breathes 60% through its skin, which is supplied with fine blood-vessels, like a frog's skin. While in water the eel gives out carbon dioxide through its gills, but when out of the water, as when travelling overland at night, this is given out through the skin. Both the intake of oxygen and the giving out of carbon dioxide become less efficient at temperatures above 16°C/60°F.

Greedy flesh eaters

Eels feed mainly at night. They eat almost any animal food, alive or dead. Two kinds of eels can be recognised, the broad-nosed, which is predominantly a fish-eater, and the sharp-nosed, which feeds on small prey. Cannibalism is usual in crowded conditions, which acts as a check on over-population. Males remain in the lower reaches of the river, while females go higher up and also migrate over land to lakes and ponds. The males move down to the sea at 4—8 years, according to how well fed they are. The females remain until 7—12 years old. In all mature eels, feeding stops prior to migration in autumn. Eels are prey to the usual fish-eating birds and mammals that hunt in freshwater. They are a favourite food of otters.

Heading for mid-Atlantic

Before migration, the eel goes through drastic bodily changes. Feeding ceases and the heads of all mature eels become pointed. Their colour changes from yellowish-grey (the so-called yellow eels) to olive-green or dark brown and silvery-white on the belly (silver eels). The eyes grow large. The pectoral fins enlarge, become pointed and black. The eels make their way to the mouths of the rivers and head for mid-Atlantic.

How do they breed?

The mystery of the breeding of the freshwater eel is at least 2 000 years old. Aristotle may have known that adult eels go down to the sea and young eels return to fresh water. But between his time and the latter part of the 18th century, the how and why of their breeding habits was a subject for speculation, much of which was pure fantasy. The reproductive organs of eels remained undiscovered until C Mondini, at Bologna, in 1777, identified the ovaries in a female eel, and it was not until 1874 that a Polish naturalist, Simone de Syrski, found a sexually-mature male. Meanwhile, in 1856, a German naturalist, Johan Jacob Kaup, gave the name *Leptocephalus brevirostris* to a small fish caught in the Straits of Messina, which, 40 years later, the Italians Giovanni Batista Grassi and Salvatore Calandruccio proved was the larva of an eel. Since that time the larval eel has always been spoken of as a leptocephalus.

In 1904, the Danish zoologist Johannes Schmidt, in the research ship *Thor*, caught a leptocephalus off the Faeroes. The following year, working farther south, he caught leptocephali not in ones but in hundreds.

He caught them by the hundred in 1906 in the Bay of Biscay, and during the period 1906—1920 Schmidt brought together evidence which made a coherent story. Briefly, in late summer and autumn the adult eels of Europe and the Mediterranean countries make their way down the rivers to the sea, to go 3 000 miles or more to the Sargasso Sea to spawn. They do not return, but the larvae or leptocephali hatching from their eggs make the return journey. Reaching the coasts of Europe they change into elvers, just under 3 in. long and, by now, 3 years old. These ascend the rivers to feed and grow before setting off in their turn into the Western Atlantic on their own breeding migration.

Sorting themselves out

The American eel carries out a similar migration to spawn in an area in the Western Atlantic which overlaps the breeding ground of the European eel. Its leptocephali return to the eastern coasts of North America, taking only a year on the journey.

The larvae of both species may be found in the Western Atlantic, and the natural question is how the two species sort themselves out. The orthodox explanation is that if a larva of the European eel happens to travel in a westerly direction it will reach the American coast long before it is ready to change into the elver. Conversely, if the larva of the American eel should migrate in an easterly direction it would undergo metamorphosis in mid-Atlantic. The assumption was that in either case the misguided larvae would perish.

There is no direct evidence for this hypothesis, since no leptocephali of the American species have been found in mid-Atlantic and none of the European species found off the American coast. Another gap in the evidence is that no eggs have been found, except four collected in 1925 from 3 000 ft, at a point northwest of what is supposed to be the spawning ground. These were kept

Glass-clear elvers try out their paces on reaching their freshwater home. After crossing as larvae from their mid-Atlantic birth place their bodies become thicker and their eyes and fins larger.

△ *A freshwater eel heads overland during the first stages of its long trek to the Sargasso Sea. Bottom: Heavyweight — a large specimen in the shallows. The females can grow up to 5 ft long.*

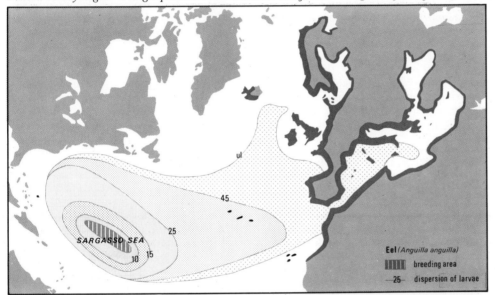

△ *Spread of the growing European eel: figures indicate larval sizes in millimetres. The line — ul — shows the farthest extent from the breeding ground at which unmetamorphosed larvae are found.*

under laboratory conditions but only one larva was reared, which had the number of vertebrae of the American eel. Two other gaps in the evidence are that no adult eels have been taken in the open ocean, and no eels in full breeding-dress have been seen, although eels injected with hormones experimentally have shown what this should be.

Nobody doubts that the account of the breeding migrations of the two North Atlantic species, so carefully and laboriously put together by Schmidt, is anything but substantially correct. There can be no doubt that the two species are derived from spawning grounds in the Western Atlantic, and that no adult eels return from their breeding migration.

All the same family?

Writing in *Nature* for February 21, 1959, Dr Denys Tucker suggested how some of the anomalies in the story might be explained. He stressed that American and European eels are extremely closely related, and that their larvae are outwardly so alike as to be difficult to tell apart. He pointed out, however, that the American eel, with only a short distance to go to its spawning ground, is nowhere near as advanced into breeding condition when it enters the sea as is the European eel which has the longer distance to go. This, as he justifiably points out, is the reverse of what should be expected. He suggests, therefore, that the adult European eels never reach the spawning ground but die off in the ocean, that the American and European eels belong to one species, that the eels found in Europe are recruited from larvae hatching from eggs laid exclusively by American eels, and that the differences, as in the number of vertebrae, are solely the consequence of environmental conditions in the early larval stages.

It is known that changes in the temperature of the water in which other fish larvae develop can induce changes in the number of vertebrae, even in larvae from the same parents. Since the spawning ground of the two eels extends from 20 – 30 degrees North and between 1 200 to 2 100 ft deep, those larvae hatching in the southern part of the grounds will be subject to different temperatures from those hatching in the northern part. This could be sufficient to account for the difference between the 103 – 111 vertebrae of the American eel and the 110 – 119 vertebrae of the European eel. Added to this, the current-system in that part of the Atlantic is such that larvae hatching in the southern part of the spawning ground will be carried towards the American coast. Those in the northern part, which because of the lower temperature in those waters will have the larger number of vertebrae, will be carried on the inside of the current-system east and northeast across the Atlantic, towards the coasts of Europe.

This ingenious theory has so far received little acceptance by ichthyologists.

class	**Pisces**
order	**Anguilliformes**
family	**Anguillidae**
genus & species	***Anguilla anguilla*** *European eel* ***A. rostrata*** *American eel*

Electric catfish

Electricity is linked with the very nature of living matter. Every time we blink an eyelid or move any other muscle we are using electric impulses in our nerves. Fishes alone among vertebrates can generate an excess of electricity, using it to catch food, to beat off enemies or to find their way about. Three of the best-known are the electric catfish, electric eel and electric ray, but there are others.

The electric catfish, in a family on its own, lives in rivers and lakes of tropical Africa except for Lake Victoria and East Africa, as well as the Nile Valley. Up to 3 ft or more long, and 50 lb weight, it has a plump body, rounded tail fin and no dorsal fin. It has 3 pairs of barbels around the mouth, very small eyes, and its colour is greyish-brown becoming flesh-coloured around the head and on the belly. It remains hidden by day, resting among waters or in natural cavities, and comes out at night to feed.

The electric catfish, on this bas-relief from Sakkara, Egypt, is seen directly behind the boating pole.

Aggressive neighbours

Electric catfish feed voraciously on almost any animal food, from worms to smaller fishes, and are noted among aquarists for pugnacity and aggressiveness. One result is that only juveniles can be kept in aquaria with other fishes, since electric catfish are docile until they begin to grow up.

There is no obvious distinction between the male and the female, and because of its quarrelsome disposition—it cannot easily be kept in captivity—practically nothing is known of its breeding.

Skin-deep batteries

The electric organ is formed from a layer of muscle that lies like a jacket just under the skin of the trunk and part of the tail. It is divided into compartments containing electroplates. Each of these receives the branches from a large nerve cell in the spinal cord. The positive pole is at the rear end of the organ, the negative at the head end, and a large catfish can discharge up to 350 volts, the first discharge being followed by several lesser shocks. The discharge will stun other fishes in an aquarium with a catfish, and in the wild it is used to capture food and deter enemies.

Known to the Egyptians

The Ancient Egyptians must have been very familiar with this fish since it is figured on their bas-reliefs and tomb paintings, dating from 2 750 BC. Even earlier, from 4 000 BC, it was known in the hieroglyphics as 'He who releases many', the implication being that a fisherman hauling in his net, receiving a jolt from this fish, would drop the net and liberate his catch. They clearly had a respect for it although they also ate it, as Africans have done since. It has also been used in tropical Africa as a remedy for aches and pains, the live fish being placed on the affected part, so giving the patient an electric shock. The Arabs have used this same electro-therapy since the 11th century and their name for the electric catfish is *ra'ad*, the shaker. Had we been writing about this before the days when electricity entered so much into medical treatment we would have thought it sheer nonsense for African and Arab healers to clap a fish on a patient's head to cure a headache!

Painstaking research

One of the major difficulties in finding out how extinct animals lived is that usually only the hard skeleton is preserved, so we have difficulty in telling whether any extinct fishes used electricity. The soft parts, such as the internal organs, have long since decayed. Nevertheless, a Swedish Professor, Erik Stensiö, thought that the Ostracoderms, forerunner of the fishes that died out well over 300 million years ago, had electric organs. Although he later changed his mind, the story of his researches is worth telling.

Most Ostracoderm fossils are crushed flat, but Stensiö found small ones in the sandstone rocks of Spitzbergen which were not. He took one after another of these, ground it at the tip of the snout and photographed the surface under oil. Then he ground away another tissue-paper-thin layer and photographed this. Patiently he continued grinding and photographing until the fossil was gone. In its place he had a large number of photographs. From these he could reconstruct in the round the head and all its organs even down to the fine, almost microscopic markings on and throughout the skull. He could make out where there had been nerves, blood-vessels and muscles, and he could also see what he had at first thought were electric organs like those of living fishes. Unhappily, further research showed that although these were sense organs they were not electric organs.

class	**Pisces**
order	**Siluriformes**
family	**Malapteruridae**
genus & species	***Malapterurus electricus***

The electric catfish remains hidden by day, coming out at night to feed on almost any animal food.

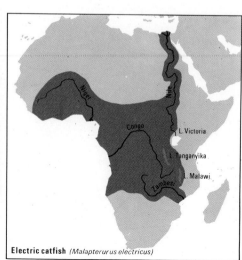

Electric catfish *(Malapterurus electricus)*

The electric eel, unrelated to the true eels, emits high-voltage discharges which stun or kill fishes or frogs, those dying near the eel being eaten.

Electric eel

The South American electric eel, which can kill a horse with an electric shock, is not even related to eels. It has less than 50 relatives, the gymnotid eels and knife-fishes (page 120), all tropical American and probably generating electricity to a greater or lesser extent; but the most spectacular and notorious is the electric eel itself, which can discharge up to 550 volts when fully grown.

The electric eel has a cylindrical body, a uniform olive-brown, up to 6 ft long—the largest recorded 9½ ft—running to a pointed tail. It has no fins on the back, only very small paired fins behind the gills, and a long conspicuous anal fin running from the tip of the tail almost to the throat. Its eyes are very small. About ⅞ths of the body is tail, with the internal organs crowded into a small space behind the head. The tail contains the electric organs, made up of 5–6 thousand electroplates (elements) arranged like the cells in a dry battery. Moreover, there are three parts to the electric organ, two small batteries and the main battery. The electric eel is positive towards the head end, negative at the tail end, the reverse of what we have seen in the electric catfish.

Poor gills, no lungs

The electric eel lives in waters poor in oxygen. It comes to the surface from time to time to gulp air. In its mouth are patches of superficial blood vessels which take up oxygen from the air gulped at the surface, so acting as auxiliary breathing organs.

It swims by undulating the long anal fin and is said to be able to swim forwards or backwards, up or down, with equal ease. So long as it is still its main electric organ at least is not working, but the small battery in the tail is working continuously. As soon as the eel starts to move it gives out electric impulses at the rate of 20–30 a second which later increases to 50 a second. These are used for direction-finding, it is now known, although they do not form an electric field, as in the Nile fish.

High-voltage jolts

It has been said that the second of the small batteries probably fires the larger battery, which gives out a series of 3–6 waves at intervals of 5/1000 of a second, each wave lasting 2/1000 of a second. These are the high-voltage discharges which stun or kill fishes or frogs, those dying near the eel being eaten. Larger animals coming into contact with a large electric eel are stunned. A stunned horse falls and is liable to be drowned. A man can stand the shock, but not repeatedly.

Unknown breeding places

Little is known of the breeding; there is no obvious difference between the sexes and the breeding places are unknown. The eels disappear from their usual haunts in the breeding season. When they return young eels 4–6 in. long come back with them, still guarded by the parents. Young eels are light brown with bands. Later they become marbled and finally olive-brown with the throat brilliant orange.

Millions of years ahead

Even more remarkable than the electric eel is the story of the first man to study its electrical discharge. From the beginning of the 16th century Spain had refused all non-Spaniards permission to visit her American colonies. In 1800, when rapid strides were being made in the study of electricity, the German naturalist, Baron Friedrich von Humboldt, applied for and was granted permission to visit South America. With a companion he arrived at the upper reaches of the Orinoco River and Calabozo, a town of exiles.

Von Humboldt took with him a large amount of scientific apparatus. Oxygen had only recently been recognized and von Humboldt took the latest apparatus in order to analyse the gases in the swim-bladders of fishes. He also took the latest electrical apparatus, only to find that Carlos del Pozo, resident in the town of exiles, had begun making similar apparatus thousands of miles from the centres of learning in Europe—a remarkable coincidence. And there also von Humboldt found large fishes that had developed their own electrical apparatus, but millions of years in advance of del Pozo and the European scientists.

This gifted German gave the world the first scientific accounts of the behaviour of the electric eel. He stood on one of these fishes and experienced a painful numbness. He also found that for the rest of the day he was afflicted with a violent pain in the knees and in the rest of his joints. Having studied the eel he made a remarkable prophecy: 'The discoveries that will be made on the electromotive apparatus of these fishes will extend to all the phenomena of muscular motion subject to volition. It will perhaps be found that in most animals every contraction of muscle fibre is preceded by a discharge from the nerve into the muscle.' He also predicted what we saw in the opening lines of the account of electric catfish: that electricity is the source of life and movement in all living things.

class	**Pisces**
order	**Cypriniformes**
family	**Gymnotidae**
genus & species	***Electrophorus electricus***

The South American electric eel lives in waters poor in oxygen. It comes to the surface from time to time to gulp air. In its mouth are patches of superficial blood vessels which take up oxygen from the air gulped at the surface, so helping with breathing.

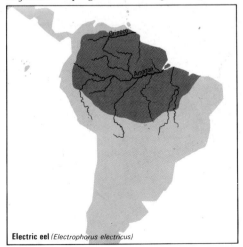

Electric eel *(Electrophorus electricus)*

The electric ray **Torpedo torpedo**, which may grow up to 2 ft in length, is found in the warmer areas of the Atlantic as far north as the Bay of Biscay. It is identified by the dark blue eye-spots on its back. It prefers to live on sand and is often found near sea-grass.

Electric ray

A man-made torpedo is a fish-shaped missile fired from a warship, but the original torpedo was a flat fish related to the skate, much used in medicine in the days of Ancient Greece and Rome. The torpedo was often represented on Greek pottery, either on its own or among other fishes. The Greeks believed it was bad luck to dream of this fish swimming among other fishes. Alphabetically this is the last of the electric fishes, but historically it comes first, since it was the comparison between this fish and the amber (Greek **elektron**) rubbed with fur that gave us the name 'electric'.

There are three dozen species of electric ray, the largest being **Torpedo nobiliana** of the North Atlantic, up to 5 ft long and 200 lb weight, the smallest, **Narcine tasmaniensis** of Australia, no more than

17 in. long. They are disc-shaped, the head, body and large pectoral fins being joined to give an almost circular outline, with a short slender tail behind. The oddest of them is the Australian crampfish **Hypnarce subnigra**. This is nearly oval and has no tail.

Electric rays are found in all tropical and temperate seas, from the intertidal zone down to 3 000 ft, but never in large groups like the stingrays and skates.

Stunning their prey

Electric rays eat fish which they catch by pouncing on them, wrapping their pectoral fins around a victim and stunning it with the discharge from their electric organs. These organs are therefore the centre of interest. Otherwise there is little to be said about their daily habits because they do no more than lie on the seabed, except when hungry. They usually feed on small crustaceans, some electric rays siphoning them into their mouths.

Jelly-filled batteries

Most, if not all, skates and rays have electric organs in the tail, but in the electric ray there are two large electric organs on each side of the head. The current passes from the lower to the upper surface of the body. Each organ is made up of a large number of hexagonal columns forming what looks like a honeycomb, but each column is a pile of plates filled with a jelly. The number in each pile in one column may be 140 to a thousand or more, and in a large ray it may be half a million. The organs are controlled by four nerves from each side of a special lobe of the brain, known as the electric lobe and coloured differently—yellow in some species—from the rest of the brain. The main nerves branch repeatedly and their fine end branches reach the lower side of each plate. So the batteries represented by the hexagonal columns are arranged in parallel.

It is the rule that in all marine fishes the batteries are in parallel, and in all fresh-water fishes they are in series, giving a higher voltage.

Torpedo marmorata swimming slowly on the lookout for food such as fish, crustaceans and molluscs. Dorsally it is yellowish brown with its ventral surface white with a darker fringe. Its short, powerful tail has a triangular fin at its tip. There are electric organs on both sides of the body

An average torpedo can electrocute a large fish with the pulses it puts out of 50 amps at 50—60 volts, but large individuals may put out 200 volts. There is less need for a high voltage in marine electric fishes because salt water is a better conductor than fresh water.

Baby rays take shape

Young are born alive but little else is known about the life history apart from scattered records. One female nearly 16 in. long contained ten eggs each about 1 in. diameter. The smallest young ray so far measured was just over 5 in. long, others ranged up to 10 in. Since these still bore traces of a yolk sac they were fairly new-born. One feature of the embryo which helps our understanding of the shape of the fish is that early in development the pectoral fins are not joined to the head. As growth proceeds they grow forward to fuse with the sides of the head to give the rounded outline typical of rays. Sometimes the fins fail to join with the head and the ray remains abnormal throughout life with a notch either side of the head.

Link with the Leyden jar

Until the mid-18th century scientists were unable to explain what happened when an electric ray was touched. The Greeks had known that there was something peculiar about the fish. They thought it drugged its prey. The Romans were equally puzzled. Claudian described how a torpedo took the bait on a bronze hook and emitted from its poisonous veins an effluence which spread far and wide through the water and also crept up the line to the fisherman's hands and congealed his blood, so that he threw away his rod. Yet the Roman physicians used the fish to treat gout, headaches and other ailments. The patient either stood on a live torpedo or had the live fish clapped to his temples.

In 1746 the Leyden jar was invented and soon after a Dutchman, Laurens Storm van's Gravesande, and a French naturalist, Michel Adanson, almost simultaneously realized there was a similarity between it and a torpedo. Then in 1791 Luigi Galvani suggested there was a likeness between the emanations from a torpedo and the elec-

tricity he thought he had discovered in the muscles and the nerves of animals.

The batteries of the torpedo, which was now becoming known as the electric ray, continued to excite attention by scientists, as it had the Greeks.

Today the fish is seldom heard of outside the realm of zoology, or the fishing industry when a fisherman sorting his catch inadvertently puts his fingers on one of these fishes, gets a sudden shock that slightly numbs his arm—and swears volubly.

class	**Selachii**
order	**Batoidei**
family	**Torpedinidae**
genera	***Torpedo, Narcine, Hypnarce,*** *others*

In the ring: two wary males circle each other during a lull in combat, seeking an opening to attack.

Fighting fish

Many fish fight, but the celebrated species is the fighting fish **Betta splendens** *of Thailand. This is one of 7 related species in southeast Asia, ranging from Thailand to Borneo. It has been selectively bred for fighting qualities and used for sport, with bets placed, in Thailand.*

The wild ancestor is 2 in. long, yellowish-brown with indistinct dark stripes along the flanks. In the breeding season the male becomes darker and rows of metallic green scales on its flanks become brighter. Its dorsal fin is medium-sized, metallic green tipped with red. The anal fin is large and red edged with blue and the small pelvic fins are red tipped with white. The tail fin is rounded. The female is smaller, less colourful, mainly yellowish brown.

Short-lived

Fighting fish live in clear but weedy rivers and lakes, in irrigation ditches and ponds, and two species are also found in mountain streams. They mature rapidly and grow quickly, and they do not live much longer than two years. Because of their rapid growth they feed heavily on all kinds of small aquatic animals such as water fleas, mosquito larvae, worms or small pieces of dead flesh.

Endurance tests

Male fighting fish are pugnacious towards each other—one species has been named *Betta pugnax*—but to nothing like the extent of the selectively bred descendants. Wild fighting fish rarely keep up their fights for 15 minutes and usually it is much less. The cultivated varieties are considered to be poor samples if they fight for less than an hour and some will continue to attack for up to 6 hours.

A raft of bubbles

Mating is preceded by the male swimming around the female, with heightened colours and fins spread. There follows what can only be called dancing and embracing. Before this takes place, however, the male has built a nest, a raft of bubbles. He takes in bubbles of air at the surface and these become enclosed in a sticky mucus in his mouth, so the bubbles last a long time.

The courtship ends with the male turning the female on her side and wrapping himself round her. Then he tightens his grip, turns her upside down, and in a short while lets go and, as she remains suspended in the upside-down position, he stations himself beneath her. She begins to lay 3–7 eggs at a time, to a total of several hundred. As these slowly sink the male catches each in turn in his mouth, coats it with mucus, then swims up to his raft and sticks it on the underside. This is repeated until all the eggs are laid, the male looping himself round the

female each time to fertilise the eggs as she lays them. Finally, the male drives the female away. After that the male guards the nest. The young hatch 24–30 hours later, when the male's parental duties are at an end.

Head-on crash

The first *B. splendens* to be bred in Europe appeared in France in 1893 and in a very few years it was being kept by aquarists over a large part of the world. One of the earlier varieties was cream-coloured with flowing red fins. Then came the famous Cornflower Blue. After that there were various shades of blue, lavender, green and red ending in the best-known, the rich purplish-blue. All these varieties had flowing veil-like fins and, whatever their colour of body, all had red drooping pelvic fins.

There have been many stories, usually highly coloured, about the way the males fight. The facts are dramatic enough. When two males are put in an aquarium together their colours heighten and they take up position side by side, heads pointed in one direction, one fish slightly in advance of the other. Their fins are erected, their gill-covers expanded. Then, with lightning speed they attack. They try to bite each other's fins and in the end one may have some of its fins torn down to stumps. They may also bite patches of scales from each other's flanks. Sometimes they meet in a head-on clash with jaws interlocked.

Above: Male on the right surveys female. Below: Under the nest, a raft of bubbles, male mates with a female by wrapping himself round her.

The greatest damage is done when the cultivated fighting fish are unevenly matched. A small one matched against a large one is bound to suffer. So is a long-finned variety matched against a short-finned variety. Long flowing fins make it hard for their owner to turn quickly. Moreover, the fishes attack the rear half of their opponents, where the flowing fins are.

Exploding with rage

One of the more exaggerated stories to be published was collected by the distinguished American fish specialist, Hugh M Smith. It is quoted in *Exotic Aquarium Fishes* by WT Innes. It tells how you go out and catch your fighting fish—assuming you live in Thailand—and bring it home in a bottle. Your neighbour does the same. You stand the two bottles together. The two fishes see each other, flash their colours at each other and blow themselves up. They hurl themselves in vain at each other, until finally one of them becomes so angry it literally bursts. If this is your fish you lose your bet!

class	**Pisces**
order	**Perciformes**
family	**Anabantidae**
genus & species	***Betta splendens*** ***B. pugnax*** *others*

Firemouth

The firemouth has nothing to do with dragons or other mythical beasts. It is the popular name for one of the most beautiful freshwater fishes, which belongs to the family Cichlidae, and it refers to the fiery orange colour which extends along the underside and forwards even into the mouth. The species is singled out for special treatment from among several species of Cichlidae on which the Dutch zoologists G P Baerends and J M Baerends-van Roon based their pioneer studies.

The firemouth, up to 4 in. long, lives in the rivers and in the subterranean connections between natural springs in Guatemala and Yucatan. Its back is high, markedly convex in outline, with a large head and prominent dorsal and anal fins. Its ground colour is a bluish-grey with a violet sheen, darker on the back than the flanks, on which are dark bands. Its scales have red edges so the body appears to be covered with a red network, and there is a brilliant splash of orange on the belly and throat.

△ *A firemouth shows its gaudy throat—and its confusing 'false-eye' colour pattern.*

Dredging for food

As with other cichlids the firemouth moves about very little, spending much of its time near the bed of the river. It takes animal food, either by sucking in small animals swimming or floating by, or digging for food in sand or mud. In digging it stands on its head bringing the mouth near the bottom, scoops sand or mud into the mouth, and after making chewing movements it spits out the indigestible parts. At times it may drop into a more horizontal position and with open mouth plough its way through the sand. Having travelled about 3 times its own length it then reverses the beat of the pectoral fins to swim backwards and while doing so spits out the indigestible sand, having sorted from it any edible material.

Digging and spawning

The courtship and spawning are both elaborate. The male stakes out a territory, driving out any other males straying into it but eventually pairing up with a female wandering in. The courtship includes swimming round each other, with the male displaying, as well as other movements including both partners digging a pit in the sand. The female leaves her pit from time to time to investigate possible surfaces on which to lay her eggs. The male also leaves his pit to swim over and inspect the sites. Finally the female lays eggs one by one, each sticking to the chosen surface. Every time she breaks off egg-laying he swims over from his pit and fertilises the new batch of eggs.

'Talking' with gestures

Baerends and Baerends-van Roon studied the bones and muscles of each kind of fish they were observing and traced in detail how the movements of these were linked with behaviour. They were able to divide the fishes' everyday movements into those used in moving about, comfort movements (such as yawning and stretching) and those used in feeding and spawning. Finally, there are signal movements which serve as a language. This last group includes exaggerations of everyday movements which are therefore conspicuous. They are also conventional, and so they cannot be misinterpreted. Colour and colour changes, associated with the movements, emphasize their meaning.

For example, if a male firemouth enters the territory held by another, the occupier raises his fins, as he would do in swimming, and raises his gill-covers, as he would in breathing. But all these are exaggerated as compared with normal swimming and breathing movements. The result is that the fish's head looks bigger than usual and the body seems to bristle with fins. At the same time the normal colours become brighter and, moreover, with the gill-covers standing out and the fins fully spread, all colours show off to greater advantage. To the intruding male this says 'Get out', as clearly as it could be said in words.

Baby firemouths on trial

Signals are not used only between adults. When the baby fish begin to swim they follow one or other of the parents, usually the mother. Baerends and Baerends-van Roon set about finding what things influenced the young fishes. They made a number of models which they could move about in the water in front of the fry. These ranged from a perfect replica of an adult firemouth, through discs, circles, rectangles, horseshoes, triangles—a range of 17 different shapes. The baby firemouths followed them all equally readily provided one thing: that they were moved through the water in the slow jerky way of a small fish swimming in leisurely fashion.

If the models were moved rapidly or violently the babies fled in all directions, so the next thing to test was whether it was sight or some other sense that made them do this. The simple experiment was to move the models outside the aquarium, so the baby fishes saw them through the glass. They still followed when the movement was slow and jerky but did not flee when it was violent. So they appreciated the slow movements by sight and the violent movements through the disturbance made in the water.

Another set of models of very varying sizes showed that size made no difference, the baby fishes would follow any 'parent', large or small, or of whatever shape, provided it had slow jerky movement.

Then came the tests for colour. These used many more models, coloured red, orange, yellow, green, blue, black and silver, and for each colour they were graded also for brightness. The tests were made on the young of several species of cichlids. Some of the babies followed certain colours by instinct. The babies of one species were actually frightened by black. Baby firemouths followed almost any colour, of any brightness, so long as the model moved slowly and jerkily. This was unexpected; having parents with such a vivid patch of colour that we give them their common name because of it, we would naturally expect the babies to recognize it from birth. It seems, on the contrary, they have gradually to learn to recognize it, and do not do so until 15 days old. Only at that age will they follow red in preference to any other colour.

class	**Pisces**
order	**Perciformes**
family	**Cichlidae**
genus & species	***Cichlasoma meeki***

Flying fish

There are two types of herring-like flying fishes: the two-winged and the four-winged. In the first only the pectoral fins are enlarged. In the second the pelvic fins also are enlarged, making two pairs of wings, and it is this type that is noted for the colours of its fins.

*The commonest species is the two-winged **Exocoetus volitans**, 10 in. long, found in all tropical seas. The commonest four-winged flying fish is **Cypselurus heterurus**, 1 ft long, found on both sides of the tropical Atlantic. The largest four-winged type is **C. californicus**, 18 in. long, which in summer provides an attraction for visitors to California's beaches. In spring and summer it is fished commercially, most of the catch being used as bait for swordfish and tuna fishing.*

Dangers above and below

Little is known about the biology of flying fishes apart from their journeys through the air which have been the subject of much debate. When swimming, their long fins are folded against the body. They feed on plankton, perhaps also on small fishes, and in turn will be the prey of larger, predatory fishes, and also of seabirds. The flying habit must have evolved largely in response to heavy predation. Yet ironically, whenever a flying fish leaves the water for the air, seabirds, such as frigate birds, albatrosses and gulls, are liable to attack. Among the predatory fishes the main enemy seems to be the dolphin fish (page 68).

Butterflying fishes

Flying fishes spawn on floating seaweeds and on other floating objects. Some seem to use sargassum weed almost entirely. On it they make nests by drawing the weed together with white elastic strings, and the eggs are fastened to one another and to the nest by similar but thinner threads. The young flying fishes are so unlike the adults that they have been described as different fishes. Besides being patterned in many colours, which prompted the American

oceanographer William Beebe to call them butterflying fishes, each young fish has a pair of large flap-like barbels, or whiskers, which hang down from the tip of the lower jaw. In the young Californian flying fish the barbels form a red, many-fingered outgrowth. In the young 2in.-long Caribbean flying fish the barbels extend back beyond the tail, like streamers.

Vibrating wings or gliding?

For many years it was hotly debated whether flying fishes vibrated their wings while in the air, or whether they merely glided. The reason why this doubt continued for so long was largely due to the fishes being so hard to photograph. Also there is an illusion of wing-flapping when the fishes are taxying for the takeoff and are washed by wavelets. At this time also the rapidly moving tail vibrates the body and makes it quiver, so that the fins appear to be beating the air.

Studies of the anatomy, however, suggested that the fishes had the wrong muscles to be able to beat their wings. Experiments in wind tunnels pointed to the same conclusion. Finally stroboscopic photography showed conclusively that flying fishes are gliders, not true flyers. In stroboscopic photography a camera is used that makes repeated exposures at short intervals of fractions of a second. The pictures it takes show the successive positions of a moving object. The results are better than in a ciné film, in which each separate frame gives a blurred picture.

Takeoff at 40 mph

To become airborne, the flying fish swims rapidly forwards and upwards to the surface. As its body lifts above the surface it spreads its fins and taxis along the surface with the lower lobe of its tail fin moving in a sculling action. The lower lobe is longer than the upper lobe and is vibrated at a rate of up to 50 beats a second. After a short while the pelvic fins are spread and this gives enough lift to raise the tail fin clear of the surface and the fish is then fully airborne.

The average speed in the air is about 35 mph. At the start it is about 40 mph and this falls off to about 20 mph at the end as momentum is lost. The fish may land on its belly with a splash, or it may dive headdown, drop back into the water tail first or even land on its back. If it lands tail first it may resume the sculling action and taxi once more for another flight. Usually one or two flights only are made but there are records of up to 11 flights in succession, covering a distance of 1 000 ft or more. Each flight, or leap, may cover up to 450 ft and last about 10 seconds. The longest recorded lasted 42 seconds. Most flights are made just above the water but flying fishes have been known to land on the decks of ships up to 36 ft above sea-level. These higher flights may be when a fish strikes an up-current of air if the takeoff is into the wind.

The usual estimate is that 3 times out of 4 the fish takes off into the wind, but in 1965/6, NJB Plomley, of University College, London, made several journeys across the Indian Ocean, from the Red Sea to Australia, studying flying fishes disturbed by the ships he was on. He came to the conclusion that the direction and force of the wind had little bearing on the flights of flying fishes. What he did find was that they were less likely to become airborne if their course lay towards the sun than when it was away from the sun.

At times it seems that flying fishes have little control of their movements in the air but Carl Hubbs, distinguished American ichthyologist, maintained otherwise. According to him they sometimes fly straight towards the side of a ship and, when about to crash into it they suddenly plunge into the water, turn about almost directly, and make away in the opposite direction, either in the water or in the air. The four-winged flying fishes would have the advantage in such circumstances because their large pelvic fins act as ailerons for banking and as elevators for nosing down or for climbing.

Once aloft, the fish presents a perfect glider's silhouette. Flights can last up to 42 seconds.

Desperately evading the enemy below, a flying fish struggles to get airborne. Sculling across the surface with its tail to gain flying speed, it spreads its fins for lift-off.

class	**Pisces**
order	**Atheriniformes**
family	**Exocoetidae**
genera	***Exocoetus, Cypselurus***

What's in a name? The flying gurnard is, at best, a weak flier, and is not a true gurnard. Both species are aggressive, despite their size; this is the Atlantic species.

Flying gurnard

There are two species of flying gurnard, one in the tropical Atlantic, the other in the Indian Ocean. Whether in fact they do fly is in doubt. Another problem is whether or not they should be classified with other gurnards, which they closely resemble.

The Atlantic species is up to 15 in. long. It has a large head and large, wing-like pectoral fins. It is greenish-blue with orange-edged dark spots on the head and body. The large pectoral fins are greenish-blue ornamented with the same orange-edged spots. The Indian Ocean species, up to 12 in. long, is a dull reddish with pink underparts, blue spots down the back and a dorsal fin covered with brown spots. The pectoral fins are bright blue with brown and pale green spots. These descriptions of colour are, however, only approximate because in both species the colours vary with age as well as from one individual to another, and in any individual the colours vary somewhat according to what is happening. In the Atlantic species, for example, the young has a large white-edged black ocellus or eye-spot on each of

the pectoral fins, and in the adults the colours, especially of the pectoral fins, become much more brilliant in moments of excitement.

Familiar—yet little known

Flying gurnards are familiar fishes on account of their colours and because in the Indian Ocean they are caught for food, from canoes fishing in deep water. Yet little is known about them. We know they are mainly bottom-living and that they feed on prawns and other small crustaceans.

A pugnacious fish

The flying gurnard swims slowly just off the bottom with its large pectoral fins laid back along the sides of the body. It may also crawl over the sandy seabed using the small lower lobe of each pectoral fin as a foot aided by the thin pelvic fins, which are said to be moved alternately like small legs. Skin divers report that when they approach to within 4 ft of one of the Atlantic flying gurnards it spreads its pectoral fins to the full extent and their turquoise-blue patches become brilliant. At the same time it grunts, with a noise not unlike a raucous version of the clucking of a barnyard hen. In the Indian Ocean the flying gurnard has many local names, all expressing that it makes

noises when caught in a net. After this show of bad temper the fish relaxes and folds its fins back along the sides. When the skin diver approaches to about 2 ft from the fish it does not swim away as other fishes do, but goes into an even more vigorous aggression, even advancing towards its adversary. A woman collecting shells in shallow water in the Caribbean met a flying gurnard. It spread its pectoral fins, came over to her and butted her ankles, which became numb immediately afterwards. It is suggested that the spines on the gill-covers may be poisonous, or perhaps it is the spine on the front of the dorsal fin which lies just behind the head. Certainly the fish is feared by the local people in the Caribbean.

Skilled at evading capture

Anyone trying to catch a flying gurnard with a net finds it very agile and skilful in evading capture, swimming away quickly. When caught and put in an aquarium it swings its body from side-to-side and it taps on the bottom with the hand-like lower lobes of the pectoral fins, tapping first with one 'hand', then with the other.

Do flying gurnards fly?

Those who maintain that the flying gurnard flies agree that its flight is more clumsy and less sustained than that of a flying fish. Dr PH Greenwood, distinguished ichthyologist, has described seeing Indian Ocean flying gurnards 'flying' out of the bow wave of a ship. About 4 in. long, their pectoral fins spanned 6 in. full spread, and he describes them as airborne for about 2 seconds. In that time, however, they seemed to be gliding in a controlled manner, not merely jumping out and plunging in again in the manner of other fishes. Opponents of this view argue that almost any fish will at times jump out of the water and it is quite accidental that the gurnard has large fins which act as planes to keep it airborne.

Near relatives?

Some students of fishes claim that flying gurnards and gurnards, which we deal with later (see page 99), are closely related but should be kept in separate families. Others maintain they are not closely related and should be placed in separate orders, which is the view followed here. The two kinds of fishes differ in the bones of the skull. They also differ in the way the front spines of the pectoral fins are arranged, as well as in some of their behaviour. If they are not closely related then they give us a wonderful example of convergence in evolution—that is, of two kinds of animals that have come to look alike externally because they have the same way of life.

class	**Pisces**
order	**Dactylopteriformes**
family	**Dactylopteridae**
genus & species	***Dactyloptera volitans*** *Atlantic flying gurnard* **D. orientalis** *Indian Ocean flying gurnard*

Four-eyed fish

This remarkable fish has two eyes each divided into two. Even more remarkable, 'left-handed' males must mate with 'right-handed' females and vice versa.

A minnow-like fish, 6—8 in. long, sometimes reaching 1 ft, it lives in freshwater from southern Mexico through central America to northern South America. It is long-bodied with a rounded tail fin but otherwise undistinguished in shape except for its large goggling eyes. It spends most of its time cruising at the surface with only the upper half of each eye above the water.

Divided eyeballs

Each eye of the four-eyed fish is divided horizontally by a partition, and the fish swims with the surface of the water level with this. The partition divides the cornea. Anything underwater is seen by the upper retina through the lower cornea. Vision through water requires a thicker lens than vision through air, so the lens is oval, and anything viewed underwater is seen through the thicker part of it.

Land animals have a tear duct to keep the eye moist but the four-eyed fish has to dip its head from time to time to keep its eyes from drying out.

Looking for prey

The four-eyed fish feeds on small swimming animals. It would be reasonable to suppose that with the double vision it could look for food under the surface and also for any insects falling on the water. This, however, seems to be in some doubt. Its usual way of feeding is to swim down, catch its prey, then immediately swim up to lie once again just under the surface with half of each eye above the waterline. We can only suppose also that its aerial vision helps in keeping watch for enemies from above, such as water-birds.

Compatible mating

The females bear between 1—5 living young. One female 6 in. long gave birth to one baby 2½ in. long, and another of similar size gave birth to 4, each of which was 1½ in. long. Fertilisation is internal; the male must inject his sperms into the female. He does this using a tube formed from modified rays of the anal fin. In any male this tube can only be moved either to the left or to the right.

The sexual opening of the female is protected by a special scale, so it can be entered only from the left or from the right. As a result a 'left-handed' male can mate only with a 'right-handed' female, and vice versa.

Bifocal blenny

Anableps anableps and *A. tetrophthalmus*, the two species of four-eyed fishes so far discussed, are not alone. There is a four-eyed blenny, 3 in. long, living on the rocky shores of the Galapagos Islands. Its eyes are divided by a vertical partition, and for a long time we have been told that this blenny

Two-tier vision: the compound eyes of the four-eyed fish scan both air and water.

spends much of its time in a vertical position with its nose out of water and the partition in the eye coinciding with the waterline. In 1963, however, the German zoologist, Ebehard Curio, studied this blenny *Dialommus fuscus* at first-hand in the Galapagos and found it does no such thing. It feeds on small crustaceans and it comes out onto rocks at low tide. It has a skilful way of moving about. The blenny rides the crest of a wave and lets this wash it into a crevice. If the crevice is unsuitable the blenny moves over the wet rock with sculling movements of its tail. When returning to the sea it waits for the run-off to carry it back. This and more Curio learned, but he could not find out what use the 'four eyes' were.

Although *Anableps* was the first fish to be called four-eyed the only one that truly deserves the name was brought up from deep water in the North Pacific only a few years ago. Given the name *Bathylychnops exilis*, it is a slender pike-like fish, 1½ ft long, living in the twilight zone of blue light, between 300 and 3 000 ft down. From its shape it is a hunter that catches other fishes by short swift spurts. It needs good eyesight and the large eye has a retina made up of millions of rods, the light-sensitive cells. This gives wide vision and also keen sight for detail. Each large eye has a small eye on its lower part which looks downwards. These have their own retina and probably give greater sensitivity, especially in judging distances. Behind the small eyes are two smaller eye-like organs that are no more than swellings on the cornea of the large eye. They lack a retina and probably do no more than bend the light rays into the large eye. Yet this is only a guess and we may have to wait a long time for an explanation why such an unusual fish exists with four eyes on each side of its head.

class	**Pisces**
order	**Atheriniformes**
family	**Anablepidae**
genus & species	*Anableps anableps* *others*

Anableps anableps, *the freshwater four-eyed fish of central America (actual size).*

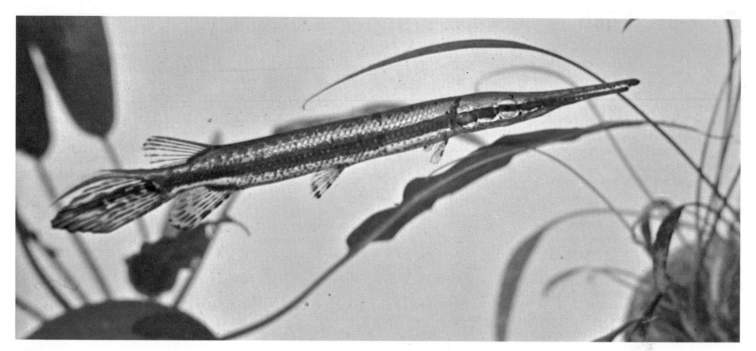

Gar

These slender pike-like fishes are living fossils of a family that reached its peak in the Mesozoic period 70—220 million years ago. There are seven species living in the rivers and lakes of North and Central America.

The commonest of these species is the longnose gar, which lives from the Great Lakes southwards. It is up to 5 ft long, its slim body covered with a tough armour of close-set diamond-shaped or rhombic enamelled (ganoid) scales which do not overlap in the usual manner of fish scales. The long snout is a beak; its jaws studded with small sharp teeth recall those of the gharial among crocodilians, the beak being twice as long as the rest of the head. The dorsal and anal fins are set far back on the body. The back is olive to silver, the underside white.

The shortnose gar, up to 2 ft long, lives mainly in the Great Lakes. The tropical gar of Mexico is said to reach 10 or even 12 ft, and the alligator gar which ranges from southern United States to Panama and Cuba is about the same size. Its snout is very like that of an alligator.

Indolent fishes

The gars live mainly in still waters, where they lie almost motionless among water plants, looking more like floating logs than fish. They move quietly and slowly to stalk passing prey, which is seized with a sudden sideways slash of the snout. Although apparently so lethargic, gars can move rapidly when necessary. Their food is mainly other fishes but little animal food is refused. Frogs, salamanders and worms are readily accepted and the young gar feeds largely on water insects. They soon take to catching fish, however, and a young 2 in. gar is on record as taking 16 young minnows in quick succession. It is easy to imagine from this the predatory nature of the gar and why

fishermen hate them, and gars also take bait from their hooks. A gar can, with one snap of its jaws, seize a whole group of small fishes. With larger fish the prey must be gradually worked round in the mouth into a position from which it can be swallowed head first. All food takes 24 hours to digest, which is slow compared with most other freshwater fishes.

Eggs and babies stick to rocks

The males mature in 3—4 years, the females taking 6 years. Spawning is from March to May in shallow waters, each female being accompanied by 3 or 4 males. The average number of eggs laid per female is about 28 000 but may vary from 4 000 to 60 000 according to her size. The eggs are sticky and cling to rocks and water plants. In a few days they hatch and the baby fishes fix themselves to water plants by cement organs, adhesive discs at the end of the snout, and hang there until the yolk sac has been absorbed. After this they swim freely, feeding at first on mosquito larvae.

Rapid growth

In spite of its reputation for voracity, justified if by nothing else by its almost shark-like teeth, a gar has a low food consumption, feeds irregularly and has a slow rate of digestion. Yet it is one of the fastest growing of freshwater fishes. In its first year a young male gar grows on average just over $\frac{1}{10}$ in. a day to reach $19\frac{1}{2}$ in. by the end of the first season, the female reaching 22 in. in the same period. After that growth slows down to 1 in. a year but continues for 13—14 years in the females, which outlive the males. Because it moves about so little—even its feeding is leisurely—and because it has a high metabolic efficiency (that is, its body makes the fullest use of all its food), the energy supplied by the food goes into growing in size instead of being dissipated by moving about quickly and continuously.

Scaly armour

In all probability it is because its scales are so closely set, forming such a rigid covering, that a gar must lead an inactive life. This

△ *The dart-shaped body of short-nosed gar helps it merge with surrounding water plants.*

tough scaly armour of the gar has, however, proved very useful and been used by different peoples in different ways. The original inhabitants of the Caribbean islands are said to have used the skin, with its diamond-shaped, closely fitting scales, for breastplates. Some of the North American Indians separated the scales and used them for arrowheads. The early pioneers in the United States found gar skin hard enough to cover the blades of their wooden ploughs.

class	**Pisces**
order	**Ginglymodi**
family	**Lepisosteidae**
genus & species	***Lepisosteus osseus*** *longnose gar* ***L. platystomus*** *shortnose gar* ***L. spatula*** *alligator gar* ***L. tristoechus*** *tropical gar*

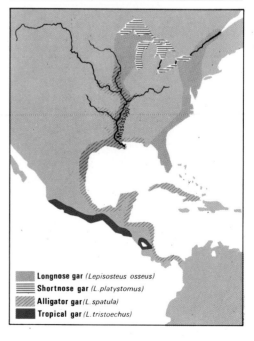

▢ Longnose gar *(Lepisosteus osseus)*
▤ Shortnose gar *(L. platystomus)*
▨ Alligator gar *(L. spatula)*
▰ Tropical gar *(L. tristoechus)*

Giganturid

This name, which looks very queer to the non-zoologist, is deliberately used to introduce a very odd deep-sea fish, one that breaks all the rules. There are several species in one genus **Gigantura,** *belonging to one family placed in a suborder on its own. The several species, which differ from each other in small details only, have been brought up from depths between 1 500 – 6 000 ft in both Atlantic and Indian Oceans. The name suggests giant fishes but they are usually between 2 – 5, rarely as much as 8, in. long. In fact, when we break up the name we find it is made up of a Latin word* **giganteus** *and a Greek word* **uros** *meaning tail. It refers not to the size of the fish but to the extraordinarily long lower lobe of the tail fin. And if the name is misleading this is appropriate because almost everything else about the fish is misleading.*

made. The shape, number and disposition of the fins of a giganturid suggests that they do not swim rapidly. On the other hand, it is a mystery why it should be silvery or why it has no scales. And the long lower tail fin is hardly more easy to explain. We are on firmer ground about the way it feeds because the strong jaws and sharp teeth mark it as predatory. Moreover, because its teeth are depressible we could suppose it swallows large prey, the teeth being lowered to allow more room for large prey to be taken into the mouth. This line of argument is supported by the elastic stomach of a giganturid and by those brought to the surface that have recently swallowed a fish as large or larger than themselves. One giganturid, appropriately named *Gigantura vorax,* itself 3 in. long, had swallowed another fish 5½ in. long. Moreover, this fish was doubled up, suggesting that the giganturid had seized it by the middle and had swallowed it bent into a V.

Then comes the question: how does a giganturid breathe while swallowing such large prey, which must take an appreciable

they are poor swimmers and, presumably, must stalk prey that cannot see as far as they can. A further theory is that the eyes, which have an accessory retina of short rods as well as the main retina, are specially adapted for picking up the luminescence from the light-organs of their prey.

Problems to be settled

The eyes of fishes are essentially like ours but there are differences, one of them being that the lens, instead of being oval, is spherical and bulges well through the pupil. Consequently, with the eyes set on the sides of the head a fish has a wide all-round vision, necessary because it has no neck and cannot turn its head to look for food or keep watch for enemies. It has, so to speak, the next best thing to having 'eyes in the back of its head'. Most fishes, also, are long-sighted despite a popular belief that they are short-sighted. In addition, many fishes can swivel their eyes forward to give better vision forwards. This can be seen when we look at a fish in an aquarium as it faces us head-on as in the angelfish,

Gigantura—tubular-eyed fish with a body 2 – 5 in. long is found in the deep waters of both the Atlantic and Indian Oceans.

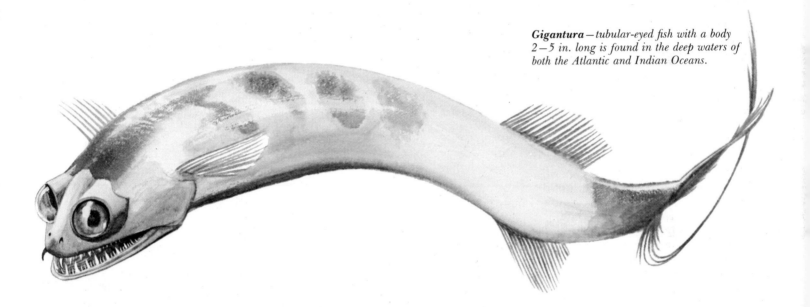

Catalogue of oddities

Giganturids have slender rounded bodies. They lack pelvic fins as well as a number of other anatomical parts, normally considered essential to the life of a fish, including several bones of the head. They also lack light-organs which are such a feature of deep-sea fishes. They have needle-sharp teeth that can be raised and lowered. The pectoral fins are unusually large for the size of the body. Their bodies are scaleless and whereas other fishes living at these depths are black or dark brown, giganturids are a bright, metallic silvery colour, like fishes that live near the surface. Above all, these fishes have tubular eyes directed forwards, as if they were wearing binoculars. There are a few other fishes with tubular eyes but usually these are directed upwards.

Breathing while swallowing

As with all deep-sea animals virtually nothing is known of the way they live except what can be deduced from the way they are

time? One suggestion is that while doing this, and so prevented from taking in water through the mouth to pass across the gills, the large pectoral fins are used to fan water into the gill-chamber for breathing.

Infrequent meals

So far as the food and feeding habits are concerned, all that has so far been deduced fits into the general pattern of what is already known for the carnivorous deep-sea fishes. That is, they are living in depths where food is not abundant so they must take whatever food presents itself even to swallowing prey larger than themselves. So they make up for the infrequency of their meals by taking huge meals when opportunity offers. What is now needed is to guess why the tubular eyes are required. One view is that they act like the telephoto lens of a camera so the giganturid can see prey a long way off, even in the murky gloom at great depths. Another is that they need this improved vision because

picture on page 14. It can also be seen on the television screen when underwater close-up pictures of fishes are being shown. These considerations show how specialised are the eyes of giganturids, which can only look directly forwards. Perhaps one day we may know how they are compensated for this loss of all-round vision, with eyes in the front of the head only. They may have other senses for detecting the approach of food or enemies from behind. Perhaps the scaleless skin means it is more sensitive to vibrations in the water. And then, there is the long lower tail fin—the giant tail—to be accounted for, one of the many problems to which answers are eagerly awaited.

class	**Pisces**
order	**Cetomimiformes**
family	**Giganturidae**
genus & species	*Gigantura vorax others*

*See-through skin and shining colours make glassfishes popular in aquaria. △ **Chanda lala**. ▷ Siamese glassfish **Chanda wolfii**.*

Glassfish

This is an obvious name for fishes that are transparent, with the skeleton and some internal organs clearly visible; yet although transparent they do not lack colour. A number of fishes are transparent or translucent but the name 'glassfish' is reserved for certain small fishes that are favourite aquarium fishes. Large game or commercial fishes, including the snooks and the Nile perch were once thought to be closely related. The glassfish and the Nile perch although so different to look at, have one thing in common: they have both, at different times, ended in the ground: the glassfish used as fertilizer, the Nile perch mummified by the Egyptians.

The body is deep and strongly compressed from side-to-side. The dorsal fin is in two parts, that in front being supported by hard rays, the rear portion having one hard ray and up to 18 soft rays. The tailfin is either rounded or deeply forked.

The 8 or more species are found from East Africa through southern Asia to eastern Australia, the majority being in southeast Asia.

The 8 species of snooks live in the seas of tropical west and east Atlantic and the eastern Pacific. They readily enter rivers and may be 4½ ft long with a weight of 51 lb. The Nile perch, up to 7 ft long and more than 250 lb weight, is only one of several related African game species. It looks much more substantial than the glassfish.

Living gems for fertilizers

The Indian glassfish looks like a piece of crystal floating and reflecting colours in water. It is up to 3 in. long, greenish to yellowish but shining gold or iridescent bluish-green in reflected light. The flanks are marked with bars made up of tiny black dots, with a delicate violet stripe running from the gill-cover to the root of the tail. The fins are yellowish to rusty-red, the dorsal and anal fins with black rays and bordered with pale blue. Rays of paired fins are red or bluish.

It is the best known of the small glassfishes, and lives in fresh and brackish waters of India, Burma and Thailand. Its uneventful life is spent among water plants feeding on small aquatic animals such as insect larvae, crustaceans and worms. Its breeding habits are almost equally uneventful. In aquaria, according to Günther Sterba, spawning is triggered by morning sunshine raising the temperature, and a brief separation of the sexes, by putting them in separate tanks for a short time then reuniting them. The pair take up position side-by-side, quivering all the time. As the female lays the pair turn over to an upside-down position. The female lays her eggs among water plants to which they stick. She lays 4–6 at a time, repeating this until 200 or more have been laid. After this the parents take no further interest. The eggs hatch in 8–24 hours, depending on temperature, the baby fishes hanging from the water plants for 3–4 days after which they swim freely. Their food is small crustaceans, such as water fleas. The young glassfishes do not go in search of food but snap up any that drifts past them. It can be presumed that if food is scarce around the area at such times many young fishes will die of starvation. Nevertheless, large numbers survive for, as William T Innes remarks in his *Exotic Aquarium Fishes,* this little gem treasured by aquarists is caught in large numbers in India and Burma for use as a fertilizer.

Family likenesses

Two people when related even distantly often share what we call a family likeness. In height, girth, colour of hair and in almost every way the two may be wholly unlike yet there is something that marks them as belonging to a family. It may be something very small, for example, a peculiarity in the way they walk, the shape of the lower lip, and so on. It is the same in classifying animals, and the family we are considering here is a fine example. Included in it are glassfishes, small, transparent, delicate; as well as snooks that are large, sturdy and not transparent and the 7ft robust giant, the Nile perch. From a casual glance they look most unlike yet each has a similar outline, and each has at least one small feature we call a family likeness. In each the lateral line, the line of sense-organs running along the flanks of fishes, goes right to the end of the tailfin, which is most unusual.

class	**Pisces**
order	**Perciformes**
family	**Centropomidae**
genera & species	***Chanda ranga*** *Indian glassfish* ***Centropomus unidecimalis*** *snook others*

Goby

*Gobies are the Lilliputians of the fish world, most gobies being under 3 in. long and many not much more than 1 in. long. The giant goby **Gobius cobitis** of the Mediterranean and western Europe does not exceed 9 in. and is usually 4–5 in. Most of them have little commercial value and so tend to be overlooked. Some of the largest among the nearly 500 species in the family are the mudskippers. Other large gobies are the guavina **Gobiomorus dormitor** of Central America, 2 ft long, and the several species of **Bunaka** of the Indo-Australian region, of nearly the same size, which are valuable food-fishes. The smallest is the Luzon goby **Pandaka pygmaea** of the streams and lakes of the Philippines, barely ½ in. long, the smallest vertebrate.*

Mainly marine, but with many species entering brackish estuaries, gobies are colourful fishes with flattened heads, large eyes and short snouts. The eyes are high up on the head, often almost touching each other. There are two dorsal fins and the margins of the pelvic fins are joined to form a sucker.

Holing up for safety

As they are small it is natural that gobies should live in places where safe retreats are near at hand. Usually each fish has its own retreat from which it sallies forth to feed and to which it returns. The habitat is variable. Many gobies are bottom living, especially on rocky shores, some being left behind as the tide ebbs and sheltering under stones in rock pools. Others live in burrows in sand or mud, or shelter among branching corals. Some gobies have been elusive, regarded as rare for years, and then turning up unexpectedly in large numbers in a bay or a fiord. Since biologists began skin-diving, so-called rare species have been found to be common. The Catalina or blue-banded goby, for example, was first found in 1890. Few specimens were seen then or later until 1938 when an early skin-diving biologist found it was common, living in crevices in the rocks. New species have been discovered which could not have been otherwise brought to light because they live among rocky reefs, spending much of their time in crevices, where nets cannot reach them. A few gobies live among seaweeds in shallow inshore waters, and fewer still live in shoals in open water. Wherever they live their food is small invertebrates, especially the small crustaceans, and they also eat any small items of dead flesh that come to rest on the seabed.

Male guards the eggs

By contrast with their retiring nature at other times the male gobies are aggressive towards each other during the breeding season. This is a matter of fighting over territories, in this case an area of rock, coral or other surface where the female will lay her eggs. After pairing, the male goby

acts as guardian to the female while she is laying her eggs. Each egg is oval or pear-shaped, about $\frac{1}{16}$ in. long, and usually has a short stalk, the clump of eggs being fastened to a solid surface as they are laid. The 'nest' may be on rock or coral or in an empty shell. Having laid her clutch of about 100 eggs the female departs, leaving the male to guard it for anything up to a fortnight. He aerates the eggs by fanning them with his fins. The newly-hatched gobies are well developed and soon look like their parents. Douglas Wilson has watched the sand goby *Pomatoschistus minutus* guarding eggs in an empty mollusc shell. If a shrimp or baby flatfish comes near he drives it off. When the shell with its eggs is removed for a few moments he swims back and forth over the spot in what seems a frenzied manner, and when the shell is put back he fusses over it like any conscientious mother to restore it to its original position, carrying tiny stones away with his mouth until the shell and the eggs are in order again.

Sold as 'ipon'

Gobies are eaten by the usual predatory fishes, as well as diving seabirds such as divers, but little more is known of their enemies. Gobies are sometimes accidentally included in whitebait but apart from the few larger species taken for food in the Far East the only important fishery is in the northern Philippines. There a freshwater goby spawns in the sea and its ½in. fry return in huge shoals to the mouths of the rivers. From September to March these are netted in the streams and rivers and sold under the name *ipon,* which is fried in oil or made into a paste called *bagoong.*

Unlikely partnerships

Gobies of the genus *Parioglossus* depart from the usual habit of keeping near their hiding places and 'hover' in mid-water in shoals of thousands. When disturbed they dive into the nearest coral heads. Related species of *Vireosa* do much the same except that they dive into the gaping shells of oysters and giant clams. Their entry alarms the molluscs which close their shells, so giving the gobies added security.

The habit of sheltering in cracks, crevices and burrows has led to several instances of commensalism (living together). The arrow goby *Clevelandia ios* of California shares

Leopard-spotted goby **Thorogobius ephippiatus** *in its shelter (fan worm* **Bispira volutacornis** *in foreground).*

holes in mud-flats with a pea crab and a burrowing worm. The goby will carry large pieces of food, too big for it to swallow, for the crab to tear apart, then wait and pick up the crumbs. The blind goby *Typhlogobius californiensis,* also of California, lives in holes dug by the ghost shrimp. Should the shrimp die its goby companion is doomed unless it can find an unattached shrimp to live with. Several species of *Smilogobius* around the coasts of the Indo-Pacific region team up with snapping shrimps which dig and maintain the burrow, constantly shovelling away the loose sand, while the goby maintains a watch near its mouth. At the slightest alarm the goby dives into the burrow and the shrimp follows. The fish is the first to leave when things have settled down, and the shrimp then comes out to resume digging. It is a perfect partnership except that the goby is apt to feed on the shrimp's babies. A less damaging relationship is found between the neon goby *Elacatinus oceanops* and several species of larger fishes; it cleans parasites from them.

Knowledge of their surroundings

It has been suggested that nocturnal animals carry in their memory a knowledge of their surroundings. Something of this sort has been worked out for a goby *Bathygobius soporator.* This lives in pools when the tide is out and can find its way down the beach to the sea, if need be, by jumping from one pool to another. It is unable to see the next pool at the moment it takes off yet can leap with precision and not get stranded on dry land in between. This was carefully studied and the remarkable conclusion was reached that as the fish swims above the seabed at high tide it learns the topography of it so thoroughly that when the tide is out it knows the layout of the pools from high up the beach to the water's edge.

class	**Pisces**
order	**Perciformes**
family	**Gobiidae**

◁ *Rock goby showing sucker of pelvic fins.*

▽ *Rock goby* **Gobius paganellus** *is a model father who cherishes the eggs until they hatch.*

A 'celestial' goldfish: his eyes are turned for ever towards the heavens.

Goldfish

Goldfish are, in fact, a domesticated form of a wild carp native to China. The wild ancestral form is a very ordinary fish, sometimes used as food, green and brown in colour but occasionally throwing up red or red-gold individuals. These were collected and cultivated by the Chinese as far back as 960 AD and by the period 1173–1240 goldfish were being kept as pets in earthenware bowls and ornamental ponds. They were introduced into Japan in 1500 but reached Europe nearly two centuries later. There is reason to believe that the first reached England in 1692 on a ship that left Macao in 1691. From then on, goldfish reached France in 1750, the Netherlands in 1753 or 1754, Germany in 1780 and in Russia there were goldfish in bowls in Prince Potemkin's Winter Garden in 1791. Goldfish did not reach the United States apparently until 1859.

The relationships of the goldfish have been variously stated by experts. That its ancestor is the crucian carp which is also known as the Prussian carp when it is lean, is one variation. The opinion now seems to be that the goldfish **Carassius auratus** *is Asiatic, and that the Prussian carp* **C. auratus gibelio**, *which is greyish-yellow to silver-grey, is a European subspecies. The crucian carp of Europe is a separate species* **C. carassius**.

Usually regarded as a small fish, the goldfish can weigh up to 10 lb, although those bred as ornamentals are usually only a few inches long. There are two types of fancy goldfish, the scaled and the 'scaleless', the latter having scales that are transparent and hard to see. At first the scaled varieties are uncoloured, that is smoky or like tarnished silver, then black begins to show and later changes to red or white. The scaleless varieties do not have the metallic sheen of the others but show more delicate colours, such as lavender and blue. They are white at first, sprinkled with dark specks, and quickly gain their permanent colours. The shubunkin is a familiar example of the 'scaleless' type, blue tinged with red and mottled with yellow, red and dark brown, or in some combination of these colours.

Food from the mud
The life of the wild goldfish is no more eventful than that of the domesticated varieties. The natural food includes animal and plant, the first including water fleas, freshwater shrimps *Gammarus*, gnat larvae and worms (especially *Tubifex*). Among the water fleas are *Cyclops* and *Daphnia*, the latter so familiarly known to aquarists as a food for aquarium fishes that the name is anglicized, usually to daphney. The plant food includes duckweed and in the aquarium the small green algae that tend to coat the wall of the aquarium. This is augmented by mouthfuls of mud, the fish chewing this over by churning movements of the jaws. The inedible matter is spat out and the fragments of dead plant and animal matter swallowed. By what extraordinary means the two are sorted is not fully understood.

Pearl organs
Male and female become recognizable at the breeding season because the female is then swollen with eggs while the male develops tubercles known as pearl organs on the gill covers and pectoral fins. These are difficult to see without viewing the fish from a certain angle. The female lays 500–1 000 eggs, each $\frac{1}{16}$ in. diameter, between May and August, which are fertilised after they have been laid, the male following the female around all the time she is spawning. The eggs stick to the water plants. They hatch in 8–9 days when the temperature is 16–18°C/60–65°F, in 5–7 days at 21–24°C/70–75°F. The larvae, $\frac{1}{5}$ in. long and tadpole-like in shape, hang on to the water plants for the next 48 hours, by which time the yolk sac is emptied, the fins have grown and the baby goldfish are able to feed on infusorians (microscopic protistans). When 18 days old they will be 1 in. long and will feed on water fleas, especially 'daphney' In the aquarium they are usually given packaged foods, especially ants' 'eggs'.

Danger of infancy
Pet goldfish can be long-lived, up to 25 years having been recorded, but life for the wild form is more precarious. The enemies are predatory fishes, fish-eating birds such

as herons and kingfishers, as well as aquatic mammals. The losses from these may represent perhaps 5–10% of the adult population. The real wastage takes place in the early stages of life, especially among the baby fishes, where the death-rate is 70–80% during the first 6 months to a year. The enemies then are many both for the wild stock and for goldfish in ornamental ponds.

Wherever in this encyclopedia the enemies of freshwater fishes are considered they must include much the same as those now to be listed for the baby goldfish. What follows here can, therefore, serve as a standard for the general run of freshwater fishes, with the advantage that those who keep goldfish in ornamental ponds can know who their enemies are. The freshwater hydra, leeches, pond skaters or water striders, water scorpions and water boatmen or backswimmers, as well as a variety of beetles are the main enemies, together with dragonfly larvae. On top of these there are bacterial and fungal diseases. The enemies that do the most damage are probably the various beetles, the whirligig, the great diving and the great silver beetles. The larvae and the adults of the first two attack baby fishes, and so do the larvae of the third. The larva of the great diving beetle *Dytiscus* has been called the water tiger, the larva of the great silver beetle *Hydrophilus* is called the spearmouth by American aquarists. Both names are justified.

Beautiful freaks

The more fancy breeds of goldfish are freaks, no matter how attractive some of them may look. To recite their names is enough to make this point: veiltail, eggfish, telescope, calico, celestial, lionhead, tumbler, comet or meteor and pearl scale. There are also the water bubble eye, blue fish, brown fish, brocade, pompon and fantail and many others. Some breeds are monstrosities rather than freaks. The veiltail with long curtain-like tailfins, doubled in number, is a reasonable freak. The eggfish has a rounded body and has lost its dorsal fin. The telescope has large bulging eyes which may, rarely, be tubular. The lionhead has not only lost its dorsal fin and grown a rounded body but its swollen head is covered with rounded bumps and looks more like a raspberry.

Students of fishes have sometimes noted that certain freaks arise more or less frequently in nature. Under domestication natural mutants or freaks, or monstrosities that appear are selected and bred to produce new strains. In goldfish the most frequent are the doubling of the tail fin or of the anal fin, the loss of the dorsal fin, and eyeballs that are outside the sockets. Where goldfish have gone wild, however, as they have in southern France, Portugal, Mauritius and the United States, the descendants of the more normal goldfish quickly revert to the wild form, in colour and in shape. Under these conditions the more freakish varieties are at a disadvantage and soon are eliminated – which is what happens to the freaks in any wild species.

class	**Pisces**
order	**Cypriniformes**
family	**Cyprinidae**
genus & species	***Carassius auratus***

A beautiful freak of nature bred by man, a veiltail would never survive outside the artificial world of the aquarium.

Grouper

There are 400 species of related fishes forming the family Serranidae which are variously spoken of as groupers, sea bass, sea perch, or rock cod. Some among them have more exclusive names such as wreckfish, jewfish and soapies. The name 'grouper' has nothing to do with living in shoals but is from the Portuguese name for the fish **garupa** which may in turn be derived from a South American Indian name.

Serranids (groupers or sea perches) live mostly in tropical seas, but a few live in temperate waters and some in fresh water. Most of them are similar in appearance, heavy-bodied with large heads, strong jaws and capacious

mouths armed with many strong, needle-sharp, backward-pointing teeth. In some species the teeth are arrow-headed. When the mouth of a large grouper is gaping its interior has the same wicked look as a shark's mouth, and like sharks they snap up any animal food. The fins are typically perch-like, with two dorsal fins, the one in front being spiny, the rear one having soft rays. Serranids range in size from those that are little more than an inch long when fully grown to the Queensland grouper **Epinephelus lanceolatus** of the Indo-Pacific said to grow to 12 ft long and nearly half a ton in weight. It is reported to stalk divers as a cat does a mouse and one has actually rushed a diver in an apparent attack. There are unconfirmed stories about this giant swallowing skin-divers.

Active and passive

The habits of groupers are varied. Some lurk on the bottom and wait for prey to come to them; others swim about, actively searching. An example of the first is a serranid known as the wreckfish or stone bass *Polyprion americanus*, up to 6 ft long, common in the Mediterranean and tropical Atlantic. It takes up position near rocky reefs and is also noted for haunting wrecks where it has at times been caught in large numbers. By contrast, the striped bass *Roccus saxatilis* swims about, and because of its active nature makes a good sporting fish which gives the fisherman something to test his mettle. Its original home was the Atlantic seaboard of North America but it has been taken across the continent and released off the Pacific coast. There, it quickly became established and is now the basis of a commercial fishery. The striped bass ascends rivers to spawn, but several of

◁ *Giant swallower—the Queensland grouper may grow to 12 ft long and weigh nearly half a ton. There are unconfirmed reports that this giant has swallowed skin-divers.*

△ *An inquisitive 30lb brown spotted grouper swims unafraid by cameraman and comrade.*
▽ *Golden striped grouper, small by comparison, being only 5 in. long, frequents rock pools.*

its relatives in North America are wholly freshwater. These include the yellow bass *Morone mississipiensis* and the white bass *R. chrysops,* each 1 ft or more long.

Another grouper with a commercial value is the 10in. golden-striped grouper *Grammistes sexlineatus,* of the Indo-Pacific seas, that is a favourite with some aquarists. The name 'jewfish' has been given to several different fishes but really belongs to a grouper *Epinephelus itajara,* which also has a commercial value of sorts. It grows to 6 ft long and 600 lb weight and is a dark green, heavy-headed and sluggish fish with rough scales, living in fairly deep waters of the Caribbean and Mexican coasts. Its flesh is not highly valued but it is prized by the sports fisherman. The name 'jewfish' is believed to have been given because the fish has very obvious fins and scales and therefore qualifies as a clean fish according to Levitical law. Around Bermuda groupers make up three-quarters of the commercial fish catch.

Unusual members of the family are the soapfishes *Rypticus* living on both sides of the Atlantic. When alarmed they give out a slime from the skin and also thresh about, the slime becoming beaten up into foam like soapsuds.

Females become males

The family Serranidae is remarkable for having several members that are hermaphrodite. A true hermaphrodite is an individual that has both male and female reproductive organs. The young groupers mature at 2—5 years of age, depending upon the species. They then are females, able to lay eggs, but they also have the beginnings of organs that will later produce sperm. For all practical purposes, however, they are females. At 7—10 years the females finally turn into males, having passed

through a period when they were both female and male—or neither female nor male—and incapable of breeding. Once they have turned into males there are still the remains of egg-producing tissues in their reproductive organs, but for all practical purposes they are males. This unusual situation has not been fully explored in any one species of grouper, and it has been studied in only a few species, but it is suspected that all groupers show this unusual reproductive change to a greater or lesser extent.

Remarkable colour changes

As well as their unusual sex behaviour groupers are noted for their remarkable colours and changes in colour. Many of them are covered all over with hexagonal reddish-brown spots bordered with white or blue, a pattern that reminds us of the colouring of a giraffe. The hamlet *Hypoplectrus* of the Caribbean is generally orange with black spots or blotches and with blue lines, the fins being checkered with orange and blue. A complete list of the colour changes it can undergo becomes, however, almost a catalogue of rainbow hues: deep indigo blue with bands and bars of black and dark blue; pink-brown or violet-black body with yellow or black fins; orange with blue, black or violet spots; yellow and black body with a blue head. The Nassau grouper *Epinephelus striatus* (see pages 30–31) has 8 colour phases, including dark, creamy-white, dark above white below, back banded and belly white, light brown all over, pale with faint dark markings, light-coloured body with dark bands and mottlings and blue with vertical brown bands. None of these can be called normal and a collection of groupers in an aquarium may show all these colours and each fish may pass from one to the other. No two photographs of Nassau groupers ever show the same colours, and the individual fish may pass through several of these phases in a few minutes. Whatever the meaning of these colour changes, and we are not certain what it may be, all the vari-coloured Nassau groupers in an aquarium will become light coloured with dark bands and mottlings when they are alarmed and dash for security among the crevices in rocks. A fisherman who speared a grouper in the Indian Ocean saw the fish take shelter in a clump of coral and refuse to leave it. As it lay there the red spots on its body exactly matched the coral polyps. Perhaps the biggest surprise came to someone who watched a grouper, blue with brown bands, swim into a clump of coral. When it came out a few minutes later it was brilliant yellow with black dots.

class	**Pisces**
order	**Perciformes**
family	**Serranidae**
genera & species	***Epinephelus lanceolatus*** Queensland grouper ***Grammistes sexlineatus*** golden striped grouper ***Epinephelus sp.*** spotted groupers others

Beached for breeding: grunion masses make an impressive sight as they gather at high tide on a Californian shore. These fascinating scenes occur from late February to early September following a new or full moon. The certainty of large numbers makes for an easy harvest for seabirds and humans.

Grunion

A fish with most spectacular breeding habits that attract hordes of visitors to the coast of California, the grunion belongs to the family Atherinidae, related to the mullets. The members of this family are also known in Britain as sand smelts, and in the United States as silversides.

The 150 species of atherinids are not true smelts and the name 'silversides' is more descriptive of them. They are mainly marine fishes of tropical and temperate seas. They differ from true smelts in having two dorsal fins, the front one spiny, in lacking a lateral line, and in having a broad silver band along each flank. Some silversides live in the brackish waters of estuaries, others in rivers or lakes. Freshwater species in Central America are important food-fishes.

Best known of the family, the grunion is 5–7 in. long, and lives in the inshore waters of southern and Lower California.

Beaching themselves to spawn

For 3–4 nights following a new or a full moon, when high tides occur, grunions can be seen from Californian beaches, riding in on the surf at extreme high tide. For 1–3 hours, until the tide begins to ebb, the females leap from the surf onto the beach, wriggle into the sand and lay their eggs at a depth of 2 in. Each is accompanied by a male, sometimes two or three. They wrap themselves around her and fertilise her eggs as they are laid. Having spawned they flop back into the water.

With the next tide, and for days following, the water does not reach so high up on the beach. The eggs are ready to hatch a week later but nothing happens until, at the next spring tide, a fortnight later, the surf goes into the sand and washes the eggs. These then hatch in about 3 minutes. Succeeding waves wash the young grunion out of the sand and carry them down the beach and away into the sea.

This happens from late February to early September. One species spawns only at night and they seem to have an uncanny knowledge of the state of the tides. A second

species, living along the coasts farther north, spawns by day, also on extreme high tides, and in doing so is exposed to attacks by seabirds.

Legendary dancing fishes

Bruce Arthur Woodling, in *Sea Frontiers*, the journal of the International Oceanographic Foundation at Miami, has described how at the stroke of midnight, under a full moon, thousands of silvery fishes leave the sea to perform a mysterious dance on the beach. They sparkle like diamonds on the beach, from Point Conception in the north to Baja California in Mexico, to the south, a distance of several hundred miles. At its highest intensity there may be more fish visible than sand, creating an illusion of a silver canopy over the beach. This is the sight that regularly draws large numbers of visitors, some to watch the sight for the first time, but most of them to gather an easy harvest of fish. If the scene is fascinating the biological facts associated with it are hardly less impressive.

Just before the spawning run, the shallow waters just beyond the edge of the tide are crowded with jostling fishes awaiting their opportunity. At first a few throw themselves on to the beach singly. These are males; there is a popular belief they are scouts, and that if they are prevented from returning to the sea the rest will not venture out. Experience suggests this may be so because when these first fishes are picked up by over-eager visitors the spawning run may fail on that part of the beach. It is believed also that the light from hundreds of fires along the more popular beaches, lighted to cook the fish, may inhibit the run.

Each female grunion is out of the water for several minutes but the actual spawning takes less than a minute. During that time she thrusts her tail into the sand, anchors herself by her pectoral fins, arches her body and waggles her tail in a drilling action so she is finally half-buried. At this point she lays her 1 000—3 000 eggs, according to her age, a process each female repeats 4—8 times in a season.

Far from being chaotic, as the poetic account of sparkling dancing fishes suggests, for each individual fish it is a matter of precise timing. Not only must it be aware of the day and time of extreme high tide, it must not be too early. As the waves of a flowing tide tend to remove sand from the beach and the ebb tide throws up sand the eggs must be laid after the tide has turned. Otherwise the eggs would be uncovered and washed away. Full advantage must be taken of the ebbing tide before it has receded too far down the beach, so spawning should start as early as the ebb, and here also the fishes need an awareness of what is happening.

Impeccable timing

If the eggs were washed out of the sand without time to develop, they would not survive. Experiment has shown that grunion eggs develop normally when embedded in sand and die when floating free in water. What makes them hatch on the next high tide? If allowed a week in which to develop the eggs will hatch as soon as they are shaken. This, in nature, is what happens when the next high spring tide stirs up the sand. The eggs are shaken and hatch, and the young escape to the sea before the first females come out to lay their fresh batch of eggs. It is all so beautifully and automatically timed, with adequate safeguards all along (except against the human marauders!) in a rhythm that fully justifies the comparison with a dance. And any eggs the waters may not reach on one tide will almost certainly be shaken by another a fortnight later or by one a fortnight after that. In the meantime growth of the baby fish within is suspended, but is ready to be resumed and the eggs hatched as soon as they are shaken. The advantage of this complex spawning is that the eggs develop safe from the many hungry mouths in the sea.

class	**Pisces**
order	**Atheriniformes**
family	**Atherinidae**
genera & species	***Leuresthes tenuis*** *spawns at night* ***Hubbsiella sardina*** *spawns by day*

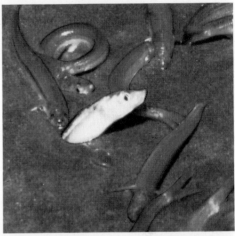

Grunions riding in on the surf at extreme high tide on a Californian beach. This occurs for 3—4 nights following a new or full moon when high tides occur. Until the tide begins to ebb, for 1—3 hours, the females leap from the surf onto the beach, wriggle into the sand to lay their eggs at a depth of 2 in. (above). Each female is accompanied by a male who wraps himself around her and fertilises the eggs as they are laid (right). After the rigours of spawning, a female grunion issues a final burst of energy and wriggles out of the sand, returning to the sea until she is ready to spawn again. During her spawning activity, a female may, however, be surrounded by as many as nine males. This is seen below, where the female's head can be distinguished poking out from the mass of males.

△ *Barbel searches for food using its barbels.*

▽ *Gudgeons frequent slow freshwaters of Europe.*

Gudgeon

The gudgeon is a small member of the carp family, rarely longer than 6 in. or 5 oz in weight. It is grey-green to blackish-grey on the back, lighter on the flanks but silvery with dark spots underneath. Its scales are large and there is a barbel at each corner of the mouth. The gudgeon is found in streams, rivers and lakes across Europe except in Spain and Greece.

The bronze to green gudgeon has been described as a smaller and prettier edition of the barbel, which grows up to 3 ft in length and 20 lb weight in England, although in continental Europe it grows up to 33 lb, and even 50 lb fish have been reported from the Rhine and Danube. Conversely, the barbel has been called a giant gudgeon. In England it was once common in the rivers Thames and Trent, but is generally much smaller in size in the first and has disappeared from the second. It was introduced into the Stour 50 years ago and has from there reached the Hampshire Avon, while other barbels were introduced into the Severn.

Bottom-dwellers

The gudgeon lives in slow waters, often keeping near the bank in large shoals near the bottom. Sand or gravel beds are preferred. The barbel keeps at the bottom, also in shoals, but in deeper water, being found especially in weir pools, in early summer. It favours especially well-aerated waters. In winter it lies torpid in deep water, and tends to hide away by day.

Both fishes, as the shape of the snout and mouth, as well as the presence of barbels indicate, are bottom feeders. The gudgeon is wholly carnivorous. The barbel feeds mostly at night, on insects and their larvae, snails, worms, sometimes small fry. It also eats plant food, rooting for this in the mud of the banks or in the bottom with its pointed snout. It will also eat the roots of water plants. Its method of feeding and the wide diet taken caused Frank Buckland to speak of it as a 'regular fresh-water pig'.

Spawning over gravel

The gudgeon spawns in running water in May and June. Each female lays 1 000 – 3 000 transparent eggs that stick together in small clumps on the bottom, only a few eggs being laid at a time. These hatch in 10 days, the baby fishes carrying at first a large yolk-sac. Barbel spawn at the same time of year but on gravel beds in deep water. Each female lays on average 9 000 eggs which she covers with gravel, and these hatch in about a fortnight.

Fighting fish

Although so similar, except in size, there is a marked contrast between the two fishes in the fisherman's eyes. Gudgeon are described as fish that are caught by accident, or with a red worm or even bread paste. The barbel has fighting qualities that make it a splendid fish, which may in the end break quite strong line if care is not taken. Partly this comes from its larger size but it is more due to its lightning rushes, its rolling tactics and dogged persistence, and to some extent to its living where there are underwater snags. It has been credited with trying, when hooked, to saw through the line with its dorsal fin or break it with blows of its tail.

Differences of opinion

The opinions expressed about the palatability of the two fishes have been conflicting. At various times, and by various writers, gudgeon have been described as fit only for bait to catch better fishes. Another writer thinks they make a delightful dish when cooked in hot fat, and garnished with red pepper and lemon juice, while a third writer recommends cooking them on the river bank. This last is sound advice if only because the more quickly fish are cooked after being landed the better (by far) is the flavour. This may also explain the popularity of gudgeon in former times — and there used to be a regular fishery — because it was a fish easy to keep alive in fresh water until it was required. This may also account for the various descriptions of it: sweet, tender, delicate flavour, delightful, tasty, wholesome.

Its larger relative, the barbel, has been called all manner of names, from evil fish to uninteresting, a fish of medium quality flesh only to be tolerated if made palatable by elaborate cooking. It is true that the hard roe is poisonous and may affect the flesh adjacent to it. Yet in the days of Elizabeth I, Queen of England, the barbel was of sufficient value as a fish to be protected by special statute.

class	**Pisces**
order	**Cypriniformes**
family	**Cyprinidae**
genera & species	***Gobio gobio*** gudgeon ***Barbus barbus*** barbel

Guppy

The guppy was originally called 'the millions fish', because it was present in such large numbers in freshwater from the Caribbean islands of St Lucia, Barbados and Trinidad to the northern part of South America. It also deserves the name because it must have led millions to keep home aquaria. Another name used to be rainbow fish. It was first named **Girardinus guppyi** after the Reverend Robert Guppy who found it in Trinidad in 1866. Then it was discovered that it had already been described in 1859 and that its correct scientific name was **Poecilia reticulata**. By then, however, everybody was calling it guppy.

The male is little over 1 in. maximum length but the female may grow to twice as long. He is colourful, hence rainbow fish, in patches of red, orange, yellow, green and violet, with a few black spots. The wild female guppy lacks the bright colours and is largely whitish.

Hardy favourite

First imported alive into Europe in 1908, into Germany, the guppy's popularity has since grown, and it is almost domesticated. Certainly it is established as a laboratory animal widely used for experiments in genetics, in physiology and for the study of breeding behaviour. There are few fishes that surpass it for these purposes. It is prolific, matures rapidly, is active, thrives well in small aquaria, can stand extremes of temperature from 5° – 38°C/40° – 100°F, can live in foul water, will take a wide variety of food and is subject to few diseases.

Guppies prevent malaria

The guppy eats aquatic insects, algae and the eggs of other fishes. In many places it has been accidentally liberated or put down by aquarists. On the island of Mauritius, where this has happened, it is said to harm local fish population by eating their eggs. It has, however, been deliberately introduced to places as far apart as Argentina, Hawaii, Tahiti, Borneo, Singapore and Ceylon, for controlling malarial mosquitoes, because guppies feed on the larvae and pupae. These are especially vulnerable because they must rise to the surface and hang suspended there to breathe. Guppies have a sensitive area in the floor of the eye by which they quickly see food at the surface.

Unusual breeding habits

Guppies' breeding habits are remarkable. The males grow to maturity at about an inch and then stop. The females reach maturity at the same size but they continue growing. The males, from the time of reaching maturity, are almost incessantly sexually active. At first they will court and try to mate with inanimate objects and the females of other species, as well as with female guppies. In time they learn to court only their own females. Fertilisation is internal, part of the anal fin of the male being converted into a gonopodium for the transfer of sperms to the oviduct of the female. These are stored and females isolated from males have been known to have as many as eight broods of young from a single mating.

Mother eats young

The guppy is ovo-viviparous, that is, the eggs hatch just before leaving the mother's body and the young are born alive. As the time for this draws near, the female's abdomen becomes swollen and a dark patch appears near the anal fin. The young are nearly always born at night or early in the morning, usually head-first but often tail-first especially when 2 or 3 are born in quick succession. They are expelled with considerable force. Once a female has given birth it will be at least 23 days before she does so again and usually it is 28 days or more.

As each fry is born it quickly sinks towards the bottom. Usually it swims upwards rapidly before touching bottom and takes a gulp of air at the surface. This is forced down the gullet and into the swimbladder, expanding it. Then the young fish can swim normally. As each fry is expelled the mother turns round and tries to catch and eat it. She usually succeeds if she can overtake it before it has taken its gulp of air. Aquarists argue that this happens only when there are not enough water plants in the aquarium in which the fry can hide. This seems doubtful, but at all events guppy-

Below: The birth—female guppy bearing one of many babies. Bottom left: Male guppy in the full glory of his mating colours. Bottom right: A male guppy, all fins fanned in full display and gonopodium extended, approaches a female immediately before mating.

breeders often use a maternity cage which allows the fry to escape while holding the mother back.

The mother guppy's infanticide may explain why for so long the size of the broods was in doubt. Estimates varied from 2 to 50. In 1960, Robert J Affleck, of London, showed that the number varied with the length of the mother: a female guppy 1⅛ in. long might have 2–4 at a birth, whereas one 2 in. long would have 100 or more.

Living longer

Usually guppies live to the age of 2 or 3, but at least one lived to be nearly 7. An old idea is that fishes do not age as readily as land animals, which is why there are exaggerated stories of long-lived carp and pike. This was tested with guppies a few years ago by Dr Alex Comfort. He found, among other things, that a female fed once a fortnight grew less rapidly than one fed once a week, but she lived longer. It was already found from experiments with rats that underfeeding meant a longer lifespan. He also found that the more he coddled the guppies the more quickly they died. Cleaning out the aquarium, giving it crystal-clear water and adding chemicals as a matter of hygiene—all shortened the lifespan. The guppies that did best were those that were left severely alone. One surprising result was that old females kept in cramped quarters might take on male colours and grow tails the shape of the male's. Others would give birth to litters without having been in a tank with males, and these were all-female litters. Moreover, when such females died and were dissected it was found that their ovaries contained not only eggs but sperms as well. Another point of this study was to see whether, as the old idea had it, fishes could live indefinitely. Dr Comfort found they certainly did not but from the statistics he was able to construct scales of growth and age. Applying these to other fishes it seemed that sticklebacks probably live for 5 years, a cod 20 years, a plaice 60 and a sturgeon 120. These figures fit fairly well with what is known from other sources, and they show fishes as far from immortal, although some may live to what would seem to us a very ripe old age.

class	**Pisces**
order	**Atheriniformes**
family	**Poeciliidae**
genus & species	***Poecilia reticulata***

△ *Manufactured splendour: natural changes of form, which in the wild would usually result in death for the unfortunate fish, are exploited by aquarists to produce specimens like this prizewinning male guppy.*

▷ *The 'millions fish': a shoal of guppies swims among the roots and decaying vegetation at the edge of a mangrove swamp. Dirty environment means little to these fishes; guppies are so hardy that they have been used to control mosquito larvae in the stagnant and fetid waters of tropical swamps. It is this hardiness which has made them one of the most popular of fishes with aquarists, and many colour varieties have been bred from this insignificant little fish.*

Gurnard

The gurnard or sea-robin differs from all other fishes by its wing-like pectoral fins in which 2 or 3 rays are separated into long feeler-like 'fingers'. It is not related to the flying gurnard (page 82). It has a heavy, almost box-like head protected by bony plates and spines, and the eyes are set well up on the head. It has two separate dorsal fins and some species have spines along the bases of these as well as along the lateral line. There are other species in which the body is also covered with bony plates beset with spines. The armoured sea-robins, as they are called, used to be placed in a separate family but are now classified with the gurnards. They live in deeper water than the gurnards, which inhabit shallow waters and those of moderate depths in tropical and temperate seas.

The grey gurnard is up to 18 in. long and, despite its name, may be coloured from a dark grey to a rosy pink. The largest in British waters is the yellow gurnard, also called the tub or latchet. Nearly 2 ft long, it is golden-brown and its pectoral fins are a deep blue. The young of this species is known as the sapphirine gurnard from the brilliant colouring of its pectoral fins.

Noisy sea-robins

Gurnards spend much of their time on the seabed, using the 'feelers' of the pectoral fins to move about. They press the tips of these into the sand, at the same time folding the winglike parts of the pectoral fins flat against the body. Then they press backwards with them, so driving the body forwards, much in the way a pole is used to propel a punt, the body being lifted from the bottom buoyed-up by the large swimbladder. Some gurnards can move quite quickly on these false legs. According to one observer a gurnard can move easily backwards, to right or left or forwards. The large head of the gurnard is kept steadily on course by the large tail fin. Indeed, a large tail fin is a feature of all fishes with large heads or stout bodies.

The name of these fishes is said to come from the French *grogner*, to grunt, and gurnards have a reputation among fishermen for grunting when taken from water. One gurnard *Trigla lyra* is named the piper from the noises it makes, and a general name for the whole gurnard family is sea-robin. An earlier name was gurnet and soused or pickled gurnet was not held in great favour. Shakespeare implies this in making Falstaff remark, in *Henry IV* 'If I be not ashamed of my soldiers, I am a soused gurnet.' In the mid-17th century Thomas Muffet, in his *Healths Improvements*, however, rates the 'curr' high—a contemporary name for the fish, curr meaning to murmur softly. The grunting noises are, as in many other 'musical' fishes, made by the walls of the large swimbladder being vibrated by the contraction of special muscles. The sounds vary from grunting and snoring to crooning. One of the noisiest is *Prionotus carolinus* of the shallow seas of Atlantic America, from Nova Scotia to Venezuela. This is said to be at its noisiest during the breeding season from June to August.

Tasting with its fins

The long finger-like spines on the pectoral fins are also used to search for food, probing the sand. In most vertebrates the taste buds

Seabed stilt-walker
The gurnard or 'sea robin' is a distinctive fish with a massive, box-shaped head, and pectoral fins whose lower rays are divided into 'fingers' which are spread even when the fish is swimming (below). But the gurnard is essentially a bottom dweller and hugs the seabed (right), using the stalk-like feelers of its pectorals to creep over the sea floor. These 'artificial leg' fins have another purpose, however: probing the sand to 'taste' for food.

are on the tongue. Many fishes, however, have them also on the outside of the head. Gurnards have taste buds on the spines of the pectoral fins. What they eat depends on the species. Some gurnards feed largely on crustaceans, such as small crabs, detected with their 'feelers'. They also take small fishes, detected by sight, and some species prefer these. The yellow gurnard feeds mainly on fishes and especially on the sole-nette and dragonet. The grey gurnard eats mainly crustaceans but also takes sand eels. Gurnards that eat small animals on or in the sand bring their bony mouths down to scoop up the food after the pectoral spines have located it.

No mistaking parentage

Spawning is in spring to summer, some species in April to June, others June to August. The eggs are small, about $\frac{1}{12}$ in. diameter, with a pink or red oil droplet which buoys them up to the surface where they hatch in 5–6 days. The fry live on the contents of the yolk sac for the next 1–3

weeks, and reach 4–6 in. at the end of their first year. From the beginning the heavy, sculptured head is noticeable in the fry and becomes more pronounced as the baby fish reaches $\frac{1}{2}$ in. long. At this stage the pectoral fins become enlarged and spiny, fore-shadowing the characteristic pectoral fins.

Origins of names

It is an entertaining pastime trying to trace the origins of unusual animal names. Good dictionaries are a great help but sometimes these fail us. There was the name 'para-moudra', for example, that appeared in the scientific literature of the last quarter of the 19th century. The name was given to large ring-shaped stones sometimes exposed at low tide on the west coast of Ireland. An English scientist being driven along the coast by an Irishman asked what these were called. The driver replied without hesita-tion 'Paramoudras'. The word has never been used since, and there is a suspicion he made the name up on the spot.

In the 1840s a Monsieur Deslongchamps

had been studying gurnards in artificial sea ponds on the coast of Normandy. Dr William Buckland, Dean of Westminster and also a geologist, became interested and it happened that he was sent a piece of flag-stone from Chester bearing impressions which he supposed to be the trackways of some fish crawling, like M Deslongchamps' gurnard, along the bottom which had be-come fossilized. He called them ichthyo-patolites (fish-tracks). Fortunately the word died almost at birth, and does not appear in any dictionary.

class	**Pisces**
order	**Scorpaeniformes**
family	**Triglidae**
genus & species	*Aspitrigla cuculus* red gurnard *Trigla lucerna* tub gurnard *Eutrigla gurnardus* grey gurnard, *others*

Haddock

The haddock is better known to many as the finnan or finnan haddie. Although haddock have been fished and eaten for centuries, little was known of their breeding behaviour until 1967 when live haddock were kept in an aquarium. Related to the cod and very like it, the haddock, one of the more important commercial fishes, is greyish-brown with a white belly. It can be easily recognized by its three dorsal fins, the small barbel on the chin and, most of all, by the dark patch on the flank just behind the gills — the celebrated St Peter's thumbmark. Smaller than the cod, its maximum size is 44 in. long and 36 lb weight. It also has a darker lateral line than the cod. It lives on both sides of the North Atlantic and in Arctic seas. On the European side it becomes rapidly less numerous from the North Sea through the English Channel and into the Bay of Biscay. Other important fishing grounds for haddock are off the Skagerrak, Faeroes, northwest Scotland and Iceland. On the American side of the Atlantic haddock are fished off Newfoundland and off the New England coast.

Egg-eating fishes

Haddock move about in shoals spending all their lives roaming over the bottom searching for food. They feed less on fish than on crustaceans, shellfish, sea-urchins and worms. At times they gorge themselves with herring eggs. The spawning grounds of the herring were first located by trawlermen catching 'spawny' haddock, with stomachs crammed with herring eggs.

Mapping the spawning grounds

The fish spawn from mid-January to mid-June, with a peak from the middle of February to the middle of March. One of the main spawning grounds is in the northern North Sea, another is off Iceland. These and others had been located by studying where the eggs and larvae were found and by noting where 'ripe' fish were caught. Something was known also about the eggs, which can be netted and taken to the laboratory for study. They are about $\frac{1}{20}$ in. diameter and they float some way off the bottom, perhaps even in midwater, the spawning grounds being at depths of about 300 ft. The young fishes remain in midwater until they are 2 in. long. Then they become bottom feeders.

Aggression between males

In February 1967 four haddock were caught with a handline off the Isle of Skye and taken to the Torry Marine Station at Aberdeen where they were put into a large glass-fronted aquarium. One was a female, and she spawned in April. Before she did so the males became very aggressive towards each other. They faced each other or swam broadside on to each other with their fins spread to the full. At the same time they made knocking sounds. From these encounters one of them emerged as the dominant, or boss fish, and it was he who finally mated with the female.

The show of force between the males brought the female swimming towards them. Her fins were pressed against her body, in the usual way of a female fish choosing her mate. He can tell she is a female simply because she is not showing fight, which, in effect, is an invitation to him to court her. The male begins to swim round followed by the female and as this happens two more black patches appear on his flanks behind the 'thumbmark'. The sounds

Top left: A male haddock, showing 'Saint Peter's thumbmark'—the distinct black mark just behind the gills.

Bottom left: Having established himself as 'boss' fish by a series of aggressive displays a haddock, with fins still erect, turns towards a female; she has been attracted by the behaviour of the males.

Above: Finale: the two haddock mate.

he is making increase in frequency until he is humming, and he swaggers before her in a flaunting, exaggerated swimming action. Then they pair. They swim upwards together the female laying her eggs, the male shedding his milt to fertilise them.

She lays about 12 000 eggs and then swims away. About 30 hours later she swims back to the male and they pair again, and she lays another 12 000 eggs. There may be a dozen spawnings over the next 2 weeks, at an average interval of 30 hours, and an average of 12 000 eggs laid each time. The number of eggs laid is larger with the older and bigger females, and the total laid in one season may be as many as 200 000 or more.

Caught between wind and tide

Not all the hazards facing the haddock come from the many animals, especially fishes, that feed on fry and young fishes. An even greater danger to the species may come earlier. It happens sometimes that large numbers of eggs are carried by currents into inshore waters and estuaries. Although conditions there are highly unfavourable and the eggs perish, this probably does not affect the stock. Wide fluctuations in the catches of haddock over the years had been noted, and the cause has been studied. The first study suggested that changes in the strength and direction of the wind were the cause. When the water movements caused by persistent winds carried eggs and fry into places where they could not survive there would later be a dearth of marketable fish. They might, on the other hand, be carried into places where conditions are so favourable there is a high rate of survival. Now it is generally accepted that year-class fluctuations are a result of differing weather conditions from year to year, producing more or less food for the early larvae. This applies to haddock, bass and perch.

Doubtful benefactors

Baby haddock, like the fry of the related cod and whiting, shelter under the umbrellas of large blue jellyfish, gaining pro-tection from their stinging tentacles. Occasionally one swims against a tentacle, is stung, paralysed and devoured, showing that they are not immune to the poison but merely manage to keep clear of the tentacles. The main food of the jellyfishes is, however, the planktonic larvae of molluscs, crustaceans and sea-urchins and other animals living on the bottom which haddock at a later stage feed upon. When the jelly-fish are numerous there are severe inroads into the larvae, which means a shortage next year of the bottom living animals, and therefore less food for the growing and grown-up haddock. Nobody has followed the cycle through to see exactly what happens but it looks as though any protection the baby haddock enjoy through the good offices of the jellyfishes is apt to be offset by a short-age of food later on because of their benefactors.

class	**Pisces**
order	**Gadiformes**
family	**Gadidae**
genus & species	***Melanogrammus aeglefinus***

Hake

A close relative of the cod, the hake is a deep-water fish living at depths of 300– 2 400 ft from Norway to northwest Africa and in the Mediterranean. The silver hake, a very similar fish, lives in the Atlantic off North America. There is another species in the Pacific off North America and one off Chile. The stockfish of South Africa, which may be up to 4 ft long, is another hake.

Hake have streamlined bodies and large mouths armed with sharp teeth. Instead of the three dorsal fins of the cod the hake has a short fin and a long second dorsal fin with a notch in the middle as if two fins have joined. The single long anal fin has a similar notch. The pelvic fins are farther forward than the pectorals, and all fins have a black margin. The lower jaw is longer than the upper jaw and there are no barbels on the chin. The scales covering the body are large. The back is brownish grey, the sides and belly silvery-white.

Daily and seasonal migrations

There are two main movements in the life of the hake. The first is a daily migration. During daylight hours the hake swim near the bottom and do not feed. As night comes on they swim upwards to varying depths in midwater. They are then well spread out, some rising nearly to the surface. This is their feeding time. The second movement is seasonal. During winter and spring most hake are living at depths of 450–1 800 ft. They move into shallower waters for spawning.

Mainly fish-eaters

Hake are voracious and given to cannibalism. They have remarkably sharp teeth with elastic hinges so they easily bend backwards to allow prey into the mouth, but spring up once it has passed through. Their feeding is closely linked with the daily and seasonal movements. For example, hake rarely eat bottom-living fish, but feed entirely on prey in the middle depths of the sea. Also, their prey varies with the seasonal migration. Large hake take only fishes and squid. The most important of these is

Merluccius merluccius, a deep-water fish.

the blue whiting, then mackerel, smaller hake, horse mackerel, squid and herring, in that order, taking the year as a whole. There is an old saying: 'What we gain in hake we lose in herring.' This refers to the hake chasing shoals of herrings. During winter and spring they eat mainly blue whiting, hake and squid, and 21% of the total is the smaller hake. When in shallower waters, in summer and autumn, they eat herring, mackerel, horse mackerel, smaller hake and some garfish and pollack.

Spawning in shallower waters

Some of the spawning grounds are off the southwest coasts of England and the west coasts of Ireland and Scotland. The males are ripe for nearly the whole year. The females may be ripe from January to November but they are mainly in spawning condition from April to August. The ovaries –the hard roe–are made up of a mass of eggs but not all are shed at a time. Some ripen and are laid, then another batch ripens and is laid. Altogether, throughout the season, a female will lay 500 000 to 2 million eggs. Fertilisation is external, the males shedding their milt–from the soft roe–into the sea. Spawning is exhausting, the fishes having to call upon food reserves in the body to supply the reproductive organs for eggs and milt to ripen. As a result, bodily growth ceases for 2 months at the end of a spawning.

Helpless baby hake

At the beginning of spawning time the eggs in the roe grow larger, become opaque and are turned white or pink by the yolk and oil being stored in them to feed the developing embryo. As they are being laid they absorb water and swell, becoming glassy clear except for an orange-coloured oil drop. The eggs float at or near the surface and a week later they hatch. For the first 6 weeks of life the babies are part of the plankton, drifting with the currents and being carried inshore. At this stage they have no proper fins and neither the mouth nor the intestine has opened. Then the fins begin to form and later the mouth and intestine open. Until that happens the fry are feeding on the yolk in the yolk sac. Now they begin to catch their own food. At first this is small crustaceans and tiny squid, and, later still, small fishes. By the end of the first year

of life the young hake will be 4 in. long, and 8 in. by the end of the second year. They then behave like mature hake, swimming over the sea floor by day, swimming up to feed at night. The rate of growth continues at $3\frac{1}{2}$ in. a year except that the male grows slightly more slowly after his third year. He matures in his fourth year when about 11 in. long; the female matures in her tenth year when 27–30 in.

Persistent cannibalism

Hake are their own worst enemies. They cause a tremendous destruction of their own eggs, which is usual in the sea, especially among floating eggs. There is also the usual heavy loss among the babies. Hake are slightly unusual in that they so consistently prey upon their smaller brethren. Cannibalism, especially among fishes, is by no means novel, but the hake's score of 21% is unusual.

Contrasting values

The flesh of the hake is somewhat soft and does not keep as well as that of other food fishes. This is one reason why in some parts of the world the commercial use of hake has been slow. There is, however, a flourishing fishery for the South African species and there has long been a fishery for the European hake, which is showing signs of being overfished. In mediaeval times hake was regarded as the cheapest food one could buy. When dried and salted it was called poor-John. In *The Tempest* Trinculo, seeing Caliban crouching in fear on the sand, exclaims:

'What have we here? a man or a fish? Dead or alive? A fish; he smells like a fish; a very ancient and fish-like smell; a kind not of the newest poor-John.'

By contrast, the South African hake or stockfish is regarded as the most valuable single commercial fish of that region.

class	**Pisces**
order	**Gadiformes**
family	**Merlucciidae**
genus & species	***Merluccius bilinearis*** *silver hake* ***M. merluccius*** *European hake* ***M. capensis*** *stockfish, others*

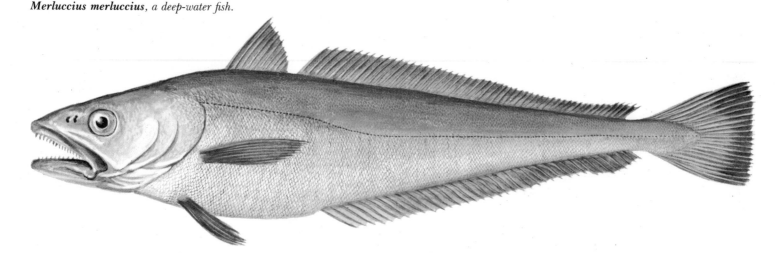

Hippoglossus hippoglossus
The halibut is a rather mixed-up fish—being halfway between an ordinary fish and a proper flatfish.

Halibut

The halibut is little more than halfway between an ordinary fish and a thorough-going flatfish. It is longer in the body and more plump than most flatfishes, such as the plaice and the flounder. Its jaws have kept their original shape instead of being distorted, with one jaw weaker than the other, and they are armed with sharp teeth. The fringing fins (dorsal and anal) are somewhat triangular and the tail and tail fin are well-marked and powerful. The upper surface, which is in fact the right side, is uniformly olive brown, dark brown or black, the underside being pearly white.

There are two species, one in the North Atlantic, the other in the North Pacific. Exceptional heavy-weights have reached a length of 12 ft and a weight of 700 lb. Small halibut live inshore but, as they mature, move into deeper waters, onto sandy banks for preference, at depths of 1 200 ft or more.

Matching its background
A halibut lies on the seabed where it can pass unnoticed by its prey because of its colour. It leaves the bottom to chase after smaller fishes. Most flatfishes swim by undulations of their fringing fins, but halibut do so by vigorous movements of the body and the powerful tail. While on the bottom the halibut's upper side is coloured like the seabed. Lying on mud a halibut will be black. If it moves onto a patch of sand it begins to grow pale. One with its head on a patch of sand and its body on mud will have a pale head and a black body. These changes are governed through the eyes. A flatfish blinded by injury remains the same colour whatever it is lying on. If we watch a flatfish in an aquarium we see the eyes standing well out on the head, each moving independently of the other, and commanding a view of the bottom all around its head.

Bludgeoning its prey?
Halibut eat crabs, molluscs, worms and other bottom-living invertebrates, but their main food is fishes, especially herring, also flounder, cod, skate, and many others. The fish evidently has a reputation as a killer with fishermen. Dr GB Goode, former Commissioner of Fisheries in the United States, has stated that fishermen declare a halibut kills other fishes with blows of its tail. Whether this is true or not, it tells us something of what fishermen think of the halibut.

Floating eggs
Spawning takes place in the Atlantic during May to July at depths of about 1 200 ft. The Pacific halibut spawns in winter at depths of 900 ft. The female roe is large. In a 250lb fish it may be 2 ft long and weigh 40 lb. A mature female may lay $2\frac{3}{4}$ million eggs, each $\frac{1}{8}$ in. diameter and buoyant, so they float to the surface. The eggs hatch in a few days, the baby fish being the usual fish shape at first, with an eye on each side of the head. It remains at the surface and is carried by currents to inshore waters. After a while the left eye begins to migrate over the top of the head until it comes to lie close to the right eye. At the same time the young halibut turns more and more on to its left side while the dorsal and anal fins grow longer to become the fringing fins. As these changes are taking place the fish is sinking towards the bottom finally to rest on it, left side down. In about one in 5 000 it is the right eye that migrates and the fish then comes to rest on the right side. Until it comes to rest the young halibut is transparent, then it changes colour to become brown or black on the upper side. The halibut is fairly long-lived. One 4 ft long will be about 12 years old, and as much as 35 years of age has been recorded.

Evolution of flatfishes
In the Indian Ocean is one flatfish of the genus *Psettodes* that is more like sea perch to look at. The migrating eye stops short on top of the head, the dorsal fin begins farther back than in other flatfishes and both dorsal and anal fins have spiny instead of soft rays. They rest on their side on the bottom and, like the halibut, swim up to catch prey. Some sea perches also lie on their sides on the bottom to rest, although their shape is normal, and they and *Psettodes* suggest how the flatfish condition probably arose during the course of evolution.

Enemies of halibut?
There are few details known about the enemies of halibut but we can be reasonably sure, by comparison with what is known about other fishes laying huge numbers of eggs, that there is a heavy loss of eggs, fry and young. Later, the growing halibut will suffer from fish-eaters among other species of fish, doubtless also from porpoises, dolphins and seals. There is a steady drain on their numbers from commercial fisheries, halibut being taken by trawl and long line.

Name is mediaeval
Halibut must have been fished for a very long time since the name dates from mediaeval times. It is believed to mean holy turbot, from the Scandinavian word *butta* used for turbot. Captain John Smith, founder of Virginia, wrote of 'the large sized Halibut, or Turbot', and followed this with the strange remark that some are so big 'that the fisher men onley eat the heads & fins, and throw away the bodies'. Later, the halibut became known as the workhouse fish. This may have been a term of contempt or a reference to the fact that one halibut could be large enough to feed many hungry mouths. The fish finally came into its own, not only for the table but for medicinal purposes, in the present century. As we have noted the cod was finally recognized in the 1920s as a supplier of cod liver oil for medicinal purposes. A decade or so later halibut oil became popular and almost displaced cod liver oil.

class	**Pisces**
order	**Pleuronectiformes**
family	**Pleuronectidae**
genus & species	***Hippoglossus hippoglossus*** *Atlantic halibut* **H. stenolepis** *Pacific halibut*

Hammerhead shark

There are five species of shark in which the sides of the head are drawn out to form more or less a hammerhead, with an eye at the end of each lobe and a nostril beside it. In one species, the shovelhead or bonnet shark, the head is nearly kidney-shaped. It is hard to see what is gained by these curious shapes. One suggestion is that they help the sharks to turn quickly while travelling at speed. Again, the distance between the nostrils may help in locating odours.

The largest of the hammerheads is 20 or more feet long and weighs 2 000 lb. In such a shark the width across the head, from eye to eye, is about 3 ft. The bonnet sharks rarely exceed 5 ft long. Their colour is grey above, paler on the underside. Apart from the strange head these sharks look like their relatives, the usual large sharks.

Singly or in companies

Hammerhead sharks live in warm seas although occasional individuals wander, in summer, into temperate seas. One of 13½ ft length was caught off Ilfracombe, in Devon, in 1865. Usually they keep to deep water so their incursions into temperate seas may be more frequent than the records show. When at the surface they swim with dorsal fin and the upper part of the tail fin showing above water. They are said to be swift and vigorous swimmers. Hammerheads are usually caught singly or seen at the surface in small groups of half-a-dozen. It is possible that they also congregate in shoals, especially when half-grown, or when attacking stingrays. The rays often cover the seabed, even in depths of 8–12 ft, in their thousands, and hammerheads would be drawn to them, certainly a dozen or so at a time. In 1962, a fisherman saw off the coast of Florida what looked like a large school of Spanish mackerel in 8 ft of water. He and a helper shot a net, encircled the fish and, after an hour, pulled in the net containing 700 bonnet sharks 2–3 ft long.

Seabed feeders

Hammerheads under 10 ft long probably get most of their food, such as crabs and barnacles, from the seabed, but they doubtless also take fish and squid. More is known about the feeding habits of the large hammerheads. These also take crabs and small animals of that kind but they feed largely on other fish, including bass, skate, small sharks and stingrays. One celebrated hammerhead, 12½ ft long, harpooned off Beaufort, North Carolina, had its stomach filled with half-digested stingrays and had about 50 of the ivory-like, saw-edged stings embedded in its neck and back or in its mouth, even in its gullet. From the description given by Dr WE Gudger, some of these

The unusual shape of the head of this otherwise ordinary shark makes the hammerhead very easy to recognise. No conclusive explanation for the development and function of these lobes on the head has yet been found. They may serve as balancers making up to a certain extent for the shortened pectoral fins and lack of stabilizing keels along the sides of the tail (right). The eyes and nostrils are at the end of each lobe (left).

The large distance between the nostrils may help in locating odours. The position of these sense organs is a distinguishing feature used in the classification of the different species of this shark. The shape of the forward edge of the head, which may be straight, rounded, or indented, is also used to identify the types of hammerhead.

Another mystifying characteristic of the hammerheads, apart from the peculiar shape of their heads, is their aggressive nature. There are conflicting views held on whether these fish are dangerous or not but there have been several reports of attacks by hammerheads along the American Pacific coastline, some of these being fatal.

had been recently implanted, others had been embedded in the flesh for some time, and had become encysted.

Large broods
These sharks bear live young but nothing more is known about their breeding. One female, 11 ft long, caught and opened up, contained 37 embryos and another of similar size had 31.

Hammerhead fisheries
Nothing is known about enemies apart from the inroads made by man. Even these are slight. There was formerly a shark fishery in Florida and there the hammerhead was favoured because of the richness of its liver oil. In the Indian Ocean hammerheads are sometimes brought to the surface in nets containing catches of other fishes. The hammerhead, with its fine-grained flesh, is fairly widely eaten in Japan.

Dangerous to man?
Hammerheads have been credited with being dangerous to man. Reports of this are few and the reputation of hammerheads as a whole seems to have suffered badly from the capture of one off the American coast which was found to have human remains as well as pieces of man's clothing in its stomach. Dr VM Coppleson, an Australian doctor who has made a study of shark attack, and Dr Gilbert P Whitley, formerly Curator of Fishes in the Australian Museum, both regard hammerhead attacks as rare in the extreme. There was one attack, on a woman bather in 1931, at West Palm Beach, Florida, 20 ft from the shore. She was rescued by a life guard who said the shark was a hammerhead. The woman had jagged lacerations on the right thigh and leg. Skin-divers have reported that they were compelled to drive hammerheads away because they persistently 'hung around' and

Dr Irenäus Eibl-Eibesfeldt has recounted how, at the Galapagos, five hammerheads cruised around their boat and followed it up to the landing place. He described the sharks, which were 6—9 ft long, as 'very forward and impudent'. Other skin-divers operating off the Galapagos were also bothered by them. Eibl-Eibesfeldt explained that in that area hammerheads were used to large-sized prey, such as sea lions.

class	**Selachii**
order	**Pleurotremata**
family	**Sphyrnidae**
genus & species	*Sphyrna mokarran* great hammerhead *S. tiburo* bonnet shark *S. zygaena* common hammerhead others

Hatchet fish

Tiny, strangely-shaped fishes, looking like strips of shiny, crinkled tinfoil—such is the best description of the 15 species of deep-sea hatchet fishes, all of them distant relatives of the salmon. Most of them are 1—2 in. long, the largest being 3½ in. There are 450 of the smaller ones to the lb. Hatchet fishes have high bodies flattened from side to side, resembling the head of a hatchet, the lower surface corresponding with the sharp edge of the hatchet blade. They are covered with large scales which in a few species are missing from the breast and belly, leaving those parts transparent. In all of them the colour of the body is silvery and iridescent. Their eyes are large, their fins are of moderate size and transparent except for the rays supporting them, and along the lower edge of the body and on the underside of the tail are many closely-set light organs. The light from these is usually blue but in some a bright ruby red light has been seen.

The marine hatchet fishes should not be confused with the freshwater fishes given this name (see page 43).

Sensitive telescopic eyes

Marine hatchet fishes live in the twilight zone of the oceans, where only the green and blue rays of light penetrate. They can be found between 300 and 1500 ft in all tropical and temperate seas. The human eye can detect light at these depths although sensitive photographic plates lowered into the sea register that a very small amount of light penetrates even farther, down to 3000 ft. Since the human eye can detect a faint light down to 1500 ft we can suppose the large eye of hatchet fishes, with its large lens, and retina composed of long rods only, is at least as sensitive as the human eye.

How much the light from the hatchet fish's own light organs (which are on the lower edge of the body) help the eyes is problematic. They probably help little, since the eyes are well up on top of the head or directed upwards in some species. In some of these last species the eyes are tubular and are usually described as telescopic. It is even suggested that they may truly be telescopic, magnifying objects seen by the fishes because their focal length, the distance between the lens and the retina, is greater than in the normal eye.

Submarine weightlessness

Hatchet fishes are very light, weighing on average about $\frac{1}{35}$ oz. They have a well-developed swimbladder. These two things together mean they have neutral buoyancy, that is, they neither float up nor sink, but maintain a balance. We are used to the idea of weightlessness in space travel; neutral buoyancy means much the same thing. So hatchet fishes can swim easily and make considerable vertical migrations daily, coming up almost to the surface at night and going down again by day. In these migrations they are following their food, which consists of planktonic animals such as copepods and the fry of other fishes. At the same time the hatchet fishes themselves become the prey of carnivorous fishes living near the surface and they are an important part of the food of tuna.

Submerged islands?

Since the end of the Second World War, with the refinement of the echo-sounder, observers on ships of the US Navy in the Pacific noted that their echo-sounder traces showed, in addition to a profile of the seabed, a second, sometimes a third or a fourth profile far above the seabed. During the day these 'deep scattering layers', as they came to be called, were at depths of 700–2 400 ft. At nightfall they moved up nearer the surface and became more diffuse. They proved to be made up of the larger animals in the plankton. They need to be about $2\frac{1}{2}$ in. long to reflect back the echoes of the echo-sounder, and the animals giving the traces that make up the deep scattering layers are jellyfishes, large numbers of crustaceans and the larger arrow-worms. In the trace of a deep scattering layer are blobs and marks like an inverted V. These marks were first called tent fish and blob fish, but were later found to be caused by hatchet fishes and lantern fishes. This is an indication of how numerous these two kinds of deep-sea fishes are. When echo-sounders were first being used they often indicated shoals where there should have been deep water. These submerged islands, as they were thought to be, are now known to be deep scattering layers, strata of plankton with the hatchet and lantern fishes feeding under them and forming a temporary and movable ceiling over the vast recesses of the abyssal depths of the oceans.

class	**Pisces**
order	**Salmoniformes**
family	**Sternoptychidae**
genera & species	*Argyropelecus gigas* *Sternoptyx diaphana* others

△ *Dense masses of hatchet fishes help form the phantom sea floor of the deep scattering layer on echo-sounder screens.*
◁ *These are preserved museum specimens.*

▽ *Freshwater hatchet fishes, which do a butterfly-like dance in courtship. Like the marine version, they are named for their shape. These are pygmy hatchet fishes* **Carnegiella marthae.**

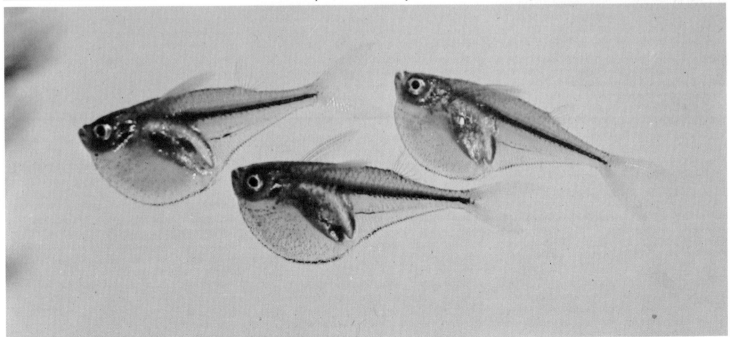

Herring

No single fish has had more influence on the course of human history or existed in greater abundance than the herring. It is estimated that 3 000 million are caught in the Atlantic and adjacent seas each year.

A description of the herring is rarely given on the assumption that it is familiar to everyone. It is what might well be called the typical fish, with its torpedo-shaped (fusiform) body, forked tail fin, single dorsal fin, single anal fin, pectoral fins on the breast and pelvic fins in the pelvic region, a very prototype of fish-form. Up to a foot long, its back is grey-green to golden-brown according to the colour of its background, and silvery on lower flanks and belly. Its scales have only a delicate layer of skin, and are readily rubbed off.

Shoaling fish

Herrings are pelagic fishes—that is, they spend much of their lives swimming near the surface. They feed by taking water into the mouth which passes across the gills. The plankton in it is strained off by a fine mesh-work formed by the gill-rakers and swallowed. They have small, feeble teeth. Herrings are shoaling fish living in schools, each fish spaced evenly in the school with room to swim but not to turn round. Schools are of two kinds. In the first the fishes lie with their heads level. In the second, of which herring schools are an example, the head of each fish lies opposite the middle of its neighbour's body.

Deceptive migrations

It was once thought that these vast shoals of herrings migrated from north to south, with the fishing fleets putting out from successive ports to catch them. Now we have a different picture. Herrings flourish in water temperatures of 6−15°C/43−59°F. Each year the Gulf Stream moves northeast across the Atlantic, reaching successively in summer the coasts of France, the British Isles, the Low Countries, Scandinavia and Iceland. Herrings live in colder waters. When, in summer and autumn, the warm waters withdraw, the shoals appear in the surface waters first off Shetland, then in successive areas in the North Sea and finally off the coast of Brittany in January.

We now know the herring exists in a number of races, distinguished by the number of vertebrae, speed of growth and age of sexual maturity. Also Icelandic, Norwegian, North Sea and Channel herring can be recognised, and each of these includes forms spawning at different times of the year. There are winter spawning herrings, shedding their eggs close inshore, and summer spawners laying in deeper waters. The pattern is complicated further because the different races migrate to a varying extent to spawning grounds or to feeding grounds. The race which spawns at the entrance to the Baltic remains within that area. The Norwegian race may move from southwest Norway northwards into the Arctic, into the Barents Sea, and back again.

More where they came from: about 3 000 million herring are caught every year around the Atlantic.

Mass spawning

What happens to herrings when they are in deeper waters is uncertain. Possibly the schools are more spread out. The schools are most compact when they are made up of young fishes and when adults are coming together for spawning. The act of spawning is random, the females shedding their eggs, the males shedding their milt to fertilize the eggs, the parents then moving on and paying no more attention to them. Spawning appears to be accompanied by some excited swimming about but there seems to be no courtship. The eggs, $\frac{1}{25}$ in. diameter, are laid in sticky clumps which are heavier than sea water and sink to the bottom, coming to rest on a shingly sea bed. Only 21 000−47 000 are laid by each female, a very small number compared with the millions laid by some other marine fishes. This is a sure sign that they are relatively immune from attack, lying on the shingle beds, as compared with floating eggs.

The eggs hatch in 8−9 days at temperatures between 11°−14°C/52°−58°F but take 47 days at 0°C/32°F, while at lower temperatures they fail altogether. The larvae, $\frac{1}{8}$ in. long when hatched, are transparent and still carry the remains of the yolk sac. They have no mouth or gills and only a single fin down the middle of the back and round the rear end. Development is rapid, however, and in a month the baby fish may be $\frac{2}{5}$ in. long and looking almost like its parents. The growth rate then begins to slow down, the young fish being at most 2 in.

long, usually much less, by the end of the year. Maturity is reached in 4−5 years.

Influence on history

The fishing grounds of the northern hemisphere, as well as supplying nations with food, have greatly influenced their history. The herring is an outstanding example. It has been suggested that wherever the shoals of herrings came in towards the coast of Norway there sprang up a village. The same seems to have been true for Scotland and Newfoundland, and for Alaska, Japan and Siberia with respect to the Pacific herring. The villages may now have become towns, and in addition to these there are towns that were deliberately founded to cater for the fishing. Charlemagne, in 809 AD, founded Hamburg as a herring port. Viking descendants, the Normans, established Ostend, Dunkirk, Etaples, Dieppe and Fécamp for the same purpose: Fécamp is said to be derived from the Viking name *Fisk havn*, the fish harbour.

Cause of a war

Along the coast of North Prussia, and extending to Norway and Belgium, were many free cities and small states carrying on general trade which were compelled to supply armed escorts for their merchandise, especially against pirates. In the 13th century they banded together to sail their great merchant fleets in convoy under protection. This co-operative group became known as the Hanseatic League, with Lübeck as head-

quarters. Their ships carried herrings from the Baltic ports and brought back wool, timber, wine and other merchandise. The herrings were fished by Danes off the south coast of Sweden, but the curing and exporting were the concern of merchants in the north German towns. The League monopolised almost the whole of the export trade of Europe and for two centuries was a dominating influence in northern Europe.

Then suddenly the stocks of herring in the Baltic disappeared, the result it was supposed of some natural catastrophe, now believed to have been a lowering of the temperature. In any event the stocks never recovered. But about this same time the Dutch had begun to export salted herrings fished in English waters. This new fishery prospered and in 1610 Sir Walter Raleigh estimated that the Dutch employed 3 000 ships and 50 000 people in their herring industry. The Dutch fishing led to friction with England who wanted to extract a tribute for herrings taken in her waters, and the friction led also to the founding of the Royal Navy in Stuart times and to the 1652-4 war in which England wrested sea power from Holland.

Friction over fishing

In the 19th century friction arose between the fishermen of New England and those of Newfoundland over the fishing on the Grand Banks, which the Newfoundlanders regarded as their natural rights. In 1877, under the Halifax Commission Treaty, the United States paid Great Britain $5\frac{1}{2}$ million

Some of the herring family, like the Pacific herring, lay their sticky eggs around any suitable rock or plant on the seabed (left). Others, like the Atlantic herring, let their eggs sink from the spawning levels to the shingle sea floor (above) where they are quite well camouflaged. The babies within develop quickly; the ones at right are about halfway.

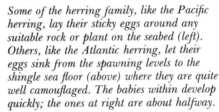

Herring spawning grounds
○ spring ● autumn & winter

dollars for their fishermen to be able to fish for herring within the 3-mile limit off the Gulf of St Lawrence and Newfoundland. Nevertheless, one Sunday morning in Fortune Bay, the Newfoundland fishermen cut the seines of two of the New England schooners, so the entire catch was lost; another New England schooner saved its catch only by threatening to shoot, and the rest of the fleet sailed for home. The incident is known merely as the Fortune Bay Riot, but it is yet another example of the constantly recurring friction over fishing.

Even the Russo-Japanese war of 1902 was inspired by a Japanese claim to the herrings off the Russian territory of Sakhalin Island. More recently there has been the friction between British trawlers and the Icelandic gunboats. Iceland's anxieties over her fishing can be appreciated when it is recalled that she employs nearly 7 000 fishermen and that 95% of her exports are fish products.

class	**Pisces**
order	**Clupeiformes**
family	**Clupeidae**
genus & species	***Clupea harengus***

111

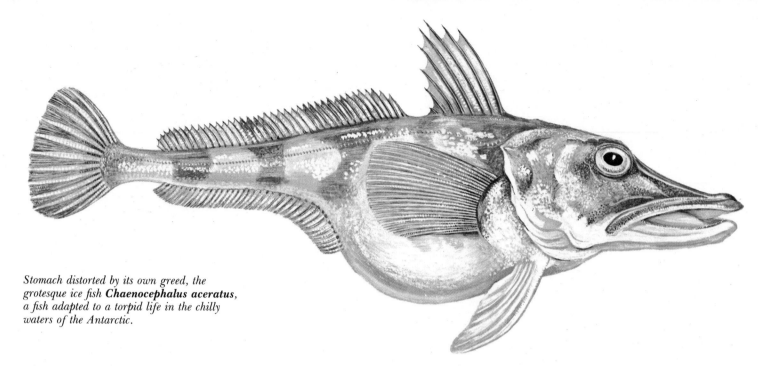

*Stomach distorted by its own greed, the grotesque ice fish **Chaenocephalus aceratus**, a fish adapted to a torpid life in the chilly waters of the Antarctic.*

Ice fish

The first reports of ice fish were made by Norwegian whalers working in the Antarctic, who brought back stories of 'bloodless' fishes they caught near their shore factories. The fishes do, in fact, have blood but it is almost transparent with a just perceptible yellowish tint. It lacks haemoglobin, the red pigment that in many other animals carries oxygen from the lungs or gills to other parts of the body. The problem of how these fishes survive without the oxygen-carrying capacity of haemoglobin has led to speculation ever since the fish were discovered but only in the last few years has it been possible, in the remoteness of the Antarctic, to carry out the necessary detailed work for its solution.

The name ice fish was given by British whalers in allusion to the translucent appearance of the body. Ice fish have no scales and the body is very pale brown or white, and slimy. A second (and also descriptive) name is crocodile fish. The front of the head is drawn out into a beak with a large, gaping mouth edged with thick lips. The eyes are large and goggling. The dorsal fin has two parts; the front part in the middle of the back is sail-like and the second part is ribbon-like, similar to the anal fin on the underside. The pectoral fins form paddles just behind the gills and the fleshy leg-like pelvic fins lie in front of them under the belly.

*There are about 18 species of ice fish, all but one of them confined to the Southern Ocean. The exception ranges north as far as Patagonia. The largest ice fish **Chaenocephalus aceratus** measures up to 2 ft long and can weigh $2\frac{1}{2}$ lb.*

Sluggish carnivore

The fishes of the Antarctic are now being studied intensively by scientists of several nations but by comparison with other kinds like the Antarctic cod very little is known of the habits of the ice fish. It has recently been caught with nets at depths of about 200 ft, in some numbers, and so more is likely to be known about it soon. Its muscles are weak and its ribs soft which suggest that the fish is not active. It probably spends much of its time on the sea bed resting on its leg-like pelvic fins, engulfing passing fish or picking up carrion. Like large snakes such as the anaconda, it probably takes in big meals at long intervals. The large mouth can close over a fair-sized Antarctic cod and the stomach and skin of its belly can stretch to accommodate a large meal. The proof of this is that ice fishes are sometimes caught when they have engulfed an Antarctic cod already hooked. Ice fish also catch krill, the crustaceans that abound in the cold, oxygen-rich waters, supporting whales and many other Antarctic creatures.

Breeding in the Antarctic autumn

Ice fish spawn in the Antarctic autumn, between mid-March and late April. Each fish lays about 2 000 large yolky eggs, $\frac{1}{6}$ in. in diameter, on the sea floor.

Oxygen problems

The discovery that ice fishes have no haemoglobin in their blood posed several questions. The first was how they manage to transport oxygen to their tissues, for in red blood 90% of the oxygen taken into the body is carried by the haemoglobin and the rest is dissolved in the blood plasma. Ice fishes must carry all their oxygen in the plasma and they must be able to live on very little oxygen. They are helped by the high concentration of oxygen in the Antarctic seas. One of the reasons for the vast amount of plant and animal life in the Southern Ocean is that gases can dissolve in cold water better than in warm water. As a result the organisms living in the cold seas, where temperatures rarely rise more than a few degrees above freezing point, have a greater supply of oxygen and they oxygenate their bodies more efficiently. Ice fishes are probably able to absorb oxygen through the skin as well as through the gills.

Despite these advantages, ice fish must still absorb less oxygen than other Antarctic fish and it was presumed that this ties them to their sluggish existence. Recent experiments, however, have shown that, weight for weight, ice fish use as much oxygen in their bodies as do Antarctic cod. Some ice fishes and Antarctic cod were caught alive and put in sealed, water-filled containers. Samples of water were drawn off at intervals and the amount of oxygen in them analysed to find out how much the fish were using. It turned out that the ice fish were using as much oxygen as the Antarctic cod, so they do not seem to be labouring at a disadvantage but have a system for carrying quite enough oxygen for their sluggish way of life. The haemoglobin of the Antarctic cod would seem, then, to be an unnecessary luxury, and this may be the case for other fish. Goldfish, for instance, are able to survive indefinitely when their haemoglobin has been put out of action by carbon monoxide.

Ice fishes also have large hearts, about three times the size of the hearts of red-blooded fishes. This must enable them to pump blood very rapidly through the body and so compensate for the small amount of oxygen in the blood. A similar adaptation is found in people living in the rarefied atmosphere of high mountains.

The absence of haemoglobin in the blood of ice fish and the discovery that in other fish haemoglobin appears to be superfluous, raises awkward questions. One can ask either why ice fish lost their haemoglobin, or why so many other fishes have haemoglobin. Even when we know more about the habits and physiology of the fish, these questions may remain debatable.

class	**Pisces**
order	**Perciformes**
family	**Chaenichthyidae**
genus & species	*Chaenocephalus aceratus* *others*

Jack Dempsey

This dazzling fish once enjoyed, among aquarists, a high popularity which still persists, but to a lesser degree. It is very aggressive and can create havoc in a mixed tank, with other kinds of fishes so it needs to be kept in a separate aquarium and to be made a special pet. The fighting between males is, however, ritualized and has the appearance of a boxing match. The fish was accordingly named after the world heavyweight boxer at the time it first became popular.

Young fishes are brown but mature males, which are up to 8 in. long, are deep brown to black peppered with light blue spots, and some yellow spots, all over the body. They also have a round black spot at the centre of the body and another at the base of the tail. The upper edge of the dorsal fin is red and the iris of the eye is also red. The females are slightly smaller than the males and have fewer blue spots and shorter fins. The body of both is deep and slightly flattened sideways. The head is large, with a jutting lower jaw. The forehead of the male bulges as it gets older.

The Jack Dempsey lives in slow flowing waters of the basins of the Amazon and Rio Negro in South America.

Rules of fighting

Almost nothing is known about how the Jack Dempsey lives in its natural habitat. It has, however, been closely studied as an aquarium fish, especially in regard to its rules of fighting and its breeding. These two aspects of its behaviour are closely linked, as they are in other species of animals. When a male Jack Dempsey comes into breeding condition he establishes a territory. Should another male swim into that territory the owner faces the newcomer, swims over to him and begins what is known as a lateral display; swimming beside him so the two are nose to tail and lying alongside each other, separated by only a short distance. At the same time he raises his dorsal and anal fins, spreads his paired fins and raises his gill-covers. From the side he now looks very much bigger. At the same time his colours grow brighter, and this masks the two black spots. The total result of this is that he looks much more terrifying to his opponent.

His opponent may do one of two things. He may retreat, in which event he is chased across the boundary of the territory. He may, and usually does, respond to the display by raising his own fins and his own colours grow brighter. In that event the two circle each other, trying to butt each other with the sharp edge of the jaw. The two may later seize each other by the mouth in a trial of strength. In the end it is almost invariably the intruder that finally gives up and retreats, being then chased by the owner of the territory. Slight injuries may be sustained in the fight — very occasionally these may be serious.

Female inferiority

Should a female wander into the territory something of the same sort takes place, but everything depends on how near she is to being ready to spawn. In any case, the male displays at her as if she were a male, but instead of raising her fins she lowers them. This indicates to him that she is a female. It is what is called a show of symbolic inferiority. It does not prevent him attacking her, butting her with his jaw, but she accepts these blows and does not fight back. In the end she leaves the territory, chased out, if she is not ready to spawn, but if she is ready to spawn the male's aggressiveness dies down and he accepts her as a mate. Given plenty of space, as they would have in the wild, a female not ready to mate would have room to get away. In a tank a female, in these circumstances, would be beaten up. The usual procedure, in bringing a male and a female together in an aquarium, is to put a sheet of glass in the tank to separate them. They do all their displaying through the glass which prevents them harming each other. In due course this turns to courtship as the female comes into breeding condition, and when the glass is finally taken out they come together peacefully as a pair to spawn.

Preparations for breeding

'Coming into breeding condition' means more than merely getting ready to spawn. Especially in the male there is a build-up of energy which is largely dissipated in fighting. Like many cichlid fishes he digs pits in the sand, as described for the firemouth (page 80). Instead of digging several small pits as some cichlids do, the Jack Dempsey digs one big pit. This is interpreted by some scientists as the result of the female taking a long time to come into breeding condition. They compare it with the way some birds build extra large nests when their mates are slow to reach mating condition.

Aquatic boxer: because of the ritualised fighting which occurs between males during the breeding season, the Jack Dempsey, when it first became popular, was named after the world heavyweight boxer. During display the large black spots become masked as other colours heighten.

Eventually, both male and female Jack Dempsey choose a flat surface and start cleaning it with their mouths. Then the female moves over this surface laying her eggs, the male following her and fertilising the eggs as they lie stuck to the surface. The eggs take 51 hours to hatch, during which time both parents fan them with their fins. For some 96 hours after hatching the babies are feeding on their yolk sacs, unable to swim. They are then known as wrigglers, and the parents take each wriggler in turn in their mouths and place it in a pit in the sand, where they guard their family. As the babies begin to swim out of the pit the parents pick them up in their mouths and spit them back into the mass. There comes a time, however, when the young swimmers are too big for the parents to keep spitting them back and so they give up doing so. Instead, they direct their efforts to keeping their family of several hundred bunched together for protection. Some 1 000 or more eggs may be laid in a season.

Foster broods

One thing scientists have tried to find out is whether Jack Dempseys recognize their own babies. They have taken away their eggs and replaced them by eggs laid by a related species. From these experiments it seems that provided the foster broods grow at the same rate and are about the same size all will be well. So it seems the Jack Dempseys are not recognizing their own babies but are recognizing that the family they are guarding are the same size and have the same growth rate as they should have. Sometimes, in swapping the clutches of eggs, the scientists have overlooked a batch of eggs on the underside of a slab of rock. When, therefore, hatching time comes the wrigglers are half Jack Dempseys and half the babies of another species. All goes well at first but after a few weeks the two sets of babies begin to differ in size, one set growing slightly more quickly than the other, and these larger babies eat their smaller foster-brethren. Although they have lived with them all the time these babies can recognize when one of their foster brothers or sisters is slightly smaller than themselves and so can be overpowered.

class	**Pisces**
order	**Perciformes**
family	**Cichlidae**
genus & species	***Cichlasoma biocellatus***

Training session: young immature 3in. Jack Dempseys circle one another in their aquarium. Almost nothing is known of their behaviour in the wild, but from observations in the aquarium their rules of fighting and their breeding are now known. These two aspects of their behaviour are closely linked as in many animal species.

This jewel-spangled African cichlid is a favourite among aquarists. Although it is only 4 in. long when fully grown it will bully other fishes in a tank and so for this reason is best kept in a separate aquarium. Even so a group of jewel fish makes a beautiful display.

Jewel fish

This is one of the most beautiful of African cichlids and a favourite with aquarists as well as with those studying fish behaviour. The adults are gorgeously coloured and seem to be spangled with jewels. They are up to 4 in. long and the colouration is similar in both male and female although at times the female is the more brilliant. The male has, however, more 'jewels' especially on the gill-covers and a more pronounced crescent on the tail fin. The general colouring is dark olive to grey brown with a greenish sheen and there are 6—7 rows of sky-blue spots along each side of the body. There are also 3 larger dark spots on each side, one on the gill-cover, one in the centre of the flank and one at the base of the tail fin. These are more pronounced in the male than the female. There are scarlet edges to the fins, and the body more especially of the female is tinged with red or scarlet over the head, shoulders and belly. These remarks on colour can only be general because there is so much change, with the breeding season and with the mood of the fish, and it can happen sometimes that the male is the brighter of the two.

The jewel fish is found in rivers over most of tropical Africa, from the Niger and Congo to the Nile.

Pugnacious character

The colours of the beautifully patterned jewel fish play an important part in its life. They help it find a mate and protect it as a baby. As the time for egg laying approaches the red on the body becomes more intense and covers a larger part of the body. Male and female spend much time lying side by side on the sandy bottom during a period of 2—3 days then they begin to clean a hard surface for the eggs. These, $\frac{1}{20}$ in. long, are laid in rows, looking like small strings of tiny pearls, the male following to fertilise each row, until a rounded patch of eggs covers the surface, 500—700 in all. The female fans the eggs with her pectoral fins to aerate them, the male taking over when she leaves to feed. When the baby fishes are about 7 days old they begin to feed, first on protistans, then on rotifers and small crustaceans. After a month they look like the parents and although small they start to fight, their pugnacious character coming out at an early age. They grow $\frac{3}{4}$ in. a month.

Experiments with colour

The behaviour of the jewel fish is very like that of the Jack Dempsey, which has also been much studied in aquaria. Attention will be given therefore to other features of the behaviour, notably to the part colour plays in keeping the baby fishes with their parents. It will be of interest to describe how the experiments are carried out.

The parent jewel fishes, like the parent Jack Dempseys, herd their brood when they are able to swim. This is a necessary protection because if left on their own the

babies will soon be eaten, so the parents must have some way of calling their broods to them when danger threatens, and the babies must have some way of recognizing when their parents are calling them.

In some of the earliest of the experiments three glass aquaria were placed side by side with their long sides touching. Some baby jewel fish were put in the middle tank and in each of the end tanks was put a disc on a long rod, the rods being fixed above on a converted windscreen wiper. When this was set going the disc in each of the end aquaria moved back and forth in sight of the baby fishes. One disc was painted scarlet, the other was painted black. As soon as the discs started moving the young jewel fish moved over towards the scarlet disc.

When young fishes leave home

Having done this the experimenters then used different sizes of discs, 1—3 in. diameter. They also used different coloured discs and they tried the effect of having the discs merely hanging in the end tanks or having them move quickly or slowly. They also experimented with broods of different ages. This meant hundreds of tests and the results show the following. Baby jewel fishes are born with a preference for scarlet over all other colours. Some colours, such as yellow or dark blue, did not attract them in the slightest. Their preference for scarlet becomes even stronger as they get older, so besides having the built-in preference for the main colour on the mother's body, this grows stronger as the young fish grows in size. There comes a time, however,

when the baby fish's liking for red declines. This is when it is several weeks old, and when it is time for the young fish to leave its parents' care. The waning effect of red makes it stray farther from its parents. As this is happening to all members of the brood the family eventually breaks up.

Size is important

The results of the experiments also show that size is important. A baby jewel fish will swim over to any disc coloured red but will swim over more slowly to one that is only 1 in. diameter than it will to one that is 2 or 3 in. diameter. Parent jewel fishes are about 2—3 in. long. Movement also makes a difference. A scarlet disc that is not moving will not attract the baby jewel fishes, or will not attract them strongly. In the same way a sluggish parent will not be able to call its brood together effectively. An active parent, sensing danger, moves more quickly and so imparts a sense of urgency to its brood. Moreover, at such times, the mother jewel fish raises and lowers her unpaired fins several times in succession and this fin flicking acts as a signal to bring her babies rapidly towards the red on her body.

In other species of cichlids which herd their broods as the jewel fish do the same results have been obtained except that the babies respond most to discs coloured like their parents, to black discs if the parents have black blotches or large black spots, and so on. Similar tests made on courting fishes show similar results. For example, a jewel fish is more attracted to a partner which not only shows red but moves quickly than to one that shows even more red but moves sluggishly. It is an advantage for a female jewel fish to choose a mate that moves quickly. He will be much more likely to protect her eggs after they are laid.

No two alike

The detailed colour pattern of the jewel fish has its value as well as the general colour. Once two fishes have paired they recognize each other even when among a crowd of their own kind which to our eyes all look alike. A male jewel fish will know his own mate when there are several females in his territory. He will drive the others away but will not molest her, and tests have shown that he recognizes her by small differences in the pattern of her colours. When the male of a pair is taken out of an aquarium and one or more strange males put in the female will attack these and try to drive them out but will welcome her mate when he is put back into the aquarium. There have been instances in which a female fish, after mating with a male, sees him the following year in a nearby aquarium and tries to get to him although another male has been put into her aquarium. So while the jewels of ornate fishes may be a joy to the human eye they play an important part in the life of a fish.

class	**Pisces**
order	**Perciformes**
family	**Cichlidae**
genus & species	***Hemichromis bimaculatus***

△ *The eggs are laid in rows on a clean rock. Once fertilised both parents take it in turns to fan the eggs with their pectoral fins.*

▽ *An attentive parent spits tiny straying baby jewel fish back onto the nursery stone. If allowed to stray they would soon be eaten.*

John Dory

This fish, of curious shape and habits, is included in an order known formerly as the Zeomorphi but now called Zeiformes. The non-classical scholar may be forgiven for translating these two names as god-like or god-shaped.

The John Dory has a very high and narrow body, flattened from side to side and rounded in outline, it is shaped like a plate. The large head has a mournful expression due to the drooping mouth and the jawbones are such that the mouth can be shot forward when seizing prey. The dorsal fin is in two parts, the front portion being high with the spines strong and, in older individuals, long and carried backwards to end in a line with the tail. The rear part of the dorsal fin and the anal fin that lies opposite it are soft and flexible. Along the bases of the dorsal and anal fins are spines, but the scales on the body are small and spineless, and the skin is smooth. There are also 8–9 spiny plates along the belly. The John Dory is grey to fawn or golden yellow with long blotches of reddish-purple, and on each flank just behind the gill covers is a large black spot with a yellow margin. The maximum length is $22\frac{1}{2}$ in. and it can weigh up to 18 lb.

It lives in the Mediterranean and eastern Atlantic as far north as the southern and southwestern waters of the British Isles and sometimes reaches Norway.

Cat-like stalking

The John Dory with its high plate-like body cannot chase its prey. Instead, it stalks its food, keeping its body rigid, swimming by waving its second dorsal and its anal fin, using the tail fin as a rudder. Its plate-like shape means it can slip easily through the water for short distances. Keeping its eyes on its prey, it gradually draws nearer and nearer to it, finally seizing it by shooting out its protrusible toothless mouth. While stalking it shows signs of excitement. It holds its dorsal fin erect and quivers its fins, its colours blushing and fading all the time. These signs of supposed excitement may have an added value. Seen from head-on the high and very narrow body looks like a thin vertical stripe. The colours coming and going and the quivering of the fins tend to blur even this, so the small fish being stalked is oblivious of impending danger and makes absolutely no attempt to swim away.

The John Dory lives at depths down to 300 ft and little is known about its way of life apart from what has been seen of occasional individuals kept in aquaria. It feeds almost exclusively on small fishes, especially young herring, pilchard and sand eels, although it has been seen to take shrimps in captivity. It takes only live food; a John Dory in an aquarium was seen to spit out a dead fish it had seized. Nevertheless, Dr Douglas Wilson at the Plymouth Aquarium was able, in due course, to persuade a captive John Dory to take strips of squid which looked like fish when dropped into water and slowly floated down.

Sexing the John Dory

There is no outward difference between the sexes. Only by dissection and by examining the roes is it possible to distinguish female from male. In the same way we learn that the eggs are $\frac{1}{10}$ in. diameter. The eggs are pelagic (that is to say that they float), and are laid at any time during the period from June to August.

Origin of the name

The John Dory is used as a food-fish but people are divided on the quality of its flesh. There is also a division of opinion so far as its name is concerned. It seems to have a romantic ring, almost reminding one of the tang of the sea, so one suspects the fish might have been named after some swash-buckling buccaneer or other adventurous seadog. Then there is the story that the black marks on its flank are where the finger and thumb of St Peter pressed when he took the coin from the fish's mouth, so getting the name *Peterfisch* in Germany. But there is the same legend about the haddock, and also about a species of *Tilapia*, but since the John Dory and the haddock are both marine, the *Tilapia*, being a freshwater fish, should take the credit.

Two other suggestions rob it of any glamour it might have. One is that its name is a corruption of the Italian word *janitore*, for a doorkeeper, the other that it is from the French *jaune dorée*, because of its golden yellow colour. The scientific name is *Zeus faber,* the first name being that of the overlord of the Greek gods; the second is Latin for a blacksmith.

△ *Never seeing the bright side of life the John Dory swims around with a permanent gloomy expression on its face. Apart from the unfortunate pout this fish has exquisite dorsal fin spines which grow trailing filaments and the large black flank spots. The legend goes that St Peter made these marks with his finger and thumb.*
◁ *Because of its high plate-like body the John Dory cannot chase its prey. Instead it stalks its food and seizes it by rapidly shooting out its toothless mouth.*
▽ *Head of John Dory with the mouth retracted (left) and protruded (right).*

class	**Pisces**
order	**Zeiformes**
family	**Zeidae**
genus & species	***Zeus faber***

Kissing gourami

This is a popular aquarium fish that has achieved fame for a single trick of behaviour that looks uncommonly like a familiar human action. Other than this the species would have remained in relative obscurity. 'Kissing' is by no means confined to this gourami, which is chosen here to show an interesting facet of animal behaviour.

There are several species of gouramis, all from southeast Asia, where they grow to a foot or more and are used for food. The kissing gourami may grow to a foot long, but when kept in an aquarium it is usually well short of this. Its body is flattened from side to side, oval in outline, with a pointed head ending in a pair of thickened lips. The greenish to grey-yellow dorsal and anal fins are long and prominent and both slope upwards from front to rear. The normal colour of the body is silvery green with dark stripes on the flanks but there is another colour phase, pinkish-white and somewhat iridescent.

Thick lips for breathing and eating

The kissing and other gouramis belong to the labyrinth fishes, which means they have an accessory breathing organ in the gills for taking in air at the surface, as well as breathing by gills. The kissing gourami not only rises to the surface from time to time to gulp air, and therefore can live in water that is slightly fouled, but it also feeds at the surface. The thickened lips probably have an advantage in these two respects. The food

consists of both animal and plant matter and in an aquarium kissing gouramis eat dried shrimps and powdered oatmeal, water fleas and dried spinach. To some extent they will feed on the small algae that grow on the sides of the aquarium.

Life history little known

There is still some doubt about their breeding habits. Many labyrinth fishes build bubble nests for their eggs but so far as we know kissing gouramis build no nest but lay 400–2 000 floating eggs. They seem to ignore these as well as the young which hatch in 24 hours. The baby fishes eat ciliated protistans for their first week, taking water fleas after this, graduating to the mixed diet as they grow older. They begin to breed when 3–5 in. long.

Mystery of the kiss

Nobody seems very clear whether this is an aggressive action or part of the courtship. Probably it enters into both. When several kissing gouramis are kept together in one aquarium the larger of them bother the smaller by 'sucking' at their flanks. They will do the same with fishes of other species. This is probably aggressive. When a pair are together, however, they can be seen to face each other, swaying backwards and forwards, as if hung on invisible threads, and then they come together, mouth to mouth, their thick lips firmly placed together in an exaggerated kissing action. Like other labyrinth fishes the male wraps himself around the body of the female when mating. This is preceded by the two swimming round and round each other in a circling movement, after which they again come together, lips to lips, in a seeming kiss.

A touching scene—like mirror images of each other two gouramis 'kiss'. It is not fully understood why this fish, a favourite among tropical fish fanciers, makes this familiar human action. It may be one of aggression or, as we tend to think, a sign of affection.

Mouth wrestling

The use of the mouth as a test of strength in fighting is common among the higher animals. It is frequently seen in aquarium fishes, especially among cichlids and labyrinth fishes. One fish butting another with its mouth is often used in courtship, especially by the smaller freshwater fishes, and it seems likely that the mouth-wrestling and the butting lead on to the kissing. At all events, A van der Nieuwenhuizen, in his book *Tropical Aquarium Fish*, takes the view that in the cichlid, known as the blue acara *Aequidens latifrons*, mouth-wrestling is used to defeat a rival as well as court a mate. He maintains that when a pair indulge in a bout of mouth-wrestling which ends in stalemate this means the two are physically and psychologically suited and the chances of their breeding are high. The mouth-tugging, as he calls it, may last for hours and be repeated day after day, to end in a genuine lovers' choice. The chances are that the kissing of the gourami has exactly the same importance, so it is a true lovers' kiss.

class	**Pisces**
order	**Perciformes**
family	**Anabantidae**
genus & species	*Helostoma temmincki*

119

*Aptly named: South American apteronotid knife-fish **Sternopygus macrurus** moves backwards and forwards by undulating its long anal fin.*

Knife-fish

For a fish to be called a knife-fish its body must be deep and thin. The knife-fish of tropical Africa and southern and southeast Asia, belonging to the family Notopteridae, is very much flattened from side to side and the blade-like body ends in what is almost a point. There are three other families of knife-fishes, which live in South America, and they belong to a different order. They are the Gymnotidae, Apteronotidae and Rhamphichthyidae. Together they give us an excellent example of convergent evolution, in which two or more unrelated animals have come to look alike. The last three families are related to carp (order Cypriniformes), the Notopteridae being nearer to the arapaima (order Osteoglossidae).

Knife-fishes are often kept in aquaria, where they will flourish when shaded or given dimly lit places into which they can retire. Anyone wishing to air his knowledge or, conversely, not wishing to expose his ignorance — needs to take a second look to know whether the particular fish he is looking at is from South America or from tropical Africa and Asia. Knife-fishes are separated into families on the basis of their anatomy, and one thing that helps us tell straight away whether a knife-fish in the aquarium before us comes from the Old World or the New World is that the South American knife-fishes have a well-marked tentacle lying in front of each nostril.

Forward and backward swimmers

In all knife-fishes, the abdominal cavity and digestive organs occupy a small part of the body behind the head so the vent is well forward, where the pectoral fins would be in an ordinary fish. All the fins are small, even the tail fin, and only one is prominent: the anal fin, which runs from behind the vent along the underside of the body, and is continuous, or nearly so, with the very small tail fin. Knife-fishes, from wherever they come, swim by wave-like movements of the anal fin. When the flow is reversed the fish moves backward with equal ease. This is swimming reduced to a simple formula. With the body held rigid the knife-fish moves forward or backward, using only one fin, the long anal fin.

Two ways of breathing

All knife-fishes live in quiet weedy waters, in the side reaches of large rivers or in stagnant backwaters. In an aquarium they do best when shaded or given dimly lit places into which they can retire. They need to come to the surface to gulp air. In the South American knife-fishes the swimbladder has been transformed into a kind of lung. In the knife-fishes of the Old World, at least in the species studied, air is gulped into the gill cavity and the spent air is later given out through the stomach, intestine and vent. All knife-fishes feed at night or in twilight, on animal and plant food. In aquaria they are fed with chopped meat, worms and rolled oats, as well as small invertebrates such as water fleas, insect larvae and small fishes, although little is known for certain about what they eat in their native habitats. There is no way of telling male from female and little is known about their breeding.

Electric currents

The Nile fish, with similar movements and shape to knife-fishes, is a species that has been intensively studied because of the special use it makes of electric organs. It is of interest to note that the South American knife-fishes also generate electricity, from organs derived from outer parts of trunk and tail muscles. These generate impulses at frequencies between 1 and 1 000 per second. Some species produce 1—5 pulses per second while resting, increasing this to 20 per second when excited. Others produce up to 1 000 pulses per second. These electrical pulses set currents flowing in the water around the fish, the pattern of the current being altered by objects in the surrounding water. Animals have a higher conductivity than water, rocks have a lower conductivity. An animal concentrates the current so increasing the current flowing through nearby parts of the knife-fish's body. A rock has the reverse effect. So the fish can tell animal from mineral, food from an obstacle — but the current is not strong enough to kill prey.

class	**Pisces**
order	**Osteoglossiformes**
family	**Notopteridae**
genera	***Notopterus, Xenomystis***
order	**Cypriniformes**
families	**Gymnotidae, Apteronotidae, Rhamphichthyidae**
genera	***Gymnotus, Sternarchus, Hypopomus**, others*

*False feather **Xenomystus nigri**. Its sole claim to generic recognition is the fact that it lacks the dorsal fin common to the rest of the family.*

Lancet fish

The lancet fish takes the place of the barracuda in the twilight zone of the oceans. It has been called the 'sea-wolf' of the deep seas. There are only three species, two in the Atlantic, the other in the Pacific. The body of a lancet fish is scabbard-shaped with a long, high, sail-like dorsal fin reaching from just behind the head almost to the adipose fin that lies in front of the well-developed tail fin. The rest of the fins are small or of only moderate size. The mouth is wide and armed with fang-like or lancet-shaped teeth. Although the largest individuals known go up to 6 ft long, none weighs much over one lb, showing how long and thin the body is.

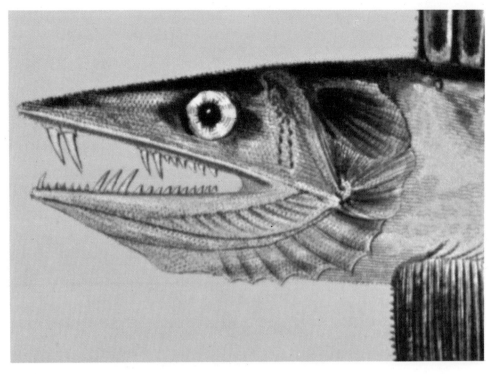

Voracious appetite

The shape of the lancet fish's body and the high dorsal fin remind us of the surface-living sailfish, which is among the swiftest of fishes. Its teeth suggest the arch-hunter and its scaleless skin is typical of fishes able to swallow large prey because the stomach and skin are elastic. It is easy to imagine from these details the lancet fishes flashing through the water, snapping up anything they meet, probably solitary except at the breeding season, lone wolves in the truest sense of the term. There are no details known of their breeding but such information as we have of their feeding is illuminating. For example, the stomach of one lancet fish contained several octopuses, a number of crustaceans—perhaps prawns—several of the jelly-like salps, 12 young boarfishes, a horse mackerel—and one young lancet fish. A swift predatory fish of this kind probably has few enemies once it is adult and cannibalism, as is usual in such species, would act as a natural check on its numbers. Another insight into their voracity is given by the finding of lancet fishes at the surface ballooned up by the food they have eaten. Other ways in which specimens are obtained is by the lancet fishes coming to the surface when sick or heavily parasitized or by being washed ashore. They are also sometimes caught on longlines off Japan, Portugal and Madeira.

Deep-sea collectors

While lancet fishes have little to offer in terms of their own biology their capture is associated with a romantic story of one of the ways in which research into marine zoology progresses. In the large collections of marine animals in the British Museum one comes across, every now and then, a jar containing specimens collected off Madeira. On the label will be the name R T Lowe or J V Johnson, as the collectors. These were British naturalists who are virtually unknown beyond these museum labels and the pages of minor scientific journals in which they published the results of their work. From 1835 to 1860 the Rev R T Lowe collected marine animals off Madeira. Mr Johnson continued his work from 1862 to 1866. The fishes they collected were mainly those caught by local fishermen on their longlines, set at depths of about 600 ft. Others they found at the surface. They included lancet fishes and other deep-sea fishes with their stomachs distended with food. Dr Albert Gunther, Keeper of Zoology at the British Museum, began to compare these with surface-living fishes and gave us the first comparison between deep-sea fishes and those in shallow-seas. He was able to draw attention to the fragile tissues, thin muscles, feeble bones with a 'diminished amount of earthy matter' (that is, calcium), large eyes (or else degenerate

Killer in closeup: its looks reflect its savage nature. The discoverer wrote in a letter which accompanied this drawing in 1833 of 'its violence and ferocity when taken into the boat' and went on to say that fishermen damaged it with blows struck, they said, in self-defence.

eyes) and light organs of deep-sea fishes. It was what we would call today, a breakthrough in knowledge, all the result of the patient years of work of two men beyond the limelight of fame. About a hundred years after Lowe started his collecting Dr G E Maul, of the Municipal Museum of Funchal, Madeira, used lancet fishes caught by local fishermen, to enlarge our knowledge of other deep-sea fishes by studying specimens taken from their stomachs.

class	**Pisces**
order	**Salmoniformes**
family	**Alepisauridae**
genus & species	***Alepisaurus ferox*** Atlantic ***A. brevirostris*** Atlantic ***A. borealis*** Pacific

Savage lightweight: the lancet fish can grow to 6 ft long, but weighs no more than 1 lb.

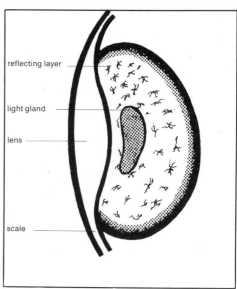

△ Diagram of lantern fish light organ. Light is generated at the central organ, reflected by the surrounding layer and magnified by the lens.
◁ Submarine lamps: lantern fish **Electrona rissoi**.

Diagram labels: reflecting layer, light gland, lens, scale

Lantern fish

Lantern fishes are minnow-shaped with a normal compact fish-like shape. Coloured brownish, greyish or silvery, they are 1–6 in. long, some species never exceeding 1 in., and weigh $\frac{1}{20}$ – $\frac{1}{40}$ oz. They have large eyes, and take their name from numerous light organs.

There are over 250 species of lantern fishes and their populations play a major role in the life of the sea. Although typically deep-sea fishes, living between 600 and 3 000 ft, they make daily vertical migrations, coming to the surface at night and going down again at dawn. While at the surface they are attracted to lights on ships, although they carry light organs of their own and normally shun the light. Even on moonlit nights they fail to come right up to the surface.

Depend on sight
The light organs, the most conspicuous feature of lantern fishes, are like tiny pearl buttons arranged in one or more rows along each side of the body. Each species has its particular pattern, so one of the first uses of the light organs is for lantern fishes to recognize their fellows. The large eyes of lantern fishes have large lenses, wide pupils and highly sensitive retinas showing that these fishes depend much on sight. The males have one or more luminous plates on the upper side near the tail fin and the females have similar plates on the underside near the tail fin. The luminous plates serve for sex recognition but may have other uses. For example, William Beebe found that when lantern fishes switched on these luminous plates in an aquarium the entire darkened room was momentarily illuminated, enough to read small print.

Beebe found that when he placed the luminous dial of his wrist watch against the side of the aquarium a male lantern fish flashed his light organs at it, but did not respond in the same way to the beam from an electric torch. This suggests that the light organs are used by males for intimidating rivals. Beebe also saw small plankton animals swim towards a lantern fish and, on coming within range of the light from a light organ, swim towards it. The lantern fish then quickly turned and snapped them up. One species has light organs on its tongue, presumably attracting food into its mouth. Most lantern fishes have, as well as the light organs mentioned, one or more large luminous patches on the front of the head which act like miners' lamps. They send out beams of light forwards to a distance of 1–2 ft. Beebe found that when the head or tail lights were suddenly doused his eye had difficulty in picking out the fish in spite of the smaller light organs glowing.

Attracted to electric light
Sir Alister Hardy has described how, when powerful electric lights are hung over the side of a stationary ship, the chances are that many lantern fishes will swarm to the surface under the lights, like moths round an electric bulb. They flash silvery in the lights and they also show bright red lights which are their eyes, reflecting the light as cats' eyes do in the headlamps of a car. Each light organ is backed by a silvery reflecting layer, and has a luminous gland in front of this which is served by a nerve, and is overlaid by a thickening of the scale covering it that serves as a lens. The luminous gland is switched on by the nerve, possibly to some extent also by hormones.

Daily journey upwards to feed
The daily vertical migrations bring the lantern fishes up to the surface waters that are teeming with plankton. Lantern fish eat mainly copepods but they also take euphausians, amphipods, sea butterflies (pteropods) small squid and arrow-worms, and they even nibble bits off jellyfish. Their movements up and down, to get the best of two worlds, bring double the risks. At the surface lantern fishes are preyed upon by tuna, bonito, albacore and dolphin fishes in tropical waters. The sealions of the Pribilof Islands, off Alaska, feed on them. Since lantern fishes eat krill (euphausians) which forms the food of large whalebone whales, it is not surprising they are sometimes accidentally eaten by whales. Lantern fishes are sometimes a main food of hake; and down in the deeper waters, during the day, they are preyed upon by many kinds of deep-sea fishes such as anglerfishes.

Going deep with age
Spawning takes place during winter to summer, with a peak in spring. Each female lays 200–4 000 eggs. The larvae hatching from these, $\frac{1}{4}$ in. long, stay in the surface waters at first. As they grow they go deeper until at $\frac{3}{4}$ in. length, when they have reached a depth of 300 ft, they change to the adult shape and make a quick retreat into the depths of the twilight zone, their normal adult daytime habitat.

Delicately beautiful
The lights of lantern fishes may be blue green or yellow, with the eyes glowing red, as we have seen. The fishes usually go about in small shoals, so their lights usually are not a spectacular sight although delicately beautiful. Some years ago the weather ship *Weather Observer* was steaming for Glasgow following a spell of duty in the western Atlantic. One evening she steamed for 5 hours through an immense shoal of small fishes, among which were a number of squid 1 ft long. A dip net was lowered over the side and came up with the occasional squid but full of lantern fishes.

class	**Pisces**
order	**Salmoniformes**
family	**Myctophidae**
genera	*Myctophum, Electrona Lampanyctus*

Leaf fish

In 1840 an odd little fish was added to the collections in the Vienna Museum. It came from the northern part of South America and was given the scientific name **Monocirrhus polyacanthus**. Nothing more was known of the species until 1921 when an American collector, visiting that region, saw a mat of dead leaves at the bottom of a sluggish brook overhung with dense vegetation. He saw some of the leaves move although the water was still, so he took a closer look and caught three more **Monocirrhus**. The local South Americans call it the leaf fish. Between 1822 and 1964 eight species of leaf fish were discovered with a curious distribution: four in India and southeast Asia, one in tropical West Africa, and three in the Amazon basin.

Leaf fishes are 3—4 in. long, the largest 8 in., with bodies flattened from side to side, roughly oval in outline, with a pointed snout and rounded tail fin. The dorsal fin is spiny with a soft-rayed portion at the rear, and the anal fin is similar. Judging by their scattered, or discontinuous, distribution they are primitive. Presumably they evolved as a group in freshwater many millions of years ago before the continents were separated. Not all are called leaf fishes: some are known as nandids, after the family name Nandidae. This is because not all are equally leaf-like. Another similar species, the badis of India, is subject to great variation in its bright colours. It may be brown with a black or red chain pattern, pale blue fins edged with pink and with yellowish markings on the body, or it may be dark brown with black markings, blue fins and buff markings on the body, even a pale flesh colour with dark markings, blue fins, red blotches and fawn patches—or anything between these. The best example of a leaf fish is the one discovered in 1840 and rediscovered in 1921. This, like most of the others, is drab, its body brown, greenish or yellow, marbled with darker tints.

Fascination—a nandid, **Polycentrus schomburgki,** *watches guppies from its hiding place.*

Remarkable camouflage

Leaf fishes generally live in still or very slow-moving waters, keeping to shaded places. They move about little except when about to capture prey, and tend to hold a position, often with the body pointing obliquely down. The fins may be kept folded, or extended to show the saw-edge of the spiny parts of the dorsal and anal fins. At all times they look like leaves, the resemblance being enhanced by the mottled colour and by the fish swimming with the body at angles to the perpendicular. In the Amazon leaf fish, and to some extent in other species, the eye is obscured because dark lines radiate out from it, masking its outline. The male of this species also has a barbel on the chin that looks like a leaf stalk, and in most species the tail fin and the rear soft-rayed portions of the dorsal and anal fins are so delicate that they seem to vanish, making the body look less like a fish than a dead and sodden leaf.

Habitual over-eating

As well as looking like a dead leaf the leaf fish behaves like one when moving in on its prey. It drifts slowly towards a fish then suddenly shoots out a very extensible and capacious mouth to claim a victim. Even more voracious than most predatory fishes, any of the nandids is likely to be able to swallow another fish up to three-quarters its own size. Normally it will eat its own weight of food in a day. So although leaf fishes live well in aquaria they should not be put in mixed tanks; they also tend to be cannibalistic, especially when young.

Cleaning up before spawning

In all species there is no obvious difference between male and female, but the breeding behaviour differs somewhat within the family. The Amazon leaf fish has no courtship display but the two partners clean the surface of a broad leaf of a water plant, or of a stone, and the eggs are laid on this. Only a few eggs are laid on the cleaned surface, and these hatch in 3—4 days. To begin with, the male takes care of the eggs, fanning them with his fins. The babies, which are almost transparent, feed on water fleas. At about 1 month old the members of a brood, having grown at different rates, become destructive, the larger eating the smaller. At about this time, also, white spots

△ *The blue perch or 'chameleon fish', so called because of the amazing variety of colours into which it can speedily change, ranging from solid to intricate mottled designs.*

▽ *A mottled nandid,* **Nandus nandus,** *hiding among the water weeds in an aquarium.*

△ *Pair of leaf fish,* **Monocirrhus polyacanthus.** *The barbel on the male looks like a leaf stalk.*

cover their bodies, as if they were diseased. These disappear later. The spots may serve as a camouflage, but this can only be guessed at. Most species spawn in pits in the sand or gravel, but one makes a bubble nest (see fighting fish, page 78). At least one lays the eggs in crevices among stones.

Sensing the female

When a pair of fishes look so closely like dead leaves that either of them can drift undetected towards its prey an interesting question arises. How do they recognize each other as fishes—and therefore potential mates—especially in a dim light? Clues are found in the courtship of one of the species, the blue perch. The male chooses a cavity among rocks or stones, with a dark interior. He digs a hole in the sand on its floor by twisting his body, swimming backwards and forwards and fanning all the time with his paired fins, throwing the sand outwards from a centre. If the floor is a rock surface, he uses the same actions to clear it of algae. A female draws near the entrance and the male stops work, as if sensing she is near. He drives her away and returns to his task. She comes back and is again driven off. This goes on repeatedly until the male has completed his preparations. When the female now returns she tilts her body towards him, presenting to him her swollen abdomen. The male turns black but the female goes pale as she enters the nesting cavity. They swim round each other, and for a brief moment they meet mouth to mouth in a kissing action, after which he wraps himself round her middle and the two drop to the floor of the cavity, she shedding her eggs in the hole he has prepared or onto the cleaned surface. Sometimes she scatters her eggs as the two hang suspended in an embrace a little way up from the bottom; or she may turn upsidedown and lay her eggs on the roof.

There have been other changes of colour during the courtship on the bodies of both partners. These are almost certainly visual signals as is the female's action of turning her swollen abdomen towards him. We still have to account, however, for the way the male 'sensed' the presence of the female. This is the really important point. Tests have been made, taking water from an aquarium in which there is a female ready to breed. When this is poured into a tank in which a male, on his own, is preparing a breeding cavity, he behaves as if there is a female in the tank making amorous approaches. It seems therefore that as she comes nearer and nearer to spawning condition she exudes something, possibly a pheromone, a sort of external hormone, into the water—which no dead leaf would do.

class	**Pisces**
order	**Perciformes**
family	**Nandidae, Badidae**
genera & species	**Monocirrhus polyacanthus** *Amazon leaf fish* **Badis badis** *blue perch*

Cold-water carnivorous marine fish — young **Cyclopterus lumpus**, *largest species of lumpsucker.*

The pelvic fins form an elaborate sucker.

Lumpsucker

There can hardly be another animal to exceed the lumpsucker fish in parental devotion. Even more surprisingly, the male gives us this remarkable instance of self-sacrifice.

The lumpsucker is stockily built, being up to 2 ft long and 13 lb weight. Its body is rounded and humped, ornamented with rows of tubercles. Its head is massive. The male is smaller than the female, a dark blue, almost black, with fins almost transparent and tinged with red, and he has a reddish belly, especially in the breeding season. The female is greenish with dark bluish patches, there is a reddish tinge on the pectoral fins and her belly is yellowish. On the underside of both is an elaborate and efficient sucker formed by the pelvic fins.

The largest species, which is also known as the sea-hen or henfish, from the tenacity with which the male sits guarding the eggs, is widely distributed in shallow seas on both sides of the North Atlantic. There are other species of smaller size and there is a second group of species known as snailfishes or sea-snails. These have flabby or jelly-like bodies covered with small spines instead of tubercles. One of them, the common sea-snail, is also found on both sides of the North Atlantic.

Clinging like a leech

Lumpsuckers spend much of their lives clinging to rocks or, in the smaller species, to other less solid supports, such as seaweeds. The description of the strength of the sea-hen's sucker given by Thomas Pennant in his *British Zoology*, written in the 18th century, cannot be bettered and is usually quoted. 'By means of this part it adheres with vast force to anything it pleases. As a proof of its tenacity, we have known that on flinging a fish of this species just caught into a pail of water, it fixed itself so firmly to the bottom that on taking the fish by the tail the whole pail was by that means lifted, though it held some gallons, and that without removing the fish from its hold.'

Eight months' fasting

The feeding habits of the lumpsucker have not been fully studied but apparently it feeds mainly on crustaceans. During the breeding season and even beyond it takes no food, so there is a period of fasting from April to November, during which time the stomach is distended with water. Dr J Travis Jenkins, in *The Fishes of the British Isles*, tells us that when the stomach is perforated the water spurts out violently and the stomach walls collapse.

Male guards eggs

The female lays up to 136 000 pink eggs in April, on the shore between mid-tide and low-water marks. So at every tide they are uncovered for a period of time. The eggs are not in a solid mass but spread over a rock surface, and are guarded by the male. While they are covered with water he fans them with his pectoral fins to ensure that eggs in the centre of a clump will be fully aerated. He probably eats or otherwise removes any infertile or diseased eggs. In due course, the time being as yet uncertain, the eggs hatch and the tadpole-like larvae, as active as the parents are sluggish, swim around. They rest at intervals holding on with their sucker and wrapping the tail round their large head so they look like anything but a fish.

Danger of lack of oxygen

So far the story of the lumpsucker seems to be one of large numbers of eggs and larvae guarded securely by a male parent with an unusual sense of responsibility. In fact, the reverse is true. When the tide is out the eggs are eaten by gulls, crows, rooks, starlings and rats. When the tide is in they are eaten by a variety of fishes. Once the surviving eggs have hatched the larvae must face the same dangers. The male guarding the eggs may be attacked by crows and rooks or be torn from his perch by spring storms and battered on the rocks or be cast well up the beach, where he will die.

On one occasion watch was kept on a particular male lumpsucker for several weeks. Day after day, each time the tide went out, there was the lumpsucker at his post. The experiment was then tried of removing the lumpsucker and putting him a couple of yards from his eggs. He immediately wriggled back to take up position for guarding the eggs. When taken to a greater distance he still struggled back as soon as he could and fixed himself by his sucker in his former position with his snout almost touching the nearest eggs. On another occasion it was the eggs that were removed, by stormy waves that flung them well up the beach. When the storm subsided the father lumpsuckers were seen moving about over the shore, presumably searching for the lost eggs.

We always say the male lumpsucker is guarding the eggs. He is doing nothing of the kind. This sort of language is a relic of the times, two centuries or so ago, when naturalists first wrote about it. And writers since have slavishly copied them. A lumpsucker has no means of defending his eggs. He cannot even defend himself. What he does is to aerate the eggs. In the execution of this duty he has a built-in impulse to stand by the eggs no matter what happens. This much we can admire and marvel at the extraordinary instinct that pins him to his post even at the cost of his own life. We should stop saying he is guarding the eggs though unless we say he is guarding them against the danger of lack of oxygen. But this story of the lumpsucker is a first-class example of parental devotion.

class	**Pisces**
order	**Scorpaeniformes**
family	**Cyclopteridae**
genus & species	*Cyclopterus lumpus* *others*

△ *Helped by their streamlined shape and powerful tail, shoals of mackerel move very fast as they scour the upper waters for food.*

Mackerel

Diminutive relatives of the mighty tunas, mackerel share with them the streamlined shape, voracious feeding, and agile swimming which have made them favourites with fishermen and with anglers all over the world.

The common European mackerel has a plump but streamlined body, blue green on the back, silvery below. The back is patterned with darker ripple marks, but two varieties are occasionally seen. In one, the dotted mackerel, the ripple marks are replaced by spots. In the other, the scribbled mackerel, the ripple marks are finer and look like marbling. There are two dorsal fins, the one in front being spiny, and the pelvic fins are well forward, almost level with the pectoral fins. A line of finlets runs from the second dorsal to the tail fin, with a similar row of finlets on the underside of the body.

The range of the common mackerel in the eastern Atlantic is from Norway to the Canaries. The same species occurs in the western Atlantic from Chesapeake Bay to the Gulf of Maine. The Spanish or chub mackerel occurs in these same areas but does not extend so far north. The Pacific mackerel ranges from Alaska to the Gulf of California, and on the other side of the Pacific, with a similar distribution, is the Japanese mackerel.

*The pygmy mackerels live in the Indo-Australian region. These are similar fishes, more deep bodied and up to 15 in. long. **Rastrelliger kanagurta**, of the Indian Ocean, known as **kembong**, is fished in large numbers all the way round the coasts of the Indian Ocean from East Africa to the Malay Archipelago.*

The horse mackerel is not a mackerel but a member of the family Carangidae, although its habits are similar to those of true mackerel.

Spawning cycle

Mackerel live in shoals, but to a lesser extent than, for example, the herring. At the end of October they leave the surface waters, go to the bottom and lie densely packed in the troughs and trenches. Towards the end of December they spread outwards over the surrounding seabed. At the end of January they move up to the surface, coming together in shoals, and start moving towards the spawning grounds. One of the main spawning grounds is near the edge of the continental shelf, in a wide V to the south of Ireland. The period of spawning is from March to June, after which they move into inshore waters breaking up into small shoals, and they stay there until October, when they go down to the bottom again to repeat the cycle.

Seasonal change of diet

On the seabed, mackerel feed on shrimps and smaller crustaceans, marine bristleworms and small fishes. When they return to the surface in January they change their diet, taking animal plankton, especially the copepod *Calanus*, selectively picking these from the water, snapping them up as a swallow snaps up flies. From June to October, while in inshore waters, the mackerel feed on small fishes, especially young herrings, sprats and sand eels. Mackerel hunt mainly by smell, as is shown by the Breton fishermen who lure them by pouring stale fish blood overboard and scooping up the mackerel attracted to it. They must use sight at close quarters, however. With their pelvic fins well forward they can turn in a tight circle to catch prey as fast as themselves but less manoeuvrable.

Sinking eggs

The female lays about half a million eggs, each $\frac{1}{20}$ in. diameter. Each egg has a small oil globule in it and floats at the surface for 2 days. Then it sinks slowly down to midwater where it remains suspended for a short while. If the temperature is right, about 15°C/58°F, the eggs hatch and a larval mackerel $\frac{1}{10}$ in. long, still bearing a yolk sac, is born. The yolk lasts for about

9 days, after which the young mackerel begins to hunt minute plankton. Mackerel take 2 years to mature, at about a foot long.

Important food fish

Mackerel are preyed upon by fast swimming predatory fishes, especially in the young stages, their first two years of life, about which little is known. They are caught in nets or on long lines, or by spinning. Mackerel are only second in importance to herring among pelagic fishes. They are caught in seine nets from March to June and by hook and line from July to October.

Diver's discovery

Dr J Travis Jenkins tells us that it is a belief among fishermen that the first mackerel of the season are blind, that they have a cloudy film of skin over the eyes, which disappears in summer. One reason for this belief is that mackerel will not take bait until the summer. It used to be thought by marine zoologists that mackerel strained plankton from the sea, as a whalebone whale does. This seemed reasonable because mackerel have slender gill-rakers beset with fine spines making an efficient filtering apparatus. Both these beliefs were corrected in 1921 when an officer of the Royal Navy was hanging below a ship in a diver's suit during salvage operations. In the shadow of the ship the plankton animals showed up in dark silhouette against the sunlit waters beyond. The mackerel appreciated this advantage and the diver was able to watch them distinctly snapping up individual copepods — at a time when they should have had a film over their eyes.

class	**Pisces**
order	**Perciformes**
family	**Scombridae**
genus & species	*Scomber japonicus* Spanish or chub *S. scombrus* common others

Maneater shark

A single species of heavy-bodied shark bears the ominous name of maneater, or great white shark. It grows to 20 ft long or more and is bluish-grey to slate grey above, shading to white below, with fins growing darker towards their edges. It also has a conspicuous black spot just behind where the pectoral fin joins the body. Its snout is pointed and overhangs an awesome, crescent-shaped mouth which is armed with a frightful array of triangular saw-edged teeth. In large individuals the largest teeth may be 3 in. high. The pectoral fins are large. The pelvic fins, and the second dorsal and the anal fins, which lie opposite each other, are small. The tail fin is nearly symmetrical instead of having the upper lobe larger as in most sharks. There is a large keel along the side of the tail in front of the tail fin.

The maneater belongs to the family of mackerel sharks, which includes the porbeagles and mako shark. These are similar to the maneater but smaller, up to 12 ft long being about the limit. They feed on fishes such as mackerel, herring, cod, whiting, hake and dogfish. They also provide sport for sea anglers because of the fight they put up when hooked. Most mackerel sharks are dangerous to man.

The maneater is found in all warm seas and occasionally strays into temperate seas. It lives in the open sea, coming inshore only when the shallow seas are near deep water. One maneater was caught at a depth of 4 200 ft off Cuba and other evidence also suggests the shark is a deepwater fish.

Not as big as was believed

Maneaters may be much maligned monsters. They are neither as big as is generally said nor as voracious. Very little is known about the habits of the maneater except what can be deduced from its shape and the contents of the stomachs of individuals caught and dissected. Its shape suggests it can swim rapidly, but from those hooked and landed with angling tackle it is fairly certain the maneater is not as swift as the smaller mako. Since young have been found in a female's body the species is presumed to bear its young alive. The maneater is said to be of uncertain temper, yet skin divers report it to be wary and even easily scared. It is probably less dangerous than the mako which is known to attack small boats as well as swimmers. The maneater's bad reputation probably rests on its large size and fearsome teeth, coupled with occasional attacks that look deliberate. On the first of these two points it is hard to speak with certainty. The largest maneater of which we have reliable information measured 36½ ft long, and this one was caught a century ago, off Port Fairey, Australia. Most of the others are between 20 and 25 ft. One that was 21 ft long weighed 7 100 lb; another 17 ft long weighed 2 800 lb. Maneaters have been said by authoritative writers to grow to over 40 ft but there is no solid evidence.

Nothing refused

Several books have been published in the last 10 years which give details of shark attacks. Two are devoted solely to the subject. They are: *Shark Attack* by V M Coppleson, an Australian doctor who has collected the case histories of injuries from sharks, and *Danger Shark!* by Jean Campbell Butler, whose narrative is based on the New Orleans Shark Conference of 1958, at which shark researchers pooled their findings. Putting the information from these and other sources together, there is the general impression that sharks, the maneater in particular, will try to eat anything that looks like food. As a result they snap at living animals, including bathers or people who have accidentally fallen into the sea, as well as corpses and carrion, even inanimate objects such as tin cans. The attacks on boats, as in the attack on the 14ft cod boat off Nova Scotia in 1953, by a maneater, which left some of its teeth in the timbers, are probably due to mistake rather than malice. Several times whole human corpses have been taken from sharks' stomachs but they proved to be of people who had been drowned.

Maneater or corpse swallower?

There are several instances of maneaters found to contain the intact bodies of other animals. These include a 100lb sea-lion, a 50lb seal, and sharks 6−7 ft long. While human beings have been badly bitten, usually producing frightful wounds, some of which have proved fatal, there is little evidence of limbs being severed, and less of a person being swallowed whole. Two things have also emerged from the studies so far made. The first is that sharks digest food very slowly and animal remains swallowed take days, even weeks, to be digested. The other, which seems linked with this but is learned more from sharks in captivity, is that sharks seem to eat little.

Extenuating circumstances

When one speaks of malice in relation to shark attack one is only reflecting the attitude of mariners to these beasts. As a class they are hated. There are many stories of captured sharks being treated with savagery, being disembowelled and then thrown back live into the sea. Yet in the economy of the sea they are scavengers rather than evil predators. Moreover, in areas where shark attack is heavy there is reason to suppose man has not been blameless. For example, in the region around Sydney Harbour, Australia, and again at Florida, blood from abattoirs seeps into the sea, and sharks are drawn by the smell of blood. In the Bay of Bengal, where human corpses are floated down the Ganges from the burning ghats, shark attack is again high.

None of these things lessens one's sympathy for victims of shark attack, nor lessens one's own fear of the sharks themselves, but they put the subject in perspective zoologically. One of the first scientific conclusions we are led to is that while sharks may be ferocious they seem not to be voracious, as they are so often described. In fact, because they will engulf almost anything they come across, sharks have at times aided the course of human justice.

Silent witness

The classic example of this concerned the United States brig *Nancy* which was captured on July 3, 1799 by HM Cutter *Sparrow* and taken to Port Royal, Jamaica, Britain and the United States then being at war, to be condemned as a prize. The captain of the *Nancy* produced papers at the trial which were, in fact, false and he was about to be discharged when another British warship put in at the port with papers found in a shark caught on August 30. They proved to be the ship's papers thrown overboard by the captain of the *Nancy*, when capture seemed inevitable. They led to the condemnation of the brig and her cargo.

class	**Selachii**
order	**Pleurotremata**
family	**Isuridae**
genus & species	***Carcharodon carcharias***

Maligned monster: the maneater shark's bad reputation stems from its large size and supposed voraciousness. Most maneaters measure between 20 and 25 ft and not 40 ft as often quoted. They seem to eat anything that looks like food which results in bathers, corpses, carrion and rubbish being taken.

Swiftest hunter: with spear-like bill and streamlined body a marlin executes a magnificent jump off La Paz, Baja, California, being able to achieve speeds of up to 50 mph or even more.

Marlin

A fish combining grace with power and size, the marlin is among the most popular gamefishes. There are half a dozen species, including the spearfishes. The body is long and flattened from side to side, and the snout and upper jaw are drawn into a slender beak which is round in cross-section. The dorsal fin is low and continuous in young fish but with age the front part increases in height and the first few spines become greatly thickened. The anal fin is divided into two parts and the pelvic fins are at first longer than the pectorals but become relatively shorter with age. The tail fin is strongly forked, and there are keels found at the base of the tailfin.

The back is bluish, dark brown or black and the underside silvery, silver-grey or yellow. In some species the back and flanks are marked with narrow blue or silver bands.

The real number of species is uncertain but it includes the Atlantic white marlin, up to 9 ft long and 106 lb weight with a record of 161 lb, the blue, striped and black marlins of the Pacific, up to 14 ft long and 1 560 lb weight, the Cape marlin of South Africa, and the spearfishes. These last include the short-billed and long billed spearfishes, of the Pacific and Atlantic respectively, and the Indian spearfish, or goohoo, of the Indian Ocean and Malay Archipelago, up to 6 ft long and 60 lb weight.

Rapid movement

Marlins are very powerful and are probably the fastest of all swimmers. They can reach speeds of 40–50 mph or even more. Such speeds are possible because of their shape; the body is streamlined, with the beak forming a highly efficient cutwater, and when the marlin is going at full speed all the fins, apart from the tail fin, are folded down into grooves in the body so there are no obstructions to an easy passage through water. Having the pelvic fins far forward, on a level with the pectoral fins, means that marlin and spearfishes can turn suddenly in a tight circle. Rapid movement through water places a great strain on the skeleton, especially when the fish has to brake suddenly. The backbone is made up of relatively few vertebrae and each of these has flattened interlocking processes that give strength and rigidity to the whole body.

Some indication of the speed and of the thrust of a marlin is seen in the way the beak has at times been driven through the timbers of ships. One whaler had a spear from a marlin or a spearfish that was driven through 13½ in. of solid timber. In another case a 'spear' was driven through 22 in. of wood. There has long been speculation whether such incidents are due to accidental collision or deliberate attack. The former seems more likely.

Marlins lead solitary lives, well scattered about the ocean. In spring and summer they form pairs, so this is probably their mating and spawning time.

Rises in temperature

The main food of billfishes, as marlins and spearfishes have been called, is other fishes, especially mackerel and flying fishes, but squids and cuttlefishes are also eaten. The billfishes pursue the shoals for days on end, striking to left and right with the beak and then feeding at leisure on the dead and injured victims. It seems that the billfishes pursue, then stop to feed, overtake once more to take their toll, stop again to feed, and so on. A fish which moves at great speed needs a large amount of food to supply the necessary energy for this. Moreover, the muscular action generates heat and tests showed that the temperature of a five-striped marlin, about 9 ft long and weighing nearly 300 lb, was up to 6°C/11°F higher than the surrounding water. The marlins were tested with a thermopile harpoon—a harpoon carrying a device for registering temperature. They were played for a half hour or more before being landed, which would drive their temperature up, but it means that any billfish swimming fast has temporarily slightly warmed its blood.

Caught when exhausted?

It is something of a surprise to learn that the only enemies of these fishes are large sharks, especially the tiger shark and the maneater. Sharks are not especially fast swimmers. The blue shark has been estimated to reach 26½ mph and the mako at 35 mph is probably as fast as any. Perhaps a comparison can be made between the fastest animal on the land, the cheetah, which can keep up its great speed for only a few hundred yards, and the fastest fishes, the marlins and spearfishes. Possibly they also only use speed in bursts and must then recover, and this would be the time when they are vulnerable to the slower but relentless sharks.

Spearing their food

Clearly, to try to probe the secrets of an oceanic fish moving at speeds of 40–50 or more mph offers unusual difficulties. This has led to arguments in the past among deep-sea anglers as to whether marlins and other 'billfishes' ever spear their prey. In 1955 the *John R Manning*, longline ship of the US Fish and Wildlife Service, caught a marlin south of Hawaii. It weighed 1 500 lb and in its stomach was a freshly dead yellowfin tuna, 5 ft long and weighing 157 lb. The tuna had been swallowed headfirst and it had two holes through the body that corresponded with wounds from the marlin's spear. This more than justifies the name 'marlin', which is a shortened form of 'marline spike'.

class	Pisces
order	Perciformes
family	Istiophoridae
genus & species	*Makaira albida* white marlin *M. brevirostris* short-nosed spearfish *M. mitsukurii* striped marlin others

Minnow

Although this name in its strict sense is used for a small European freshwater fish it has been widely used for many large-headed fishes. These cannot be ignored, so here we shall include with the original minnow a number of related fishes of the carp family.

The minnow is one of the commonest and best known freshwater fishes in Europe and it extends into Asia from Siberia to Lake Baikal. It has a cylindrical body, seldom more than 4 in. long, marked with dark bars and covered with small scales. There is a single, small, dorsal fin and the anal and paired fins are small and slightly tinged with red. The colour is brownish-green to silver grey, to silvery white on the belly. Minnows live in the deeper parts of clear brooks and streams where there is a sandy or gravelly bottom. Spawning is in May to July when the male, slightly smaller than the female, becomes almost black, with a scarlet mouth, belly and fins, and has whitish tubercles on the head. These growths are sometimes called pearl organs.

Many species

There are many kinds of minnows, some are active swimmers, some lethargic, some are small, some large. They are found in both temperate and tropical waters, where they occupy many kinds of habitat, from small brooks and ponds to broad rivers, mountain streams, glacial lakes and warm springs. They all agree in certain features: they have no teeth in their jaws but have strong throat teeth; their fins have soft rays; the pelvic fins are set far back on the body, and in the breeding season the males in many species, sometimes the females also, develop tubercles on the head.

Many species live in North America where they are known under a variety of names: squawfish, fathead, split tail, hardhead, shiner, fallfish, stoneroller. Most of them are used as bait and some of the larger species are used as food fishes. In parts of the United States there are minnow farms, where small fishes are cultivated to be sold for livebait. One that is used for bait is the common shiner, up to 8 in. long but very like the European minnow in shape. The split tail, with a deeply forked tail, of California, grows to 12 in. and the hardhead of the same area may be up to 3 ft.

Chub and dace

The chub's name refers, in several European languages, to the shape of its head, and 'chub' almost certainly refers to the chubby cheeks. The chub of Europe and southwest Asia is a surface-living fish up to 2 ft or more long and commonly weighing up to 7 lb, but up to 12 lb has been recorded in Continental rivers. In North America there are over a score of chubs, most of them less than 4 in. long, with the flathead chub going up to 12 in. The dace, of Europe and parts of Asia, closely resembles the chub but with a

more slender body and a more forked tail fin. It is up to a foot long and very rarely more than 1 lb weight. It lives in clear streams with rapid water and, like the chub, is often found in trout streams. The bleak, up to 6 in. long, can be mistaken for a small dace. Shoals of bleak often feed at or near the surface in slow rivers. There are several dace in North America and some of these are brightly coloured, like the southern red-belly dace, 3 in. long, with a red stripe with dark borders on each flank.

The doctor fish

Another well-known minnow-type is the tench of Europe and western Asia, distinguished by its two barbels and golden-yellow scales. It lives among water plants in quiet ponds with muddy bottoms. Normally slow-moving, it passes the winter in a torpid state in the mud. Up to 28 in. long and 8 lb, rarely 17 lb, weight, it is considered a tasty fish and has been introduced into the United States. The tench has been called the doctor fish. This name came from the belief that injured fishes touching it will have their wounds healed, by the curative properties of its slime.

One American minnow, the stoneroller, is remarkable for its very long intestine which is looped several times round its swimbladder.

Mound builders

Most minnows and their near relatives feed on small prey such as water fleas, freshwater shrimps and insect larvae, but others feed on smaller fishes. Their breeding habits are even more varied. Many, including the common European minnow, shed their eggs onto gravel or sand or among water plants and show no parental care. In a number of species the males dig shallow pits in the sand for the females to lay in, or the females lay their eggs on the under surfaces of stones or submerged logs. A few species gather small stones and pile them to make nests for the eggs and the most remarkable of these is the fallfish. The males, smaller than the females, and never more than 18 in. long, move stones as much as 3 in. diameter, making nests 6 ft across and 3 ft high.

Very vulnerable

The enemies vary with the size of the fishes and the situations in which they are living. The fact that so many minnows are used as livebait tells its own story. In the wild these small fishes are the prey of waterside birds such as heron, bitterns or kingfishers as well as of larger fishes. The tench, for example, is soon cleaned out of ponds by other fishes, especially pike, unless there is a good growth of plants in which they can

Top: Common minnow. This small fish is used by many anglers as bait. A trick of some anglers is to paint the inside of their minnow-can white, the minnow assumes the lighter colour and so is more conspicuous to pike and perch in deep dark water.
Centre: Dace, **Leuciscus leuciscus,** *a silvery coloured fish. It frequently feeds from the surface of the water.*
Bottom: Tench. A large fish that lives in quiet ponds where the bottom is muddy.

hide. The common minnow is particularly vulnerable when it gathers in shoals over shallow sand or gravel banks, each female laying 1 000 small sticky eggs. On the continent of Europe these shoals are the occasion for a regular fishery, the minnow being used for food. They are good to eat if caught in sufficient numbers, and they used to be served at table in England. In 1394, for example, 7 gallons of minnows were served at a banquet given by William of Wykeham for King Richard II.

Danger signals

Because minnows are numerous, easily caught, and easy to keep in aquaria, it is natural they should be used as laboratory animals. One thing about them that has been especially studied is their reaction to danger. When one of the shoal is seized by a predator the rest of the shoal bunches together, then swims away, and does not come back to the place for a long time. In the laboratory they do the same if an injured minnow is put among them. Further study showed that a substance given out into the water when the skin is broken or cut is smelt by the rest, causing them to behave this way. They will do the same if a little juice is extracted from a piece of minnow skin and, in dilute solution, is poured into the water. Tests showed that extracts from the intestine and liver had no effect, that extract from muscle had only $\frac{1}{20}$ the effect of skin extract and from the gills $\frac{1}{5} - \frac{1}{10}$ that of skin extract. Further tests revealed that minnows showed this fear reaction to extracts from the skin of other species of minnow, but to a lesser extent than to that from skin of their own species, and that extracts from the skin of fishes in other families had little or no effect. Moreover, if a minnow dies of injuries and its body lies in the water, this 'alarm-substance' continues to be given out for several days, keeping the other minnows well away from the spot.

class	**Pisces**
order	**Cypriniformes**
family	**Cyprinidae**
genera & species	***Campostoma anomalum*** *stoneroller*
	Chrosomus erythrogaster
	red-belly dace
	Hybopsis gracilis *flathead chub*
	Leuciscus cephalus *chub*
	L. leuciscus *dace*
	Notropis cornutus *common shiner*
	Phoxinus phoxinus
	common minnow
	Semotilus corporalis *fallfish*
	Tinca tinca *tench*
	others

▽ *Lively, colourful, good community fish, the white cloud mountain minnow* **Tanichthys albonubes** *is popular with aquarists.*

Moorish idol

This is one of the most striking of the small reef fishes. It has given inspiration to artists, designers and decorators and has been figured on wallpapers and fabrics. It is said to have been sold in the fish markets of Hawaii, and may still be sold there. It is mentioned and depicted in almost every book on fishes although practically nothing is known of its way of life or its life history.

There are three species of moorish idol, the largest being up to 8 in. long but 4 in. is more usual. The body is strongly flattened from side to side, and when looked at from the side it is nearly circular. There is, however, a high dorsal fin in the mature fish and a triangular anal fin, making the outline almost diamond-shaped. In front the snout is drawn out and ends in a small mouth with small, very fine teeth in both upper and lower jaw. Two bony horns grow out over the eyes. The tail is short and it carries a tail fin that is almost triangular. The most striking feature is the colour pattern, the body being white and pale yellow with broad bands of brownish black running from top to bottom. The skin is shagreen-like, being covered with small sharp scales which make it feel almost like fine sandpaper to the hand.

Moorish idols spread halfway round the world in tropical seas; they are found from East Africa around the coasts of the Indian Ocean, the East Indies, Melanesia, Micronesia and Polynesia to the coasts of Japan and the various islands off the Pacific coast of Mexico.

Hiding among coral

These fishes are often seen in shallow inshore waters but their real home is on the coral heads in deeper waters, in coral lagoons, especially in the surge channels through coral reefs, and along the outer edges of the reefs. Although the outward appearance and colours, the shapes of their fins and other physical features have been repeatedly described in great detail in one scientific paper after another, nothing has been recorded of how they swim or what is their food. At best we can only deduce something of this. They probably swim by waving their tails, dorsal and anal fins, with the tail fin used as a rudder. This is how the butterfly fishes and marine angelfishes, to which they are distantly related, also swim. It is the way fishes swim that spend their time among irregular reefs or coral where quick movements and sharp turns are needed rather than swift forward movement.

Tweezer jaws

The narrow jaws of a moorish idol, with small teeth in front, act almost like tweezers. The snout is very like that of the butterfly fishes. From looking at moorish idols in aquaria, as well as guessing from the shape of the jaws and teeth, they probably feed on small crustaceans and other small invertebrates picked out with the 'tweezers' from small crevices.

Knife-like spine

The spawning times and mating behaviour are unknown. Young moorish idols are seldom seen, probably because of the difficulty of collecting them from among the coral heads. The few that have been caught show that the young fishes, up to $\frac{1}{2}$ in. long, have much the same shape as the adults but with long, low dorsal and anal fins and only one black band running from the top of the head, through the large eye

△ *At home among the colourful corals—the moorish idol has a very striking colour pattern and an exquisitely shaped dorsal fin.*

to the throat, where the pelvic fins are situated, the small pectoral fins being just behind the eye. In the front of the dorsal fin are three spines. Two of these are very short but the third is long and thin, about $1\frac{1}{2}$ times as long as the body, streaming out behind. As the fish grows this gets shorter and finally the whole dorsal fin assumes the well-known triangular shape. Another feature of the young fish is that it has a knife-like spine behind each corner of the mouth. These drop off when it has grown to about 3 in. long.

Why moorish idol?

Not the least puzzling aspect of these fishes is their common name. 'Moorish' is usually associated with the western Mediterranean region, where the Moors are best remembered for the way they spread across North Africa and into Spain centuries ago. But moorish idols do not live there. Moreover, the Moors would have nothing to do with idols. A possible key to the origin of the name may lie in the association of the word 'Moorish', meaning Mohammedan, with the language of southern India on the coasts of which the fish does live. This word is now obsolete but it was once used by Englishmen living in that part of India. Perhaps it would have been better to have adopted the name which the Hawaiians give to these fishes—*kihikihi*.

class	**Pisces**
order	**Perciformes**
family	**Acanthuridae**
genus & species	*Zanclus canescens others*

△ *A moray eel, one of the* **Lycodontis** *species, floats jauntily into view, flaunting its crest.*

△ *Stars and stripes? A starry moray eel* **Echidna nebulosa** *emerges from its hole in the coral.*

Moray eel

One of the ogres of the deep according to early divers' stories, the moray eel has a far worse reputation than it deserves. There are 120 species, living in the warmer seas, especially around coral reefs. They range in size from 6 in. to 10 ft or more. The front part of the body and the head are bulkier than the rest of the body and the mouth is large. In most species the jaws are armed with slender sharp teeth, some of which are long, making the open mouth somewhat like that of a snake. The skin is thick and scaleless. The gill pouch has a small opening. There are no pectoral or pelvic fins but the dorsal fin starts just behind the head and is often high on the front third of the body. In some species, however, the dorsal and anal fins, and sometimes the tail fin as well, are very small and indistinct or even hidden under the skin, so increasing the snake-like appearance. Some moray eels are sombrely coloured but many have gaudy colours and patterns, and because of this they are sometimes called painted eels. Some morays are a uniform brown or olive, others are yellow with a brown network, or whitish with dark spots and blotches. The dragon moray of the Pacific is reddish brown with a bizarre pattern of white spots and bars as well as dark blotches. The green moray is brown but its natural colour is usually obscured by a film of green alga covering the body. The zebra moray of the Indo-Pacific has a rich ochre body marked with 50—80 white rings.

Morays live in tropical and subtropical seas, down to 150 ft, and are rarely, if ever, seen in the open seas.

Ill-founded reputation

Morays have the reputation of being venomous, but so far there is no evidence to support this. They also have the reputation of being aggressive, of attacking bathers and divers, and people searching the reefs for lobsters, abalones and other shellfish, and even of taking a tenacious grip of a man's arm and holding him underwater till he drowns. The present-day evidence, especially from skin-diving biologists, is that morays usually try to avoid a man as anxiously as a man tries to avoid them. If cornered or speared, however, a moray will lunge and bite in a tremendous effort to escape. There are a number of authentic records of severe wounds sustained in encounters with morays. In attacking, the moray's actions seem to be like those of a venomous snake, rearing its head and the front part of the body and striking down. It will do this underwater and also when the front part of the body has been raised out of the water.

Moray eels spend the day in cavities and crevices among rocky or coral reefs. They come out at night to feed and will come out by day if disturbed. Many morays feed on octopuses and GE and Nettie MacGinitie, well-known American marine biologists, have suggested that when a man puts his hand among rocks, searching for shellfish, his moving fingers look like the arms of an octopus, and this could be one reason why a moray lunges and bites. Others suggest that as morays eat shellfish of various kinds, when a human hand grasps one of these it catches the moray's attention so the eel lunges to grasp the food, and incidentally seizes the man's hand.

They must bolt their food

The food of many morays is made up of almost any animal, dead or alive, that it can swallow whole. This includes crustaceans, molluscs and fishes. The members of one genus *Echidna*, of which the zebra moray is one, have flattened grinding teeth for eating clams and sea-urchins. One reason why morays must take only food they can swallow quickly is that they need a continuous flow of water through the mouth for breathing. As a result, they seem to be panting, especially when actively exerting themselves. This is the strongest argument against the stories of morays holding men under water.

Irritable at breeding times

It seems possible that the people attacked by morays without having provoked them

▽ *Moray eels do not always live up to their reputation, which condemns them as being extremely vicious and aggressive.*

▽ *A legless zebra of the deeps. This moray* **Echidna zebra** *is a deep ochre colour with 50—80 white rings around it.*

△ *A painted eel? A Java moray eel daubed with spots. Many morays are strikingly coloured, hence their alternative name of painted eels.*

△ *The sensory pits which decorate the face of this moray eel contain sense cells which respond to vibrations in the water.*

may have been attacked during the eels' breeding season. When the *Kon Tiki* raft was wrecked on an atoll in the Pacific, its crew was chased from the lagoon by morays. The scientific members of the Royal Indian Marine Survey Ship *Investigator* had a similar experience on the Betrapar Atoll, in the Indian Ocean, in 1902. On that occasion it was noted that the eels were breeding. Apparently there is no breeding migration as in freshwater eels. The females lay large numbers of heavily-yolked eggs from which hatch ribbon-shaped leptocephalus larvae (see page 72) a few inches long.

Flesh rarely poisonous

Morays are caught and eaten in many parts of the world. In the Mediterranean there is the time-honoured story of the Romans keeping them in specially built reservoirs near the sea, to serve at their banquets. The Romans are also reputed to have thrown the bodies of dead slaves, or even living slaves guilty of small misdemeanours, to be nibbled by the morays. These stories are, however, rather doubtful and the piscinas, as the reservoirs were called, probably held congers as well as, or instead of, morays. All this helps to build up and maintain the unjustifiably evil reputation of morays. Even the supposed venomous nature of these eels probably springs from the few occasions when people have died after eating their flesh. John E Randall, writing in *Sea Frontiers*, in 1961, tells how 57 people in the Mariana Islands sat down

to a meal of moray. They felt a scratchy sensation in the mouth and throat as they ate it and 20 minutes later some felt their lips and tongue growing numb. Ten minutes after that some were unable to speak and medical help was sought. Yet in spite of stomach pumps, by the next day their hands and feet were tingling, they vomited and found difficulty in breathing. Many of the men had convulsions, eleven became comatose and two died. When we remember that at one banquet given by Caesar 6 000 morays were eaten and that morays have been eaten in Mediterranean countries ever since, as they have in tropical and subtropical countries around the world, such misadventures must clearly be very rare.

Sea dragons

There is a suspicion that the sea serpent story is founded on the sightings of many commonplace objects seen at unusual angles at various times and places. One could be the moray eel. For example, when disturbed they will sometimes swim at the surface with the forepart of the body and the head held high above the water. We do not know the greatest size to which they grow. Morays 7–8 ft long have been caught, but estimates of larger individuals are for 10 ft or more. A large moray with bizarre colours swimming like this, with the front end of the dorsal fin looking like a mane, would come very near the conventional picture of a sea serpent. The illusion would be helped by the snakelike set of teeth seen as it

opened and shut its mouth. Then there is a further adornment. Most bony fishes have 4 nostrils, in 2 pairs on the top of the head. In some morays, the nostrils have leaf-like flaps sticking up from them. In others they are tubular, with the rear pair of tubes standing well up from the top of the head.

Morays have a trick of throwing their bodies into a knot and letting this knot travel forwards to or backwards from the head. One used this trick to free itself from an octopus clinging round its head, slipping its body back through the loop to force the octopus' tentacles off its head. A moray hooked on a line will try to do the same to free itself and in doing so will sometimes climb the line, tail first. William M Stephens has recorded that off Palm Beach, Florida, three anglers jumped overboard as a large brown moray came writhing tail-first aboard their boat.

class	**Pisces**
order	**Anguilliformes**
family	**Muraenidae**
genera & species	***Echidna zebra*** zebra moray ***Gymnothorax funebris*** green moray ***Muraena helena*** Mediterranean moray ***M. pardalis*** Hawaiian dragon eel others

▽ *The cleaners. The shrimps, which live with the moray eel in its hole, keep its skin clean by removing parasites.*

▽ *Panting moray. They often swim with their mouths open as they need a continuous flow of water through their mouths to breathe.*

Umbra limi lifesize

Mud minnow

This name is given to small North American fishes quite unrelated to minnows. Their nearest relatives are the Alaska blackfish and the pike. They are remarkable for the way they bury themselves in mud.

Mud minnows have a stocky, slightly compressed body and head, covered with cycloid scales. The snout is rounded instead of being long and scoop-like as in pike. The single dorsal fin is set far back and the tail fin is rounded. There are 3 species in the eastern United States and one in southeast Europe, including the lower Danube and the Black Sea. Those in the United States range from the area south of the Great Lakes to the Mississippi basin and Florida. The largest, the central mud minnow, is usually about 2 in. long but may reach 6 in., slightly less than the maximum for the European species. The western mud minnow does not exceed 4 in. and the eastern mud minnow, found in rivers of the Atlantic seaboard, does not exceed 3 in. The colour is yellowish-brown to green with narrow stripes running along the flanks and back or with broad bars running across the back. Mud minnows usually live along the sides of streams under dense floating vegetation.

Life in mud

The most remarkable feature of mud minnows is their habit of burying themselves in the mud, digging themselves in tail first. At any moment there will be as many buried in the mud as are swimming between the mud and the mat of vegetation

Distribution of the American mud minnows. A fourth species is found in Europe. This unusual situation is paralleled by that of the related pike which has a similar distribution.

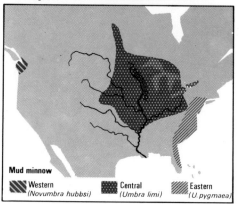

Mud minnow

Western
(Novumbra hubbsi)

Central
(Umbra limi)

Eastern
(U. pygmaea)

above. They can survive for days or weeks in sticky mud and can live successfully in water deficient in oxygen. Unfortunately it is not known how they manage to do this: the breathing methods of mud minnows have still not been fully investigated. We know, however, that they have a swim bladder that is used as a sort of lung and that it has its special system of blood vessels, like a true lung. We also know that the European mud minnow will dart to the surface, gulp in air and then give out bubbles through its gills as it is going down again.

They feed on any small animals they can swallow or overpower. Their mouths are lined with what are called villiform or velvet-like teeth, on the jaws, the roof of the mouth and in the throat.

The European mud minnow is like its North American relatives in being at home in mud. It lives in peat bogs and marshes and in the muddy bottoms of deep pools. One writer has said it can move through soft mud as easily as other fishes move through clear water. This could be largely due to the way the fish makes its way through water. It moves its pectoral and pelvic fins alternately, as a dog moves its legs when trotting, while its dorsal fin makes wave-like movements, such as we see in the fins of an eel.

Guarding the nest

The breeding season is in early spring and in one species at least, the central mud minnow, the male develops a bluish-green iridescence on the anal fin, which is larger in the male than the female. The female carries anything from 220 to nearly 1 500 eggs. The female of the European mud minnow makes a simple cavity in the mud among the tangled roots of plants, and having laid her eggs she closes the cavity—with mud, presumably—and remains near the nest, apparently standing guard over the eggs. The babies hatch in 6–10 days and in the smaller pools they are apt to be cannibals, so only 4 or 5 survive from the brood. The European mud minnow probably has few serious enemies in its specialised habitat in the muddy water. The North American species seem to be mainly preyed upon by their near relatives, the pikes.

Tail-wagging signals

Malcolm S Gordon has described an interesting piece of behaviour in juvenile mud minnows under an inch long. At the tail end of the spine in fishes is a bony structure known as the urostyle which supports the tail fin. In very young mud minnows the urostyle projects backwards for a greater length than is usual between the lobes of the tail fin. Gordon saw that whenever a

group of juvenile mud minnows was about to move one of them vibrated its urostyle independently of the tail fin for a fraction of a second. This was immediately repeated by others and the whole school then began to swim. It is a feature of juvenile mud minnows that they may move about in well spread out schools of 10–12 and it looks as though this vibrating of the urostyle is an 'intention movement', a signal to the rest that one is about to swim and instinctively all the others start to swim with it. As the mud minnows grow the urostyle is absorbed and they become solitary.

Suspended animation?

From the small amount of information we can glean on the mud minnows, they must be quite remarkable little fishes. Yet the many books dealing with fishes either say nothing about them or give only scanty notes. The scientific literature is little better, and we can only suppose that because of their habit of living hidden among vegetation or in mud their study is difficult. One extraordinary account is given by JR Norman, in his *History of Fishes,* of a Dr Gill who had some mud minnows in a large glass jar of water, which froze solid during an exceptionally cold spell, the jar itself being broken. He allowed the lump of ice to melt gradually and every one of the fishes revived and swam about normally. However, the same stories were told about the Alaska blackfish and, for this fish, they were scientifically disproved.

Another remarkable feature of the mud minnows is that there should be 3 species in North America and one in southeast Europe, thousands of miles away. Mud minnows are related to pike, which are found throughout North America and Europe. It seems that both types of fishes sprang from a common ancestor about 150 million years ago. It is likely that formerly mud minnows lived over the whole northern hemisphere in muddy streams and bogs, and that they have died out except in these restricted areas in North America and Europe. Why they should have died out is another question; because when the eastern mud minnow was introduced into a pond in France in 1913 it flourished.

How do they manage to live in muddy waters and mud? Günther Sterba tells us that the European mud minnow may hang suspended in water for hours at a time with the head pointing obliquely up or down. This and the few other things we know about their breathing, and the way they burrow into mud, suggest that mud minnows may have the secret of voluntary suspended animation—or a sort of hibernation they can turn on or off!

class	**Pisces**
order	**Salmoniformes**
family	**Umbridae**
genera & species	***Novumbra hubbsi*** *western* ***Umbra krameri*** *European* ***U. limi*** *Central* ***U. pygmaea*** *eastern*

Mullet

Mullets are fish with elegantly elongated and compressed bodies covered with smooth scales. They are up to 2 ft long, even 3 ft in the striped mullet. Females are slightly longer than males. They have two short dorsal fins, the front one having 4 spines.

The pelvic fins lie halfway along the underside, and the tail is somewhat forked. The mouth is small, somewhat narrow, and toothless except for a fringe of minute bristle-like teeth. Some of the mullets have an adipose eyelid; that is the skin over the eyeball is thickened with a fatty material and although still transparent it covers most of the outer surface of the eye.

Mullets live in tropical and subtropical seas around the world and some move into temperate seas in summer. The 100 species of mullets are sometimes called grey mullets to distinguish them from the red mullets or surmullets. Three species, the thicklipped, thinlipped and golden mullet, enter the coastal waters of the British Isles in early summer and leave again in autumn.

Sleeping on the sea bed

Although mullet swim in shoals, individual members dip down to the bottom from time to time to scoop up or suck up a mouthful of mud, spitting out the inedible part of the mud as they continue swimming. They also feed at the surface, with their mouths wide open, by sucking in small items of food. They do this especially where there is garbage and sewage, and will gather inshore as the tide is going out to pick up insects and grubs, particularly on the edges of beaches with piles of rotting seaweed.

At night the shoals break up and each mullet goes to its own spot on the bottom, the whole group well spread out but all facing the same way. At any disturbance they gather into shoals once more.

Difficult to catch on hooks

Rapid changes occur in the body system of mullets which enable them to go from salt to fresh water and back again, as they frequently swim into estuaries, often going considerable distances up rivers, usually with the tides. Exactly what these changes are is not known. In some parts of the world advantage is taken of this readiness to enter rivers and coastal lagoons. Walls are built across the entrances to narrow inlets with openings to let the small mullets in. The fish are then farmed, or cultivated in ponds. Mullet are difficult to catch on a hook as their lips tend to tear away as they struggle, and the usual way of catching them is with seine nets. In some places a tangle of net is placed on the outer side of the seine to prevent them jumping the nets. Mullet jump out of water holding their body rigid, in contrast with the curved body of, for example, a salmon leaping a weir. The moment one mullet jumps all the rest follow like sheep.

Long intestines

Mullets suck up sand and mud with their soft thick-lipped mouths and strain it through a sieve formed by numerous gill rakers, to extract the decomposed animal and vegetable matter. They will also eat small molluscs and scrape the fine filamentous green algae from the surfaces of stones and the piles of harbour and piers. Craig Phillips, in *The Captive Sea*, tells of a mullet in a seaquarium that cleaned a film of alga off the body of a manatee. They have taste buds, with which they find food, on the outer surface as well as inside the mouth. The food is ground to fine particles by a gizzard like that of a chicken. Its walls are so thick that the cavity inside, which is lined with a horny covering, is no more than a crack. The intestine is very long and closely coiled, a foot-long mullet having nearly 7 ft of intestine.

Clustering to breed

Spawning is in shallow waters, the time of year varying with the species. The mullets cluster in tight pods, all touching each other. Little more is known of the breeding habits. Young mullets, an inch or more long, are found in tidal pools.

Swimming upside-down

From time to time there are reports of one mullet in an otherwise normal shoal swimming upside-down. These reports are usually received with scepticism but we have support for them in the notes published in 1953 by Dr Donald P de Sylva in the scientific journal *Copeia*. He saw, off the coast of Florida, a school of 15 mullet and one was swimming upside-down. At first he thought it was an albino and he tried to net it but as soon as he approached the school it reacted in typical fashion by forming into a tight bunch which swam round and round him. The one fish continued to swim upside-down and at the same speed as the rest. This was on September 16, 1952. On October 10 of the same year, at another point off the Florida coast, Dr de Sylva saw a larger school, and this also had one member swimming upside-down. He followed the school for 5 minutes and at last the upside-down fish dropped back, apparently exhausted, and was netted. It was put into a freshwater aquarium but died some hours later, perhaps from having been transferred so suddenly from salt to fresh water. A post mortem showed no injury, sickness or disease.

It is usually assumed that upside-down fish are sick or dead, except for a catfish *Synodontis batensoda*, living in the Nile and other African rivers, which always does so, and its belly is coloured while its back is light. But there is a record of a school of blue runners *Caranx fusus*, one of the jacks of the family Carangidae, chasing anchovies, and all were swimming upside-down.

class	**Pisces**
order	**Perciformes**
family	**Mugilidae**
genus & species	***Crenimugil labrosus*** *thicklipped grey mullet* ***Liza auratus*** *golden mullet* ***L. ramada*** *thinlipped grey mullet* *others*

◁▽ *Not knowing which way to turn two very young grey mullet fry seem bewildered by the galaxy of bubbles surrounding them.*
▽ *In the same predicament, slightly older fry stranded in a pool. Previous page: Grey mullet shoal in silhouette.*

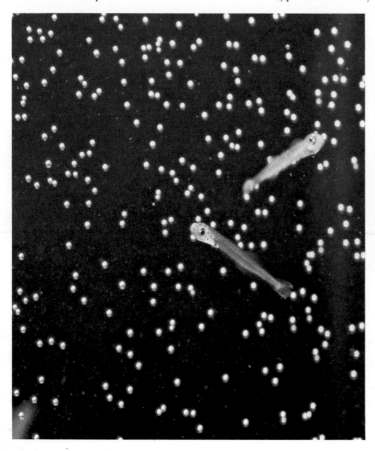

△ *Freshwater halfbeak, small, playful relative of the needlefish. The large fin area at the hind end drives this torpedo-shaped fish.*

Needlefish

Needlefish is an alternative name for garfish, which avoids confusion with the North American gar or garpike. Garfish is Old English for spearfish. It is apt not only with reference to the shape of the fish but also to its habit of launching itself into the air. The garfish has a long slender body and its jaws are drawn out to form a beak-like snout. The total length may be 3 ft or more, and up to $4\frac{1}{2}$ ft in tropical species. The mouth is armed with many sharp teeth. The back is blue-green, the belly silver. All the fins are small, the unpaired, soft-rayed fins, and the pelvics being set well back. Garfishes are noted for having green bones, hence their alternative name of greenbone.

Related to needlefishes are the halfbeaks and skippers and some indication of the evolution of the related flying fish can be drawn from their study. Halfbeaks are usually smaller, up to 18 in. long with a stouter body. The upper jaw is very short while the lower jaw is long, as in the garfish. Some tropical species may, however, reach 6 ft or more. Otherwise the two kinds of fish are very alike except that some of the halfbeaks live in freshwater, although most are marine.

The skippers, sometimes known as sauries, have only a very short beak and they have 5 – 7 finlets behind the dorsal fin and the same behind the anal fin.

There are 60 species of garfishes in tropical and temperate seas, 70 species of halfbeaks and 4 species of skippers. All three of these fishes are, however, most numerous in tropical seas.

Skipping and skittering

Garfish, halfbeaks and skippers often leap in and out of the water or skitter along the surface for quite a distance. They skitter with the head and forepart of the body out of water with their submerged tail vibrating rapidly from side to side. Garfishes, which are very fast swimmers, often feed in shoals, skimming along at the surface, and frequently transfix smaller fishes with their spear-like beak. Their jaws are armed with numerous teeth, not to masticate the food, but to prevent the prey, which is swallowed whole, escaping. The stomach is straight so it can take in whole prey. Halfbeaks are even more adept at skittering and they probably do so when trying to escape from enemies, such as tuna and swordfish. It is possible that they may also skitter along when feeding as they are vegetarian, eating mainly green seaweed. Their open mouths would also take in a certain amount of planktonic crustaceans and molluscs which often float at the surface.

Playful fishes?

Garfishes, also known as longtoms in some parts of the world, sometimes leap over the back of a turtle or a floating log, often performing somersaults. This action has all the appearance of play. The antics of halfbeaks are even more playful: one of them will swim rapidly at a floating object and, just as the tip of its long lower jaw is under the object, it flips itself over, usually to land the other side, facing in the opposite direction. Sometimes it repeats this several times.

Evolution of flying fishes

Whether leaping and skittering are necessary for feeding, escape or merely play, it is easy to see how, if garfishes, halfbeaks and skippers had large paired fins, they could remain airborne by gliding on spread fins. This is precisely the case with their relatives, the flying fishes. This sequence is an indication of how the large pectoral fins of flying fishes (page 81) could have evolved.

Halfbeak baby garfishes

Spawning takes place in shallow water, in spring or early summer. Garfish eggs, $\frac{1}{6}$ in. diameter, have sticky filaments which anchor them to each other and to objects such as seaweeds. They hatch in 5 weeks, in the species *Belone belone*, of the eastern Atlantic, the larvae being $\frac{1}{2}$ in. long on hatching. They are shaped like the adult except that only the lower jaw is prominent, so they look more like young halfbeaks. The lower jaw

△ *Netted skipper* **Scomberesox**. *Skippers are 12—14 in. long at the most and can be distinguished from the rest of the family by their short jaws. They got their name from the way in which they skitter over the surface of the water with their submerged tail vibrating rapidly from side to side.*

continues to grow longer, while the upper jaw remains short until the young garfish are just over 2 in. long, when the upper jaw begins to elongate. At the end of the first summer the young fishes, moving in shoals, go farther out to sea, and this annual migration continues throughout their lifetime with great regularity. Off the coasts of Europe this brings them inshore with the mackerel, on which they feed, and into contact with the herring shoals.

Halfbeaks lay eggs similar to those of the garfish and development follows much the same lines except for some of the freshwater halfbeaks of the Indo-Australian region which bear live young. Some young halfbeaks look like floating seaweed. They react

to danger by going stiff and floating passively so they look like dead pieces of seaweed.

Tragic encounter

That the fish should have been called garfish, or spearfish, from early times, may have been connected with something more than its spearlike shape or its habit of leaping from the water like a spear launched through the air. In the *Malayan Nature Journal*, May 1968, is an account of a Singapore customs vessel taking in tow a Sumatran rowing sampan with seven Indonesians on board. After a while one of the sampan's crew collapsed, bleeding profusely from the neck. He died before the boats reached the shore and an autopsy showed there was a frag-

ment of bone in his neck. It was part of a garfish jaw, the fish having leaped out of the water, not with aggressive intent but in the normal way of garfishes, stabbed the Indonesian and fallen into the sea again. Apparently the people of Malaysia have long been aware of this danger but their ideas have hitherto been treated as folklore.

class	**Pisces**
order	**Atheriniformes**
families	***Belonidae*** *garfishes*
	Exocoetidae *halfbeaks*
	Scomberesocidae *skippers*

▽ *Fish hooks. Many unsuspecting fish have been impaled on these teeth before being swallowed whole. Garfish, also known as longtoms, are fast swimmers and often feed in shoals. They are noted for the way in which they leap playfully over floating objects, sometimes doing somersaults over turtles' backs.*

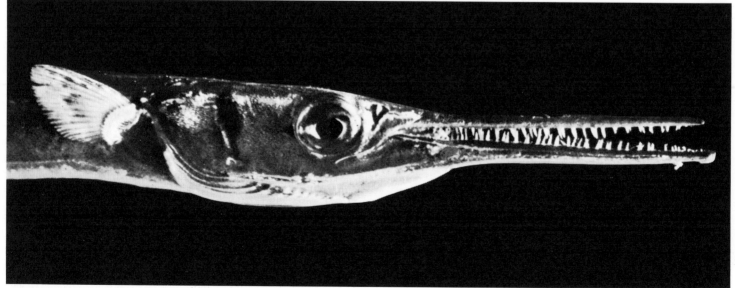

Nile fish

There are several fishes living in the Nile and in rivers in tropical West Africa that can swim backwards and forwards with equal ease. Little notice was taken of this until, within the last 20 years, it was found that each fish can generate its own electric field. One of these is **Gymnarchus niloticus**, which has been called the Nile fish but is more often called by its scientific name, as it is of special interest to students of biology.

The Nile fish is 5 ft long, flattened from side to side and ending behind in a slender 'rat's tail'. The only fins it has are a pair of very small pectorals and a long ribbon-like dorsal fin starting just behind the head and ending well short of the slender tip of the body. The head is rounded with small eyes, blunt snout, wide mouth and strong teeth. Its body is covered with very small scales.

The other species, belonging to the family Mormyridae are more 'fish-shaped'. The body is compressed and while the pelvic fin are absent and the pectoral fins small, both dorsal and anal fins are well-developed and the anal fin is usually longer than the dorsal. The tail fin is forked. Some species have a finger-like process on the jaw which is used as a feeler for searching for small animal food in the mud. Others have a long proboscis-like snout which gives the fishes a most unusual appearance. Mormyrids swim by waving the dorsal and anal fins and keeping the body rigid. Like the Nile fish, they also have a weak electric system which they use to sense their surroundings.

The Nile fish ranges from the upper reaches of the River Nile to the Chad basin and beyond to Senegal and the basin of the Niger river. The mormyrid fishes occupy much the same area but also spread into the Congo.

▽ **Gymnarchus niloticus** rises to the water surface to breathe. This series of photographs clearly shows how the fish swims with graceful ease propelled by the undulating fin along its back. It does not lash its tail from side to side as most other fish do, but keeps its spine straight. It keeps its body rigid so as not to disturb the electric field generated in the tail. The tail of this remarkable fish is naked, and it is from this characteristic the fish gets its name, for 'gymnarchus' means 'naked tail'.

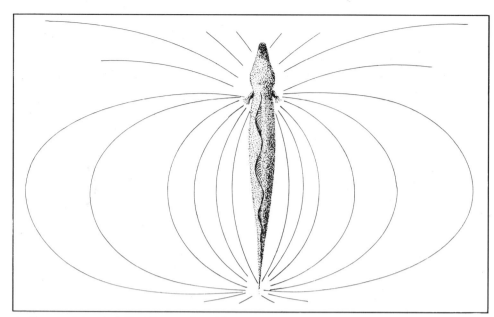

△ *Pattern of electric field of* **Gymnarchus**. *The electric generating organs are in the rear end of the body while the electric sensory organs are in the head region. The fish responds to changes in the distribution of electric potential over the body surface.*

Electric generators in the tail

The most remarkable discovery of an electric field surrounding the Nile fish was first published in 1951 by Dr HW Lissmann, of Cambridge University. Muscles on either side of the tail form electric generators which throughout the life of the fish are constantly giving out pulses at the rate of 300 a second. Lissmann found that when he lowered a pair of electrodes, connected to an oscilloscope, into the water containing a Nile fish, these electric discharges were picked up. Each discharge spreads out through the surrounding water forming an electric field like the field around a bar magnet, with the positive pole at its head and the negative pole at its tail. Any object in the water disturbs the field as when the two ends of a U-shaped copper wire were dipped into the field near the fish. The fish was disturbed and swam away, but would remain still and undisturbed if a similarly shaped non-conducting material was used.

Surrounded by an electric field

Later it was found that the sense-organs with which the fish picked up the disturbances are minute jelly-filled pits in the skin of the head, each with a receptor at the bottom. These are like the lateral line sense-organs of other fishes. The sensitivity of these organs is such that, as Lissmann has said: 'combing one's hair with a vulcanite comb and waving such an electrified insulator near an aquarium containing these fishes causes much excitement amongst the inhabitants'. They will also respond to a bar magnet placed near the aquarium. Conditioning experiments were carried out in which two porous clay tubes were put in the aquarium, one filled with tap water or some other conductor, the other with a non-conductor such as wax or glass. The fish was trained to come to the conducting tube by rewarding it with a piece of meat. It soon learned to come to the conducting tube and to ignore the non-conductor. By changing around the contents of the clay tubes the sensitivity of the Nile fish could be

shown. It was, for example, able to detect the presence in a tube of a glass rod $\frac{1}{12}$ in. diameter, which would cause only a minute change in the fish's electric field. When the fish's own discharges were recorded and played back it attacked the electrodes, as if they were one of its fellows.

A fish that cannot bend

The electric field enables the Nile fish to detect the small fishes on which it feeds without seeing them. It has little use for eyes anyway in the muddy waters of the swamps in which it lives. With the electric field the fish can move backwards as well as forwards with confidence because it can detect obstacles in its path. It swims in a smooth glide with a rigid body, driven by a wave passing through the long dorsal fin. A Nile fish swimming forward merely reverses the direction of the wave to swim backwards. The rigid body is necessary, for

were it to move the body, as most fishes do, this would disturb the electric field around it.

Floating nest

The Nile fish makes a floating four-sided nest of grass and other pieces of plant, with three sides out of the water and the fourth submerged to a depth of 4–8 in. The female lays about 1 000 large amber-coloured eggs. The larvae have long gill filaments and the remains of the yolk-sac are still attached. They stay in the shelter of the nest for 5 days, by which time the yolk is used up and the baby fishes are then 3 in. long.

Large brains

How the Nile fish interprets the messages from the sense-organs, to tell the position of an obstacle or other object is not yet known. The part of the brain linked to the sense-organs is very large so we can suppose it is able to analyse the complicated data coming from the sense-organs. The mormyrids also have large brains, said to bear the same proportion to the body as the human brain. Those who have kept these fishes in aquaria tell of their playing for hours on end with a leaf or a ball of tinfoil. They also turn on their backs and glide alternately backwards and forwards. We do not normally think of fishes playing in this manner and it reminds us of some of the antics of needlefishes (see page 139). Whether it was the curious 'elephant trunk' of some of the mormyrids, or whether it was their playfulness that caught the attention of the Ancient Egyptians, nobody can say. The fact remains, however, that as early as 2500 BC mormyrids were painted on the murals in tombs and figured on bas-reliefs.

class	**Pisces**
order	**Mormyriformes**
family	**Gymnarchidae**
family	**Mormyridae**

▽ *An elephant-trunk fish,* **Gnathonemus petersi.** *This species has only its lower lip elongated. The mormyrids and gymnotids, although not closely related, have some very similar behavioural characteristics. Both can swim backwards and forwards and both have electric organs.*

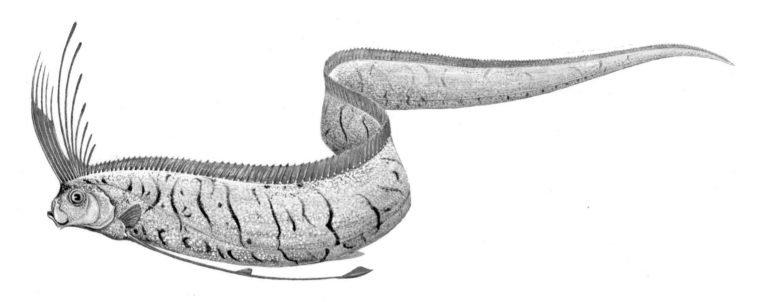

An oarfish with its oars, the pelvic fins, trailing at its side, and its crest, the first 10 rays of the continuous dorsal fin.

Oarfish

This has been described as one of the most mysterious of the larger sea fishes, and has often been linked with stories of sea-serpents. Its real interest, however, lies in its extraordinary shape, its large size and how little we know of its way of life. There is only one species, but oarfishes large and small have been found floating on the surface or washed ashore in warm and temperate seas throughout the world.

Sometimes called the ribbonfish, the oarfish has a flattened body up to 1 ft deep and only 2 in. across; it is up to 20 ft or more long. Hard knobs stud the skin, which is silvery with a bluish tinge on the head and is marked with dark streaks, sometimes with dark spots. The eyes are large. The fins are coral red. The dorsal fin starts on top of the head between the eyes and runs all the way to the hind end of the body. Because the first 10—12 rays of this are long, it makes a spectacular mane or crest over the head. People who have had first hand encounters with living oarfishes report that when the fish is touched it raises this 'mane', almost as if it were an aggressive display. The tail fin is very small or missing altogether. The pectoral fins are small but the pelvic fins, lying just under them, are long and slender, broadening at their tips, like oars.

An elusive king

Varying opinions put the oarfish's home anywhere between the surface and 3 000 ft deep. It is generally believed, however, that when an oarfish is seen at the surface it is sick or dying. A report of an oarfish swimming towards the *Florida*, in 1958, pursued by a shark, suggests that not all oarfishes seen at the surface are weak or moribund. Moreover, the oarfish has been called the

King of the Herrings because it was once believed that it swam in front of the herring shoals, as if leading them. This must mean they were not unfamiliar to fishermen. No adult oarfish has ever been caught in a net, however, possibly because of the speed at which it can slip through the water with wave-like movements of the long thin body.

Washed ashore

Oarfish are rarely reported; only 16 were captured in British waters from 1759 to 1878, according to Dr Albert Günther, and since then they have been caught about once every 10 years. Sir Alister Hardy thinks that oarfishes have 'been taken as often in our waters as anywhere else in the world, except perhaps off Japan'. Nevertheless, in the newspapers and magazines, as well as in the scientific journals of the world, there are a number of records of oarfishes, from 2 ft long to 20 ft or more, being captured or washed ashore, and there must be many more seen but not captured. So wherever it lives, this unusually shaped fish comes close enough to land to be familiar to sailors and fishermen everywhere.

Small mouth

An oarfish has a very small mouth and no teeth. It has a large number of long spiny gill-rakers, the number varying from 42 to 58. These strain very small crustaceans, especially those known as euphausids, from the water passing over the gills.

Remarkable streamers

The larvae, which hatch from small, floating eggs, have remarkable streamers, ornamented with small tags of skin. These streamers are made up of the much elongated rays of the front part of the dorsal fin and of the similarly elongated pelvic fins. What purpose they serve is unknown.

Can survive without tail

Except for the shark seen chasing an oarfish there is no direct evidence about its enemies.

A high percentage of captured oarfishes, however, have either lost a part of the tail or have scars from old wounds somewhere on the rear half of the body. It seems that an oarfish can lose nearly half its body yet still survive. The internal organs are all packed into the front quarter of the body, although there is a large bag connected with the stomach, an accessory digestive organ, which extends back among the muscles of the tail to about the centre of the body. Therefore —or so it seems from studying the captured specimens—an oarfish can survive provided only the rear half is bitten, even if it is bitten off completely.

King of the Salmon

Related to the oarfishes are the dealfishes, family Trachipteridae. These have a similar shape to the oarfishes but are shorter and higher in the body. They also lack the 'mane' and have only small pelvic fins. They have a small fan-shaped tail fin which points obliquely upwards. Dealfish grow to 8 ft long and there are a number of species. *Trachipterus arcticus* lives in the North Atlantic, *T. iris* is in the Mediterranean, and there is one which is sometimes seen off the Pacific coast of North America, where the big runs of salmon occur. This is named *T. rex-salmonorum* because the North American Indians living on the coast there had similar beliefs to the herring fishermen of Europe. They believed that the dealfish led the salmon, so they misleadingly called it the King of the Salmon.

class	**Pisces**
order	**Lampridiformes**
family	**Regalecidae**
genus & species	***Regalecus glesne***

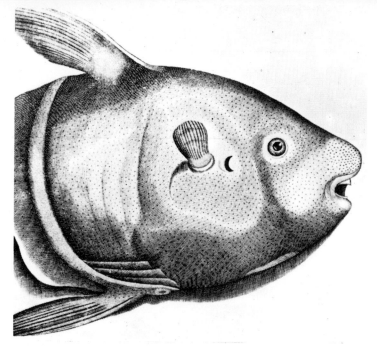

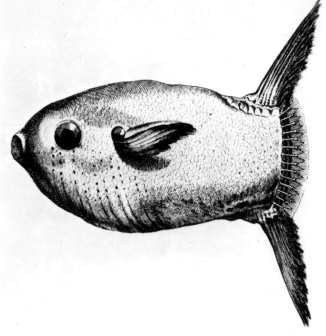

△ *Fins folded back so as to fit on the page! 17th century,* **Mola mola.**   △ *Artistic rendering of oblong sunfish. 18th century,* **Ranzania laevis.**

Ocean sunfish

Shaped like a millstone—its scientific name **Mola** *is Latin for millstone—this fish has been described as weighing a ton although it has a spinal cord only ½ in. long, which is, in fact, shorter than the brain.*

It looks all head, and these fishes are sometimes called headfishes. Its body is oval and covered with a thick leathery skin, grey, olive-brown or nearly black with silvery reflections. The snout projects beyond the small mouth in which the teeth in both upper and lower jaws are joined to form a single sharp-edged beak. The dorsal and anal fins are large and high and the body ends abruptly in a low tail fin. In the ocean sunfish **Mola mola** *the tail is rounded and wavy, but it is slightly different in the two related species. In the pointed-tailed sunfish* **M. lanceolata** *it is drawn out into a point in the middle, and in the oblong or truncated sunfish* **Ranzania truncata** *it has a rounded margin. The first of these species is up to 10 ft long and weighs a ton or more. The other two are smaller, the third seldom exceeding 2 ft long. All three are found in the warmer seas and occasionally in temperate seas, throughout the world.*

Colour changes

Ocean sunfish will sometimes lie at the surface somewhat obliquely with the dorsal fin above the surface, as if basking in the sun, or so the stories have always said. Doubts were raised about this during the last quarter of a century when people began to think that when ocean sunfishes are seen on the surface they must be either dead or dying. Several times these fishes have been seen well up rivers, as if carried in helplessly on the tide, and in Monterey Bay, in California, in October 1960, there was a very heavy death rate among ocean sunfishes close inshore. Skindivers went down and saw a hundred of them in 50 ft of water and all had their fins bitten off and most of them had lost their eyes. On the same day a little away from that spot a score or more were seen floating on the surface and in these also the fins and eyes had been damaged. The cause of death is unknown but Daniel W Gotshall, who investigated this event, concluded that when sunfishes are seen floating at or near the surface they are probably sick or dying.

Underwater observations made by the Italian, L Roghi, seem to bear this out. He tells us how, when the sunfish is at rest, it lies stationary in the water with its tail down and its mouth pointing upwards. While in this position it goes a darker colour except for the fins and a large area around the throat. He then describes how, as soon as the fish starts to swim, it immediately, and very strikingly, changes to a very light colour. If sunfishes came to the surface to bask we should expect, from what Roghi tells us, that they would be light in colour and would rest nose up. A few years ago two Dutch zoologists who listed the 57 records of ocean sunfishes taken off the coast of Holland during the years 1836–1959 showed that the great majority were caught in the months of November and December. No healthy warm-water fish would allow itself to drift north in winter.

Although often at or near the surface, especially in calm weather, ocean sunfish may possibly go down to depths of 600 ft at times. The ocean sunfish is usually seen singly or in pairs but it may come together in schools of a dozen or more at certain times of the year.

Small train

Ocean sunfish wave both dorsal and anal fins in unison from side to side, in a sculling action, the fins twisting slightly as they wave. The small pectoral fins flap continually but they probably act only as stabilizers. The tail is used as a rudder, while the sunfish steers with its gills by squirting a strong jet of water out of one gill-opening or the other, or out of its mouth. Sunfishes have no need for speed because their food is mainly plankton and includes jellyfishes, planktonic molluscs, small crustaceans and fish larvae. Leading this kind of life it does not need much intelligence, and not only is its spinal cord short, its brain is very small. In fact, the brain is smaller than either of the two kidneys that lie just behind it, instead of farther back in the body, as is usual.

Normal infancy

Although so like a caricature of a fish when adult, the baby ocean sunfish is a normal shape. From dissection of captured sunfish it is estimated that the female's ovary may contain 300 million eggs. The larvae are about ⅒ in. long and almost the usual shape of a fish. This soon changes as the dorsal and anal fins begin to grow and the body becomes covered with spines. Then this coat of spines is lost until only 5 long spines are left. These then shorten until they are lost completely, and the bulky, disc-shaped body begins to take form. The baby fish is then about ½ in. long.

Tough coat of gristle

In the past people have tried to harpoon or shoot sunfishes, but they have had the greatest difficulty in doing so. The sunfish made no attempt to escape by diving, or by swimming away as they could not go any faster than a rowing boat. All they did was to make sounds like pigs grunting, or else they just sighed. One was described as making hideous groans. These sounds, which are made by grinding their throat teeth, may or may not indicate distress, but the reason the sunfish takes no evasive action probably lies in the 2–3 in. coat of gristle under its tough skin. Even expert harpooners have had to try a dozen times before piercing this tough coat, and one sunfish lying off the coast of New South Wales, Australia, was proof against bullets. Its 'tough hide rendered it impervious to bullets fired from Winchester rifles!' Presumably, therefore, ocean sunfishes have no enemies except when they are very small.

class	**Pisces**
order	**Tetraodontiformes**
family	**Molidae**
genus & species	*Mola mola*

Old print of ocean sunfish, **Mola mola**.

△ *Suffering from exposure: waste eggs trapped in stream debris. Eggs are usually covered by sand.*

Pacific salmon

There are six species of salmon in the North Pacific, by contrast with the North Atlantic where there is only one species, the Atlantic salmon (see page 22). Except for the Japanese species, the masu, these range from about Kamchatka in Siberia to the American west coast as far south as California. Of these the chinook, also known as the tyee, quinnat, king, spring, Sacramento or Columbia River salmon, weighs 10–50 lb, with a maximum of 108 lb. The sockeye, red or blueback salmon weighs 5–7 lb, but may weigh up to 15½ lb; the silver salmon or coho weighs 6–12 lb, going up to 26½ lb; the chum, keta or dog salmon weighs 8–18 lb; but is sometimes as much as 30 lb, and the humpback or pink salmon which is 3–5 lb, may weigh up to 10 lb.

Drastic changes for spawning
Pacific salmon return to spawn in the same river in which they hatched, and when they do so they become brilliant red, and their heads turn pea green. The males grow long hooked snouts and their mouths become filled with sharp teeth. The females do not grow the hooked snout. Most of the returning salmon are 4–5 years old. The humpback matures the earliest at 2 years, the silver salmon at 3, but some of the sockeye and chinook may be as much as 8 years old.

The salmon return in early summer, even in late spring, or in autumn in the case of the chum. They stop feeding as their digestive organs deteriorate and head for the coast from their feeding grounds out in the Pacific. On reaching the mouth of a river they head upstream, except the chum which usually spawns near tidal waters. The silver salmon moves only a short distance upstream. The chinook, on the other hand, has been known to travel as much as 2 250 miles up rivers. One exception to this is a subspecies of the sockeye which is non-migratory. In contrast with the Atlantic salmon, however, Pacific salmon never survive the spawning run.

Mating ends in death
By the time the salmon near the spawning grounds, they are mere bags of bones housing the eggs or the sperms. The males often look the worse for wear as they fight with each other. The females look for a place in the sandy or gravelly shallows where the water is clear with plenty of oxygen. Then they start digging troughs (redds) in the river beds with their tails; each one lying on her side and flapping with her tail. When her trough is deep enough, she lies in it to spawn, her mate swimming over to her to shed his milt to fertilise the eggs. Each female lays several batches of eggs, to a total of 3–5 thousand, in different troughs, by the end of which time she is completely exhausted. With her tail fins worn to stubs, her skin blackening and with blotches of grey fungus attacking it, she dies. The males share the same fate, and the carcases of both drift downstream or are stranded at the edge.

Down to the sea as infants
Each batch of eggs becomes buried under sand as fresh redds are dug and the loosened sand is wafted over them. Thus protected, the orange-pink eggs hatch 8 weeks later. The alevins or young salmon remain under the gravel feeding on their yolk sacs for some weeks before wriggling to the surface as fry. They feed heavily on water fleas and other small animals and in the following spring are carried downstream by the current. The humpback and chum go to the sea as fry but the sockeye may go as fry or as 1–3 year fish, and the quinnat and coho go when 1–2 years old.

Finding their way home
There has always been a great interest in how salmon find their way back to the streams where they were hatched. The full story has not yet been pieced together but sufficient is now known to sketch in many of the details. There is evidence, for example, to show that the thyroid gland plays a part in the salmon's changing preference for water of varying salinity. When the coho was injected with a certain hormone it sought sea water. When the injections were stopped it sought fresh water. The opposite effect was found in the humpback. Probably other glands are involved, as well as the length of day and possibly the diet. The sense of smell may play a part, as it does in finding food. Temperatures also influence the fish, certainly once they have entered fresh water. When these are too low or too high the fish make no effort to surmount obstacles. There is some evidence also that celestial navigation, using the sun by day and the stars by night, as in migrating birds, keeps the salmon on their compass runs along the coast to the mouths of the rivers they came from.

Expert water-tasters
Of the different ways that salmon find their way back, one of the easier to test is the odour, or the taste of the water from which the fishes originated. Laboratory experiments have shown beyond doubt that fishes, including salmon, can recognize waters of only slightly different tastes; smell and taste are closely linked. This is not so very surprising since water-tasters dealing with the purification of drinking water are able to tell by tasting, in an almost uncanny way, where a particular glass of water came

△ *The remains. Reduced to blackened bags of bones after spawning, dead sockeye salmon are washed up at the river's edge.*

△ *On home ground. A pair of sockeye salmon, having swum from the Pacific Ocean up to the head waters of the river in which they hatched 4 or 5 years before, are now ready to spawn themselves — then die, starved and exhausted by their marathon journey on which they do not feed at all.*

from. These same tests show that the memory of a particular type of water persists for a long time in a fish, and that the younger the fish the longer the memory will probably be.

Controlled fishing

Many people living a long way from the Pacific are familiar with the Pacific salmon — in canned form. The salmon fishery is commercially highly valuable, with 2–10 million sockeye alone being caught and canned. The salmon are taken in gill nets, reef nets and purse seines on their way to the Fraser River in British Columbia. Unrestricted fishing could kill the industry,

so by an agreement between Canada and the United States, 20% of each race of fish are allowed through to continue their journey to the spawning grounds. This is taken care of by a joint International Pacific Salmon Fisheries Commission, which also arranges for the catch to be divided equally between the two countries. There is co-operation also in providing concrete and steel fishways to assist the salmon up the rivers. The Pacific salmon fishery is therefore as near as it has so far been possible to an actual husbandry of a wild resource. Moreover, research is being carried out to produce strains of salmon that can tolerate less favourable rivers than they

use at present, and to transplant fry which, when mature, will return to spawn in waters earmarked for cultivation.

class	**Pisces**
order	**Salmoniformes**
family	**Salmonidae**
genus & species	***Oncorhynchus gorbuscha*** *humpback*
	O. keta *chum*
	O. kisutch *silver salmon*
	O. masou *masu*
	O. nerka *sockeye*
	O. tshawytscha *chinook*

American paddlefish looks menacing but is really quite harmless, feeding on small planktonic organisms which it probably detects with its long snout.

Paddlefish

The paddlefish, a large freshwater bony fish, is related to the sturgeons. It has a long body, and looks like a shark. The skin of the paddlefish is naked except for a few scattered vestigial scales and patches of scales on the tail fin. It has a fairly large head drawn out at the front into a flattened snout shaped like the blade of a canoe paddle. The snout is between one-third and one-half the total length of the fish. At the base of the snout are the small eyes and beneath them a very wide mouth. The gill covers are large and triangular with the apex to the rear, and are drawn out into a point. The pectoral and pelvic fins are medium-sized, as are the single dorsal fin which is set well back on the body and the anal fin which is opposite it. The tail fin is only slightly forked.

There are only 2 species: one, also known as the spoonbill sturgeon, lives in the Mississippi Valley of North America, the other in the Yangtse river system in China. The first is up to 6 ft or more long and weighs 170 lb. The Chinese species, sometimes called the swordbill sturgeon, is reported to reach 23 ft long.

Paddling for food

Some people say the paddlefish uses its paddle to probe in the mud for food, while others say it uses the paddle to stir up the mud, but as others have suggested, this seems unlikely for such a sensitive and easily damaged organ. They maintain, and this seems more likely, that as the paddle-fish swims slowly along, it swings its highly sensitive paddle from side to side to detect its food. When it opens its large mouth, the back of the head seems almost to fall away from the rest of the body as the gill

covers sag, revealing the capacious gill chambers. This sudden opening of the mouth and gill cavities probably produces a suction which draws in small plankton. As the fish swims forward, the plankton is strained from the water by the long gill rakers on the inner sides of the gills. They sometimes eat other fish; shad, for example, have been found in their stomachs.

Vanishing mystery

Although paddlefish are living in a region where there are many people fishing and where there are many naturalists capable of keeping a watch on it, its breeding and spawning behaviour were unknown until a few years ago. Then CA Purkett, in 1960, noticed paddlefishes assembling over a gravel bar in the Osage River when the water level had risen several feet during a spate. He could see them swimming just over the gravel bottom and every now and then one would come to the surface, waggle its tail, and then go down to the bottom again. He assumed correctly that they were spawning and he was later able to work out the story, so ending a long-standing mystery.

The eggs are $\frac{1}{8}$ in. diameter. As they are laid they sink down to the pebbles and stick to them. The larvae hatch within 7 days at ordinary summer temperatures and they are then $\frac{1}{3}$ in. long, with a large head, no eyes, no paddle and no barbels, and each feeds on its large yolk sac. The larvae are encumbered with this yolk sac until it has been used up. They can be seen swimming erratically up to the surface and down again and when the flood waters begin to subside they are carried downstream or are washed among the rocks. Now we see why the spawning had escaped attention. It takes place on a flood, and when the flood waters recede, there is nothing left to show what has taken place.

The larvae begin to grow their eyes and their barbels within a few hours of being hatched but the paddle does not begin to grow for 2—3 weeks. At first it is only

a small bump on the snout but once it appears it grows rapidly. The paddle of one individual that Purkett had under observation grew to 2 in. long in 29 days and had a paddle $\frac{1}{3}$ in. long. Paddlefish kept in ponds grew 6—12 in. in a year, some growing as much as 2 ft in a year, but they are 7—8 years old before they begin to breed.

Missing links

In the early days of the settlement of North America, the paddlefish was not regarded as a fish worth eating. Even today it ranks as only second rate, although the greenish-black eggs are used as caviare. The chief interest in the fish is in its relationship with other fishes. It is classified in the class Pisces, which are also known as bony fishes, yet its skeleton, like that of sharks, is made of cartilage. It also has a short straight intestine with a spiral valve, like sharks. There are other small details of the anatomy which link the paddlefishes with the sharks although in most other respects they are more like bony fishes. They are, in fact, 'missing links', connecting these two main groups. They and the sturgeons are the only surviving members of an order dating back about 100 million years, which was an offshoot from the common ancestors of sharks and bony fishes. The fact that there are only 2 species, one in one part of the world and the other in a widely separated part, suggests that they are a dying race. If so, their end is being hastened, at least in North America, where the building of dams and river pollution have even further restricted their range.

class	**Pisces**
order	**Acipenseriformes**
family	**Polyodontidae**
genera & species	***Polyodon spathula*** *American* ***Psephurus gladius*** *Chinese*

Paradise fish

This is the fish that first made tropical aquarium keeping popular. People have been keeping goldfish for a long time but it was in the mid-19th century that home aquaria became the rage. At first marine animals and a few freshwater fishes were kept in them. Then in 1861, the paradise fish was brought to Paris. Before long it had reached England and other European countries and in 1876 it was introduced to the United States. At first aquarists were afraid the new fish would injure their goldfish. But in fact it was the paradise fish that started the fashion of keeping 'tropicals'.

The paradise fish can be up to $3\frac{1}{2}$ in. long and has a body that is flattened from side to side. It has flowing dorsal and anal fins, a large rounded tail, small pectoral fins and pelvic fins about the same size as the pectorals and lying beneath them. The male is brown to greenish-grey with marbling on the head and a large blackish spot ringed with orange on each gill cover. The flanks are banded blue-green and carmine. The fins are reddish, the pelvics white-tipped and the dorsal and anal fins have dark spots. The female is similar but paler.

The range of the paradise fish is from Korea through eastern China, including Formosa, to South Vietnam. A second species, the round-tailed paradise fish, similar but slightly smaller, has much the same range but does not go so far south. A third species, also small, with two longitudinal bands on the flanks, ranges from India and Ceylon, through Burma to South Vietnam.

Wild or tame

Much has been written about the paradise fish in scientific and aquarist journals, discussing two aspects of it: whether it is the wild form or one bred by the Chinese, and what is the purpose of its bubble nest. No firm conclusions have been reached. On the whole it seems that the fish as we know it in the aquarium is much the same as the fish that is wild in the rice fields. The aquarium breeds have been only slightly altered from the wild forms although there are also special breeds. There is, for example, a dark variety, *concolor*, and there is an albino strain, white with pink eyes and pink bands on the flanks which breeds true.

Eggs sealed in bubble nest

As in many other labyrinth fishes, paradise fishes build nests of bubbles. The male blows out bubbles of air and mucus which rise to the surface and there form a raft. Then follows an elaborate mating. The colours of the male become brighter as the breeding period draws near, the female becomes paler. When the female is about to spawn the male wraps himself round her while she lies in the normal position just under the bubble raft. As the eggs begin to be laid

△ *Fashion makers — paradise fish made tropical aquaria popular. Species:* **Macropodus dayi**.

the pair make a barrel roll, which brings the female upside-down with the male still wrapped round her, so he fertilises the eggs as they leave her body. Then he releases the female and trembles for a few seconds before gathering any slowly sinking eggs in his mouth, rising to the underside of the bubble nest and spitting the eggs onto it. Unlike other bubble nesters whose eggs are heavier than water, those of the paradise fish mostly float upwards when laid. Only a small percentage fail to do this and slowly sink. When the clutch is complete he blows more bubbles to make a second layer under the eggs, sealing them in. This may be repeated time and time again.

There are several opinions about the purpose of the raft. One is that it protects the eggs from the heat of strong sunlight beating down on the rice fields. Another is that it shades them from strong light. A third is that it protects the eggs from bacteria. The fourth suggestion, and the most likely, is that it keeps the eggs together, and also the fry when they hatch, making it easier for the male to guard them. The eggs hatch in 2 days at a temperature of 26°C/80°F.

Paradise fish can respond to sounds of frequencies between 2 637 and 4 699 cycles per second and there is the possibility that they make sounds, perhaps inaudible to us, which stimulate breeding.

Reason in their quarrelsome habits

Little is known about the enemies of paradise fish in the wild. More is known about their pugnacious nature in aquaria, where they will tear the fins of other kinds of fishes if placed in a mixed tank. They feed on any small animals, being very predatory, and they readily attack members of their own kind. In aquaria care must be taken to keep male and female apart until they are ready to breed, and it may happen that, after mating, the female may be savaged by the male if she has too little

space to get away from him. What purpose is served by this internecine strife is hard to say. Perhaps clues can be found from experimental work that has been carried out on paradise fish in the laboratory. It has been found that they eat more food when grouped together but grow faster when placed in tanks on their own. Their aggressiveness may be purely a matter of keeping each fish spaced out, to give them growing space, or it may be a natural means of controlling numbers.

Females take over

Although the building of the bubble nest and care of the young is normally the work of the male, females have been seen to do both. Presumably, should a male be killed after the eggs are laid a female can take over his work. That, however, cannot be the whole story. In aquaria females ready to lay but having no male present will build a bubble raft and lay their eggs, unfertilised. It has even been known for such a female to be helped by another female. In one instance an aquarium keeper kept a male and female apart, by sliding a sheet of glass between them. The male started to build a bubble raft one side of the glass and the female started one the other side. When the aquarist noticed this, and before he could move the glass, the female had laid her eggs under the raft and was trying to keep the male, on the other side of the glass, at bay.

class	**Pisces**
order	**Perciformes**
family	**Anabantidae**
genus & species	***Macropodus opercularis*** *others*

149

Colourful coral fish—parrotfish appear as blue-green patches moving around the tropical reefs on which they feed. With their parrot-like beaks (below) they bite off chunks of coral leaving distinct tooth impressions behind. Because of this feeding habit parrotfish slowly erode the reefs.

Parrotfish

These brilliantly coloured fishes do not in fact get their name from their gaudy colours but from their teeth, which are joined to form a 'parrot's beak' in the front of the mouth. Nobody knows how many species there are: 350 have been named but there are probably fewer than 80.

Parrotfishes live around tropical reefs. They vary in adult size, from 1—6 ft; a few have reached 12 ft. When merely cruising around they swim with their pectoral fins, using their tail only when they need to swim more quickly.

Herds of fishes

Parrotfishes of the genus *Sparisoma* may live solitary lives or they may come together in small groups without any social organisation. Some species of the genus *Scarus* move about in large schools of up to 40 when feeding, rather like herds of cattle. Because of this parrotfish are sometimes referred to as the 'cattle of the sea'. Often they are seen near the shore with their backs out of water. The schools are made up of fishes of about the same size, the smallest keeping together, and similarly with the medium and large sized individuals. In some species of *Scarus* the groups are smaller and are made up of several females with a mature male acting as leader, like cows with a bull. Should another male join the group he is chased away, the boss male sometimes trailing him 20 ft away for a distance of 100 yards before rejoining his harem.

Different coloured sexes

For a long time parrotfishes were separated into species on the basis of colour. Then it was found that the same species could appear in different colours. Some species go through at least three different colour phases in the course of a lifetime. In others there is a marked difference between male and female. For example, *Scarus taeniopterus* is striped with orange and blue while *S. croicensis* is striped brown and white. Then it was realized they both belong to the same species, the first being the male, the second the female. This was tested by taking the female parrotfishes and injecting them with male sex hormones. *S. croicensis* so injected turned from brown and white striped to orange and blue striped. Where males and females are differently coloured the young fishes are coloured like the females. As they mature the females keep these colours but the males take on the colours of the mature males. Another change that can take place with age, in some parrotfishes, is that the males become bumpheaded. Instead of the forehead sloping it becomes a large bump, so that old males have heavy blunt snouts.

Homing by the sun

Some parrotfishes spend the nights under overhanging ledges of rock or in caves. When alarmed during the day they swim straight for their night quarters, in a direct line. Tests were made to see how they homed so accurately. First a net was hung in front of a cave and when the fishes were disturbed they swam straight for the net and continued trying to swim through it. When it was lifted they swam straight into the cave. The next test was to net some of the parrotfishes that were known always to swim in a south-easterly direction to their caves. They were then taken farther along the coast and put back into the sea. They immediately swam on a south-easterly course, to where there were no caves. When this experiment was repeated it was noticed that if a cloud passed across the sun the fish were temporarily lost. They swam about in different directions until the sun shone again, when they once more swam unerringly on a south-easterly course. Finally, the experiment was tried of blindfolding the fishes, by putting suction caps over their eyes. They swam in all directions, quite confused, but when the caps were removed they swam straight for their caves.

Eroding coral reefs

With their parrot-beak teeth they browse the eelgrass and seaweeds, often nipping pieces off the coral. In this way they erode the coral reefs. The pieces of coral swallowed are ground by flattened teeth in the throat. The undigested coral fragments are passed out and dropped in special places along the route the parrotfishes follow to and from their caves, accumulating in heaps. The sound they make when crunching the coral can be heard by anyone standing nearby.

Several kinds of courtship

It is not easy to generalize about the behaviour of parrotfish as they differ so much from one species to another. It is the same with their breeding habits. The eggs of *Scarus* species are elongated and oval, those of *Sparisoma* are spherical. In the one species *Sparisoma rubripinna* in which the spawning habits have been closely studied it was found that it bred all the year round but only in the afternoons. Then, a milling mass of fishes leaves its feeding ground close inshore and assembles in depths of 65—70 ft, the mass keeping a few feet up from the bottom. Most of the fishes assembled there are males, so while the spawning is going on there is a preponderance of females inshore. Every now and then groups of 4—13 swim upwards from the main mass and circle rapidly around to release eggs and milt. There is, however, a second type of spawning in which a solitary male mates with a solitary female. The bulk of the eggs come from the group spawning, however. In another species a male and a female swim up to the surface, circling round each other as they go. As they get near the surface they are rotating round each other, and then they release a cloud of eggs and milt. The eggs of all species contain an oil drop, so they float near the surface. They range from $\frac{1}{25}-\frac{1}{10}$ in. diameter, and they hatch in a day, to release the usual fish larvae.

Mucous envelope

When some parrotfishes *Scarus guacamaia* were kept in aquaria in 1954 they were seen as night fell to give out mucus, or slime, from glands in their skin. Later, other parrotfishes were seen to do the same thing. The mucus formed a kind of loose shroud with an opening in the front guarded by a flap that allowed water in and a hole at the back which let it out. So the parrotfish can draw water in and pass it across its gills to breathe even while enclosed in what is almost a plastic cover. In the morning the parrotfish breaks out of its 'nightdress' and goes about its normal activities. When a parrotfish rests at night its breathing drops to a low rate. It is to all intents sleeping. The mucous envelope may be a way of preventing the gills silting up while the fish is resting on a sandy bottom, or it may be a protection from enemies. It is not known whether all parrotfishes do this, or even whether those species that have been seen to do it always do so. Whatever the situation is, a fish that wraps itself up for the night like this must be unique.

class	**Pisces**
order	**Perciformes**
family	**Scaridae**
genera	*Scarus*
	Sparisoma
	others

Properly dressed for the night, a sleeping parrotfish **Scarus guacamaia.** *At night certain parrotfish reveal a remarkable phenomenon—they secrete a loose mucous envelope around themselves. This envelope may take half an hour to secrete and the same time to break out of at daylight.*

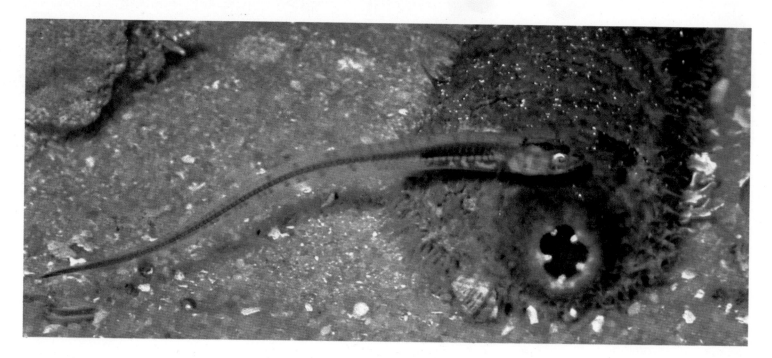

Pearlfish

These fishes were so named because they are often found embalmed in pearls in oyster shells, and also because their bodies are transparent with a pearly lustre. They are familiar to biology students as **Fierasfer,** *a fish that lives in the body of a sea-cucumber. The two dozen species of pearlfishes are thin and eel-like, usually only a few inches long. The longest is 12 in. They have scaleless, rounded bodies or are compressed from side to side. The tail tapers almost to a point. The dorsal fin starts just behind the head and continues round the tail to join the long anal fin. The pectoral fins are very small and there are no pelvic fins. The body is transparent so the internal organs and the backbone are visible.*

Pearlfishes live mainly in tropical and subtropical seas, although a few species occur in temperate seas. They inhabit shallow water down to depths of 600 ft.

Most remarkable partnership

Adult pearlfish shelter in cracks and crevices in rocks, inside the shells of bivalve molluscs or inside the bodies of sea-squirts, sea-urchins, starfishes and sea-cucumbers. Most of them come out to feed but a few live permanently and parasitically inside the body of another animal. Sometimes pearlfishes are caught in nets which suggests that some of them may spend a larger proportion of their time swimming freely than hiding in crevices. Some species of pearlfishes will shelter in a variety of hosts, like *Carapus homei,* of the Malay Archipelago, which will readily go into a starfish, sea-urchin, clam or other animal, whereas *C. bermudensis* of the Caribbean uses only three species of sea-cucumber. These spend only part of their time within the host, but others, such as *C. acus* of the Mediterranean, live permanently in it.

Experiments show that a pearlfish that normally uses a sea-cucumber for a host will enter an artificial sea-cucumber so long as water is flowing out of it and some mucus from a live sea-cucumber has been added to the aquarium water. A sea-cucumber breathes by drawing water in through its vent, passing it through its gills, and then driving it out again. Young pearlfishes swim in headfirst, the head keeping the vent open while the tail is being inserted. Should the sea-cucumber try to close its vent before the fish is in, a pearlfish may twist its long tail like a corkscrew to insinuate itself inside. More than one pearlfish may live in the same sea-cucumber, and as many as seven have been seen to enter, one after the other.

Regrowth of eaten organs

For the most part pearlfishes shelter by day and come out at night to feed on copepods, small shrimps, small crabs and probably other small invertebrates. The parasitic species feed on the reproductive organs of their hosts, and possibly other of their internal organs. This may not be as bad for the sea-cucumbers as it appears because they have the habit of casting out their internal organs in moments of crisis and growing a new set. So presumably they can re-grow any parts that are nibbled away.

Four stages

The eggs are laid in sticky, roughly cylindrical masses, 2–3 in. long. After this each fish passes through four stages, with changes at each stage in the shape of the body, colour and behaviour. In the Mediterranean pearlfish the first or vexillifer larva is very slender and has a long lobe on its back. This is not a fin but a flag-like outgrowth of the body (*vexillifer* means a standard-bearer). As the larva grows in size the 'flag' becomes small, disappearing when the baby fish is $2\frac{1}{2}$ in. long. All this time it has lived in the plankton. The next stage, the tenuis, or slender larva, has a larger head relative to the rest of the body and it begins to grow long teeth. It must now enter a sea-cucumber. It cannot change from one sea-cucumber to another and it cannot

△ *Pearlfish at its front door—a sea cucumber.*

survive outside. When it has reached a length of 8 in. the tenuis larva changes to a juvenile, which is much shorter, and can leave its host for a while each day, but it feeds on the gills and the reproductive organs of the sea-cucumber. The fourth and last stage is the adult. The shelter of the sea-cucumber is still necessary but when older it is used only as a temporary day refuge.

High mortality rate

Nothing definite is known about their enemies, but once the pearlfishes have started to shelter, whether in rock crevices or in living animals, their daily risks must be much reduced. No doubt some fall prey to predatory fishes when they are feeding, but these losses are probably small. The heaviest mortality is almost certainly during the planktonic larval stage.

Patchy distribution

Although pearlfishes are found in all tropical and subtropical seas their distribution seems to be patchy, even in localities where there are plenty of sea-cucumbers. In one study off Hawaii, of 122 sea-cucumbers examined only 2 had a pearlfish inside. Several hundred examined off the Marshall Islands, in the South Pacific, yielded only one fish, and off Florida 100 sea-cucumbers yielded only three pearlfishes. William M Stephens reports that after collecting hundreds of sea-cucumbers off Miami, in some places half of them had pearlfishes inside while in other places only 2 in every 100 contained fishes, and off the Bahamas 1 in every 3 had a fish inside.

class	**Pisces**
order	**Gadiformes**
family	**Carapidae**
genus & species	*Carapus acus*
	C. bermudensis
	C. homei
	others

Perch

*This fish, which originally gave its name
to the largest order of fishes, the Perci-
formes, was the freshwater perch of Europe.
The name is derived from Greek and
Latin, through the French, and it was
known to the Romans as* **perca**. *There are
many perch-like fishes known today, so the
main attention here will be concentrated
on the European perch. This plump-bodied
fish is dark greenish with a yellowish tinge
on the flanks and dark bars. The undersurface is silvery blue to yellowish, and the
anal and pelvic fins are reddish. The
colour varies, however, from one place to
another, and in some localities the bars
may be missing. The front dorsal fin is
spiny, but both are well developed. There is
a medium sized anal fin, the pelvic fins are
well forward and the tail is almost square-
ended. It usually weighs about 1 lb
although the record is about 10 lb.*

*The perch is found in freshwater in
much of Europe, western Asia and Siberia,
and in slightly brackish waters around the
Baltic. Its counterpart in North America,
east of the Rockies, is the yellow perch,
which is golden with dark bars, a silver
belly and orange anal and pelvic fins. A
near relative in northern Europe, including
the British Isles, is the ruffe, which is a
somewhat smaller fish with a marbled
pattern and lines of distinct dark spots on
the fins. The walleye or pikeperch of North
America is considerably larger than the perch
but has a blotched pattern and prominent
eyes. The pikeperch of Europe and Asia is
about the same size as the walleye. In
North America there are also small darters,
fast-moving, brilliantly coloured fish, only
a few inches long.*

Lying in ambush

These well camouflaged predatory fish lurk
among the stems of water plants, suddenly
dashing out to seize their prey. The mouth
is small but opens into a wide gape. Their
main sense is sight but perch can hear and
smell. There are two nostrils on each side of
the head, one which takes water in and the
other at the rear which lets water out of the
nasal pouch. Inside this pouch is a rosette
of sensitive tissue.

Perch live in shoals in slow-flowing rivers
and lakes. The smaller the fishes, the larger
the shoals, so at 3 years old they swim in
small groups of a half-dozen or less, and
later may even be solitary. In winter they
retire to deeper water, as deep as 30 ft in
lakes, and remain quiescent there. They
may possibly be able to draw upon the
oxygen in the swimbladder for breathing.

Tendency towards cannibalism

The adult perch eat smaller fishes, which
they usually seize from behind with their
sharp teeth, damaging the tail. They then
swallow the fish head-first. The fry, up to
one month old, feed on waterfleas and other
small plankton, after which they eat bottom-

living invertebrates, such as midge and mayfly larvae, freshwater shrimps and occasionally a leech. During July, when the small perch are about 2 months old, there is a tendency towards cannibalism. Perch feeding only on fish grow faster than those forced to eat other food when fish are scarce.

Strings of eggs

Spawning takes place during April and May, the fishes shoaling according to size. The eggs, like those of the American yellow perch, are laid in long strings which become entangled with water plants. In laying them the female glides over the water plants with her fins lowered, shedding the eggs which are then fertilised by one or more males. A large female may lay 200 000 eggs. They hatch in about 18 days, or in only 8–10 days if the weather is warm. The transparent larvae are $\frac{1}{5}$ in. long. On hatching, each larva spirals to the surface to fill its airbladder. After this they hang for a while on water plants, and then float at the surface. Perch mature at 3 years. The maximum recorded life span is $10\frac{1}{2}$ years.

Do fish feel pain?

One of the questions often asked is whether fishes feel pain. The story usually told, to show they do not, is about the angler whose hook fouled the eye of a perch. In freeing the hook the eye was removed and the angler used it as bait, catching the perch it belonged to almost immediately. It is an unpleasant story, yet a point is made. Almost equally unpleasant reading is the fact that since 1825 a dozen or more scientists have tried the experiment of removing the forebrain of fishes, mainly of perch—probably because they were easy to get. The forebrain is the 'thinking' part of the brain. In these experiments it was found that the fishes soon recovered from the operation and, so far as one could see, led quite normal lives. Presumably, therefore, if they feel pain at all, it cannot be to anything like the same degree as human beings.

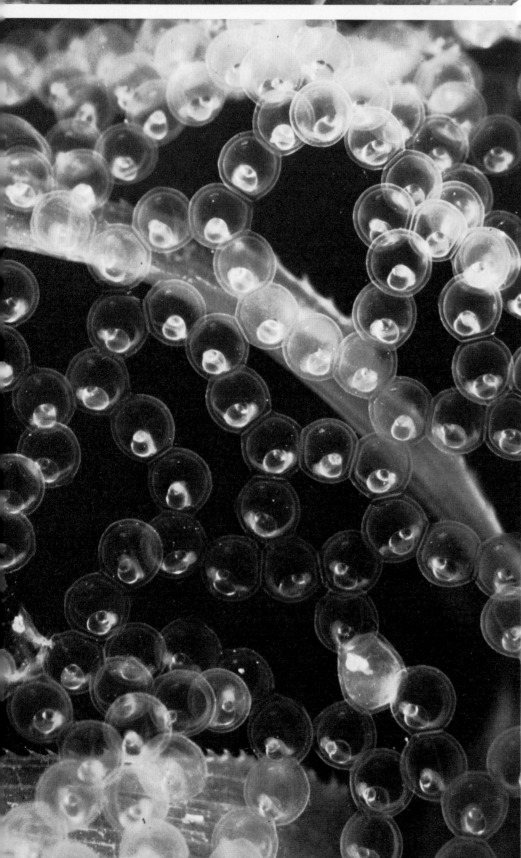

△ A rather drab relative, the walleye's most notable feature is its prominent eyes, the chief sense organ of perch.

◁ Design in eggs. Part of an egg rope of European perch wrapped around a water plant. Developing embryos can be seen inside the translucent eggs.

class	**Pisces**
order	**Perciformes**
family	**Percidae**
genera & species	*Gymnocephalus cernua* ruffe *Etheostoma nigrum* johnny darter *Perca fluviatilis* European perch *P. flavescens* yellow perch *Stizostedion vitreum* walleye others

Ambush: a northern pike in hiding. It will wait here until prey is near enough for it to dart out rapidly to seize an unsuspecting fish.

Pike

The pike, aptly nicknamed the 'freshwater shark', is the fiercest predatory fish in the fresh waters of the northern hemisphere. It and its relatives, the pickerel and muskellunge of North America, are held in awe by some fishermen, contempt by others; to many they present a challenge, backed by the legends of size and ferocity—often very tall stories. The record of the largest pike caught is of a 53lb specimen.

The pike—or northern pike, as it is sometimes called—is long bodied with a large flat, almost shovel-shaped head with large jaws and large mouth bristling with teeth. Its dorsal and anal fins are set far back. Its colour ranges from olive to dark green with pale yellow spots. It grows up to 4½ ft long and weighs up to 53 lb. The muskellunge of the Great Lakes is very like the pike but has scales on only the upper part of the cheek instead of all over it. It grows to 8 ft long and can weigh up to 110 lb. The grass pickerel, from Nova Scotia to Texas, grows up to 2 ft long, and has dark bands on the flanks. The smaller chain pickerel of the eastern United States grows up to 14 in. long and has a chain-like network of dark markings on the side. The black-spotted pike, which is sometimes called the black-spotted pickerel, lives in eastern Siberia, and very little seems to be known about this fifth member of the family.

Ambush

Pike live in still and running water, spending most of their time motionless among water plants with which their colours harmonize. The pike usually stay in one place and dart out to ambush their prey. Having the dorsal and anal fins set far back on the body gives great thrust to the tail and rapid acceleration, sending the pike out 20–30 ft to seize prey. A pike detects its prey by sight rather than by smell, at distances of up to 50 ft by day, but is probably warned of its approach by vibrations in the water, for a blind pike can also catch food. A pike can see at night as well as by day. Its habit is to lie well down in the water because its eyes are set in the top of the head and look mainly forwards and upwards. It has two sighting grooves running to the tip of the snout. A pike's brain is relatively very small, $\frac{1}{1305}$ of the total body weight, much of this being taken up by the optic lobes. This reflects the little effort the pike needs to make a living.

Teeth point backwards

When very small, pike feed on water fleas, worms and the fry of other fishes. As they grow they take progressively larger fish and are less and less tempted by small prey unless it comes so close they can snap it up without moving. They are almost exclusively fish-eaters, especially of fishes belonging to the carp family Cyprinidae and trout. Large pike will also take other water dwellers such as ducks, moorhens, coots, water voles and frogs. There are many authenticated reports of pike eating prey their own size. This is possible no matter how much it struggles because of

the pike's teeth. Those on the sides of the lower jaw are strong and stick straight up. They are used for seizing prey. There are no teeth in the upper jaw, only on the roof of the mouth. These are smaller than in lower jaw, most numerous in the front and curved backwards. They prevent prey slipping out of the mouth. The mouth itself has a wide gape. Sometimes large prey may become jammed in the pike's throat with fatal results for the pike, which cannot get rid of it because of the backwardly directed teeth. Large prey successfully swallowed takes a long time to digest, and after a big meal the pike lies inert for a week or more, often near the bottom, taking no notice of prey or the fisherman's bait. A pike can take in large prey because its intestine is more or less straight, its stomach being merely a dilatation of the front part of it.

Unusual digestive juices?

A hungry pike will seize prey of a certain size depending on its own size and usually providing its quarry does not move too slowly, although an angler will catch a pike using stationary dead bait. Pike learn, however, not to go after sticklebacks once they have had experience of their spines. It is sometimes said that the digestive juices of a pike 'are phenomenal', because even hooks are eaten away by its stomach acids. This is, in fact, illusory. When digesting a fish the pike's acidity is high on the surface of the prey, very low inside it, and a pike takes 3–5 days to digest a moderately sized fish. A similar high acidity on the surface of a hook would soon erode it.

155

High egg wastage

Pike spawn from February to May, the younger individuals spawning first. They are stimulated to spawn by the increasing day length and light intensity. They assemble in shallow water, each female attended by several males. Estimates of the number of eggs laid by each female vary from 40 000 to 500 000, the number depending probably on the size of the female. Many fail to be fertilised because the micropyle, the hole in the egg membrane through which the sperms enter, closes 30–60 seconds after they are laid. At first the eggs are sticky and lie singly on the bottom, later rising just off the bottom. They hatch after 2–3 weeks, the larvae feeding on the remains of the yolk sac for 10 days, before starting to catch their own food. The parents take no care of their eggs or young.

Automatic control of numbers

As pike are at the apex of a food pyramid they probably have few enemies except when very young. There is, however, considerable cannibalism which keeps a proper balance. The more richly a water is stocked with other fish the less the cannibalism; and the end result is that pike are seldom so numerous as to deplete the waters, in which they live, of other fish.

Tall stories

Most pike live about 7 years once they have survived the massacre of infancy but they have been known to live 10 years or more and Dr C Tate Regan once asserted that possibly 'fish of sixty or seventy pounds weight are at least as many years old'. There have, however, been many exaggerated claims, like the one, first told by Gesner in 1558, about the famous Emperor's Pike. This pike was supposed to have been caught in a lake in Württemburg in 1497 with a copper ring round its gill region with an inscription saying it had been placed in the lake by the Emperor Frederick II in 1230. So it would have been more than 260 years old. What was not explained was why the ring fitted it so well as pike continue to grow until they die. Had it been put on 260 years before the ring would surely have been a tight fit by 1497.

The pike was said to have been 19 ft long and to weigh 550 lb, and there was a painting of it in the castle of Lautern in Swabia. What appears to be a copy of this still hangs in the British Museum (Natural History). Its skeleton is said to have been preserved in the cathedral in Mannheim. When scientists studied it in the 19th century it was found to have too many vertebrae in its backbone!

class	**Pisces**
order	**Salmoniformes**
family	**Esocidae**
genus & species	**Esox americanus** *grass pickerel* **E. lucius** *northern pike* **E. masquinongy** *muskellunge* **E. niger** *chain pickerel* **E. reicherti** *black spotted pike*

◁ *Gin trap jaws: a pike can eat prey its own size with the help of its well appointed dental set.*

157

Shark's jackal? Pilot fishes swim alongside a whitetip shark Carcharhinus longimanus. *It was believed that pilot fishes guided sharks and rays towards suitable prey, receiving in return protection from enemies because of their closeness to a formidable companion. In reality, however, both fishes are in search of food, the pilot no doubt benefiting from the efforts of its big companion but never leading the foray.*

Fatal shelter

So little is known for certain about the way of life of pilot fishes, and what is known seems extraordinary. It is always supposed that by swimming under the bells of jellyfishes or among the tentacles the baby pilot fishes are protected from enemies. This may be true but they are also exposed to the dangers of being eaten by animals which feed on jellyfishes. These are more numerous than one would think. They include seabirds, such as frigate birds and fulmars and the large fishes, including the large ocean sunfishes. Indeed, there must be the suspicion that these animals may be taking the jellyfishes more for the fishes sheltering under them since jellyfishes are 99% water.

Maximum speed with minimum effort

There is also uncertainty about the protection a pilot fish gets from swimming near a shark. It is usually taken for granted that it does get protection because the shark itself is so voracious that potential enemies are unlikely to come near, but a pilot fish would get no protection from swimming with a whale or a shoal of tuna, less still from a bunch of Sargasso weed, a piece of floating wreckage or a sailing ship. Pilot fishes sometimes accompany large rays which do not afford them any more protection. It may be they sometimes enter the mouths of sharks—but do not live to serve as evidence! All the signs are that pilot fishes have the instinct to swim near a body larger than themselves; when young it is a jellyfish, when adult it is anything from a shark to a schooner. The very early idea that they are friendly to man is not far from the truth if by being friendly we mean they like to keep close to us—or to our ships.

The researches of the Soviet scientist VV Shuleikin, published about 1957, give the only valid reason for pilot fishes swimming beside sharks and ships. Shuleikin calculated that sharks swim three times as fast as a pilot fish possibly can. How then does a pilot fish keep up? Over the surface of any body moving through water there is a 'boundary layer' of water moving forward at almost the same speed as that of the body. This is thickest over the tail half of a shark, which is where a pilot fish usually swims. So presumably the pilot fish is able to travel hundreds of miles in a boundary layer carried along by it, with a minimum of effort.

Pilot fish

The pilot fish is so named because it was believed to guide sharks and whales, and to lead ships or solitary swimmers to land or to a port when they had lost their way. These beliefs go back at least to the time of the Ancient Greeks.

The pilot fish can grow up to 2 ft long. It has a strongly forked tail that is blackish with white tips, a prominent dorsal fin with 4 strong spines in front of it, a prominent anal fin and small pectoral and pelvic fins. Its body is marked with 5—7 dark bands, brownish to black, on a background of white to bluish-white. It is widespread through tropical and temperate seas and is occasionally caught off the coasts of the British Isles.

Accompanying not guiding

So far as one can tell, pilot fish do nothing else than swim about in company with large sharks, whales, giant mantas, large schools of tuna and sailing ships. They have sometimes been caught in mackerel and herring nets. Although the ancient belief is that they lead, and therefore guide or act as pilots, they more commonly swim at the side or even follow other fish. Nevertheless, the association is a very persistent one. Pilot fishes accompanying a shark which is then hooked and hauled on board ship have swum around its tail, the last part of the shark to leave the water, as if distracted. Again, a pilot fish is recorded as following a sailing ship continuously for 80 days. The idea that they piloted a ship to port was fostered to some extent by the way the fish

left it as it neared land or after it had entered harbour. One explanation for this, which does not seem unreasonable, is that they turn away when they feel the freshwater brought down by rivers.

Why pilot fishes should accompany large animals and other objects is something of a mystery. One explanation put forward is that, with their better eyesight, they see food before the shark does and lead it to it, taking the scraps as the shark feeds. This is, however, almost entirely guesswork dating at least from the 16th century when pilot fishes were called the sharks' jackals. What seems more certain is that a pilot fish may suddenly dart from a shark's side to snap up something, but it quickly returns to take up station once more. On the few occasions that pilot fishes have been caught and their stomachs examined they seem to have been eating small fishes rather than scraps of food.

Different babies

Spawning seems to take place in the early summer well away from land. It is always said that the eggs float at or near the surface but a note from the Soviet scientist AI Svetovidov, published in 1958, says that pilot fishes always lay their eggs on the skin of sharks or the submerged hulls of ships. The parents then stay with the eggs until they hatch. The larvae hatching from them are so unlike the parent that they were originally thought to belong to a separate species. They have large eyes and numerous spines on the head, and they shelter under the bells of jellyfishes and among the tentacles of the Portuguese man-o'-war, under bunches of Sargasso weed and pieces of floating wreckage.

class	**Pisces**
order	**Perciformes**
family	**Carangidae**
genus & species	*Naucrates ductor*

Pipefish

These eel-like fishes were given their name in the mid-18th century, when pipe stems were long and very thin. Today they would probably have been called pipe-cleaner fish. The shape of the body has led to such names as worm pipefish, snake pipefish and threadfish. There are over 150 species from 1 to 18 in. long, in tropical and temperate seas. All are long and very slender with long heads, tubular mouths and tufted gills. Instead of scales, they have a series of jointed bonelike rings encircling the body, from behind the head to the tip of the tail. Some have a small tailfin, in others there is none. The main fin is in the middle of the back.

The colours of pipefishes are usually dull: greenish or olive, like the seaweeds among which they live. Most have a slight banded pattern, which is particularly well marked in the banded pipefish of New Caledonia. Some are mottled and spotted. Some pipefishes can change colour, like the Florida pipefish, which is normally dark green when among eelgrass but goes light when among pale green weed. Others in American seas are muddy brown but turn brick-red when among red weeds. The sea dragon of Australian coasts has leaf-like flaps and spines, and it looks like a piece of floating seaweed.

Most pipefishes are marine or estuarine and a few are freshwater. The marine species live chiefly inshore, in shallow seas, but some live at depths of 50 ft or more, and there is also one which lives among the weed of the Sargasso Sea, off the coast of Florida.

Vertical swimmers

Pipefishes in shallow waters and estuaries often live among eelgrass, the only flowering plant in the sea, with long swordlike leaves. They swim in a vertical position with the dorsal and pectoral fins vibrating in time with each other, driving the fish through the water in a leisurely fashion. The vibra-

△ Pipefish portrait: **Syngnathus** shows off its intricate patterning. They often swim in a strange semivertical position with their pectoral fins vibrating so rapidly as to be almost a blur.

▽ A group of banded pipefish **Dunckerocampus caulleryi** patrol a coral reef off New Caledonia in the South Pacific.

tions of the dorsal fin are so rapid as to give the impression of a tiny propeller. They can also slip through the water with snake-like movements of the body. They can turn their heads from side to side, and use these movements for steering. The eyes can be moved independently of each other, as in chameleons. Pipefishes may also be found among seaweeds, at times in rockpools, in holes and crevices, and there are species in tropical seas that live in the interstices in coral rock rubble, almost like earthworms.

Locked jaws

Pipefishes have no teeth and they have been described as suffering from permanent lock-jaw, with the locked jaws supporting the tubular mouth. They cannot pursue prey but do the next best thing. The mouth acts as a syringe and can suck in a small plank-tonic animal from 1½ in. away. When searching for food they may swim upright or in a horizontal position, wriggling and twisting the body, turning the head this side and that and thrusting among tufts of weed or into cracks and crevices. They seem to be selective, apparently scrutinizing each cope-pod or other small animal, tasting the morsel, and ejecting it forcibly if not satisfied. Some spiny larvae of crabs are inspected but left severely alone.

Reversal of sex roles

The main interest of pipefishes is in their breeding. They are related to sea-horses, the males of which have a pouch in which the female lays her eggs. The pipefishes are less simple. In some species the female merely lays her eggs on the underside of the male and there they stick. At the other extreme are species in which the male has a long pouch formed by folds of the surface growing down and meeting in the middle line. There are grades between the two; in some species there are merely two folds of skin in which the eggs lie. All pipefishes have, however, one thing in common: the male carries the burden of the offspring. In many of them the female does all or most of the courting.

Courtship has been fully studied in the Florida pipefish. The two swim round each other in the vertical position but with the head and front part of the body bent forward. They swim in decreasing circles until their bodies touch, when the male bends farther forwards and caresses the female with his snout. He becomes excited, wriggling his body in corkscrew fashion as he continues to caress the female with his snout. Finally, their bodies become entwined, she inserts her ovipositor into his pouch and lays some eggs. The male wriggles his body to work the eggs down into the pouch, after which the female lays more eggs, and this is repeated until the pouch is full. The eggs hatch and the larvae are shot out, one or a few at a time, by the male making convulsive movements. Even when able to swim freely the baby pipefishes may dive back into the pouch in times of danger.

Male mistaken for female

It is not surprising that for a long time the male pipefish should have been mistaken for the female. It was not until 1831 that this was corrected, and it was many years later before they had been studied sufficiently to show how completely the roles of male and female were reversed, even to the female doing the courting. The female broadnosed pipefish of the Mediterranean, for example, courts the male for several hours before he responds. Then he swings his body from side to side, through a right angle, reminding one of the wriggling and swaying of the bashful suitor. This facetious idea receives support from the further behaviour of the female of this species who seems to flirt preposterously, courting one male after another, even mating with several in turn.

class	**Pisces**
order	**Gasterosteiformes**
family	**Syngnathidae**
genera & species	***Nerophis aequoreus*** snake pipefish
	Phycodurus eques sea dragon
	Syngnathus acus great pipefish
	S. floridae Florida pipefish
	S. typhle broadnosed pipefish
	others

△ *Moment of birth for a father! In some pipefish the male carries the developing eggs in a pouch, the female inserting them as the climax to an intimate caressing courtship.*
▽ *Some **Syngnathus griseolineata** have pregnant pouches seen halfway along their bodies.*

Piranha

Few accounts of travel in South and Central America fail to contain some references to the piranha or piraya, the small but allegedly very ferocious fish that inhabits the rivers of this region. In some places it abounds in such vast numbers as to be a serious pest, making the infested streams either very hazardous or quite impossible for fording or bathing.

The name piranha applies loosely to about 18 species, of which only 4 seem to be dangerous to humans. All are members of the genus **Serrasalmus,** having a general similarity of appearance and habits. Some scientists, however, classify them differently. Most of the

species average 8 in. in length but **Serrasalmus piraya,** of the River São Francisco in eastern Brazil, one of the most dangerous, may reach 2 ft. Most of them are olive-green or blue-black above and silvery or dark grey on flanks and belly. Some species have reddish or yellowish tinted fins. The colours seem to vary considerably from place to place and with age. For example, old specimens of the white piranha **Serrasalmus rhombeus,** found in the Amazon system and north-eastern South America, are often dark enough to be called black piranhas.

The body of the piranha is deep, short and rather compressed from side to side. A large bony crest on top of the skull supports a keel on the back, and a similar keel on the belly is strengthened by a firm

Red piranha (**Serrasalmus nattereri**) ; close-up of fish lurking among weeds.

row of enlarged scales bearing sharp, backwardly-directed points, so the deep and heavy forepart of the fish is provided with a cut-water above and below. There is a fleshy adipose fin on the back between the dorsal and tail fins. The tail is slender and muscular and together with the broad, tough, blade-like tail fin helps to drive the body through the water with great force. As in all really swift fish the scales are very small. The most striking feature is the mouth. The massive lower jaw has relatively huge muscles operating it. The teeth are large, flat and triangular with very sharp points. These points merely pierce the skin, the rest is done by the

edges, which are literally razor-sharp. The teeth of the upper jaw are similar but much smaller and fit exactly into the spaces between the points of the lower ones when the mouth is closed. The jaws are so strong and the teeth so sharp that they can chop out a piece of flesh as neatly as a razor. The fact that there is a reliable record of a 100lb capybara reduced to a skeleton in less than a minute shows the efficiency of the teeth.

A few of the smaller species are kept in aquaria, the most popular seen in tropical fish stores and public aquaria being **Serrasalmus nattereri,** the red or common piranha, up to 1 ft long and coloured red on the underside and fins.

Some piranhas are found only in certain river systems, such as the Rio São Francisco, Rio Paraguay or Rio Orinoco, while others range over a wide area.

Water alive with fish

Piranha hunt in shoals, sometimes of several thousands, so in places the water seems to be alive with them. Smaller fishes form their staple diet, but any animal entering or falling into the water accidentally may be attacked. They often attack each other. It is said that they will instantly be attracted by blood in the water but apparently anything out of the ordinary will attract them.

Waterplant hatcheries

It is thought that piranha breed when the rainy season sets in about January or February. The female deposits her eggs on water plants or roots. On hatching, the fry stay attached to the vegetation in clusters until they have absorbed most of the yolk sac, and then become free-swimming. *Serrasalmus spilopleura* is one of the few species which has been seen breeding in an aquarium. The female deposited her eggs carefully on aquatic plants, which is unlike the usual erratic spawning behaviour of most of the other members of its family. The male guards the eggs as well as the fry, when they hatch. These became free-swimming about 5 days after hatching.

Ferocity exaggerated?

The ferocity of the piranha has become almost legendary. Stories are told of a cow or a pig, falling into a river, being stripped to a skeleton in a few minutes. One of the most famous stories is that of a man, fording a stream on horseback, who was brought down and killed by a swarm of piranha. Later the bones of horse and rider were found, picked perfectly clean, the man's clothes undamaged. It is probable that a lot of the stories have been exaggerated. Some travellers now say that they have waded in or swam in rivers infested with piranha shoals and have never been attacked.

◁△*The gates of hell? A piranha displays its razor-sharp teeth which can strip a carcase to the bone with ease.*
▷ *Red piranha—one of the smaller piranhas, popular with aquarium-owners*
◁ *Piranha hurrying away, its mouth full of flesh.*

where hardly a native had not suffered the loss of a toe or finger. It is difficult to know what to believe but there must be some truth in the danger from these fish.

It is possible that the ferocity of the piranha may vary with the species and from place to place, and it may be that they are much more aggressive at the beginning of the rainy season when the males are guarding the eggs. This could also explain why it is that they will attack bathers at certain places in a river, where perhaps they have laid eggs, leaving others unmolested not far away. Nevertheless, those aquarists who keep these fishes admit to treating them with respect and taking extra care in feeding them, or when netting them to transfer them from one aquarium to another.

△ *No table manners. Piranhas have pointed teeth with razor-sharp edges which bite out neat chunks of meat from their victim.*
▽ *Cleaned out. A carcase is left to the flies.*

class	**Pisces**
order	**Cypriniformes**
family	**Serrasalmidae**
genus & species	*Serrasalmus nattereri* red or Natterer's piranha **S.** *piraya piraya* **S.** *rhombeus* white or spotted piranha **S.** *spilopleura* common piranha *others*

Plaice

The plaice is one of the best known of the flatfishes and commercially the most important. It has a flattened body, with the dorsal fin extending from the head almost to the tailfin, and the anal fin from behind the gill cover to the same point. The brownish, upper, or right side is marked with red spots, each of which is surrounded by a white ring in the adult. These may be pale when the fish has been resting on whitish pebbles. The underside is pearly white but can be partially or wholly coloured, a condition known as ambicoloration. It may take the form of scattered brown or black spots or patches on the white undersurface. Alternatively, only the hindend may be completely coloured as on the upper surface, including the red spots. When the pigmentation extends along the whole underside the undersurface of the head is usually white, but in exceptional cases even this may be coloured. The mouth is twisted, with the lower, or blind, side more developed and armed with a greater number of teeth. The small scales are embedded in the skin and there are bony knobs between the eyes. Plaice can grow to almost 3 ft long, but the usual size is much less.

They range from Iceland and the White Sea, along the coasts of Scandinavia, south through the North Sea to the coasts of France and the western Mediterranean. Plaice are not identical throughout their range but split into a number of races. They vary in area of distribution, time and site of spawning, and in their degree of pigmentation.

Living magic carpet

Plaice live on sandy, gravelly or muddy bottoms, slightly buried, swimming just off the bottom at intervals through the day and night. They are said to be demersal or bottom-living fishes. They swim with vertical undulations of the flattened body, like a living magic carpet, then, holding the body rigid, they glide down. On touching bottom they undulate the fins to disturb sand or mud, which then settles on the fins, disguising the outline of the body. In this position a plaice breathes with a suction-pump action of the gill-covers.

Young plaice seem to go into a state resembling hibernation in winter. They remain quiescent in shallow water, slightly buried in the sand. At the appropriate time they move from shallow to deeper water.

Chisel and grinder

The teeth in the jaws of a plaice are chisel-like, but the throat teeth are blunt crushers. The food is mainly small molluscs but other small bottom-living invertebrates, such as worms, are eaten. Plaice swim over the shore at high tide to feed on the cockle and mussel beds. They hunt by sight not raising the head much off the bottom, but shooting forward horizontally with great accuracy to take the prey. Very small molluscs are

△ *Face to face with the adult plaice. With distorted mouth and transposed eye it now lives permanently at the bottom of the sea, lying on its left side.*

In this plaice the upper surface is mottled light grey to suit its background of shell-gravel. The plaice in the bottom picture has a brown mottling because it is lying on differently coloured sandy gravel. A plaice can change its colour and patterns to blend in with its background. A hormone is secreted which alters the shape of the pigment cells thus changing the colour of the plaice's body.

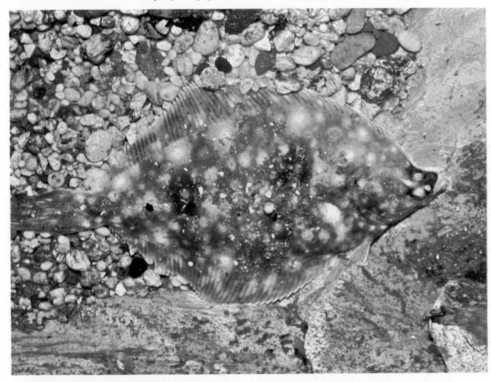

taken whole into the stomach. Larger ones are crushed by the throat teeth. They also bite off the siphons of molluscs or the heads of worms sticking out of tubes.

Prolific spawnings

There is little in their outward appearance to tell male from female, but if at any time they are held up to the light the female roe shows as a small dark triangle. The male roe is a curved rounded line. The males reach the spawning grounds first and are still there after the females have gone. Spawning time differs from one part of the sea to another. Off the east coast of Scotland it is

from early January to May, with a peak in March. In the Clyde estuary, on the west coast of Scotland, it is from February to June. In the southern North Sea it is from October to March.

To spawn, two plaice swim about $2\frac{1}{2}$ ft off the bottom, the female lying diagonally across the male, releasing a stream of eggs while he emits a stream of milt. Spawning lasts less than a minute, after which the two separate and return to the bottom. Each female lays 50–400 thousand eggs, the number depending, it seems, on the length of the fish. The transparent eggs, each in a tough capsule, are just under $\frac{1}{12}$in. diameter.

165

They float at or near the surface, and many are eaten before they can hatch, which they do in 8–21 days, according to the temperature of the water. The larvae are about $\frac{1}{4}$ in. long, without mouth or gills, and with the remains of a yolk sac attached which supplies them with food. This is the most vulnerable part of the life of a plaice. Apart from those eaten by other animals only 1 in every 100 thousand survive the first few weeks of larval life, or 2–5 for every pair of parent plaice. Although this seems disastrous the figures are put in perspective by the knowledge that in one area alone, halfway between the mouth of the Thames and the coast of Holland, 60 million plaice come together each year to spawn. The adults are probably protected by their colour and their habit of lying buried, but seals find them, and predatory fishes, such as cod, eat the small ones.

Plaice are of great economic value but of the tens of millions of plaice eaten each year in Europe, few are eaten at the right moment. Plaice has the best flavour when it is cooked immediately after being caught. The sole however, develops its characteristic taste 2–3 days after death due to the decomposition of the flesh with the formation of different chemical substances.

Baby food

As the contents of the yolk sac are being used up, the larval plaice starts to feed on diatoms. At this stage it has the normal fish larva shape, giving no indication of the adult shape to come. As it grows it graduates from small diatoms to larger diatoms then to larvae of small crustaceans, such as copepods, and molluscs. At this stage an important item is the planktonic food *Oikopleura*. After 2 months the larva gradually metamorphoses into a young flatfish, this takes about $2\frac{1}{2}$ weeks. The body becomes flattened from side to side, the young plaice starts swimming on its side, the skull becomes twisted by growing more quickly on one side than the other, causing the left eye to be swung over to the right side. At the same time the young plaice leaves the upper waters for the seabed, settling on its left side, so its right side and both eyes are uppermost. As these changes have been taking place the young plaice (still only $\frac{1}{2}$ in. long) has been carried by currents to its inshore nursery ground.

The account given above of the feeding of the larvae is only a generalization. The food taken varies in different places, the plaice taking whatever is available. In Scottish coastal waters they eat mainly worm larvae, crustacean eggs and larval molluscs. Off Plymouth, copepods and other small crustaceans are eaten, in the Irish Sea the larvae feed on small copepods, and spores of algae, and in southern North Sea it is mainly *Oikopleura*. The survival of the larvae can be seriously affected if supplies of these foods are low in the area where they form the staple diet of the larvae.

How they grow

After the $\frac{1}{2}$ in. young plaice has settled on the bottom it reaches $2\frac{3}{4}$ in. by the age of 1 year, 5 in. by 2 years, nearly 8 in. by 3 years, $10\frac{1}{2}$ in. by 4 years and 13 in. by 5 years of age. These figures are for females, the males being smaller. On average, the males reach sexual maturity in 2–3 years, the females in 4–5 years. The figures must be read as approximations because average sizes of plaice have been found to vary: 17 in. in the North Sea, 15 in. in the English Channel, 13 in. in the Kattegat and 10 in. in the Baltic. These are, again, merely examples to show how size can vary, with environmental conditions. A 2ft plaice is 20 or more years old, and a 33in. plaice, which is one of the largest recorded, would be about 40 years old.

class	**Pisces**
order	**Pleuronectiformes**
family	**Pleuronectidae**
genus & species	***Pleuronectes platessa***

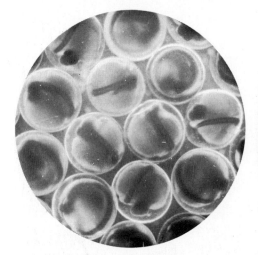
Plaice eggs with developing embryos.

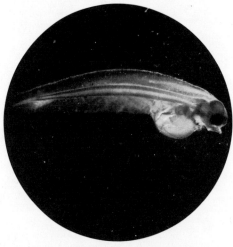
Larva lives in plankton, off its yolk sac.

As yolk sac is used up the mouth develops.

Like many marine fishes the plaice lays a large number of eggs to offset heavy predation. The dramatic part of the life cycle occurs after 2 months in preparation for life on the seabed. The body becomes flattened from side to side; the skull is twisted by growing more quickly on one side than the other, causing the left eye to be swung over to the right side; then the young plaice settles with both eyes uppermost.

Left eye migrates as larva swims on its side.

Eye migration complete, plaice settles on bottom.

Platy

This is a small tropical fish, a long-standing favourite with aquarists who shortened its scientific name **Platypoecilus** *to platy. The scientific name has now been changed to* **Xiphophorus** *but platy still persists as the common name.*

The wild platy is a deep-bodied freshwater fish of Mexico and Guatemala with a single dorsal fin and a relatively large, rounded tail fin. The males are up to $1\frac{3}{4}$ in. long, the females up to $2\frac{1}{4}$ in. The colour is brownish to dark olive on the back, the flanks being bluish and the underside whitish. The fins are almost transparent but in the male the pectoral fins are bluish at the tips and the anal and tail fins have a greenish-white band. Platys have also been called moonfish, a name seldom used now, because of the mark at the base of the tail fin which looks like a crescent moon. This mark is, however, variable and is missing in many individuals, and the colours also are variable even in the wild forms, in which black checkered and red varieties are not uncommon.

A second species, from another part of Mexico, was named **Platypoecilus variatus,** *or the variable platy, because of the range of colours it shows. It is similar to the first species and some experts treat the two as a single species.*

Rainbow colours

Platys are sometimes described as cheerful and not at all shy, which is just what an aquarist likes in his pets. They are easy to keep and they breed well, often producing colour varieties that can be selected and which breed true. They have, in fact, provided more colour varieties than probably any other aquarium fishes. Among these are the blue platys, in a wide range of blues, the red platys which at first were red, stippled with the black dots of the wild platy but are now bred in a pure deep red form, and the black platy which is green or yellow with a broad black stripe along the body, or may be all black except for the fins. Then a European aquarist found a yellow variety among his stock which became known as the golden platy, and when this was crossed with the wild form it gave the wagtail platy, which had a grey body and black fins at first, but later developed a yellow body and black fins. By breeding platys the aquarist was able to amuse himself with producing new colour varieties or even to study heredity.

Brief courtship

As well as eating animals such as water fleas and mosquito and midge larvae, platys take plant food and are especially fond of nibbling the green algae that grow on the sides of an aquarium. Courtship and mating are very brief. As the colours of the male intensify he either swims alongside the female or dashes about encircling her with outspread fins. Then suddenly they

mate, in one quick movement, while both partners are still moving forward. Fertilisation is internal and the babies are born alive, 10—75 at a time. The growth and general welfare of the young depends on the temperature of the water; for example they grow noticeably faster and survive better at 22°C/97°F than at 23°C/103°F.

In aquaria platys readily hybridize with the related swordtails, yet although these two fishes live almost side by side in their natural habitat they have not been known to hybridize there. Careful study of this suggests that courtship is not only a way of bringing the sexes into breeding condition, but is also a kind of language by which members of the species recognize each other and also learn to tell the difference between their own kind and members of another species. The courtship of the platys and swordtails is very similar differing only in a number of small details. None of these is important on its own but together they keep members of the different species apart. In an aquarium, where there is not the same wide choice of partners the 'language' breaks down and a male and a female of different species will come together and breed, giving rise to hybrids.

△ *Through selective breeding platys have probably provided more colour varieties than any other aquarium fish.*

Cancer research

From one such hybridization came a significant discovery of medical importance. When a spotted platy was crossed with a green swordtail the offspring always developed cancerous growths along the sides of the body, remarkably like certain types of cancer in human beings. Here was an example of an heritable cancer—one that could be produced to order merely by crossing two kinds of fishes. This made it possible to study the genetics of cancer in a species that bred rapidly so giving quick results. Comparable studies on humans would prove long and difficult.

class	**Pisces**
order	**Atheriniformes**
family	**Poeciliidae**
genus & species	*Xiphophorus maculatus*

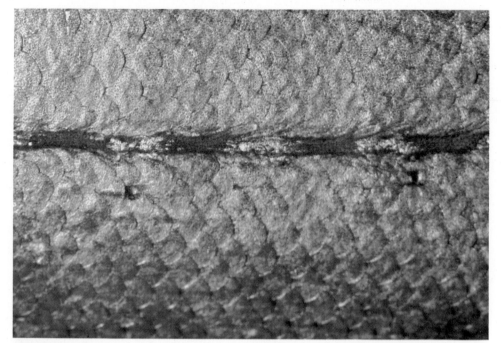

Pollack

*The pollack is probably the most
handsomely coloured member of the cod
family. It can be recognized especially by
the jutting lower jaw and the lack of a
barbel on the chin. Otherwise its shape
conforms to the typical cod pattern, with
three dorsal and two anal fins, small
pectoral fins, and very small pelvic fins
lying under the throat. It is dark green on
the back, shading to light green on the
sides, which are streaked and spotted with
yellow. The belly is white. The fins are
dark yellowish green and the eye golden.
The lateral line is dark and strongly curved
over the pectoral fin. Pollack are up to
2 ft long, exceptionally 2½ ft, and the line-
caught record is 23½ lb. They range from
Norway to the Mediterranean.*

The origins of the name are unknown,
and it has been variously altered in the past
to pollock, podlok and podley. The first
of these names was taken to North America
and given to the coalfish, (shown opposite)
the pollack's nearest relative.*

Midwater feeders

Pollack are more a coastal fish than any other
member of the cod family. They are often
taken by line fisherman from the shore and
when hooked they dive powerfully for
refuge among the rocks. The pollack is not
highly esteemed for its flesh, although it is
regarded as a good sport fish. It is plentiful
especially off Scotland where it is known as
the lythe. Pollack come to the surface at
night and are readily attracted by lights.
Mackerel fishers often catch them with
bright, moving baits. Their preference for
moving bait gives a clue to their food. They
feed in midwater on small fish, especially
sand eels, sprats, herring and pilchard.
They rarely stoop to feed on the bottom, on
worms, crustaceans and molluscs.

Long migrations

Pollack spawn from February to May. The
small, widely separated spawning grounds
are in depths of 300 ft or less. Because the
spawning grounds are so scattered — as far
apart as the western English Channel and
the Hebrides — young pollack make long
migrations as they spread out around the
coasts. The eggs, $\frac{1}{20}$ in. diameter, float near
the surface. The young fish feed on the
seabed, on crustaceans, worms and molluscs.

Loss of scales means death

Many people regard scales as a protection,
so it is worth noting a remark by Dr Douglas
Wilson in his *Life of the Shore and Shallow
Seas*. He points out that when catching
pollack for the aquarium it is better to use
hooks than a net and not to hold the fish in
the hand when removing the hook: 'a torn
jaw nearly always heals but a few lost scales
generally end in death'. Shore fishes, more
liable to be thrown about by waves, do not
easily bruise. They usually have no scales or
only tiny ones embedded in, or else firmly
fixed to, the skin.

class	**Pisces**
order	**Gadiformes**
family	**Gadidae**
genus & species	***Pollachius (Gadus) pollachius*** ***P. virens***

▽ *Pollack, the most handsome member of the cod
family swimming with bib* **Trisopterus luscus.**

△ *The coalfish: North American relative of the pollack: twin fins on the belly, three on the back, slightly jutting lower jaw, and a small barbel on the chin.*

▽ *A shoal of coalfish in east Scottish waters. They feed voraciously on their small relatives.*

Pompadour fish

This fish from the rivers of the Amàzon basin has been described as the noblest among aquarium fishes. Its name of pompadour is then quite appropriate although it is also known as the discus from its shape. The pompadour fish and its relative, which is divided into subspecies known as the green discus, brown discus and blue discus, are almost disc-shaped when fully grown and up to 8 in. long. The long dorsal and anal fins make the otherwise oval body look more nearly circular. The body is covered with small scales but the cheeks and gill covers are more markedly scaly. The mouth is small, with thick lips. There is a single row of small conical teeth in the middle of each jaw and

instead of the usual two pairs, there is a single pair of nostrils.

The colours are not easy to describe because they change with age. A young pompadour fish is brown with several vertical dark bars down each side. At 6 months old, flecks of blue appear on the head and gill covers, and these spread until the sides are coloured with alternating bands of blue and reddish brown and there are nine vertical dark bands, the first running through the eye. The fins become blue at their bases, pale blue and orange on the outer edges, and there are streaks of blue and orange between. The pelvic fins are red with orange tips. The green discus is mainly green with 9 dark vertical bars, the brown discus mainly brown with 9 dark bars and the blue discus brown with 9 blue bars.

△ Turning blue with age, pompadour fish **Symphysodon aequifasciata**. At 6 months the head and gill covers become flecked with blue and this gradually spreads across the sides.

Hanging by a thread

Pompadour fishes usually spend the day sheltering in the shadows of water plants when they are not feeding and they avoid strong sunlight. They eat water insects, especially the larvae of midges and small dragonflies, small worms and similar invertebrates. There is a brief courtship, during which the pair clean the surface of a broad leaf of a water plant. When this is ready, the female lays rows of eggs on it. Sometimes the surface of a stone is used but only after being meticulously cleaned. Once the eggs are laid the male swims over and fertilises them. The parents take it in turn to fan them with their fins and they hatch in about 50 hours. As each baby breaks out of the egg it is removed in the parents' mouth and placed on a leaf, where each hangs by a short thread for the next 60 hours. The parents continue to fan with their fins and when, at the end of this time, the babies are about to swim, they swarm on the side of one of the parents and appear to hang there. After a time the parent gives a wriggle and the fry are shaken off towards the side of the other parent, who is swimming nearby. When 3–4 weeks old the fry become independent and feed on small animal plankton such as very small water fleas or their larvae. At first they are the normal fish shape, if a little plump in the body. The discoid shape comes with age.

Feeding the fry

There can be little doubt that baby pompadours get protection by swarming on the side of the parent, although sometimes they are eaten by the parents, at least in aquaria.

The question is whether they get something more. In 1959 Dr WH Hildeman reported observations that seemed to show that the babies fed on a slime secreted by the parents' skin. This seems to have been accepted by students of tropical fishes. In the 1969 edition of their book *All about tropical fish* Derek McInerny and Geoffry Gerard not only state that the parents secrete a whitish mucus over their bodies but that the fry will eat nothing else. They quote Mr R Skipper 'who has successfully raised several spawnings' and he claims they will not thrive on any alternative food. Indeed, he maintains the only hope of raising them is to leave them with their parents. Against this we have the words of Gunther Sterba, in his *Freshwater fishes of the world*, that not only do the young of some other cichlid fishes cling to the sides of their parents but that at least one aquarist has reared young pompadours away from

the care and protection of parents.

One reason why pompadours are not more often kept in aquaria is that young ones taken in the wild are infected with micro-organisms. The frequent changes of water necessary to keep them in captivity seem to favour the parasites, which get the upper hand and kill the pompadours.

class	**Pisces**
order	**Perciformes**
family	**Cichlidae**
genus & species	***Symphysodon aequifasciata*** brown, green and blue discus ***S. discus*** pompadour fish

▽ *Floating discs of colour,* **Symphysodon discus** *swim in the shadows.*

171

Porcupine fish

When relaxed the porcupine fish has much the shape of an ordinary fish, but when it blows itself up its body becomes almost spherical with long spines bristling all over it. Its tail and mouth look very small compared with this greatly distended body. It has large eyes, and the dorsal, anal and pectoral fins are of moderate size. Porcupine fish are about 1 ft long but may be as much as 2½ ft. In the same family are the burrfishes which have short spines that are always erect.

Doubly armoured

When disturbed or alarmed, porcupine fish inflate their bodies by drawing in water. The body swells, and the spines, which have been lying flat, are erected, standing out almost at right angles to the surface. If a porcupine fish is taken out of water suddenly it blows itself up by drawing in air.

The spines, which may be 2 in. or more long, are sharp and anyone handling an inflated porcupine fish should wear gloves. Each of the long stout spines has a three-armed base, the paired arms of which overlap in the skin with those of their fellows, providing a more or less continuous 'coat of mail'. In some species the spines have only two arms at the base and can be raised and lowered without the fish inflating itself.

Porcupine fish which live in tropical seas, are slow swimmers; they swim by waving the dorsal and anal fins, helped to a small extent by the pectorals, the tailfin being used for steering.

Coral-eaters

The teeth of the porcupine fish form a continuous plate in the upper jaw with another plate in the lower jaw. Each plate has a sharp edge with a crushing surface behind it. The fishes feed by crushing molluscs and by biting off and crushing pieces of coral. The flesh of the coral is digested in the stomach. The stony matter in the coral,

△ *Submarine satellite. Free-swimming porcupine fish **Diodon hystrix** blown up with water.*

crushed by the dental plates, accumulates and one porcupine fish dissected had over 1 lb of crushed coral rock in its stomach.

Escape from shark's stomach

Nothing is known of the breeding habits or the enemies of porcupine fish. There are very few records of what happens when they are attacked but Dr William Beebe, distinguished American marine zoologist, watched some porcupine fishes threatened by a 4ft garfish bunch together for protection. They looked like one large round prickly fish. Then, for no obvious reason, from time to time one would leave the mass and swim away, to be promptly seized and eaten by the garfish. By contrast with this, Robert Hegner, in his *Parade of the Animal Kingdom*, takes the view that if a shark is foolish enough to swallow a porcupine fish it will pay dearly for it. According to him, when the prickly fish reaches the shark's

stomach it gives out what Darwin called a 'most beautiful carmine-red fibrous matter', which is supposed to protect the fish from the shark's digestive juices. Thus protected it starts to cut and crush the wall of the shark's stomach and body wall until it reaches the sea and freedom.

Sharks have been seen to swallow these fishes but we can only surmise what happens inside them. Craig Phillips, in *The Captive Sea*, says that the surest way to ruin a net is to catch a porcupine fish in it. The more tightly the fish feels itself imprisoned the more it blows itself up, and its body remains inflated with the spines sticking out. Phillips deals with this fish by inserting a plastic tube into its throat, which deflates it. Does a shark suffer the fate of the net, as Hegner suggests, or has it some trick of deflating its prickly victim?

Can be poisonous

South Sea Islanders used to make war helmets of the dried skins of porcupine fishes. In the Far East they have been used as lanterns, the dried skin hung up with a candle inside or, in more modern times, an electric bulb in it. In southern England it used to be common to see a dried dead porcupine fish hanging in a fishmonger's shop, acting as a sort of trade sign. These are about the only uses man makes of the porcupine fish except that in some parts of the world it is eaten. It has a bad reputation, however, and care and know-how are needed in preparing the fish for the table because a poison in its liver and skin can contaminate the flesh if the cook does not prepare it correctly.

class	**Pisces**
order	**Tetraodontiformes**
family	**Diodontidae**
genus & species	*Diodon holacanthus* *D. hystrix* porcupine globe fish, others

△ *Porcupine globe fish swimming slowly along the sea bed, its spines lying flat. The spines are only erected when the fish inflates itself.*
▽ *Careful guidance for a porcupine globe fish. Its spines may be up to 2 in. long.*

Port Jackson shark

The prominent nostrils either side of the snout, and a toothy mouth, permanently half open, give the Port Jackson shark a repulsive look when seen head on. It is the best known of 10 species of horn shark. They are 4½—5 ft long and are noted for the shape of their sharp front teeth and jaws.

The heavy head is blunt in front with a terminal mouth and 5 gill slits on each side. A ridge runs over the top of the head beside each eye. There are two dorsal fins, each with a stout spine in front, large pectoral fins and a single anal fin. The shark is brownish-grey.

The Port Jackson shark lives in the seas off southern and eastern Australia. Other species live in the Indian Ocean and in the Pacific, around the Malay Archipelago, Japan, the Galapagos and off California. They are a primitive race of sharks related to those whose fossils date back 150 million years, to the Jurassic period. The large spines associated with the fins were a feature of the forerunners of sharks and also of the earliest known true sharks.

Unusual teeth pattern

These fairly sluggish sharks live near the bottom of shallow waters where they feed mainly on clams and other molluscs, and crustaceans such as crabs, which they crush with their unusual teeth. The upper jaw fits into a deep groove and is attached to the cranium by strong ligaments; the lower jaw is slung from the cranium by the hyomandibular cartilage. The jaws themselves are lyre-shaped and the teeth have an unusual pattern. In the front half of each jaw they are very small, cone-shaped and numerous, crowded together and looking rather like the teeth of a file. About halfway along the jaw they begin to get larger and these larger teeth are abruptly replaced by two rows of very much larger flattened teeth, with 3 or 4 rows of medium-sized teeth beyond these at the rear end of the jaw. Although nothing is known of how these sharks feed it is reasonable to assume that the small teeth in front of the jaw are for seizing prey and passing it backwards into the mouth to be crushed by the large pavement-like grinding 'molars'.

Buried eggs?

There is a sort of courtship in which the male nibbles the female at various points on her body until mating occurs. As in all sharks the male has a pair of claspers associated with the pelvic fins. It used to be thought that these were used to clasp the female during mating but fairly recently it has been realized they are used for transferring sperm to the female, fertilisation being internal. The eggs are laid one at a time at fairly long intervals over a period of 2 months. Each is in a cylindrical capsule of a brown horny material. Around the cylinder, which narrows at the lower end, are two spiral flanges. Each capsule looks very like the end of a post-hole driller. As they float down through the water their shape probably causes them to spiral and it is hard to believe the capsules do not anchor themselves in the sand by this boring, twisting action. If they do, this may be a protection against the eggs being eaten by bottom-feeding fish—such as the Port Jackson shark! The eggs take 7—8 months to hatch, the baby fish being 8 in. long when it leaves the capsule.

Vicious spines

The spines on the front of each of the dorsal fins are formidable weapons. As well as being vicious spikes they are grooved and the tissue in the grooves gives out a poison which can cause painful, possibly dangerous, wounds in human beings. The main enemies of a 5ft shark are likely to be other larger sharks, and fishermen, as their flesh has a

△ *Dozing shark—the slightly grotesque Port Jackson shark has a large bulbous head and a sharp spine on each of its dorsal fins.*
▷△△ *150 million year old fossil relative.*
▷△ *Teeth of Californian horn shark. The small sharp front ones probably seize the prey, the flat back teeth acting as crushing plates.*
▷ *In hand—a female Californian horn shark and two of her strange corkscrew shaped eggs.*

delicate and excellent flavour when cooked. Against other sharks a sluggish swimmer like the Port Jackson shark is unable to use speed to escape. It therefore needs some form of passive defence. It is known that pike learn to leave the 3-spined stickleback alone. Perhaps in the same way other sharks learn to keep out of harm's way by giving the Port Jackson shark a wide berth.

class	**Selachii**
order	**Heterodontiformes**
family	**Heterodontidae**
genus & species	***Heterodontus francisci*** *Californian horn shark* ***H. phillipi*** *Port Jackson shark*

Puffer

Puffers or pufferfishes are known by a variety of other names, such as balloonfishes, swellfishes, globefishes and blowfishes. All express their outstanding feature, of being able to blow themselves up to twice their normal size or more, like the related porcupine fish (page 172). They grow up to a foot or more in length. The body is flattened on the underside, rounded above, when in the normal state, with a large head and large prominent eyes that give an air of perpetual surprise—or of terror, according to the taste of the observer. The dorsal fin is set far back, with the anal fin immediately below it, and these, together with the pectoral fins, are used in swimming. The skin is tough with small erectable spines which take the place of scales. The belly is usually lighter than the back, but in some puffers it is white, while in others the colours of the back extend to the belly with only a slight difference in shade. Those species that live in the open sea are greenish or bluish black on the back. Those living around coral reefs are usually blue or purple brown with white spots, marblings or stripes.

They live in tropical seas, usually inshore among coral reefs, but several species live well up large rivers such as the Nile and Congo.

Unusual swimmer

The shape of these fishes is enough to show they do not swim fast. The gill capacity is low also, showing that they use little energy when swimming. They take prey that does not move or moves only slowly, and they rely for protection on their camouflage and the defensive measure of inflating the body. In fact, the swimming muscles normally found in the rear half of a fish have virtually disappeared but those working the dorsal and anal fins are strongly developed. A puffer swims by waving the dorsal and the anal fins from side-to-side, and this is helped by the pectoral fins. The tail fin is used only as a rudder.

Probably one of the most important items in the lives of these fishes, certainly the most striking to us, is their ability to blow themselves up. Strictly speaking, this is a matter of distending the belly. When in water an 8 in. puffer takes in as much as a quart of water. This is taken into a sac leading from the stomach and kept there by a muscular valve either side of it. When taken out of the water a puffer takes in air instead of water, by a swallowing action in which the floor of the mouth acts like part of a pump, being capable of considerable expansion and contraction. When swallowing air, the puffer makes a kind of gurgling uk-uk-uk noise.

▷ *A fixed stare from a sharp-nosed puffer* **Canthigaster margaritatus**. *This small brilliantly coloured fish with its radiating blue lines is characterised by its long snout.*

△ *The marbled puffer* **Sphaeroides dorsalis**, *normal size, an ordinary small inoffensive fish.*

△ *The same marbled puffer, but now distended with water looking far more menacing and prickly.*

Rabbit-toothed shell crusher

The teeth of a puffer, like those of the porcupine fish, are fused to form a beak. In both upper and lower jaws they form a cutting edge in front and a grinding plate behind. A noticeable difference between the porcupine fish and the puffer is that the cutting portion of these dental plates has a cleft in the middle, giving the puffer, when its mouth is slightly open, a rabbit-mouthed expression. It is because they seem to have four teeth, two in each jaw, that they have been given the name tetraodon or 'four teeth'. The species living around coral reefs use these teeth to hack off pieces of coral. The coral is crushed and the living parts digested. Molluscs are crushed and swallowed, but puffers will eat any small, stationary or slow-moving animal, such as barnacles, sea snails, crabs, or worms. A number of puffers may group together to dismember a crab.

Precocious inflaters

Spawning takes place in late spring and summer. It is not certain, even for those few species in which anything at all is known of the breeding, whether the eggs are laid on the bottom or discharged and later sink. The eggs hatch in 4–5 days, and the baby puffers, ¼ in. long, can inflate their bodies almost from the time they are hatched.

Dangerous moments

Sharks and barracuda will eat puffers, in spite of their protective blowing up, but large fishes have been found with an inflated puffer impacted in the throat. Seabirds would have difficulty in eating a blown-up puffer. Therefore we can assume they have few enemies. However, it is highly likely, although we have no precise information on this, that puffers are vulnerable before they have had time to inflate and after they have deflated. As to this latter condition, there must be a time when muscle fatigue causes the puffer to get rid of the water it has taken in and return to normal size. It is probable, as with frogs and toads that inflate themselves as a protection against enemies, that some time must elapse before the inflation reflex again becomes fully operative. This would be another vulnerable period for the fish.

Poisoned food

The spiny skin and the inflatable body are the first lines of defence. Many puffers have a second line in the poison they carry. We have no information on how this affects animals eating the fishes, but a lot is known about the effects on people. Generally, puffers are among the most poisonous of all marine animals. Some of them carry one of the deadliest poisons in nature, known as tetraodontoxin. Not all species are poisonous though, and not all parts of the body carry the poison, which is usually located in the liver, reproductive organs, intestine, sometimes in the skin, and occasionally in the muscles. The poison from the poison puffer of the South Pacific is said to have been used by the Polynesians for tipping their spears. They call the fish *maki-maki*, meaning deadly death. Tetraodontoxin is a powerful nerve poison which can lead to rapid and violent death. Yet pufferfishes are eaten as a delicacy, known as *fugu*, in Japan, specially trained cooks being employed to prepare the fish. The main skill needed is to remove the liver and other poisonous parts without contaminating the flesh. Even so, there are still many deaths in Japan from eating this, and a Japanese saying, we are told, is: 'Great is the temptation to eat fugu but greater is the dread of dying.'

In the United States puffers taken in the nets were always thrown out as trash fish until it was found that the tail part of the northern puffer made delicious eating. It then became popular, in New York and Boston, as sea-squab.

class	**Pisces**
order	**Tetraodontiformes**
family	**Tetraodontidae**
genus & species	*Tetraodon hispidus* Pacific puffer *T. maculatus* northern puffer others

◁ *Polkadot fish. This wide-eyed youngster, a blue trunkfish **Ostracion lentiginosus** closely related to puffers, is just a solid bony box with holes for mouth, eyes and fins.*

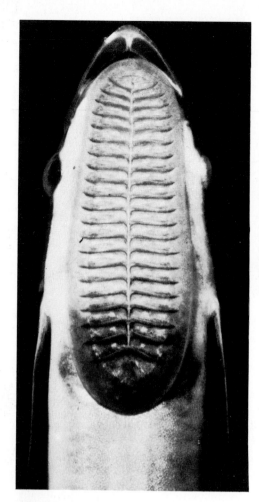

Remora

*The eight species of remora would be quite
ordinary fish but for one thing: where the
first dorsal fin should be is a large oval
sucker. This sucker is flat except for its
raised edges and ridges across its surface,
so arranged that it takes a firm hold which
can be released only by swimming forwards.
As a result, once a remora has fixed itself to
the body of another fish, the forward movement of its host cannot dislodge the remora,
but the remora by swimming forwards can
voluntarily release itself and swim away on
its own. The largest is the striped remora
3 ft long; the smallest is only 7 in. long.*

*Remoras live mainly in tropical seas.
Very occasionally they are found in
temperate waters in summer, and then
only because they are attached to large fish
that have wandered into the cooler seas.*

Ship-holders

Remoras commonly attach themselves to
sharks, and an alternative name for them is
shark sucker, but the smaller ones fasten on
to fishes such as tuna and swordfish. They
will also fix themselves to dolphins, turtles,
and even the hulls of ships. This also led to a
belief in ancient times that one of these
fishes could stop a ship from sailing, which
has given them the name, ship-holder. Mon-
taigne in his 'Essays' says: '. . . in the great
and last naval engagement, that Anthony
lost to Augustus, his admiral galley was
stayed in the middle of the course, by the
little fish the Latins call Remora . . . And

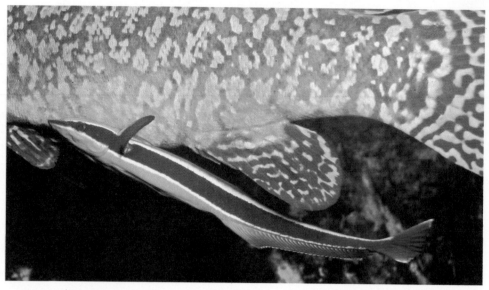

then Emperor Caligula, sailing with a great
navy upon the coast of Romania, his galley
only was suddenly stayed by the same fish'.
A probable explanation for this belief is
that there can occur in the sea patches of
dead water, which will stop the progress of
a ship. When becalmed in this way a man
was sent overboard to inspect the hull. The
chances of his finding a remora fixed on
the hull were high, so the fish was blamed.

Tests were carried out some years ago in
the New York Aquarium to show the
strength of the remora's sucker. One of
these fishes was placed in a bucket of sea-
water. It promptly fastened itself to the
side, and the bucket and its contents, weighing 21 lb, could be lifted by holding the tail
of the fish; another lifted a 24lb bucket.

Transport only

It is generally advocated that a remora
travelling on a shark will share the shark's
food, but that remoras will also eat small
fishes. The current view is that fastening itself
to the shark may be merely an easy way of
travelling, the remora letting go when it
sees a shoal of small fishes passing by. Certainly the remora could not share a dolphin's meal, and there is little guarantee of
food when fastened to a ship's hull. Some
small remoras travel in the mouths or gill
cavities of large manta rays, ocean sunfish,
sword fish and sailfish. They may be helping themselves to their host's food but a
more likely suggestion is that they eat the
parasites in these fish.

Spawning takes place in mid-Atlantic in
June and July and in the Mediterranean in
August and September. The eggs are $\frac{1}{16}$ in.
diameter and the newly hatched larvae are
$\frac{1}{5}$ in. long. The sucker begins to show when
the young fish is $\frac{3}{4}$ in. long, and by the time
it is $1\frac{1}{2}$ in. long the young remora can use its
sucker disc to hitch-hike.

Turtle-fishing

From the earliest times remoras have been
used for catching turtles in places as far
apart as Central America, Japan, East
Africa and northern Australia. We usually
read that a ring is fitted to the remora's tail,
a cord or rope is tied to the ring, and when
a turtle is sighted the fish is put into the
water. It fastens onto the turtle and both are
hauled back into the boat. The fact that a

◁ *The remora's sucking disc is evolved from
part of the dorsal fin. Remora stick to a flat
surface by applying the disc then erecting the
transverse 'ridges' to create a strong vacuum.*
△ *Thick and thin—remora fixed to grouper.*
▷ *Sand shark, with attached remora, chases bait.*

remora can lift 21—24 lb is remarkable but
a turtle worth catching weighs much more
than this. The method used today off Kenya
shows there is more to it than this.

The turtle fishers try to catch their
remoras from large fish, mainly sea perch
and snappers which they catch on a handline. If this fails they fish for remoras from
the bottom of the sea with baited lines. The
remoras are kept in a small stockade in
shallow water until needed. When out after
turtles, the fishermen put them in a basket
hung in the water at the stern of the boat.
On arrival at the place where turtles are
likely to be, a remora is put into the sea and
controlled by a line tied to a ring round its
tail. When the remora has fastened onto a
turtle the fisherman must play his line skil-
fully, not jerking it at all—a delicate operation in a choppy sea. The boat must then be
carefully brought over to the turtle. A small
metal keeper ring is clipped round the line
and a heavy line is run through this with a
grapnel at its end. The grapnel, with four
sharp claws, is let down guided by the keeper
ring. When it touches the turtle it is allowed
to drop beyond it and then it is jerked
smartly upwards. When one of the claws of
the grapnel engages, the turtle is hauled
aboard by three or four men, depending
on the size of the turtle.

There is a belief among the fishermen of
Kizingitini, a small village on an island north
of Mombassa, where the turtle fishing is
carried on, that sometimes a remora will
refuse to work. It is necessary then to give
it a few stripes with a small whip!

class	**Pisces**
order	**Perciformes**
family	**Echeneidae**
genera & species	***Echeneis naucrates*** *striped remora* ***Remoropsis pallidus*** *smallest remora, others*

Rockling

The various species of rockling are small to medium-sized members of the cod family living typically in rock pools, although some are found in deeper waters. Their maximum sizes range from 7 in. to just under 2 ft. The head is large, with a wide mouth, the angle of the jaw often being well behind the level of the eye. There are two dorsal fins. The front one is made up of a relatively long thin ray behind which are low hair-like rays set in a groove in the back. The second dorsal fin, like the anal, is long and of uniform height throughout. The pectoral fin is large and rounded, the pelvic fins, small and situated under the throat. The colour is a shade of brown or red with lighter markings. As in other members of the cod family there is a barbel under the chin, but in rocklings there are also two or more on the snout, and these have determined the names of species such as the three-bearded and four-bearded rocklings.

Rocklings are mainly northern hemisphere fishes, but also extend into the southern hemisphere. In Australia and New Zealand the name has been given to unrelated fishes of the genus **Genypterus**. The four-bearded rockling is found on both sides of the North Atlantic. Rocklings have no commercial value.

Lies on rocks

Rocklings living on the shore lie quietly in rock pools or under curtains of seaweed while the tide is out, and probably also when the tide is in. Even those in the deeper waters seem to behave in much the same way, so the chief feature of their behaviour seems to be to lie still for hours on end with as much of the body as possible in contact with a hard surface. This means they are found typically on rocky coasts, or on rocky seabeds, and not usually on sand or mud, although the three-bearded rockling which lives at depths of 30–200 ft is often caught in nets working over coarse gravel, or even, at times, over sandy bottoms. The depth at which the four-bearded rockling lives varies considerably from one part of its range to another. In the southern parts it goes down to 1 800 ft and it is only occasionally taken in waters of less than 150 ft but in the northern parts of its range it may be found in much shallower water.

Wide diet

The food varies slightly with species and with age but all types take animal food including a wide variety of invertebrates as well as smaller fishes. Its food consists mainly of crustaceans, such as shrimps and prawns, opossum shrimps and crabs. Even hermit crabs are eaten in spite of their protective shells. Some rocklings also eat molluscs and bristle worms.

▷ *A young five-bearded rockling lies curled up on rock encrusted with the red alga* **Lithothammion** *and shells of the worm* **Spirorbis**.

◁ *The name five-bearded rockling is a misnomer, as only one barbel is on the lower jaw, the others point upwards from the snout.*

Mackerel-midges

The three- and the five-bearded rocklings spawn in winter, the northern rockling in March and April and the other species in summer. The eggs, $\frac{1}{30}$ in. diameter, float near the surface and the larvae remain in the plankton. The young of the various species are difficult to tell apart. At $1-1\frac{1}{2}$ in. they form what is known as the mackerel-midge stage, with a green back, silvery sides, and long pelvic fins. It is at this stage they start to sink to the bottom. The mackerel-midge stage was thought for a long time to be a distinct type of fish called *Couchia argenteola*, after Jonathan Couch, a famous English naturalist of the early 19th century.

Prey detector

Rocklings are common fishes to those naturalists who go hunting on the shore. They are less common fishes in the nets of commercial fishermen. The three-bearded rocklings up to 21 in. long and 2 lb 13 oz weight, are often caught on rod and line. The name 'rockling' has been in use at least since the 16th century and the young of these fishes were well enough known to fishermen who gave them the nickname, mackerel-midges. All that is known of their natural history is their extraordinary equipment for catching prey. Their larger relatives in the cod family have a chin-barbel, an organ of touch that helps them find their prey on the seabed. Catfishes are so called because of their 'whiskers', feelers or barbels round the face, used in searching for food in dark and murky places. Rocklings are equally well equipped. In addition they have fair-sized eyes and seem to be able to see well. Over and above this they have a prey-detector, or food-taster, on the back. The front dorsal fin, with the low hair-like rays is constantly vibrated so wafting a current of water into the groove in which this delicate fin is set. The sides of the groove are lined with taste buds, normally found on the tongue, and presumably these detect the presence of food which is out of sight and out of contact with the barbels. So rocklings can afford to lie still doing nothing except taste the water around them for prey. It is feasible also that their very varied diet is made possible by their having so many different ways of detecting their prey.

class	**Pisces**
order	**Gadiformes**
family	**Gadidae**
genera & species	***Ciliata mustela*** *five-bearded rockling* ***Gaidropsarus mediterraneus*** *shore rockling* ***G. vulgaris*** *three-bearded rockling* ***Rhinonemus cimbrius*** *four-bearded rockling, others*

181

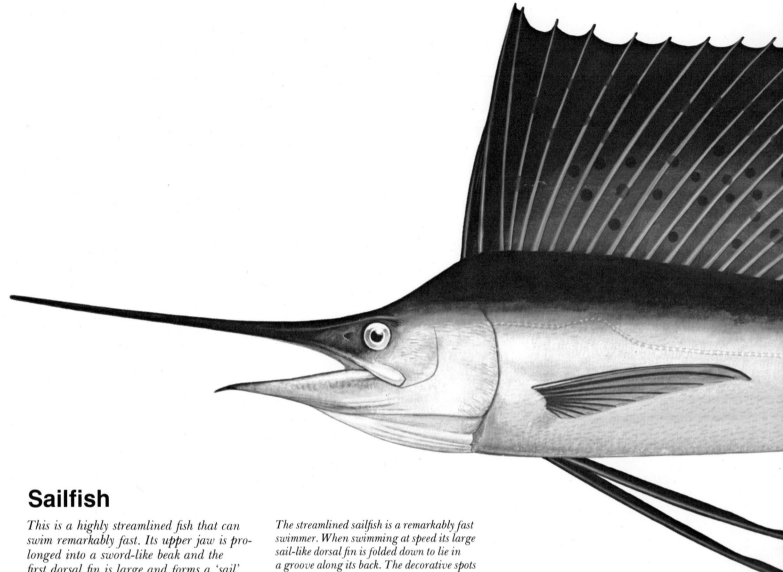

Sailfish

This is a highly streamlined fish that can swim remarkably fast. Its upper jaw is prolonged into a sword-like beak and the first dorsal fin is large and forms a 'sail' when fully raised. The second dorsal fin and the two anal fins are small. The narrow, sabre-like pectoral fin is also small and the pelvic fins, set forward under the throat, are longer, narrower and even more sabre-like. The body is flattened from side to side and the back rises in a hump just behind the head and then slopes gently towards the tail. A pair of 'bilge-keels' on each side lie just in front of the strongly crescentic tailfin. The back is steely blue or blue black and the flanks and belly are silvery, sometimes marked with pale blue crossbands or with rows of pale blue spots. The sail is usually blue with small blue spots. The length of a sailfish has been given as up to 20 ft and the weight as up to 1 000 lb, but the usual length is 7—8 ft and the weight a few hundred pounds.

There is only one species of sailfish, which is found in all tropical waters. They are especially numerous in the Caribbean and off Florida and in warm summers they go as far north as Cape Cod and the Gulf of Maine. In August 1928 a dying sailfish was found in the Yealm River in Devon—the only one known to have strayed to the European coasts of the Atlantic.

The streamlined sailfish is a remarkably fast swimmer. When swimming at speed its large sail-like dorsal fin is folded down to lie in a groove along its back. The decorative spots on this fin are very occasionally present on the body of the sailfish and the fin's rather tattered appearance is just due to everyday wear and tear.

Built for speed

The outstanding feature of the sailfish is its speed. It is one of the fastest fishes, perhaps the fastest of all, with a speed variously given as anything up to 60 knots, although conservative writers prefer to give it as 20—30 knots. When swimming at speed the sail is folded down to lie in a groove along the back. The long pelvic fins are drawn up under the body and the pectorals lie flush with the sides. Frank W Lane in his *Nature Parade* recalls that George G Schutt made various tests between 1920 and 1925 at the Long Key Fishing Camp in Florida as a result of which he believed the fish could swim at 60 mph. The 'sailfish was timed on a thin loose line. It took 100 yards in 3 seconds, which means a speed of nearly 70 miles an hour!' A sailfish may, by the speed at which it appears at the surface at one place after another, give the deceiving impression that there is more than one fish in the water.

Sailfishes live in the turbulent, well-oxygenated waters of the oceans. They have sieve-like gills which have a large surface for taking in oxygen—necessary when travelling at great speed. It seems that very high speeds are used only in short bursts and that the conservative 20—30 knots may refer to its cruising speeds. It also seems that the sail is erected, as it is in most fishes, at the end of a burst of speed, to prevent rolling and yawing. Sir Stamford Raffles, founder of Singapore, wrote that the fish 'hoists a mainsail, and often sails in the manner of a native boat, and with considerable swiftness . . . when a school of these are under sail together they are frequently mistaken for a fleet of native boats.'

Although they can swim so rapidly, sailfishes seem not to travel very far as a rule. The vertebral column is especially strong; the vertebrae are tightly interlocked by horizontal processes and the dorsal and neural spines are flattened, forming a strong and rigid backbone. These flattened surfaces also provide anchorage for the powerful muscles which drive the fish through the water.

Spear-like beaks

The upper jaw of the sailfish has many small teeth and these extend forward onto the lower surface of the sword-like beak. Sailfishes eat other fishes, especially flying fishes. They also eat the deep water false albacore, the suckerfishes *Liparis* known as sea snails, and the gurnard-like sea robins (Triglidae) that live on the bottom. They may catch needlefishes and anchovies. They also eat squid and octopus, although how they catch them is a matter for debate. Some say they beat them with their spear-like beaks, while others maintain that they snap them up with their teeth. Probably they do both, but when fishes are used as bait they are always bitten on both sides by the sailfish. When a sailfish attacks a shoal of small fishes it swims round the shoal with its dorsal fin half-raised, driving the fishes into a compact mass. Then it swims through this mass, thrashing vigorously from side to side with its beak, killing or stunning large numbers. After this the sailfish swims around slowly picking up the fishes as they sink.

Development of the dorsal fin

Many baby sailfishes have been netted and their development studied. At $\frac{2}{5}$ in. long their heads make up $\frac{1}{3}$ of their length, the jaws are of equal size and form only a short beak. The eye is large, there are short bristles on top of the head and two spiny spikes project backwards from each gill-cover. At $\frac{1}{2}$ in. long the upper jaw is slightly longer than the lower jaw and the dorsal fin is beginning to be sail-like. When it is 2 in. long, the dorsal fin rises high over the back. In these early stages the sailfishes eat tiny crustaceans in the plankton, especially copepods.

Scientific study

The sailfish gives exciting sport for the sea-angler, as it leaps out of the water and thrashes around, putting up a spectacular fight. In one year alone, in the vicinity of Palm Beach, Florida, 2500 sailfishes were caught. This is not as bad as it reads for although the sailfish is good to eat, and although there is a Sailfish Derby, with awards for the best catches, scientific study and conservation are both linked with the sport. Over 80% of the hooked sailfishes are not pulled aboard but are pulled to the side of the boat and tagged, with a cattle ear-tag fastened in one of the fins. The hook is then removed and the fish freed. Information on the migrations of sailfishes will thus be steadily accumulated, but above all the numbers of sailfishes will not be reduced. To encourage the liberation of fishes points are awarded by the fishing and conservation clubs for the numbers and sizes of the catches—with additional points for those set free again.

class	**Pisces**
order	**Perciformes**
family	**Istiophoridae**
genus & species	***Istiophorus platypterus*** *sailfish*

Sawfish

The sawfish, of which there are six species, looks like a shark but behaves like a ray and is related to the guitarfish. Sawfishes have a shark-like tail, a somewhat flattened body and large pectoral fins which are not joined to the sides of the head as in rays and guitarfishes, but like them the gill openings are on the underside of the head. The snout is drawn out into a long flattened blade with a row of strong teeth sticking out sideways on either side. These are not the true teeth, although they look like teeth and have dentine, enamel and a pulp cavity. They are like the dermal denticles, or skin-teeth, characteristic of sharks and rays. The flat blade of the sword, known as the rostrum, is made of cartilage, like the rest of the skeleton, and the teeth are in deep sockets in this. Sawfishes are up to 20 ft long and occasionally one of 30 ft or more is recorded, the sword occupying $\frac{1}{4}-\frac{1}{3}$ of this length. Weights of up to 5 000 lb have been recorded.

Sawfishes live in coastal waters in all warm seas and sometimes even go well up rivers into freshwater. The common sawfish **Pristis pectinatus** of the Gulf of Mexico goes well up the Mississippi, and there is a population in Lake Nicaragua that is believed, probably wrongly, to be land-locked. Another species, **P. perroteti**, goes well up the Zambesi and a third **P. cuspidatus** goes up the larger rivers of the Indian Peninsula.

There is also a family of saw sharks Pristiophoridae. These are true sharks with gill openings on each side of the head. They are not more than 4 ft long. The teeth in their saws are alternately large and small.

△ *Resting sawfish. The teeth on the edge of its vicious looking saw, although not its true teeth, are used when the saw is moved rapidly from side to side to stun and wound small fishes; the true teeth of the mouth then take over.*

◁ *A huge sawfish looms into view in the fishbowl tank at Marineland. Its large pectoral fins are not joined to the head as in the ray. Despite its fierce reputation, the sawfish is fairly docile in captivity.*

Automatic response

Little is known of the daily habits of sawfishes although they must be fairly numerous where the bottom is muddy. In the Indian river, in Florida, for example, one fisherman caught 300 in a season. In the sea, where food is more abundant, they are probably even more numerous. Sawfishes use their saws for grubbing about in the mud for molluscs, crustaceans and sea-urchins. Their true teeth are small with blunt crowns and are set in rows in the jaws, forming a pavement. They are used for crushing and grinding such things as shellfish. There is another method of feeding, like that used by sailfishes (page 182),

where the sawfishes swim into a shoal of smaller fishes and strike left and right with their saws, killing and stunning the fishes, then eating them at leisure. In the California oceanarium captive sawfishes are fed by hand by the diver attendants. The only thing the divers need to guard against is being struck by the saw when putting food into a sawfish's mouth. Apparently the sight of a fish nearby makes it move its saw from side to side — an automatic response.

Born with soft saw

The females give birth to live young, the eggs being incubated within the maternal body and hatching just before they leave it. The saw is still soft at birth and the teeth barely project through it. Moreover, they are covered with a membrane until the baby sawfish is born. The size of a 'litter' can be gauged from the few instances in which pregnant females have been caught and examined. One, estimated to weigh 5 300 lb, towed a fair-sized boat for several miles before she finally gave in. She had several young in her nearing the time of birth. Another sawfish, 15½ ft long, when examined was found to contain 23 young.

Dangerous?

In some parts of India sawfishes are regarded with fear because it is believed they will attack a man. There is one report of a large sawfish cutting a bather in two. Roger A Caras in his book *Dangerous to Man* does not accept this because he states that sawfishes are harmless. There is, presumably, the chance of any large animal killing someone accidentally, and we can only say that sawfishes are far more likely to be killed by man than the other way round. One danger to them is that their saws were once collected as curios. On the Mekran coast in India, according to Day, the authority on India's fishes, saws, presented by fishermen of all religions, were piled round the outsides of the temples or hung inside. The aboriginals of the Andaman Islands, in the Indian Ocean, apparently made a present of a saw to anyone they wished to honour.

class	**Selachii**
order	**Hypotremata**
family	**Pristidae**

Scad

Scad is the original name for the horse mackerel. It looks quite like a mackerel but differs especially in having the lateral line covered from the head to the tail with a row of flat bony plates, those along the hind part of the body being spiny. The head is large, the first dorsal fin is spiny, the second long and the tailfin slightly forked. The anal fin is long and its first two spines are separated from the rest of the fin. The pelvic fins lie forward, below the medium-sized pectorals. The body is compressed from side to side, up to 16 in. long, blue-grey in colour with a greenish tinge on the back, silvery on the flanks and white on the belly.

Another name for the scad is cavally, from the Portuguese for mackerel, cavalla, but the name in another form is now used for a related species, the cavallas which, with the jacks of the same family, are the most valuable food fishes in the Philippines. Both types ascend the River Pancipit to Lake Taal, where they remain for a while before returning to the sea. Some of the other 200 species in the family are also called jacks, such as the yellow jack **Gnathodon speciosus,** a 3ft fish of the Indo-Pacific, yellow with dark bands, but pure golden when young. Other species are the amber jacks, which lack the bony plates over the lateral line. An example is **Seriola dumerili** of the Atlantic. A Pacific relative is the yellowtail **S. dorsalis,** off the coasts of Mexico and California. Related to all these are the pompanos, such as the Atlantic pompano **Trachinotus carolinus** of the North American seas and the lookdown **Selene vomer** of the North Atlantic with eyes set so high up on its head it seems to be looking down superciliously on all around it. Another relative is the pilot fish (page 158).

The scad and two other species of the same genus, **Trachurus,** live mainly in European waters, including the Mediterranean and Black Seas.

▷ A shoal of torpedo-shaped common scad. They live in coastal waters in summer but move to deeper waters in winter when they are found down to a depth of 330 ft. They live mainly on the European side of the Atlantic but are also found on the American side. These 16in. long, blue-grey fish are tinged with green on the back, are silvery on the flanks and are white on the belly. They resemble the mackerel but differ in having a sharp ridge of bony plates or scutes along the entire length of the lateral line. Those at the front end are flat whereas those at the rear end are sharp. The scutes are worn down during growth, so the young fish have much sharper ones.

Carnivores from babyhood

The scad, which moves about in shoals, lives in coastal waters in summer, and retires to deeper water, down to 330 ft, in winter. Scad, particularly the young fishes, are often very numerous in summer in shallow seas with sandy bottoms, as in the North Sea off Holland. They feed on other fishes, especially herring, sprat, pilchard and anchovies, as well as squid and crustaceans. In the North Sea and in similar areas they spawn from June to August, with a peak in July. The eggs, $\frac{1}{30}$ in. diameter, contain a reddish oil droplet so they float near the surface. The larvae on hatching are $\frac{1}{10}$ in. long. They do not grow their fins until they are four times this length. They feed at first on diatoms, copepods and crustacea larvae as well as fish eggs and the larvae of other species. In the following winter their diet changes to mainly small fish and euphausians.

Fish meal fisheries

There are large commercial fisheries for scad off Spain and Portugal but elsewhere they are caught only incidentally with other catches, as they are not considered particularly palatable and are used only for fish meal, especially the young scad. Their growth rate has been studied in Spanish waters: the young fishes reach $3\frac{1}{2}-8$ in. at the end of their first year; $8-10$ in. at 2 years; and reach a length of $10\frac{1}{2}$ in. in their fourth year.

Jellyfish sanctuary

Little is known of the actual enemies of scad but it is reasonable to assume that they are eaten when adult in large numbers by predatory fishes, dolphins and porpoises. When they are $1\frac{1}{4}-1\frac{3}{4}$ in. long they have the fairly persistent habit of seeking refuge under the bells of jellyfishes. The young scad shelter under the medusoid, or bell-shaped jellyfishes, which include the common jellyfish *Aurelia aurita*, the blue jellyfish *Cyanea capillata* and the remarkable *Rhizostoma octopus*. They swim just in front of the jellyfish they have adopted and when alarmed dive for protection among its tentacles. They are said to repay their protector by eating its tentacles, even its eggs! It is possible, although this has not been proven, that the young scad eat other small animals sheltering alongside, the jellyfish thus acting as a floating larder.

class	**Pisces**
order	**Perciformes**
family	**Carangidae**
genus & species	***Trachurus mediterraneus*** *Mediterranean scad* ***T. picturatus*** *Bay of Biscay scad* ***T. trachurus*** *common scad*

187

Scalare

The scalare or freshwater angelfish often looks like a painted or artificial fish because it keeps so still. It is a very popular aquarium fish and is known to millions who perhaps have no other interest in fishes except to eat them. Its body is very flattened from side to side, and it is only a little longer than it is deep, even without the very tall dorsal fin and the equally prominent anal fin. These two fins are the 'wings' that gave the fish its other common name.

The body is silvery with a bluish sheen, and pale reddish-brown blotches. There are darker markings on top of the head, and the eye is red. Dominating these are the black bands running across the flanks. One of these bands extends up into the dorsal fin and down into the anal fin. The delicate tail with its two points and the long filamentous point on the anal fin give an impression of flow in the fish. The pelvic fins also are long, thin and backward-flowing. This gives the scalare, even when stationary, an appearance of arrested movement.

The usual aquarium scalare is about 2 in. long but the fish may be up to 6 in. long and 10 in. high including the fins.

The three species, which may prove to be no more than related subspecies, live in the rivers of northeast South America, in the Amazon, Orinoco and Tapajoz rivers. The three forms are known respectively as the scalare or angelfish, the lesser angelfish and the deep angelfish. They differ markedly in shape and colour yet readily interbreed, producing fertile offspring. They should not be confused with the marine angelfish. The distinction is made clear on page 12.

Inconspicuous among water plants

The body of a scalare is so flat that when the fish is viewed head-on it seems to have height but no breadth. When viewed broadside on the dark bands serve the same purpose as the stripes of a tiger, making the fish inconspicuous among water plants. This is probably why the scalare, although it tends to swim little for much of its time, so giving an impression of habitual immobility, is easily scared by a sudden movement when in a tank with no water plants. It is apt then to dash itself against the glass sides in panic.

Scalares eat small animals, such as water-fleas, freshwater shrimps, various insect larvae and sometimes tiny fishes.

Devoted parents

The difficulty of telling male from female is increased by the fact that in the breeding season both sexes develop a genital papilla. The males at this time may make creaking sounds with their jaws, either at a rival male or as part of the courtship. The female lays her pale yellow, oval eggs, $\frac{1}{25}$ in. long, on the broad leaf of a water plant which she and her mate first clean of small algae and grains of sediment. They both fan the eggs continually during the 24–36 hours before they hatch. The baby fishes are helped out by their parents which chew at the egg 'shells' and as each youngster leaves, one of the parents takes it in its mouth and spits it onto another leaf where it hangs by a short thread. The wriggling of the baby fishes as they hang from the leaf helps to develop their muscles and also circulates the water around them. The parents continue to care for their brood for the 4–5 days during which they are hanging from the leaf. If one falls one of the parents swims down, picks it up in its mouth, and spits it back onto the leaf.

At first the baby scalares are tadpole-like, $\frac{1}{8}$ in. long, with a well-filled yolk sac on which they feed during their first days. By the time they are 12 days old, and $\frac{1}{3}$ in. long, they look like miniature minnows, quite unlike the adult. At 20 days and $\frac{1}{2}$ in. long the body is beginning to deepen. Then 8 days later the fins are noticeably larger and the pelvic fins are growing long. When 36 days old and $\frac{3}{4}$ in. long the baby scalare is almost the same shape as its parents.

Few enemies?

Scalares, although so commonly kept in aquaria, have been little studied in their native habitat. We can, nevertheless, suppose that they have few enemies. They live in quiet streams and backwaters with plenty of water plants where the fishes stay almost motionless for hours on end. Their black stripes look like shadows among the vertical stems, and, as if to increase the camouflage effect, the fish's fins sway gently, like water plants in a slight current.

Confusion in names

When first introduced to aquarium keepers these fishes were called angelfishes. Because there were other fishes, notably the marine angelfishes, already bearing this name, to avoid confusion they were called scalare, after their scientific name *Pterophyllum scalare*. Then it was found that this species was very rarely imported by dealers and that the one most people were keeping in their aquaria was *P. eimekei*, the lesser angelfish. But the name stuck, and scalare became an accepted name for it. Because these fishes breed so readily several aquarium varieties have been produced, one being completely melanistic. These are not called black scalares but black angels.

class	**Pisces**
order	**Perciformes**
family	**Cichlidae**
genus & species	***Pterophyllum altum*** *deep angelfish* ***P. eimekei*** *lesser angelfish or scalare* ***P. scalare*** *angelfish or scalare*

▷ *Motionless* **P. scalare**: *the name angelfish comes from the dorsal and ventral wing-like fins.*

Scorpionfish

Some of the most beautiful as well as the most ugly fishes in the world are found among the 300 species of scorpionfishes. They live mainly in temperate seas, although a few live in the tropics. The family also contains some of the most poisonous fishes in the world, including the stonefishes (see page 214).

One of the most showy scorpionfishes is called the turkeyfish, lionfish, zebrafish, dragonfish or butterfly cod. The body, up to 1 ft or more long, has striped, zebra-like markings. The massive head is irregular in shape with eyes set high up, and the mouth wide and sloping down at the corners. All the fins are divided into ribbon-like strips, those of the pectoral fins being longer than the body. Among these are poison spines, 13 in the dorsal fin, three in the anal fin and one in each pelvic fin. The colours may be maroon with grey stripes, rose with blue-white stripes and brown with yellow stripes.

Another member of the family is the California scorpionfish, also known as a sculpin, a name that should properly be reserved for members of the bullhead family. It was the large ugly head of a bullhead flanked by large rounded pectoral fins and may be a foot or more long. Its body is decorated with warts, flaps and frills which with its mottled colour makes it hard to see among the seaweeds on which it lies. An even more decorative species, not only with flaps and frills but with tiny hooks and barbs, as well as patches of colour, is the barbfish. It has the same shape as the California scorpionfish but shows in patches nearly all the colours of the rainbow, from blue patches on the head, red around the mouth and throat, to a motley of reds, yellows, browns and purples on the body and fins. The orange scorpionfish, less colourful but with the same shape, is a brownish orange. In the sailback scorpionfish the dorsal fin is more like a sail than a row of spines and its colours are sombre browns, yellow and orange. The last of this family to be mentioned here are the Norway haddock or rosefish, up to 3 ft long, reddish and looking more like a normal fish because it lacks the flamboyant fins of the others; and its two near relatives the redfish and the bluemouth.

The California scorpionfish lives off the Pacific coast of North America, the barbfish off the Atlantic coast of tropical America, from New Jersey to Rio de Janeiro. The sailback scorpionfish lives around the Philippines, the rosefish on both sides of the north Atlantic and the redfish and bluemouth in the eastern north Atlantic.

▷ *The striking markings on this **Pterois antennata** act as a warning to any would-be predator.*

Poison spines

Scorpionfishes are found at varying depths, some in shallow waters, others in deep waters. In general, the deeper the water in which they live the more they tend towards a single colour. The shallower the water the more broken up and varied are the colours of the body, the more elaborate the fins, and the more irregular is the body surface. The shallow water members of the family are also more poisonous, but none is as poisonous as the stonefish. There is another difference between the stonefish and other members of the family. The stonefish raises its spines and then remains completely still when it is approached. The turkeyfish, and others, raise their spines and move them and also change the position of the body to present their spines to the best advantage to an intruder. They may even jab at the intruder with their spines. Most of them give painful wounds, but no more. The pain from a California scorpionfish, for example, lasts an hour, although the swelling may last much longer.

Small fishes the target

In all scorpionfishes the poison spines are used for defence only, not for killing prey. They feed mainly on smaller fishes. Those living in shallow waters mainly lie concealed on the bottom, snapping up small fishes that swim past their mouths. They also take shrimps, prawns and other crustaceans. Those scorpionfishes, such as the Norway haddock and the related redfish, that swim actively, feed on a wider variety of small crustaceans as well as fishes, but as they grow larger tend to eat a greater proportion of fishes.

Balloons of spawn

Most scorpionfishes give birth to live young, the eggs hatching inside the female's body. There are reports of single females giving birth to thousands at a time. For example, a 13in. female was said to give birth to 20 000. The California scorpionfish, one of the few members of the family to lay eggs, spawns several times during the summer. The eggs are laid embedded in two hollow pear-shaped balloons of jelly, joined at their small ends. These float at the surface, but the baby fishes, as they hatch, sink to the bottom of the seabed.

Untapped resources?

In spite of their poisonous spines and their unappetizing appearance, the flesh of scorpionfishes is palatable, and the redfish is fished commercially. One of the actively swimming members, the Norway haddock, has received its common name because it is fished and sold as a food fish, although it is not commercially important. Its very close relative, sometimes also known as the Norway haddock but more usually as the redfish, has achieved considerable importance in the last 20 years. It lives down to 1 500 ft and is widely distributed over the North Atlantic. Although it looks more like a normal fish than some of the shallow-water scorpionfishes, its red colour might possibly deter the public from eating it, although served. up as 'fish fingers' it is eaten and enjoyed by millions. Fishery experts suspect that the populations of redfish are far larger than we suppose. For one thing, in the North Atlantic they form the food of sperm whales, which suggests there are large numbers of them. So redfish may be one of the untapped harvests of the sea that may in the future be used to feed the untold millions of human beings that, we are told, will be crowding our planet in the 21st century.

class	**Pisces**
order	**Scleroparei**
family	**Scorpaenidae**
genera & species	***Helicolenus dactylopterus*** *bluemouth* ***Pterois volitans*** *turkeyfish* ***Scorpaena brasiliensis*** *barbfish* ***S. guttata*** *California scorpionfish* ***S. scrofa*** *orange scorpionfish* ***Sebastes marinus*** *redfish* ***S. viviparus*** *Norway haddock* ***Tetraroge barbata*** *sailback scorpionfish* *others*

▽ **S. ustulata** *lurks in a rock crevice. Its body is decorated with warts, flaps and frills which camouflage it among the seaweeds on which it lies.*

 A woeful look from a buffalo sculpin. The prominent horn-like spine on each gill-cover is the characteristic feature of this 12in. species from the American Pacific.
▷ The bizarre grunt sculpin, a fish with many comical facets. It moves across the sea bottom in a series of short jumps helped by the finger-like tips of the pectoral fins. It is able to move each eye independently and finally, it grunts when taken out of the water.

Sculpin

The name 'sculpin' has a mixed history. It is a corruption of the name Scorpaena, meaning a scorpionfish, but in the last 200 years it has become widely used in the United States for certain members of the bullhead family, and it is in this sense that it is used here.

Sculpins live in shallow seas, rockpools, and estuaries. Those living in freshwater are like the small fishes known as bull-heads in Britain and live in much the same way. Sculpins have large heads and the eyes are placed high up on the head. There are sharp spines just in front of the gill-covers. They have two dorsal fins that are either entirely separate or are separated by a notch. The front dorsal fin is spiny, the rear one soft-rayed. The pectoral fins are fairly large and fan-shaped, and the pelvic fins may be lacking but if present each has a spine and 2—5 soft rays. The skin is scaleless or has very small scales. Sculpins are mainly olive to brown, variously spotted or mottled with black, white or subdued blues and purples.

The common staghorn sculpin of the Pacific coast, from Alaska to Baja California, is plentiful in bays all along that coast. It is up to 6 in. long and has hooks on its gill-covers. The buffalo sculpin, 12 in. long, has the same range. It has a prominent hornlike spine on each gill-cover. Another type with a long horn-like spine is the longhorn sculpin of the Atlantic coast of North America. The crab-eating cabezon, ranging from British Columbia to Baja California, is 30 in. long and has a poisonous roe and

green flesh which is nevertheless good to eat. The Atlantic sea raven is purple-red to chocolate coloured, but may be yellowish-brown. It has fleshy tags on the head and there are flaps along its dorsal fin so the fish looks as if it were torn. When taken from water, it can swallow air, blowing itself up like a balloon—to float helplessly when put back.

Affected by tides

Sculpins are bottom-living fish, lurking among stones, and moving swiftly through the water when disturbed. They feed on smaller fishes as well as small invertebrates, such as crustaceans, molluscs and worms. The crab-eating cabezon will take almost anything that moves: sea snails, crabs, lobsters, worms, even small octopuses, and it will also eat the dead flesh of fish, clams and mussels. Sculpins, especially the larger individuals, come in and out with the tide, but some of them, mainly the smaller ones, stay in the deeper rockpools when the tide recedes. Some species, like the sea raven, avoid warm water as they go to deeper water offshore in summer returning inshore for the winter. Although sculpins live mainly in the tidal zones they favour certain places and go to these when the tide is in. In fact they seem to have a homing instinct.

Sea raven's eggs

Although the breeding habits vary slightly from species to species those of the sea raven can be taken as fairly typical. The females lay their eggs, about $\frac{1}{6}$ in. diameter, from mid-October to late December. The eggs are pale yellow to orange, and stick to solid objects. In one area, for example, the sea raven lays its eggs along the branches of a finger-shaped sponge. The eggs hatch after several months, the baby fishes being $\frac{1}{2}$ in. long. Growth is relatively slow, a length of only 6 in. being reached at 1$\frac{1}{2}$ years.

Strange breeding habits

To the same family belongs the 3in. grunt sculpin. It has such extraordinary breeding habits that it deserves special mention. It is called 'grunt' for the noise it makes when taken from the water. It avoids warm water in the same way as some of the other sculpins. It lives from Alaska to British Columbia in shallow water and is often found in rockpools, but southwards as far as northern California it may live to depths of 600 ft. It has an odd way of jumping along over the bottom on the tips of its pectoral fins, and when it does swim it does so awkwardly. Cecil Brousseau, Director of the Aquarium in Tacoma, has described to Earl S Herald, author of Living Fishes of the World, how, in the breeding season, from August to October, the female chases the male until she drives him into a crevice. She then mounts guard to see he does not escape. Her only purpose is to make sure he is around to fertilise her eggs—or, at least, that is what it looks like. Certainly she lays her eggs on the walls of his 'prison' and when he has fertilised them she no longer detains him.

class	**Pisces**
order	**Scorpaeniformes**
family	**Cottidae**
genera & species	**Enophrys bison** buffalo sculpin **Hemitripterus americanus** sea raven **Leptocottus armatus** staghorn sculpin **Myoxocephalus octodecemspinosus** longhorn sculpin **Rhamphocottus richardsoni** grunt sculpin **Scorpaenichthys marmoratus** crab-eating cabezon, others

Seahorse

The seahorse is a strange animal which looks like the knight of a chess set, but that is not the end of its oddities. It can wrap its tail round a seaweed or similar object, as a South American monkey wraps its tail round a branch. Each of its eyes is on a turret and can move independently. Although many other fishes can also move their eyes independently, this ability is more pronounced in seahorses. A final oddity is that the male carries the babies in a pouch.

A seahorse has a large head with a tubular snout, a moveable neck, a rotund body and a long tapering, slender tail, with a total length of not more than 8 in. The neck, body and tail are marked with circular and longitudinal ridges, on which there are bony bumps, so the fish looks almost like a wood carving. There is a pair of small pectoral fins and a single small dorsal fin. The colours vary widely but are mostly light to medium brown, scattered with small white spots, and often there are ornamental fleshy strands.

There are 20 species, half of which live in the Indo-Australian region. The others live off the Atlantic coasts of Europe, Africa and North America, with two species on the Pacific coast of America.

Swimming upright

Seahorses live in shallow inshore waters among seaweeds or in beds of eelgrass in estuaries. They swim in a vertical position, propelling themselves by rapid waves of the dorsal fin. When swimming at full speed this fin may oscillate at a rate of 35 times a second—which makes it look like a revolving propeller. The pectoral fins oscillate at the same rate, and the head is used for steering, the fish turning its head in the direction it wants to go. When a seahorse clings to a support with its tail it still keeps its body upright. If the fins are damaged they can be regenerated relatively quickly.

Tiny mouth

The seahorse eats any kind of swimming animal small enough to enter its tiny mouth. Prey is located by sight and quickly snapped up, or is sucked in from as much as 1½ in. away. It is mainly tiny crustaceans such as copepods, but baby fishes are also eaten.

Male courts male

Breeding starts with males going through actions that look like a courtship, and a male seahorse of one species has even been seen to court a male of another species. This courtship probably brings him into condition to receive the eggs. He pairs up with a female, either swimming in front of her but without actually touching her or, in some species, the two may entwine tails. He seems to be bowing to her, but this is actually a pumping action to drive the water out of the pouch on his belly. The female inserts her long ovipositor into the opening of the pouch to lay her eggs, as many as 200 in

△ *Pregnant male seahorse* **Hippocampus erectus,** *his belly pouch extended with eggs.*
▽ *Proud parent with day-old young seahorses.*

▷ *The scene is set for the seahorse ballet; one wraps its prehensile tail round another.*
▽ *Young seahorse specimen (approx. ×7).*

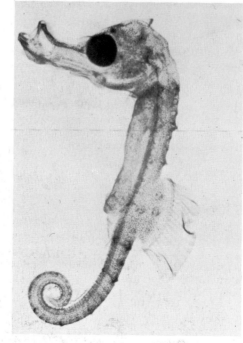

some species. During this time the mouth of the pouch is large but when laying is finished it closes to a minute pore, and stays like this until the baby seahorses are ready to be born, in 4–5 weeks. They are about ½ in. long at birth, perfect miniatures of their parents and the first thing baby seahorses do is to swim to the surface to gulp air to fill their swimbladders. They feed ravenously on extremely small crustaceans, such as newly hatched brine shrimps, and grow rapidly. In the Steinhart Aquarium in the United States young seahorses *Hippocampus hudsonius* were found to grow from ⅜ in. at birth to 2½ in. in 2 months.

Placental fishes

The inside of the pouch changes just before and during courtship. The walls thicken and become spongy, and they are enriched with an abundant supply of blood vessels. As the female lays her eggs the male fertilises them and they become embedded in these spongy walls, which then act like a placenta. As the pouch is closed there must be some way by which oxygen reaches the eggs, and it is almost certain that the network of blood vessels in the wall of the pouch passes oxygen to the eggs and takes up carbon dioxide from them. Also food probably passes from the paternal blood into the eggs, just as it does from the mother's blood in the mammalian placenta.

Male labour

We are used to the idea that no matter what happens beforehand, in the actual bearing of offspring it is always the female that has the burden. In seahorses it is the reverse. As each batch of eggs is laid in his pouch the male seahorse goes through violent muscular spasms which work the eggs to the bottom of the pouch to make room for more. It seems also that there is a physiological reaction as the eggs sink into the spongy tissue, and he shows signs of exhaustion. When the young have hatched and are ready to leave the pouch, the mouth of the pouch opens wide. The male alternately bends and straightens his body in convulsive jerks and finally a baby seahorse is shot out through the mouth of the pouch. After each birth the male rests, and when all the babies are born he shows signs of extreme exhaustion. In aquaria the males often die after delivering their brood but this does not happen in a natural state, because the male soon looks around for another female to fill his pouch with eggs.

Seahorses have been described as having the head of a horse, the tail of a monkey, the pouch of a kangaroo, the hard outer skeleton of an insect and the independently moving eyes of a chameleon. It would, however, be difficult to find a suitable comparison for the labour pains of the father.

class	**Pisces**
order	**Gasterosteiformes**
family	**Syngnathidae**
genus & species	***Hippocampus brevirostris,*** *H. hippocampus, others*

Shad

The shad must once have been a well-known fish—its English name dates from the 12th century at least—but its numbers have suffered from the effects of modern civilization. There are two species living in European seas, the allis shad and the twaite shad. There are also the common shad of Atlantic North America, the Indian shad and the Chinese shad, all of which are fished commercially. A related species in North America is the alewife, a corruption of the North American Indian name for it, **aloofe**.

Shads are herringlike with deep bodies covered with small, silvery scales and compressed from side to side. The allis shad measures up to 2 ft, the smaller twaite shad to 20 in. The upper jaw is notched in the midline with the lower jaw fitting into it and the gill cover is marked by weakly ridged radiating lines. There is a single dorsal fin, a low anal fin set well back near the tail, small pelvic and pectoral fins and a forked tailfin. Along the underside there is a row of keeled scales, almost like a row of spines. The twaite shad is the more common but it was not recognized as a separate species until 1803 because it and the allis shad are so alike. The adult twaite shad often has a row of 6—7 dark spots running along the flank from behind the gill cover, while the allis shad may have a single spot, but the only certain way to distinguish them is to count the gill-rakers on the first gill arch. The allis shad has 80—130 and the twaite shad has 40—60.

The allis shad is found from Norway through the Mediterranean to the Black Sea; the twaite shad from Iceland to the Mediterranean. The American shad, a native of the Atlantic seaboard, has been introduced three times into the Sacramento river in California and is now well established there. All shads enter rivers to spawn. The twaite shad has subspecies in the Rhône, the Italian lakes Maggiore, Como, Lugano and Garda. In the lakes of Killarney in Ireland is a landlocked shad the goureen, another subspecies of the twaite shad.

Musical shad

The allis and twaite shads are deep blue on the back with silvery flanks. They have more yellow on the flanks than herring, and are more solitary, shoaling mainly just for their spawning runs. The American shad moves about in vast shoals of fishes of about the same size, moving at the same speed and at the same distance apart, almost with military precision. Perhaps a similar shoaling was formerly seen in the European shads, when they were more numerous, yet this seems unlikely from the account given by WJ Gordon, in 1902, that German fishermen hung bells on their nets to ring underwater because shads are fond of music and would be attracted to the nets. The bells 'not only attract the fish, but keep them lost in admiration as the nets are drawn in'.

Gill-rakers decide food

Shads are plankton feeders with remarkable sieves in their throats for sorting their food. The large number of gill-rakers, particularly in the allis shad, have the same effect as fine muslin for filtering out the very smallest plankton. They also take larger plankton such as copepods and crustacean larvae, and will eat small fishes. The allis shad, with its finer gill-rakers, takes more crustacea, the twaite shad with fewer gill-rakers, takes more fish. They feed mainly in the sea but also to some extent in the fresh or brackish water on the spawning migrations up rivers in spring. The allis shad goes farther up the rivers than twaite shad, and in this respect is more like the American shad. The twaite shad tends to spawn just above tidal limits, in brackish water, as in the Nile, where it is especially abundant. The males arrive first on the spawning grounds. They mature earlier than the females, at 2—3 years instead of 4—5 in the females, so the spawning males are smaller. The eggs sink to the bottom and hatch 4—8 days later. The fry grow rapidly and move downstream. The allis shad, for example, grow from $\frac{1}{2}$ in. to $5\frac{1}{2}$ in. in a year.

Shad seem unable to surmount man-made

△ *The herring-like allis shad. This species grows up to 2 ft long. It is deep blue on the back and its body is covered with small, silvery scales. The allis shad is one of the two shads living in European seas. It is found in Norway in the north of its range through the Mediterranean to the Black Sea.*

obstacles such as weirs. Even the rafts of garbage that collect in some estuaries are a deterrent to their migrations upstream, while sewage and industrial pollution completely upset their spawning migrations. Shad are still caught in rivers such as the Severn and Shannon with stake nets but no longer come up the more polluted rivers such as the Thames.

Old English name

The origin of the name 'shad', spelt 'sceadd' in Old English, is lost in the mists of Anglo-Saxon history. Today, in England, it is probably unknown to most people apart from those who study or catch fish. On the Continent the allis shad is often named after the month in which it migrates up rivers, as in the Dutch *Meivisch* and the German *Maifisch*. The name 'shad' was, however, taken to North America and not only applied to the related American shad but to related fishes, such as the menhaden, which is known also as the greentailed, hardhead or yellowtailed shad, and to unrelated fishes, such as *Dorosoma* the gizzard shad, and *Pomolobus chrysochloris* the Ohio shad. In the United States, moreover, the name has been used for flowers that bloom, or animals that appear at the time the shad migrates up the rivers, such as the shad-berry, the shad-bush, the shad fly and the shad frog.

class	**Pisces**
order	**Clupeiformes**
family	**Clupeidae**
genus & species	*Alosa alosa* allis shad
	A. fallax (=finta) twaite shad
	A. ilisha Indian shad
	A. reevesi Chinese shad
	A. sapidissima American shad

◁ *A disappearing trick: when danger threatens* **A. strigatus** *turns its sharp underedge towards the intruder and virtually disappears.*

Upside-down swimmer

Shrimpfishes swim in small groups in shallow water. Like the seahorse they move by slight movements of their fins, and are very agile, darting about with great rapidity. They rarely swim horizontally and for a long time there has been a difference of opinion among people who have studied them whether they swim with the snout upwards or downwards. It is now believed that they do both but mostly feed head downwards. Dr Robert Rofen has described how he watched a shoal of shrimpfishes swimming along the bottom of a small underwater cave head down. Then, as they came to the cave wall, they continued up the wall but in a horizontal position until they reached the ceiling. There they continued to feed although the position of the body had been reversed and the head now pointed upwards.

Protective tricks

When really frightened shrimpfishes can streak away, swimming in a horizontal position like any normal fish. Their first reaction to danger is to turn the sharp underedge of the body towards the intruder, and virtually disappear from its sight. Another common protective trick is for several shrimpfishes to hang downwards among the long slender spines of the sea-urchin *Diadema*. The spines are about as thick as the reddish line along the shrimpfish's body, so it is sometimes hard to tell which is spine and which is shrimpfish.

No stomach

Quite obviously, when somebody has the opportunity of studying shrimpfishes there will be an unusual story revealed. Meanwhile little is known about their breeding habits, and not much more about the way they feed. Some say they feed on small particles of plant and animal matter, others that they feed on tiny planktonic crustaceans. They suck the food into the mouth as the seahorse does, and their food must be soft because they have no teeth to chew it. Moreover, they have no stomach, digestion taking place in the intestine. A surprising number of other fishes have no stomach, the gullet passing straight into the intestine, and it is not always clear how and where the digestive juices are given out or how they operate. There are also fishes that have a stomach but no digestive juices or the glands which secrete them. It is not only fishes like the shrimpfishes, which feed on soft foods, that lack stomachs, the skippers or saury pikes, *Scomberesox*, Atlantic fishes related to flying fishes and garfishes, are also stomachless.

Shrimpfish

The shrimpfish is a relative of the rather curious seahorse, but if anything, is even more curious. To begin with, shrimpfishes are so thin that when they turn sideways amongst weeds they seem to disappear. The whole head and body of a shrimpfish is flattened from side to side and is completely encased in a transparent armour made up of a number of thin bony plates, fused with the underlying ribs in much the same way as the shell of a tortoise. On its underside these form a knife edge, hence the Australian name, razorfish. At the hind end of the body is a long stout spine and the two dorsal fins, which should lie along the back, are crowded together under the spine, the second actually pointing downwards. The tail has also been pushed out of position. It lies at an obtuse angle to the trunk and ends in a small tailfin also pointing downwards. The snout is long and tubelike with a tiny pipette-like mouth at its tip.

There are two genera and two species in each genus. In **Centriscus** *the dorsal spine is long and solid and in* **Aeoliscus** *it is jointed and movable. The reason for the spine being jointed in* **Aeoliscus** *is not known.*

One species **A. strigatus** *has been observed resting at the surface head downwards, with the tip of the spine turned at right angles to the body, which possibly gives it some stability through contact with the surface of the water. There must be more to it than this, however, because this part of the spine contains nerve and sensory cells, which is most unusual.*

Most shrimpfishes are small. The largest is the Australian **Centriscus cristatus** *which occasionally reaches 12 in. in length. The body is silvery with a deep red band running from the mouth to the eye and continuing from there along the flank to the dorsal spine as an orange line. The belly is pale yellow with about 12 oblique red bars on it.*

Shrimpfishes are found in shallow waters from East Africa to Hawaii. They are completely absent from the Atlantic.

class	**Pisces**
order	**Gasterosteiformes**
family	**Centriscidae**
genera	***Centriscus, Aeoliscus***

△ A mermaid's purse: a skate's egg case.

△ A baby skate, an almost perfect replica of the adult, hatches from its egg case on the sea bed.

Skate

Skates and rays are flattened fishes related to sharks, with more than 100 species belonging to one family, the Rajidae, and the names are more or less interchangeable. The original name 'skate' dates from the 12th century and referred to one species **Raja batis**, usually spoken of as the common skate. Closely related to it is the roker or thornback ray **R. clavata**.

The body is flattened from above down and the pectoral fins are large and triangular and joined to the head, giving almost a diamond-shaped outline. The tail is slender, with a row of spines running along the mid-dorsal line and two small dorsal fins near its tip. The line of spines may be doubled in some species, quadrupled in others. The front of the head ends in a snout, short in some species, long in others. The eyes are on top of the head, with a spiracle behind each. The mouth and nostrils are on the underside, and so are the five pairs of gills. The pelvic fins are small and in males the inner edges carry a pair of so-called claspers which are intromittent organs for placing the sperms inside the female. The common skate grows to 6 ft long or more, the thornback to 3 ft. One of the largest is the big skate of the American Pacific **R. binoculata** which grows to 8 ft.

Skates and rays are found in most temperate and tropical waters except for much of the South Pacific and an area off the northeast coast of South America. They live mainly in shallow waters, sometimes down to 600 ft but **R. abyssicola,** off the Pacific coast of North America, lives down to 7 200 ft.

▽ Although the skate is mainly a bottom-living fish, it can swim well using its large pectoral fins.   ▷ A young skate glides over the seabed.

198

Food caught by pouncing

Skates live mainly on sandy, gravelly or muddy bottoms, spending most of their time lying on the seabed and only occasionally swimming up. When they do, they swim with a wavelike flapping of the pectoral fins, the free edges of which are continuously undulating. The tail plays no part. Skates do not migrate except for moving into deeper water and back again into shallow water with the changing seasons. The common skate, for example, moves into deeper water for the winter, the thornback into shallow water. All skates and rays are bottom feeders and as young fish, they take small crustaceans such as half-grown shrimps and other small invertebrates. Later they eat bottom living animals such as crabs and lobsters as well as some fishes. The larger individuals of the common ray eat gurnards, flatfishes and anglerfishes and also midwater fishes such as herring, scad and pilchard. Small squids are sometimes eaten. Prey is taken with a pounce, the skate smothering its victim with its wide pectoral fins and then seizing it with its mouth. Although skates seem to have good sight they locate their prey mainly by scent, so can hunt equally well by day or night.

Specialised breathing

When a fish spends so much time lying on the bottom with its mouth and gills on the underside there arises a special problem — its breathing. A free-swimming fish normally breathes by taking water in through the mouth; this then passes through the gill cavity and out to the exterior. When a skate is lying on the bottom its mouth is closed and water taken in through the spiracles on the top of the head, passes into the gill cavities and out through the gill slits on the underside. Thus a skate avoids swallowing sand or mud.

'Mermaids' purses'

Some time after mating the female lays her eggs, each enclosed in a capsule with a horn-like process at each corner, which in some species is drawn out into a tendril. These help to anchor the egg-cases to objects on the sea floor. In places the surface of the capsule is covered with a felt of loose fibres. In the common skate the fibres near the corners, and at the bases of the processes, are long filaments. The capsules differ in size with the species, those of the thornback being 3–4 in. long, while those of the common skate are more than double this. The baby skate when it hatches is almost as broad across the pectoral fins as the capsule it came from is long.

The capsules are amber coloured at first but turn black after the young have hatched. As the capsules are rolled about on the seabed the fibres are rubbed off. The smooth, black egg-cases of the thornback skate are often washed ashore, and are called mermaids' purses.

Once despised

Skate is a commercially valuable fish in European fisheries, but not so in America. In Britain where there is now an annual catch of around 15 000 tons the common skate was once despised and the development of the fishery dates roughly from the beginning of the present century. It is taken in trawls and on long lines, as well as on rod and line when fish up to 200 lb have been landed. The 'wings' or pectoral fins are the parts used for food.

Electric tails

Fishes are unique among the vertebrates in having electric organs. About 250 species are known to have them and the more remarkable of these have been dealt with under electric catfish, electric eel and electric ray (see pages 74–7). These organs differ in size and strength and the uses to which they are put, but in all species the electric organs are formed from modified muscles. A fairly recent discovery is that skates have electric organs in their tails. They differ in strength from one species to another. They also differ from those of the better-known electric fishes in that they are served by nerves from the spinal cord instead of the brain. Their strength is about 4 volts as compared with the 370–550 volts of an electric eel or the 350–450 volts of an electric catfish. What purpose they serve has yet to be found out.

class	**Selachii**
order	**Hypotremata**
family	**Rajidae**
genus & species	**Raja abyssicola** *deep-sea skate* **R. batis** *common skate* **R. binoculata** *big skate* **R. clavata** *roker or thornback ray* *others*

▽ *Skate ventral view in which the nostrils above the horny mouth and the double row of gill slits can be clearly seen.*

Snakehead

Snakeheads are rather distinctive fresh-water fishes of Africa and southern Asia which are not very closely related to any other fish. Their nearest relatives are the perch-like fishes. They have long bodies, cylindrical in front, and almost circular in cross section but slightly compressed from side to side towards the hind end. They have large reptilean looking heads with a jutting lower jaw and a wide gape to the mouth which is armed with numerous teeth. There is the usual pair of double nostrils and in each pair the front nostril is tubular. The dorsal fin is soft-rayed and runs from just behind the head almost to the tail and there is a similarly long anal fin. The body is usually mottled with brown, sometimes with tinges of red. There are often distinctive grey, brown, and black markings along the body in the form of irregular bands or in the African species, V-shaped markings, or else there are large spots, sometimes in a row along each flank. This disruptive pattern makes the fishes blend with their background as they rest along the water plants. The smallest species is about 6 in. long, while others are up to 3 ft, and in the larger species a few may reach 5 ft.

The Asiatic species range from Ceylon through India to southern China and southeast Asia and the Philippines.

Fishing with knives

Snakeheads live in foul and stagnant waters coming to the surface at intervals to gulp in air. Inside the gill chamber on each side are tiny pouches which are well supplied with a network of fine blood vessels that take up oxygen. Snakeheads can travel overland —by wriggling their bodies and by making rowing movements with their short, broad pectoral fins. When the ponds in which they live dry up, they bury themselves in the mud to a depth of 1—2 ft. It is then that local fishermen, armed with knives, slice out the mud to find them.

Snake throw to catch prey

When first hatched snakeheads feed on small plankton such as water fleas, rotifers and crustacean larvae. As they grow they take larger plankton including insect larvae and when about 2 in. long they begin to feed on small fishes, as well as insects and their larvae. When mature they feed almost entirely on other fishes which they stalk stealthily, approaching them from the front. Then they bend themselves into an S-shape, and throw their heads forward with a sudden jerk to seize their prey. Adult snakeheads are voracious creatures; they eat frogs and even tackle water snakes.

Frequent gulps of air

They begin to breed when about a year old. A pair of snakeheads clear the waterplants over a small area. The females then shed their eggs into the water almost at random and the males do the same with their milt. The eggs are $\frac{1}{16}$ in. diameter and contain oil droplets so they rise to the surface and float. They hatch in 2—3 days, the larvae continuing to feed on the yolk sac for another 6—8 days, during which time they float belly-up on the surface. After this they are able to swim normally and they grow fairly rapidly, but they make frequent visits to the surface to gulp air and where they are numerous the water appears coloured as a constant procession of larvae rise to the surface. In some species the males guard the eggs, and the larvae for a while, but they do not build a nest or show any other signs of parental care. Once the young fishes are able to swim on their own they hide among the water plants, a habit which then continues throughout their lifetime since snakeheads, like the pike, spend much of their time concealed among vegetation from which they emerge to seize their prey.

Live for months out of water

Snakeheads are important food fishes in southern Asia and have been introduced into parts of the United States where they are now flourishing. Because they are air breathers they can stay alive for days on end out of water and so remain fresh until they are sold or needed for cooking. This is important in areas where few families have a refrigerator. Snakeheads are said to be able to live for months out of water, breathing air and deriving nourishment from the fat stored in their bodies. In the fish markets they are put out for sale on woven trays, and Earl S Herald has described how in the Philippines the women selling the fish have to periodically belabour them with a club to keep them from squirming off their trays. She calls attention to her wares in a singing monotone, beating time at intervals by landing blows of her club on the fish.

class	**Pisces**
order	**Channiformes**
family	**Ophicephalidae**
genera & species	***Channa asiatica*** ***Ophicephalus africanus*** ***O. punctatus,*** *others*

▽ *The Asiatic snakehead—slow-stalking, serpent-striking hunter of foul and stagnant waters which breathes air and can crawl overland.*

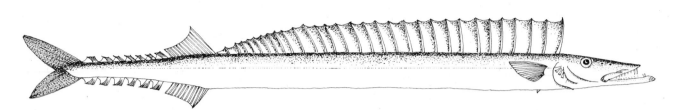

*Wandering hunter: snake mackerel **Gempylus**.*

Snake mackerel

Had a snake mackerel not jumped onto the Kon-tiki raft few people outside scientific circles would ever have heard of these fishes.

They are oceanic fishes living in moderately deep waters, and are distantly related to true mackerels. They have long, fairly slender bodies, and a long snout with a prominent lower jaw which ends in a pointed fleshy tip. The mouth is armed with fanglike teeth. The eyes are large. The body is covered with small smooth scales and small forked spines. The first dorsal fin, which begins just behind the head, is long and becomes gradually lower towards its hind end. It consists of spines joined together by membranes and just behind it is a second dorsal spine followed by a few finlets which each consists of an isolated spine with a membrane. The anal fin is also followed by a few finlets. The pectoral fins are small, the pelvics very tiny. The back is dark brown to black and there are violet tints on the flanks and belly. There are two lateral lines, one just below the dorsal fin, the other along the midline of the flank. Both are whitish in contrast to the fins and inside of the mouth, which are black.

One species **Nesiarchus nasutus,** *4 ft long, is found in the North Atlantic from near the surface to 3 600 ft.* **Gempylus serpens,** *which grows to 5 ft, is found in all tropical seas from the surface to a similar depth of 3 600 ft.*

Vertical and horizontal journeys

Like so many deepsea fishes the snake mackerels make daily vertical migrations appearing near the surface at night. The fact that the same species is found in Atlantic, Indian and Pacific oceans suggests that snake mackerels are great travellers. Little more is known of their way of life, especially in the deep waters. They are sometimes brought up on long lines and from examination of the stomach contents it is known that *Nesiarchus nasutus* feeds on the viperfish *Chauliodus*, snipe-eels and squid. Usually it is the younger individuals of this species that are found at the surface. *G. serpens* seem to feed on flying fishes. Several of those caught in the tropical Indian Ocean have had the remains of flying fishes in their stomachs and one was seen to catch a flying fish.

Another reason why it is suspected that snake mackerels are great travellers is that although they are typically fish of tropical seas, they often wander into temperate latitudes. *Nesiarchus nasutus*, for example, is sometimes taken in the Bay of Biscay and off the edge of the continental shelf to the west of the British Isles. It has several times been captured as far north as Iceland.

Year-round spawning

Gempylus serpens is believed to spawn throughout the year and two spawning areas have so far been located, one in the Caribbean and one off Florida. The young fish when $\frac{1}{3}$ in. long has a deep body of which about $\frac{2}{5}$ is taken up by the head which has very large eyes. The dorsal fin is higher in front than in the adult but otherwise the fins are much the same as when the fish is fully grown.

Attracted by light

Although public attention was focused on the two snake mackerels that jumped aboard the *Kon-Tiki*, this was not a unique event. It suggests, among other things, that the habit of jumping from the water after flying fishes must be a normal habit. The second of the snake mackerels seized the white rope Thor Heyerdhal had tied around his waist, which may have flashed in the light of the lantern, giving the appearance of an airborne flying fish, or the lantern alone may have attracted the fish as snake mackerels are sometimes attracted to ships' lights.

Castor oil fish

Another member of the same family *Ruvettus pretiosus* is the *escolar*, also known as the oilfish, scourfish, or castor-oil fish. It is deeper bodied than the others and has a more normal mouth although it is still a large one. It also is found in all tropical oceans and also in the Mediterranean, at depths of 600−2 400 ft. The fishermen of Madeira and the Canaries that use long-line fishing commonly catch it. Its flesh is very oily. It is called castor oil fish because its flesh acts as a purgative.

It used to be said that the name *escolar* meant scholar but a later suggestion is that it is from the Spanish word meaning to scour or burnish. This may refer to the roughness of the skin due to the prickles, or it may be just coincidence that another name for this fish is scourfish.

class	**Pisces**
order	**Perciformes**
family	**Gempylidae**

▽ *Raaby, of the* **Kon-Tiki***, holds the most publicized snake mackerel.*

▽ **Kon-Tiki** *under sail. The snake mackerel was attracted to her lights.*

Snapper

Some snappers are important food fishes
and are often considered as game fishes
as they are a tussle for the sea-angler
to land. There are over 250 species. They
are deep bodied fishes with a large head,
somewhat flattened on top as it slopes up
to meet the front of the dorsal fin. The
mouth is large and the jaws, with their
sharp teeth, slope down to the corners
giving the fish a disgruntled look.

The name is derived from the way the
landed fish suddenly and very forcibly
opens and shuts its jaws as it is dying,
which sometimes causes bad wounds to
the hands of an unwary fisherman
sorting his catch. They are up to 2 ft or
more long and have squarish tails. The

dorsal fin is spiny in front, soft-rayed in
the rear portion. The anal fin has several
spines in front of its leading edge, and the
pelvic fins are well forward, under the
pectorals. Some species are grey to greyish
green but many are beautifully coloured
red or rose or, like the emperor snapper,
whitish with reddish-brown bands. Yellow
is another predominant colour. The
yellowtail snapper has a yellow tail and a
yellow line along the flank; its back is blue
with yellow spots. The lane snapper of
Florida to Brazil is striped red and
yellow and the mutton snapper of the
West Indies is banded yellow and green.
Snappers are found in all warm seas.
The greatest number of species are found
throughout the Indo-Australian area although many are also found in the tropical
waters of the coast of Atlantic America.

△ Prowling through the coral on an ever-
hungry quest for anything, animal or vegetable,
that moves, a shoal of Indian Ocean snappers
Lutjanus kasmira decorates the Assumption
Island reef.

Small shoals

Most snappers move about in groups of less
than a dozen. They live mostly in coastal
waters, especially around coral reefs, at
depths of 24—90 ft, sometimes as deep as
400 ft. They are also seen near mangrove
swamps and docks, always ready to investigate a possible source of food. Snappers
feed mainly at night. Their hunting method
is to stalk living prey until a few feet from it,
then to make a sudden dash, seize the prey
and swim back in a leisurely way to the
starting point.

Refuse nothing

Snappers are euryphagous, which merely means they refuse nothing edible. They feed mainly on fish, but they will take crabs, lobsters and prawns, barnacles, octopus and squid, brittlestars, sea squirts, pyrosoma, salps, sea butterflies, worms and molluscs. They also take a small amount of plant food including algae and leaves, the last of these being eaten probably for no better reason than that they were moving through the water. Snappers will also take scraps thrown overboard from ships including vegetable waste.

The kind of food taken depends very much on which prey animal happens to be plentiful. There is also a change of diet with age, the young snappers feeding mainly on small fishes. A study of the food of one species over a period showed that of the total food taken 62% was fish and 25% crustaceans. In another it was 49% fish, 12% crustaceans and a little more than 12% for squid and for plankton.

Research into breeding seasons

In spite of the abundance of snappers little is known of their breeding habits. In tropical waters the temperature varies very little throughout the year. Off East Africa, for example, temperatures vary from 24–29°C, and snappers spawn throughout the year. In Indian waters breeding seems to coincide with the cold season following the onset of the northeast monsoon in September and October. Off the coast of tropical America there seem to be two breeding seasons for snappers.

It may seem contradictory to say little is known about the breeding habits and then to specify the breeding seasons. It is relatively easy to note when fish taken in nets are ripe. The males, even without gutting, can be tested for ripeness by gently pressing the flanks to see if milt flows out. To find out where spawning takes place, to net the eggs and larvae and to follow the life history of the fish is far more difficult.

Mature fish are not always in breeding condition. After spawning their reproductive organs are spent and the fish are in what is called a resting condition. After this the organs begin to increase in size again and the germ cells become active. A male fish not yet ripe may give out sperm, but when fully ripe—ripe running, as it is called—it gives out milt when even a slight pressure is applied to the flanks. A ripe running female gives out eggs when her flanks are squeezed but before that, when gutted, the size of the eggs shows whether she is ripe, nearly ripe or ripening.

Unpredictable poisoning

There is a kind of fish poisoning called ciguatera (see page 27). Some of the symptoms are muscular pains, cramp, nausea, diarrhoea, and even paralysis. Early symptoms are a tingling of the lips and throat and a sensation reversal in which hot things in the mouth feel cold and cold things feel hot. Snappers are among the 300 or more species of food fishes that can cause ciguatera, yet snappers are generally good food fishes.

Ciguatera is, in fact, sporadic and unpredictable and is probably caused by a fish eating a particular kind of blue-green alga, perhaps at a certain time of year or in a particular stage of the alga's growth. It can also be caused by carnivorous fishes eating herbivorous fishes that have eaten the alga, as the poison is cumulative in the fish's body. It is also persistent, for in experiments to test this poisoning snappers kept in aquaria for over a year still caused ciguatera when they were fed to animals.

class	**Pisces**
order	**Perciformes**
family	**Lutjanidae**
genera & species	**Lutjanus analis** *mutton snapper*
	L. aya *red snapper*
	L. sebae *emperor snapper*
	L. synagris *lane snapper*
	Ocyurus chrysurus
	yellowtail snapper, others

*A solitary Red Sea snapper **L. russellii** with its flattened snout and large, downward-sloping jaws shut tight, swims below an overhanging coral.*

Sole

The common sole is considered by some connoisseurs to have the best flavour of all fish but only after it has been dead 2–3 days (see plaice page 165). Soles are tongue-shaped flatfishes in which the mouth is on the side of the head which projects forward of the mouth in a smoothly rounded curve. They lie on the left side. The dorsal fin starts on the front of the head and continues round the margin of the body to join the tail fin, the anal fin being nearly as long but starting behind the gill cover. Dorsal, tail and anal fins form a complete fringe. The underside of the head is covered with little white tags crowded together.

Most soles are up to 1 ft long but some are double this length. The usual colour of the upper surface is yellow, greyish-brown or dark brown with well-spaced darker spots or blotches or with dark bands. One of the more striking species is the naked sole of the American Atlantic coasts which has a zebra pattern, with close-set, reddish-brown crossbands.

They live mainly in shallow seas, on muddy or sandy bottoms, although a few species live in deep water, such as **Bathysolea profundicola** which ranges from 900–3 800 ft. Most live in warm seas but some species, including the common sole of Europe, range into temperate seas as far north as the Faeroes. The hogchoker of America, 6 in. long with crossbands on the upper surface and spots below, lives in the sea from Carolina to Panama but sometimes enters fresh water.

Active at night

Soles lie on the bottom of the sea more or less buried in the sand during most of the day. They do this by strongly wriggling the body with an up and down undulatory movement, which digs a shallow trough and at the same time throws up sand that settles on the sole, partially hiding it. They normally become active at night, which is their main feeding time. Soles are also active by day when the skies are overcast or when the water becomes murky. Then they creep slowly along the bottom using the ends of the fin-rays with which their bodies are fringed. A sole searching for food raises its head slightly upwards and sideways, patting the sand from time to time with the underside of its head. Its eyes are small and, from the way the fish behaves, seem inefficient. A sole will stop and go back to examine any small object its undersurface has touched, feeling it with the lower surface of its head. The little white tags are sensitive, and are probably organs of touch, possibly also of taste, and the tubular nostril on the underside suggests that it may also use smell in searching for food. One nostril of the sand sole, for example, is surrounded by a rosette of swollen skin.

▷ *A common sole glides down to the sea bed.*

Diet of bottom-living creatures

The sole feeds entirely on bottom-living animals and seems incapable of catching, or even of noticing anything swimming just off the bottom. Its upper jaw and teeth are feeble and most of its mouth is on the undersurface of the head. Small crustaceans, worms and molluscs make up the main part of its diet, and to these are added brittlestars and small bottom-living fishes such as sand eels and gobies. Prey is not seized by the mouth until the sole has been able to cover all or part of it with the front part of its head. Young soles feed on smaller crustaceans such as copepods and on fish larvae.

As long ago as 1740 a Mr Collinson was fascinated to find he had bought some soles, the bellies of which were 'hard and prominent, appearing to be filled with rows of some hard substance'. He opened them up and described what he found in the *Philosophical Transactions of the Royal Society, London*. The hard substance was 'found to be shell-fish. These, from the bulging of the shells and the intervening interstices, gave the intestines somewhat the appearance of strings of beads. On further examination, some of them were found nearly dissolved, others partly so, but many of them whole'.

Left eye moves to right side

The common sole and some other species move into deeper water for the winter but migrate back to shallow inshore waters in spring and early summer to spawn. The eggs, $\frac{1}{20}$ in. diameter, float well off the bottom. Each mature female lays about half a million eggs. The larvae are $\frac{1}{8}$ in. long when hatched and, as in other flatfishes, have a normal shape. As they grow they come to lie on the left side and the left eye migrates to the right side as in plaice. By the time they are $\frac{3}{4}$ in. long their bodies have become flattened and they have settled on the bottom.

Dover sole

Relatives of the common sole are little fished: the solenette because it is too small, being only 3 in. long; the thickback because it is not abundant. The common sole is caught entirely by trawling, and off northwestern Europe around 34 000 tons are fished commercially each year, the most valuable grounds being in the central and southern North Sea and the Bay of Biscay. The name 'sole' has also been used for the lemon sole, which is a dab, and there is also the famous Dover sole. In the early 19th century a London merchant arranged for fast gigs to bring consignments of this fish post-haste from Dover, and the name has stuck for marketing the common sole, no matter where its place of origin might have been.

Imitates poisonous fish.

When dead the upper surface of the sole is a uniform sepia brown. In life most soles harmonize with the seabed on which they happen to be lying, their camouflage being helped by blotches, spots and bars, which further break up the outline of the body. The fact that a mature female lays over 500 000 eggs as compared with millions recorded for other fishes is a good indication that soles enjoy a fair measure of immunity from attack. One feature that may help is a black patch on the sole's pectoral fin. The poisonous weever fish, which also buries itself in the sand, has a black patch on its dorsal fin which it raises when a predator approaches. This is probably a warning signal to attackers that the fish is poisonous. The sole also raises its fin with a black patch and it has been suggested that this is a case of mimicry, the sole benefiting from being mistaken for a weever.

class	Pisces
order	**Pleuronectiformes**
family	**Soleidae**
genera & species	***Buglossidium luteum*** solenette
	Gymnarchirus williamsoni naked sole
	Microchirus variegatus thickback sole
	Pegusa lascaris sand sole
	Solea solea common or Dover sole

◁ *An alternating pattern: the comb-like ctenoid scales of the common sole ($\times 34$).*
▽ *A metamorphosising common sole, showing eye migration. In all soles the left eye migrates over to the right side of the body ($\times 16$).*

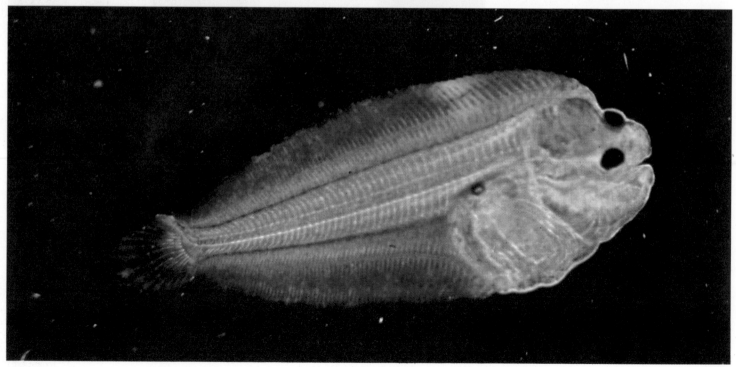

Squirrelfish

Squirrelfishes are usually bright red and they have large eyes, giving them a faint resemblance to red squirrels, and this seems to be the only reason why they were given their common name. They have deep bodies compressed from side to side, large heads, strong jaws and large eyes. The largest is 2 ft long but 1 ft is a more usual length. Their scales are large with sharp points on their hind edges. There are sharp spines on the head and on the gill covers. The front half of the dorsal fin is spiny, the rear half tall and soft rayed. The anal fin has four spines in front, the middle one large. The large pelvic fins are situated forward on the body and level with the pectoral fins. The tailfin is forked. The red body is usually ornamented with silvery spots or stripes on the flanks, running from behind the gills to the base of the tailfin. One of the most widespread in the Indo-Pacific, the red soldierfish, lives in deeper water than most, down to 90 ft. It is bright red and each row of scales along its body bears a silvery stripe. Its fins are rosy with black markings.

There are 70 species in tropical seas throughout the world, most of them living in shallow water.

Strong territorial instinct

Most squirrelfishes are nocturnal. By day they shelter singly in crevices and cracks in the coral. Each occupies a territory and shows a marked territorial behaviour. Some members of a related genus *Myripristis* contrast with typical squirrelfishes in sometimes forming shoals. Squirrelfishes are also noted for the noises they make, which are loud enough to be heard above the water. These are produced by the vibration of muscles attached to the swimbladder, which acts as a resonator. The sounds are used, it seems, for the same basic purpose as birdsong, to advertise the occupation of a territory and to bring pairs together for breeding. Their territorial instinct was made use of off the Hawaiian islands in fishing for squirrelfishes, which are an important food fish. A squirrelfish was caught, using a net, then a string was tied round the live fish which was put back into the water and dangled near the crevices in the rocks. The other fishes soon came out to fight it and, by drawing the captive fish gently to the surface, these could easily be caught by carefully lowering a net under them.

Prickly to handle

Apart from their colour and the size of their eyes squirrelfishes are remembered because they are prickly to handle. They are also notable for their nocturnal habits, which are linked with the large size of their eyes. Indeed, they could more appropriately have been called owl fishes, except that the name squirrelfish was given them in the early 18th century when people were less interested in animal behaviour and more apt to give a name based upon

△ *In close formation, a small shoal of squirrelfishes* **Myripristis** *in the Red Sea, 20 ft down.*

general appearance. This, presumably, is what led to one species being called the wistful squirrelfish.

Avoiding competition

They are predatory, catching smaller fishes, and one reason for their pronounced territorial instinct is that it keeps the individuals well spaced out, so avoiding competition with each other. This is probably when they use their sounds, to warn possible trespassers off their beat.

Pointed noses

The connection between the sounds they produce and their breeding was first discovered by accident when squirrelfishes were in a display tank in a television studio in America. During the rehearsal the sounds

were heard and a pair of squirrelfishes were seen to be courting, lying side by side with their tails pressed together and their bodies forming a V. From the eggs hatch larvae remarkable for their long pointed noses. The larvae swim to the surface and become part of the plankton. The larvae are dispersed by currents.

Few enemies

Their nocturnal habits, spininess and their tendency to keep hidden probably means that squirrelfishes have relatively few enemies. The main dangers to the adults, especially those species which have fewer spines than average, is of being caught for human consumption. The chief dangers are in the larval stage when they are eaten in large numbers by tuna fishes.

Luminous bacteria

Squirrelfishes are said to be primitive because of certain details in their anatomy. They also form a link between the large multitude of perchlike fishes living today and certain kinds of fishes that were dominant during the Cretaceous period 135-70 million years ago, which had spiny rays on their fins. Even more primitive are the alfonsinos of the family Berycidae. These are also brightly coloured but differ in having a short rounded body and a long, fairly slender tail end. They also differ in living in deep water, at about 2 000 ft. The commonest species is the 2ft long *Beryx splendens* which is worldwide in warm seas and is fished commercially.

Another relative is the pinecone fish *Monocentris japonicus* of the family Monocentridae, only a few inches long, which has platelike spiny scales and lives in deep water in the tropical Indo-Pacific. It is eaten in Japan. The only other species in the family lives in Australian waters. It is *Monocentris gloriae-maris* (the glory of the sea—which shows what a beauty it is!). These not only have large wistful eyes but have two light organs under the lower jaw—pockets filled with luminescent bacteria.

Strangest of all are the related lantern-eyed fishes of the family Anomalopidae. None is more than a foot long. They also have large eyes with a light organ beneath each eye made up of tubes of luminous bacteria. The fish cannot control the light from the bacteria but they can cover it. Some species do this by drawing a blind—a kind of eyelid—over the light organ. In other species there is a muscle which turns the light organ round so its light is no longer visible from outside.

class	**Pisces**
order	**Beryciformes**
family	**Holocentridae**
genera & species	***Holocentrus rubrum*** *soldierfish* ***Holotrachys lima*** *wistful squirrelfish* *others*

▷ *Wide eyes, sharp spines and bright colours — characteristics of all squirrelfishes; the Hawaiian striped squirrelfish* **Adioryx xantherythrus** *is no exception. Squirrelfishes are usually some shade of red but this species also sports candy stripes that look like strings of pearls. In comparison with* **Myripristis** *a schooling species (illustrated on the previous page)* **Holocentrus** *is a more solitary species and shows a strong territorial pattern. The Hawaiian striped squirrelfish is particularly renowned in that it was the first squirrelfish in which prenuptial activity was observed. A pair will hold their tails together, their heads apart, so that a V or Y is formed between them.*

Stickleback

Sticklebacks are not just tiny fishes or tiddlers caught by small boys with a bent pin on a line. They were used in some of the earliest modern studies of animal behaviour, and today they are used in testing for polluted water.

All sticklebacks have a long body, large head and strong jaws. They range in size from 2½ – 7½ in., most being only 3 – 4 in. long. The colour is usually greenish to black on the back and silver on the belly, sometimes with dark bars on the sides. They have two dorsal fins the first of which is made up of well spaced spines. The anal fin is similar to the second dorsal and lies opposite it. Each pelvic fin is one long spike and the pectoral fins are large. Most sticklebacks have a series of bony plates along each flank, the number varying with the species, and also within the species according to temperature and salinity.

There are a dozen species in the north temperate zone of the northern hemisphere and two of them range across Europe, Asia and North America. They are tolerant of salty water, at least two being found in the sea as well as in freshwater and two are wholly marine.

At home in river or sea

The 3-spined stickleback or tiddler, the most widespread, and the one we are most concerned with here, occurs throughout the northern hemisphere. It lives in all fresh waters except fast flowing mountain streams. It is also found in estuaries and along the coasts, and it has been caught 2 – 3 miles out at sea. It is not often found in stagnant or weed-choked waters, where the 10-spined stickleback, also known as the 9-spined, can live. Its distribution is similar to that of the 3-spined but is more local, both in North America and Eurasia. The 15-spined is wholly marine. In North America the 2½in. brook stickleback is found in the fresh waters of the United States and Canada, and the 4-spined stickleback is common along the eastern seaboard, from Virginia to Nova Scotia.

Swarms of sticklebacks

There is a remarkable occurrence recorded by Thomas Pennant in the mid-18th century. He tells us that in the Welland river, in eastern England, sticklebacks could be seen in 'such amazing shoals as to appear in a vast body occupying the whole width of the river'. A local farmer used them to manure his land. A man employed to catch them used to earn four shillings a day at the rate of a halfpenny a bushel. This would represent the incredible amount of about half a million sticklebacks a day.

Armoured or not

The variation in the bony plates or scutes along the flanks has led to four types being named. There is the 'trachura' type, with a complete row of scutes from head to tail, found in the north of the range and in salty waters and usually in half-grown individuals only. In the same areas live the 'semi-armata' type with scutes halfway along the body. In fresh waters in England and France are the 'gymnura' type with 3 or 4 scutes behind the head, and the 'hologymnura' form, without scutes, found in the south of the range.

Mixed carnivorous diet

The food of sticklebacks is almost any small invertebrate, the size of the prey depending on the age of the fish. It includes small crustaceans such as water fleas and freshwater shrimps, worms, small molluscs and their larvae, aquatic insects and their larvae, and sometimes fish eggs. Corresponding marine invertebrates are taken by those living in salt water, and these grow more quickly and to a slightly greater maximum size than those living in freshwater.

Nest-building fishes

As the breeding season approaches the male becomes more brightly coloured, with red on the front part of the underside. He is then called a red throat. He takes over a territory and drives out other intruding sticklebacks. In the centre of the territory he

▽ *Breeding preliminaries: a male three-spined stickleback building his nest. The nest is held together by a secretion from a modified part of his kidney.*

builds a nest of small pieces of plants g ued together with a sticky secretion from his kidneys. In the sea sticklebacks use pieces of the smaller seaweeds. The nest is lodged among the stems of water plants—among seaweeds in the sea—and when ready the male entices one or more females to lay her eggs in it. As each female lays and then departs the male enters the nest and sheds his milt to fertilise the eggs, which are just under $\frac{1}{12}$ in. diameter. These hatch in 5–12 days, according to the temperature, and during this time the male aerates them by fanning water through the nest. The 4-spined stickleback makes a nest with two holes in the top and the male puts his mouth against one hole and sucks water through the nest. The baby sticklebacks, $\frac{1}{6}$ in. long when hatched, are guarded by the male until they are ready to leave the nest. They grow to 1–2 in. long in the first year. The life span in the wild is $3\frac{1}{2}$ years.

Tapeworm

In spite of their armatures of spines sticklebacks are eaten, more especially by kingfishers and grebes. They tend to be infected with tapeworm, but this varies with the locality. In some lakes they are all infected.

Sign stimuli in courtship

The 3-spined stickleback became more than a sport for young anglers when Niko Tinbergen did his now famous study on its courtship. It provides a simple illustration, among other things, of the use by animals of sign stimuli. A male stickleback guarding his territory attacks another male because it has a red 'throat'. Even a wooden model held in a stickleback's territory will be attacked, provided it has a red throat. A female, ready to lay, on entering the territory, turns her abdomen swollen with ripe eggs towards him as he approaches. On seeing this he swims excitedly in what is called a zigzag dance. He will respond in the same way to a wooden model having the same shape. Having danced to her, the male turns and swims towards the nest. She follows and enters it after the male has indicated its position by pointing his head at the entrance. She enters and he butts her in the flank with his snout and trembles, which makes her respond by laying. He then enters the nest after she has left it and fertilises the eggs. The spawning is the result of a series of orderly stereotyped actions, each successive step being touched off by a definite signal or sign-stimulus, the red throat, swollen abdomen, zigzag dance and so on. It is, however, not so stereotyped that it never varies. For example if the female is more than ready to lay she may make straight for the nest.

▽ *A fifteen-spined stickleback: the slender* **Spinachia spinachia** *only lives in saltwater.*

class	**Pisces**
order	**Gasterosteiformes**
family	**Gasterosteidae**
genus & species	*Gasterosteus aculeatus* 3-spined stickleback, others

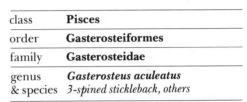

▽ *Not as dangerous as it looks: a male three-spined stickleback keeps a watchful eye on his young.*

Stingray

To say stingrays sting is an under-statement: they wound with a thrust of a poison dagger. Pliny, the Roman naturalist, wrote that the spine was as strong as iron, would pierce armour like an arrow, and driven into its root would cause a tree to wither.

The stingrays, related to skates, have a flattened body with wing-like pectoral fins and a whiplike tail bearing a long poison spine. The disc-like body may have a rounded leading edge or it may be drawn out slightly into a pointed snout. The pectoral fins and the pelvics are also rounded. The surface of the body is smooth with few or no denticles. The tail is slender and at least as long as the rest of the body. The spiracles are larger than the eyes. There is no dorsal fin, and the most obvious feature is the spine set in the tail, about a third of the way along. The upper surface is usually grey or brown, sometimes with white spots or with darker marbling. The undersurface is white to creamy white. Stingrays measure from 12 in. to 14½ ft across the fins, and weigh from 1½ lb up to 750 lb.

The 100 or more species live in tropical and temperate seas, as far north in summer as southern Scandinavia in Europe and equivalent latitudes elsewhere. They all live in shallow seas, seldom going deeper than 400 ft. Some species enter estuaries and even go up rivers, in a few instances for considerable distances.

△ *Dappled danger:* **Potamotrygon***, a species from South America which never leaves freshwater.*
▷ *An unwelcome inhabitant of the Bahamas' shores:* **Dasyatis americana** *moves off.*

Rapid action poison

Stingrays, like skates, spend much of their time on the seabed, searching for prey or merely resting. They move by wave-like undulations passing along the two pectoral fins, the tail being useless for swimming. When attacked, or even if only disturbed, the ray lashes with its tail, from side to side in some species, or bringing the tail up and over the body in others. This brings the swordlike spine into play. It is up to 15 in. long in the largest of the rays, with saw-toothed edges and grooves. The grooves are lined with a glistening white tissue which probably contains the poison.

The stab from a stingray not only injects poison, but also cuts and tears the flesh, and many people that have trodden on a stingray lying in shallow water have had to have stitches in their feet. Even a tiny puncture from the spine of a stingray has made a man faint. The effect of the poison is immediate and inflammation spreads around the wound almost as soon as the spine has penetrated. Other immediate symptoms are sharp shooting pains and throbbing. The poison affects the heart, breathing and nerves and it can be fatal although there are fairly simple remedies provided they are applied quickly. At one time washing the wound with iodine or permanganate of potash was recommended. Today, the treatment is to clean the wound, then immerse it in hot water for up to an hour, and give an anti-tetanus injection.

Clam-cracker

The mouth of the stingray is on the undersurface of the head. The jaws are wide and both have blunt teeth arranged like a pavement in rows, with several rows of broad teeth in the middle and rows of smaller teeth on each side. A North American species known as the stingaree is also called the clam-cracker. Its food, like that of other stingrays, is mainly molluscs and crustaceans, and sometimes fish.

Born alive

All stingrays are ovoviviparous. That is, the eggs are not laid but hatch in the oviduct, the young being eventually born alive. At first the young feed on the yolk in a yolk-sac hanging from their abdomens, the food passing direct into the digestive tube from the yolk-sac. Then, at a later stage, blood vessels grow out and around the yolk, and food is taken into the blood. Later tiny filaments grow out from the walls of the oviduct. Each has a network of tiny blood vessels and gives out a liquid food which the embryo stingray takes through its mouth or through its spiracles. It is the equivalent of the placenta in mammals.

Bayonet teeth

Rays and sharks do not have scales like bony fishes. Their skin is protected by dermal denticles (or 'little teeth in the skin'). Each denticle is made up of a pulp cavity inside a layer of dentine with a kind of enamel on the outside. These were once thought to be the equivalent of real teeth but with further biochemical research it is now realized they are not. For example, the 'dentine' is not true dentine. It has not yet been decided whether the spine of a stingray is a modified, and greatly enlarged, dermal denticle or not. One thing it shares with true teeth is that the spine may be replaced by a new one. Should the old spine not drop out before the new one grows out, the stingray may temporarily have two spines with which to lash its enemies, and exceptionally it may have three or four. These niceties would have held no interest for the peoples of the South Pacific who used them for spearheads. One of the dangers of being wounded by a stingray is that the poison tissue in its grooves may be left behind in the wound. Even worse, the spine may snap off and the piece left in the wound is very painful to remove. It is the equivalent of the saw-edged bayonet that was banned years ago.

class	**Selachii**
order	**Hypotremata**
family	**Dasyatidae**
genus & species	*Dasyatis pastinaca* others

212

Stonefish

The stonefish is almost the ugliest, if not the ugliest of all fishes and it is certainly the most poisonous. A stonefish is 6—12 in. long, has a heavy head which is broad and flat, and the body tapers rapidly from behind the head to the small tailfin. The mouth is wide and has a fairly large gape. The pectoral fins are large and winglike. The dorsal fin, which runs along the midline of the back, is armed with 13 stout spines. There are three more spines on the anal fin and one on each of the pelvic fins. The scaleless skin is covered with many irregular warts and a layer of slime. The colour of the fish is best described as the colour of mud, seaweed or stone—and if stones vary in colour, so do stonefishes! One stonefish even looks like a piece of rock covered with small algae.

The three species of the world's most venomous fish are found from the Red Sea to East Africa and across the Indian Ocean to the northern coasts of Western Australia and Queensland.

Defences on all sides

Stonefishes live in shallow seas, especially where the bottom is coral rock or tidal mud flats. They lie completely still even when anyone goes near them and their only reaction to a foot placed a few inches from them is to erect their spines. The stonefish is virtually invisible against its background and those who are poisoned by it probably never see it. Each of the spines has two poison sacs near its tip. Pressure on this tip makes a sheath covering it slide back leaving the point of the spine bare and exposing the grooves down which the poison flows. Although normally it is the spines on the back that do the damage, if the fish is kicked so that it rolls onto its side, the stonefish can still defend itself—with the anal and pelvic fins.

Fishermen in the Indian Ocean handle stonefishes with great care, especially as the fishes can stay alive 10 hours after they have been taken out of water. Even dead specimens lying high and dry on the beach are still able to inflict a poison wound.

Waiting for food

Stonefishes wait for their food to come to them. Any passing animal not too large to be swallowed is snapped up. They do not seem to be able to see the stonefish, which consequently never lacks a meal. The fish are snapped up in its capacious mouth faster than the eye can see. One moment a fish is swimming towards the stonefish's mouth, the next moment it has vanished, and so far as the human eye can tell, nothing has moved. The poison spines are never used for catching food, but are only used in self-defence.

It is hardly surprising, with so dangerous a fish that little is known about how it breeds. Something, however, is known about its enemies—and surprisingly it has enemies. Certain bottom-feeding sharks and rays,

with crushing teeth used for eating crabs and hard-shelled molluscs, occasionally take stonefishes. There is another disadvantage in staying very still on the seabed. In tropical seas there are large seasnails known as conchs which are both aggressive and carnivorous and stonefishes, especially young ones, fall victim to these.

Thirteen deadly spines

Reports on the effect of the spines on human beings differ. Some suggest that people have trodden on or handled stonefish and been either unaffected or little the worse for the experience. At the other extreme are reports of fatal results. It seems that one can be very slightly pricked in the finger and provided the sheath is not broken, or the wound only shallow, no poison will be injected. It seems also that once the spines have been touched and their poison ejected they are harmless, suggesting that the poison sacs, or the sheath, or both cannot be renewed. By contrast there are authentic cases on record of immediate, extremely painful symptoms, with death following. These speak of excruciating pain with the victim screaming, half mad with agony, collapse, delirium and maniacal ravings. Death follows in about six hours, but if the wounds are not fatal the agony may last up to eight hours then slowly diminish. There has been at least one case in which the patient did not fully recover for a year. In some instances the legs swell to elephantine proportions, there may be large blisters and the skin may slough. Fingers and toes are said to turn black and drop off.

Antidotes, which must be applied quickly, include a weak solution of hydrochloric acid or formalin and permanganate of potash. At the Serum Laboratories in Melbourne, Victoria, in Australia, an anti-venin has been produced.

△ *The stone mask of a stonefish* **Synanceia horrida**. *One of the ugliest and most poisonous fishes, it has been little studied.*

Fatality re-enacted

Any suspicion that reports of such grievous symptoms are exaggerated can be set aside in view of the ritual performed by some of the Australian aborigines. It takes the form of a charade, which has been described by Kelvin CB Green, of Australia, and it has been enacted since the time of the Bronze Age in Europe, that is, back in the aborigines' dream-time, their equivalent of times long past. A dancer imitates a man paddling in the tidal pools looking for fishes. He takes short steps, looking to the left, to the right. Then he takes big steps and suddenly lifts one foot, grabs it with a hand, screams and limps away. He sits down, then he lies down, he writhes and screams, while a witch doctor dances around him uttering incantations. Finally, the witch doctor throws up his hands in despair and the 'patient' wails a death song. The interesting feature of this theatrical display is that the dancer carries a clay model of a fish with 13 splinters of wood stuck into its back to represent spines.

class	**Pisces**
order	**Scorpaeniformes**
family	**Synanceiidae**
genus & species	*Synanceia horrida* *S. trachynis* *S. verrucosa*

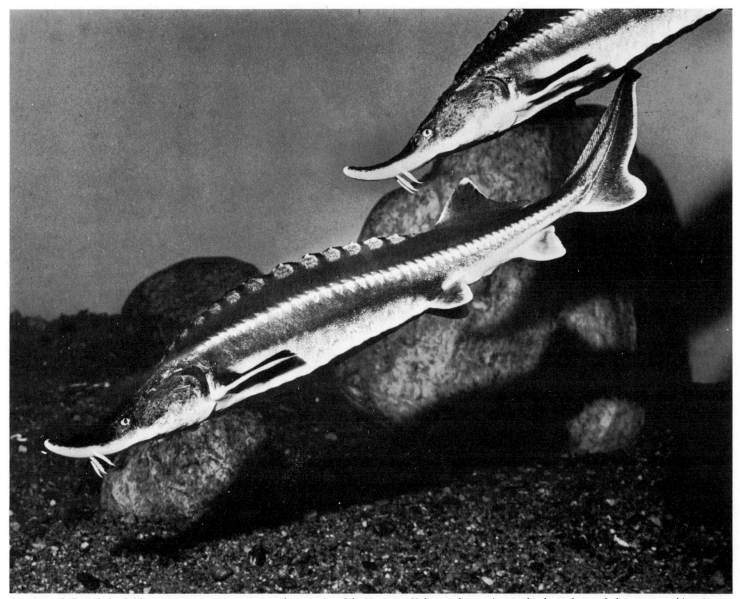

Despite a sleek and shark-like appearance, sturgeons are slow-moving fish. Here two Volga sterlets cruise gently above the sandy bottom, searching for food. They have poor eyesight and locate their food mainly by touch, using the sensitive barbels seen on the underside of their long snouts.

Sturgeon

The sturgeon is best known as the fish that gives caviare, the luxury food which could soon be a thing of the past. Of greater interest is the fact that the two dozen species are relics of a primitive race of fishes. They are more or less halfway between the sharks and the bony fishes, having a skeleton partly of bone and partly of cartilage. They are shark-like in shape and in the way the hind end of the body turns upwards into the upper lobe of the tailfin. The snout is tapered in the young fish, long and broad in adults, and in front of the mouth, on the underside of the head, are four barbels. The body is scaleless except for five rows of large plate-like scales with sharp points running from behind the gill-covers to the tailfin.

The largest is the Russian sturgeon or beluga (not to be confused with the mammal beluga, the white whale), of the Caspian and Black Seas and the Volga, Don, Dnieper and other rivers of that region. It is up to 28 ft long and

3 210 lb weight. One that was 13 ft long and weighed 2 200 lb was known to be 75 years old. It yielded 400 lb of caviare. The Atlantic sturgeon, on both sides of the North Atlantic reaches 11 ft and 600 lb. The white sturgeon of the Pacific coast of North America usually weighs less than 300 lb, but there are records of 1 285, 1 800 and 1 900 lb. The sterlet of the rivers of the USSR is up to 3 ft long. The rest of the two dozen species of sturgeon are all found in temperate waters throughout the northern hemisphere.

Numbers down everywhere

Sturgeons are slow-moving fish, spending their time grubbing on the bottom for food. Some, however, make long migrations. Individuals tagged in North American waters have been found to travel 900 miles. Most species live in the sea and go back up the rivers to spawn. The largest, the beluga, from which half the world's supply of caviare comes, is entirely freshwater. Today all sturgeons are fewer in number than they were a century or two ago, partly from overfishing and partly from the pollution of rivers and to some extent because

hydro-electric schemes have spoilt their spawning runs. In the 17th century a prosperous sturgeon fishery flourished in the New England States of America. In the mid-19th century they were still being caught, for their caviare and for a high quality lamp oil their flesh yielded. A century later the annual catch had fallen by 90%. Sturgeons were once abundant off the Atlantic coast of Europe. Now they are found mainly around the mouth of the Gironde river in western France, the Guadalquivir in Spain and in Lake Ladoga in the USSR. A few only are caught each year around the British Isles and adjacent seas. Around the Black Sea–Caspian area overfishing has brought the sturgeon yield to a low ebb and efforts have been made to establish hatcheries, to rear young sturgeon and so replenish the stock. It has been estimated that as many as 15 000 sturgeons have been caught in these seas and adjoining rivers in a day.

Rummages for food in the mud

The name of this fish in several European languages means the stirrer, from the way the sturgeon rummages among the mud for food. This it finds largely by touch, using its sensitive barbels. Sturgeon also have

215

A young sterlet barely drifts along, its sensitive barbels tracing food. As it grows the nose broadens and the fish may reach 3 ft in length.

taste-buds, which are normally on the tongue or inside the mouth in other fish, but in the sturgeon are on the outside of the mouth. These help in the selection of food. They protrude from the toothless mouth to suck in the food. Sturgeons are slow feeders and can survive several weeks without eating. In freshwater they eat insect larvae, worms, crayfish, snails and other small fishes. In the sea they take bivalve molluscs, shrimps and other small crustaceans, worms and more small fishes than are eaten in fresh water. The beluga feeds in winter mainly on flounder, mullet and gobies in the Black Sea, and on roach, herring and gobies in the Caspian.

When caviare hatches

Spawning takes place in depths of 18—20 ft. The eggs are blackish, $\frac{1}{10}$ in. diameter and sticky so they adhere to water plants and stones, or clump together in masses. A single female may lay 2—3 million in one season. These hatch in 3—7 days, the larvae being $\frac{1}{2}$ in. long but their first summer they may grow to 8 in.

Use for the swimbladder

Sturgeon have been fished for their flesh and their oil as well as for their caviare. They have also supplied isinglass. This is from the swimbladder and was first named by the Dutch in 1525. They called it *huisenblas* which became anglicized as isinglass. When prepared for use it looks like semi-transparent plastic sheets, and it is almost pure gelatin. It is still used today for special cements and water-proofing materials, but its main use is in clearing white wines, an ounce of isinglass being enough to clarify up to 300 gallons.

Royal fish

In the days of Ancient Rome the fish, garlanded with flowers, was piped into the banquet carried by slaves similarly crowned with flowers. It was, however, Edward II of England who made it a royal fish. His decree ran: 'The King shall have the wreck of the sea throughout the realm, whales and great sturgeons, except in certain places privileged by the King.' Sturgeon have ascended English rivers including the Thames

and at one time any caught above London Bridge belonged to the Lord Mayor of London. Henry I is said to have banned even that. Indeed, he forbade the eating of sturgeon at any table than his own. A royal fish indeed: and, in the 1950's, as Sir Alister Hardy recalls in his book *The Open Sea*: a sturgeon 'died in an excess of misplaced homage, and was covered with distinction, by burying itself in the condenser pipe of one of Her Majesty's aircraft-carriers: HMS *Glory*!' — a worthy burial.

class	**Pisces**
order	**Chondrostei**
family	**Acipensenidae**
genera & species	***Acipenser ruthenus*** sterlet *A. sturio* Atlantic sturgeon ***A. transmontanus*** white sturgeon ***Huso huso*** beluga others

*The aptly named shovelnose sturgeon **Scaphirhynchus platorynchus**; the bizarre snout is used to dig snails, shrimps and other morsels from the gravel.*

Sunfish

There are two kinds of sunfish. One lives in the sea and gets its name from the false idea that it comes to the surface to bask in the sun and is dealt with on page 144 under ocean sunfish. The other is a freshwater fish whose behaviour is influenced by the sun.

Freshwater sunfishes are North American. The two dozen perch-like species are variously called basses (page 30), crappies and blue gills, as well as sunfishes. They usually have a long continuous dorsal fin, the front part of which is spiny. In a few species there is a slight notch where the front and hind parts meet, and the rear portion is higher than the front part. Several species have a so-called ear flap, where the operculum extends backwards. This is often made more obvious by its colouring: white-edged in the long-eared sunfish, sometimes with dots of red on the flap itself, or with a blood-red blotch as in the pumpkinseed or common sunfish. The smallest are the banded and the mottled sunfishes, never more than $1\frac{1}{2}$ in. long. The pygmy or blue spotted is $3\frac{1}{2}$ in. long. The largemouth bass may be $2\frac{1}{2}$ ft long and up to 25 lb.

Sunfishes are most common in the central and eastern regions of the United States. The only species native to the west of the Rockies is the Sacramento perch, although others have now been introduced into the rivers of California.

Black-banded sunfish **Mesogonistius chaetodon**: a popular aquarium fish in Europe and America.

Susceptible to change

Most sunfishes live in clear lowland rivers and lakes, especially where there is a sandy bottom, and particularly in flowing waters with quiet weedy shallows. The smaller species form small shoals, the larger are solitary and predatory. All are very sensitive to changes in their environment, especially to sudden changes of temperature. The red-bellied sunfish, for example, winters in the deeper water of lakes and migrates into shallows to spawn when the temperature of the water is 10°C/50°F. They are, however, strongly influenced by sunlight, possibly largely through its effect on temperature. On a dull day they are not very active. Thus, their first act on coming to a spawning ground is to dig a redd. On dull days the sunfishes do no more than station themselves over their redd, fanning it with their fins, so preventing it from silting up. On a sunny day the shadow from a passing cloud is enough to make them stop all activities.

Swimming animals eaten

Sunfishes feed on swimming animals, rarely touching anything on the bottom. The smaller species eat insect larvae, especially midge larvae, and small crustaceans. The larger sunfishes eat small fishes.

Male guards nest

The chief interest in sunfishes is in their breeding behaviour. The male digs the redd, a shallow depression in the sand, by using his tail as a fan. He then entices the female into this to lay. The redd is usually in a spot sheltered by water plants or large stones, and the male may use bits of plant to reinforce the nest. Also, the smaller the fish the shallower the water it would choose to nest in. In some species there is no great difference between male and female, but in some the male is more brightly coloured. The female lays about 1 000 eggs which tend to stick together in clumps. They also stick to sand grains which helps to hide them. Once the female has laid, she is driven away by the male who guards the nest, fanning with his fins to aerate the eggs, and chasing away any intruder. The eggs hatch in 3—6 days. At first they lie in the redd, later they cling to the water plants, but the male remains in attendance for 2—3 weeks, shepherding the babies into the redd each night. One reason why the male must guard the eggs and young is that other young sunfishes will eat them.

Can't bear vibrations

The choice of the nesting site seems to depend on vibrations in the water. As they come into breeding condition the sunfishes that have been living in schools disperse, as if unable to bear each other's company. The reason seems to be that they are intolerant of vibrations set up by their fellows in the normal course of moving about. This was put to the test. Various objects were put into the water to act as baffles. It was found that as soon as a baffle was placed between two males, cutting off their vibrations, they were prepared to nest much closer together.

Colours and movement

One of the most colourful species is the pumpkinseed sunfish. The male is grey-green with 5—8 pearly bars on the flanks, or in older individuals the bars may be greenish-blue. There are reddish or orange spots on the head, orange-red on the throat and belly and an orange blotch on the black 'ear flap'. The gill cover itself is green with red lines and spots, and the fins are green to yellow. To test the use of these colours a male sunfish was anaesthetized and held near another male with a nest in an aquarium. The colours apparently meant nothing to it; and when the anaesthetized male was manipulated so that it went through the movements a courting female would make, the male occupying the nest courted it. Yet when a mirror was put into the water the male displayed vigorously at his image, presumably recognizing it as a male by the movements it made. To be on the safe side, tests were made with plasticine models and individuals of the same species, to see if smell had any effect. So long as the correct movements were made with the model the male would attack it or court it, according to whether it was made to move like a rival male or like a courting female. Colour must have some importance but these experiments showed that the kind of movements were equally important.

Minnows move in

A kind of cuckoo behaviour is shown by an American minnow *Notropis umbratilis*. When a male green sunfish is establishing his nest the minnows assemble above him. When a pair of sunfishes lay their eggs, the minnows lay theirs in the same nest. Tests suggested that the minnows are first attracted by the movements of the male sunfish. For example, if the male is taken away, even although his nest is still there, the minnows also depart. The stimulus that makes the minnows spawn is something given out into the water from the milt or the ova of the sunfish. Even when in an aquarium with no sunfish nor the sunfish's nest, minnows will spawn if the fluid from the male sunfish's milt or from the female sunfish's ovary is put into the water. It is probably detected by smell.

class	**Pisces**
order	**Perciformes**
family	**Centrarchidae**
genera & species	**Archoplytes interruptus** *Sacramento perch*
	Elassoma evergladei *mottled dwarf sunfish*
	E. zonatum *banded dwarf sunfish*
	Enneacanthus gloriosus *pygmy or blue spotted sunfish*
	Lepomis auritus *red-bellied sunfish*
	L. gibbosus *pumpkinseed sunfish*
	L. megalotis *longeared sunfish*
	Micropterus salmoides *largemouth bass, others*

is no more than a simple tube showing no sign of the future stomach and intestine. Later when the fins have developed, outgrowths from the dorsal and anal fins rich in blood vessels, absorb nourishment. The liquid also contains the oxygen necessary for respiration. At a later stage some of the surface cells of the walls of the ovary drop away and are consumed by the growing embryos, as are any sperms left over.

Tightly packed
The number of young varies with the species and with the size of the mother, but usually there are between 3 and 80. In the shiner or yellow-banded seaperch, for example, the number is 3–20, exceptionally 36. An 8in. mother would probably have 20, each about 1¼in. long, tightly packed within the ovary.

Commercial fishery
Some of the larger surf perch are fished commercially or for sport. The annual catch for the market is about 150 tons in the United States, and surfperch are also caught for market around Japan and Korea.

Extraordinary fishes
The first reports about the viviparity of surfperch were sent from California, in 1853, to the celebrated Louis Agassiz, professor at Harvard University. He published an account of these, calling them extraordinary fishes and, as so often follows from a fresh discovery, attention was focussed on them and they were written about in scientific journals all over the world. Perhaps, because so many remarkable things have been discovered since then, the surfperch do not excite us so much today. Yet everything about them is extraordinary. There are plenty of freshwater fishes that bear living young, but very few marine fishes, other than the surfperches. Few bony fishes copulate, other than surfperches. We have to go to bats for examples, among vertebrates, of delayed fertilisation such as is found in surfperches. Then, it is most unusual for development of embryos to take place in the cavity of the ovary. It is most unusual among viviparous fishes for the embryos to be nourished other than through a yolk sac. And then we have the unique situation of the young, or at least the young males, becoming sexually mature before birth. Perhaps it is this early maturity of the young surfperch that accounts for their being born in the surf—in a place likely to be reasonably free of enemies at the time they are pairing.

Surfperch

A hundred years ago the surfperch fishes were described as extraordinary not only because they bear their young alive but because the 'babies' are sexually mature almost as soon as they are born. Surfperch are very like the freshwater perch except that the dorsal fin, spiny in front and soft-rayed in the rear half, is continuous instead of being in two distinct parts. There is also a groove in the back on either side of the dorsal fin. Their bodies are compressed from side to side and their lips are fleshy. They are mainly silvery, darker on the back than the belly, and at the front edge of the anal fin in the male is an intromittent organ for transferring the milt to the female. Surfperch, also called seaperch or surf-fishes, are 5–18 in. long according to the various species.

Most of the 25 species come into the surf to drop their young; for the rest of the time they live in shallow seas. The pink seaperch is unusual in living at depths of about 600 ft, others may be found at times in tide pools, and the freshwater tule perch lives in the Sacramento River in California. Except for two species living off Japan and Korea, all seawater surfperch live off the Pacific coast of North America, from Alaska to southern California.

Infantile mating
Surfperch are in every way quite ordinary perch-like fishes, feeding on small crustaceans and other small invertebrates, except for their breeding, which goes on more or less throughout the summer. In some species at least, the males are slightly smaller than the females and somewhat darker in colour during the winter. The actual act of copulation has not often been observed, but it is known that it takes place, in most species, in shallow water and that the young are born the following summer at the surface. The main point is that it takes place within two days of birth, the males being sexually mature at birth, the females maturing soon after, and pairing then takes place. This is probably unique, certainly among the higher animals.

Living in the ovary
Another unusual feature is that the ova remain in their follicles in the ovary until they are fertilised. In most viviparous fishes they are shed into the oviduct before being fertilised. Moreover, although sperm are introduced into the females at copulation, the ova are not fertilised until the following spring, the sperm remaining dormant until then. The ova are small and contain little yolk but the embryos into which they grow are nourished by a fluid given out from the ovary. Once the fertilised ova drop from their follicles into the cavity of the ovary they develop rapidly and the embryos grow a gill opening. Cilia on this drive a current of liquid food through the gill and into the embryo's digestive tract, which at this stage

class	**Pisces**
order	**Perciformes**
family	**Embiotocidae**
genera & species	**Cymatogaster aggregata** *shiner* **Hysterocarpus traski** *tule perch* **Zalembius rosaceus** *pink seaperch* *others*

Surgeonfish

Most surgeonfishes are very colourful but they cause difficulties for those trying to name them because of the way they change colour. They are called surgeonfishes because they carry lancets that can cut one's flesh as cleanly as a surgeon's scalpel.

Surgeonfishes are deepbodied fishes, flattened from side to side, and almost oval in outline except for the tailfin. They have small rough scales and small gill openings. The tapering snout ends in a small mouth which has a single row of teeth in each jaw, used for scraping food off coral. Both dorsal and anal fins start just behind the head and end just short of the tail. The pectoral fins are relatively large. The 'lancets' are small, extremely sharp, bony keels, one on either side near the base of the tailfin. In some species they are jackknife hinged, the hinges being at the hind end. When not in use the lancet lies in a groove or a sheath. The lancets are used as weapons by the fish and can be quickly erected and thrust forward when needed. Some members of the family have several lancets on each side. The lancets are sharp and can cut badly anyone that handles the fish carelessly. The 200 species of surgeonfishes grow to 2 ft in length at the most. Their colours, while varied, have the subdued quality of pastel shades.

Different colours

Surgeonfishes live in shoals on and around coral reefs, so are restricted to warm seas. They crop coral for small algae, possibly eating portions of small invertebrates living on the coral, but these are taken only accidentally. Surgeonfishes range from Madagascar across the Indo-Pacific to Hawaii. A common species is the yellow surgeon which can be found in two colour phases, one yellow, the other brown. The first is found only around Hawaii, the other throughout the Indo-Pacific. The five-banded surgeonfish of the Indo-Pacific, up to 10 in. long, has a dark apple-green body with dark brown vertical bars. It is also known as the convictfish. The blue tang is blue when adult, but bright yellow when immature with a blue margin on the dorsal and anal fins. Marked changes in shape occur in some species, like the bumphead surgeon which has a smooth forehead when young but develops a large bump on its head which, with a large eye either side of it, makes it look grotesque.

Early development

The convictfish has a separate race in the seas around Hawaii, recognized by a dark sickle-shaped mark on the base of each pectoral fin. Most surgeonfishes breed throughout the year but the Hawaiian race breeds only from December to July. Each female lays 40 000 eggs which are about $\frac{1}{4}$ in.

▷ *A harmony of blue and yellow curves—a shoal of **Acanthurus leucosternon** browse a coral reef.*

diameter and contain an oil droplet that buoys them up to the surface. The larvae hatch in 26 hours and are just under $\frac{1}{12}$ in. long. They float upside down at the surface for another 16 hours, until the contents of their yolk sacs are half used up. Then they begin to sink gradually, and as they do, they start swimming. At the end of four days, the larva has grown a swimbladder and is able to swim about and capture its food of plankton.

The elongated, almost tadpole-like larva changes after $2\frac{1}{2}$ months into a diamond-shaped fish, flattened from side to side with long dorsal and anal fins. The second spine from the front of each fin is long, toothed throughout its length and venomous. The spine of the pelvic fin is similar in shape and also poisonous.

The early development of the convictfish is probably not typical since the doctorfish of Florida to Brazil passes through the larval form in a matter of days. One feature of the surgeonfish larva is the great change that takes place in the intestine. The larva feeds on small plankton animals, the adult is wholly or almost entirely vegetarian. As the larva changes to the baby fish with something of the form of the adult, the intestine grows, increasing by approximately three times its original length.

Formidable defence

The names surgeonfish and doctorfish must owe their origin entirely to the shape and the sharp edges of the lancets on the tail. There is nothing beneficent in these. On the contrary, they are weapons of offence comparable to the sting of the tail of the stingray. An outstanding feature of the stingray, the flat fish related to the skate, is that it swims with its pectoral fins and the tail is reserved almost entirely for lashing to bring the sting into action. The surgeonfishes, so different in shape, also swim with their pectoral fins, not with the tail like other fishes of their shape. As they are mainly vegetarian they do not need speed for catching food, and they have formidable weapons of defence, so they do not need speed to escape from enemies. They swim with a rowing action of their pectoral fins, the tail fin at most making leisurely waving movements. When necessary, however, they thrash the tail violently from side to side, the lancets sticking out on either side, and giving an enemy sharp, slashing cuts. As a result other fishes give them a wide berth, except for certain cleaner fishes (see page 25), which remove the parasites from their skin. When a surgeonfish feels the need for this it swims over to where the cleaner fish has its station and changes colour. In the case of the Atlantic ocean surgeon, the one on which the best observations have been made, the surgeonfish changes to a dark olive brown instead of the normal reddish purple. It is probably a signal, a sign of peace, an indication that it will not slash its benefactor. Surgeonfishes may change colour more often than we suspect. There is a record of one surgeonfish, in dispute with another, which became white in the front half and dark in the rear half; it stayed like this for half an hour—looking like a new species!

class	**Pisces**
order	**Perciformes**
family	**Acanthuridae**
genera & species	***Acanthurus caeruleus*** *blue tang* ***A. bahianus*** *ocean surgeon* ***A. hepatus*** *doctorfish* ***A. triostegus*** *convictfish* ***Naso tuberosus*** *bumphead* ***Zebrasoma flavescens*** *yellow surgeon* *others*

▽ *The yellow surgeonfish occurs in two distinct colour phases as shown by these specimens in the aquarium. The yellow phase is found only around the Hawaiian Islands, the brown phase throughout the Indo-Pacific.*

Swamp eel

Apart from their eel-shape, swamp eels are in no way related to true eels. They mainly breathe air and have more or less lost their gills. In fact it is hard to say what these unusual fishes are related to.

Some of the peculiarities of swamp eels are that they usually have no paired fins, the dorsal and anal fins are without fin-rays—they are little more than soft ridges which meet at the hind end of the body—and there is a single gill-opening on the throat. The lateral line is well marked. The scales are very small, the eyes are small and covered with skin or else are absent altogether. The colour is black, brown or green, often with spots or streaks of yellow, red or brown. Swamp eels are 1—5 ft long.

*There are about eight species in the freshwater and brackish swamps of Central and South America, tropical West Africa, Asia and Australia. One species, **Anommatophasma candidum**, was discovered a few years ago living in underground waters in northwest Australia. They range from the northern tip of Japan southwards, including the whole of the Malay Archipelago and the Philippines. There is one marine species, **Macrotrema caligans**, off the coasts of Malaya.*

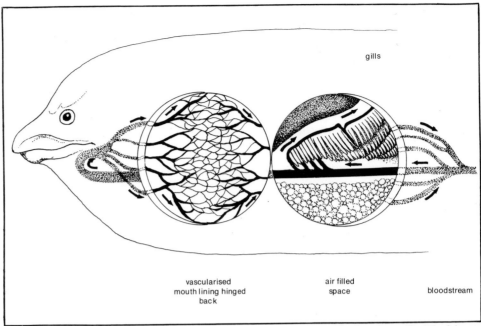

△ *Respiration system of* **Synbranchus,** *with flap of mouth lining hinged back to show gills. The fish gulps air at the surface, which passes direct into the bloodstream via the vein network and gills.*

Fishes without gills

Swamp eels mainly live in waters poor in oxygen which are liable to dry out. They avoid the light, and so tend to move about mainly at night. They do not use gills for breathing as much as other fishes. The main way of breathing is to come to the surface to gulp air, or they may even wriggle out over the surface of the swampy mud. Some swamp eels are as amphibious as many frogs and toads. In summer they burrow into the mud and go into a kind of summer sleep or aestivation.

The accessory breathing organs are different for almost each species. The cuchia of India and Burma has very small gills but it has a large lung-like sac opening from each gill cavity which extends up to behind the head and a short way along the back. These are only just under the skin and when inflated the skin behind the head bulges. Another species, the rice eel, from China and Japan to Burma, Thailand and the Malay Archipelago, uses the throat and the hind portion of its intestine for breathing. The lining membranes of these are richly supplied with blood vessels and act as lungs. More extraordinary are the species of *Synbranchus* which seem to use their gills for breathing air. They come to the surface to gulp air, the oxygen from the air passing directly, so far as we know, into the blood in the gills. Certainly when aestivating, the fish must be able to use the gills in this way.

Breathing involves not only an intake of oxygen but also the removal of carbon dioxide from the body. There are indications that in swamp eels much of the disposal of carbon dioxide is through the skin.

Fishes without eyes

The cuchia buries itself as deep as 2—3 ft in soft mud in summer, and since most fishes have no eyelids there must be some adaptation to meet this. The eyes are sunken and are covered with a thick semi-transparent skin formed of several layers of epidermal cells and a layer of connective tissue. This covering is flush with the surface of the body, so it offers no impediment to burrowing. The eye itself is degenerate. The lens is spherical and its inner surface is practically touching the retina, which consists almost entirely of cones set well apart. The structure of the eye shows it is of little use for vision, and this is confirmed by the fact that there are few blood vessels supplying the eye. Because so little oxygen reaches the eye, vision is bound to be poor. Even those swamp eels with eyes supplied with blood vessels probably use them no more than to tell light from darkness. Members of *Typhlobranchus* are totally blind.

Hearty appetites

If the gills, eyes and fins of swamp eels are degenerate, the mouth makes up for this by being strongly developed. It is relatively large with thick lips, and there are rows of teeth on the jaws and the palate. Swamp eels feed on worms, snails and other small invertebrates, or on fishes. They are said by aquarists to be snappy, rapacious and greedy, eating their own weight of food a day—when they are not aestivating.

Bubble-nesting male/female

One species, the rice eel, has been found within the last few years to be first male, later changing to female. The first sign that this species is about to spawn is when the male builds a nest of bubbles. He gulps air at the surface and spits out the mucus-covered bubbles at the surface, where they form a raft. As the female lays, the male takes each egg in his mouth and spits it on to the underside of the raft. When the clutch is complete he takes over the care of the eggs and of the young when they hatch.

It is usually said that he guards them, but a more likely role is that of supplying them with oxygen through his skin. When the young fishes first hatch they have large pectoral fins well supplied with blood vessels that are used for breathing. These drop off when the young fishes are 10 days old.

Stagnant protection

Swamp eels are largely protected from aquatic predators by living in stagnant waters but they are the prey of large swamp-feeding birds such as storks and herons. In some places they are used as food by the local people. This is especially true of the rice eel, which has also been successfully introduced into Hawaii.

Shaped to suit environment

Almost any elongate fish is liable to be called an eel, so we have conger eels, moray eels, slime eels, spiny eels, cusk eels, rock eels, and swamp eels. The usual remark made is that these fishes tend to look alike because they all live under the same conditions. In other words, the resemblance between them is due to the often-mentioned convergent evolution. We have to remember, however, that so much of biology belongs to the hen and egg realm: which came first, the hen or the egg? It may equally well be that in many instances the fishes became eel-shaped and this made it possible for them to survive in similar environments. This is probably especially true of swamp eels.

class	**Pisces**
order	**Synbranchia**
family	**Synbranchidae**
genera & species	***Amphipnous cuchia*** cuchia ***Monopterus albus*** rice eel others

221

Swordfish

Although placed in a separate family the swordfish or broadbill resembles the sailfish (page 182) in many of its habits but differs somewhat in appearance. It also is beautifully streamlined with the upper jaw carried forward into a sword-like beak, flattened from top to bottom and oval in section. The front dorsal fin is high, short at the base, and curves backwards. There are no pelvic fins. The first anal fin is fairly large and both the second dorsal and second anal fins are very small and set far back. The body is flattened from side to side and is a dark purple-blue on the back shading to silvery-grey on the underside. The sword is black above, paler on the underside. The fins are dark with a silvery sheen. Like the sailfish the swordfish is reputed to reach a length of nearly 20 ft and a weight of over 1 000 lb. Alwyne Wheeler, in his recent book The Fishes of the British Isles and North West Europe, *gives the maximum length as 16 ft and a weight of over 1 000 lb for the Atlantic and 1 500 lb for the Pacific swordfish. The more usual size is, however, between 6 ft and 11 ft, with a weight between 100—300 lb.*

The swordfish ranges through all tropical seas, wandering into temperate seas in summer. It seems to enter temperate seas more than the sailfish, as shown by its being 'not infrequently' seen off the Atlantic coasts of Europe. Moribund swordfish sometimes reach the North Sea.

Warmblooded fish

Swordfish are mainly solitary, occasionally seen in pairs, more rarely in groups, and even then there is usually 30—40 ft between the individuals. When swimming at the surface the high dorsal fin and the tip of the upper lobe of the crescentic tailfin project above water. Although no tests have been made on it, the swordfish is credited with similar speeds to those of the sailfish. It also has sieve-like gills giving a large surface for absorption of oxygen. In most fishes the amount of blood in the body is less than in the higher vertebrates and it flows sluggishly through the arteries and veins. In the swordfish, as in the sailfish and other fast fishes like the marlin and tuna, there is abundant blood in the body, which is comparatively warm. This is linked with the active life they lead. The swordfish not only swims swiftly but can take enormous leaps out of the water. It does the same when hooked and will sometimes circle the boat with only its tail in the water, thrashing it to foam as it drives its nearly vertical body skittering over the water.

Sword kept for cleaving water

The food of swordfishes and their methods of catching prey are like those of sailfishes. Smaller fishes such as herring, sardines, mackerel, bonitos and albacores are snapped up, and swordfishes are also said to swim round small shoals striking out with the 'sword' and then eating dead and stunned fishes at leisure. The stomachs of captured swordfishes have been found to contain remains of squid and of fishes that live in deep water and on the bottom. It has been suggested that the males fight with their sword-like beaks or attack larger animals such as whales. One celebrated story left us by a certain Captain Crow tells of a large whale being attacked simultaneously by thresher sharks and swordfishes but as killer whales are sometimes called swordfishes, because of the somewhat sabre-like dorsal fin, they are more likely to have been the culprits. The sword probably functions as a cutwater, for use in high-speed swimming, and secondarily as a weapon for catching food, as described above.

Covered with warts

Spawning takes place in the open sea, in water of 24°C/85°F or more, from February to April in the tropical Atlantic and from June to August in the Mediterranean. The small eggs float and hatch in 2½ days. The baby fishes follow much the same development as in the sailfish except that they are covered with small round warts arranged lengthwise. The function of these outgrowths is obscure, but they disappear when

Part of a ship's timber showing the extensive damage caused by a swordfish.

the adult shape is reached. Baby swordfishes feed in waters down to 96 ft, largely on the larvae of other species of smaller fishes which are found in great abundance in these waters.

Rich livers

The flesh of swordfishes is firm, greyish-white, of a rich flavour, and the oil from their livers is said to have a high medicinal value. The fishes are harpooned for commercial purposes. It is also taken in the tuna traps set up by fishermen.

Terrible giant of the sea

The idea that the sword of a swordfish is an offensive weapon was fostered largely by the way, from time to time, this sword has been found embedded in the timbers of ships. If, however, there is a fish with a sharp beak on the front of its head and it is able to swim at 60 mph, there are bound to be times when such a fish will collide with something, such as a ship, whale or another large fish. Nevertheless, it was the finding of these broken-off swords that earned the swordfish the name of terrible giant of the sea. What is more interesting is the extent of the damage caused by the sword and the force required to do it.

The great American bibliographer and collector of natural history curiosities, Dr EW Gudger, brought together as many examples as he could find of 'attacks' by swordfishes on ships. For example, he listed the ship off Brazil struck one night with such force that the helmsman had difficulty in keeping the ship on course. Another on his list was a ship off the Azores hit so hard the crew thought she had struck a rock. One of the more remarkable cases was that of the whaler 'Fortune'. When she reached harbour at Plymouth, Massachusetts in 1826 she had the sword of a swordfish in her hull that had penetrated a copper sheathing, 4 in. of board, solid oak a foot thick, 2½ in. of hard oak ceiling plank and the head of an oil cask. There are many similar examples. Sir Richard Owen, giving evidence in a case of damage by swordfish in 1868, said a swordfish would strike with 'the accumulated force of 15 double-handed hammers, . . . velocity equal to that of a swivel shot . . . as dangerous in its effects as a heavy artillery projectile.'

Sir James Gray once made the comparison that a 600lb swordfish travelling at 10 mph running into the side of a ship would hit it with the force of one-third of a ton per sq. in. It would be the equivalent of the blow of a 10lb sledgehammer meeting a ship travelling at 80 mph. Moreover, if a 600lb swordfish travelling at 10 mph were to meet a ship travelling towards it at 10 mph, the force of the impact would be equal to 4½ tons per sq in. A swordfish is thought to travel at times at 60 mph, although it is unlikely that this speed would be maintained for long periods of time.

In spite of all that is said here, scientists believe that swordfishes sometimes go berserk and attack deliberately. Whether this was true of the man mentioned in Daniel's 'Rural Sports' is not known. This man, in the River Severn, near Worcester, England, was 'struck, and absolutely received his death wound through a swordfish'.

△ All of the billfishes in the family Xiphiidae have long nose extensions, but the swordfish develops it to the extreme. The sword may be up to one third the body length. It is flattened, rather than rounded like those of other billfishes — giving it the common name of broadbill.

▽ An unusual catch: Mr E Leathers and the 6ft swordfish he caught in the river Ouse in England in 1969. Swordfishes are usually found in tropical and warm temperate seas but like turtles they sometimes venture north. The world record measured 15 ft and weighed 1 182 lb.

class	**Pisces**
order	**Perciformes**
family	**Xiphiidae**
genus & species	*Xiphias gladius*

Swordtail

The swordtail is one of the more important as well as most popular of aquarium fishes, not only for its beauty but because it is a good subject for selective breeding. Swordtails are live-bearing tooth-carps, so they have the shape of that family. The dorsal fin is relatively large and so is the tailfin which is broad-based and rounded at the rear edge. The pelvic fins are at about the middle of the body. The females are up to 5 in., the males being up to $3\frac{1}{4}$ in. exclusive of the sword, which is formed from much elongated rays of the lower part of the tailfin. The outstanding feature of the swordtail is its colours.

Swordtails have been bred in so many colours and colour variations that a description of these in a small space would be impossible. What follows here can, however, be taken as a sort of standard colouring, the one most likely to be seen. The back is olive-green shading to greenish-yellow on the flanks and yellowish on the belly. The scales are edged with

brown so the whole body seems to be covered with a fine net. The fins are yellowish-green, the dorsal fin being ornamented with reddish blotches and streaks. From the tip of the snout to the base of the tailfin runs a rainbow band of colour made up of zigzag lines of carmine, green, cinnabar, purple or violet. The sword of the male is yellow at the base shading to orange, bordered with black above and below.

Swordtails live in the fresh waters of southern Mexico, British Honduras and Guatemala in Central America.

Bullying males

As is usual with popular aquarium fishes more is gleaned about their way of life from individuals kept in tanks than from those living in the wild. They live the usual uneventful lives of small fishes, most of their time being taken up with searching for food – or bullying each other. Their mouth is inclined slightly upward making it easy for them to take any food floating at the surface. They can also search on the bottom, the body held almost vertical with the head downward. They also snap at small swimming invertebrates. They are, in fact, omnivorous, taking anything small, both plant and animal, swimming or floating, and in the aquarium they spend much time grazing small algae growing on the glass or stones.

There seems to be a strong social hierarchy known as peck order in a community of swordtails which reveals itself in the aquarium by one of the males tending to bully the rest. Indeed, these fishes seem to be unduly spiteful, especially in small aquaria. Dominance in a community of any species is decided and maintained by fighting, or at least, by aggressive displays, and is closely linked with the strength of the sex hormones. Experiments with swordtails have shown, however, that a female maintains her position in the social hierarchy for 1–3 months after being spayed and a castrated male retains his for $1-6\frac{1}{2}$ months. This is unusual because as a rule, when the gonads are removed, and with them the sex hormones, the individual usually drops more or less immediately to a subordinate rank in the social hierarchy.

△ *A male hybrid swordtail with a black-edged yellow 'sword' swims alongside a female.*
◁ *The male green swordtail, surrounded by red and green swordtails, began life as a female.*

Mystery of sex-reversal

Swordtails first became aquarium fishes about 1910, and not long after this the idea began to be current that these fishes undergo a remarkable sex-reversal. In 1926 Essenberg reported that females, after having had several broods, may become fully functional males. From the many reports that followed this the impression is gained that this is commonplace. There have, for example, been several authoritative books on freshwater or aquarium fishes written during the years since Essenberg's report was published, and all have given prominence to this idea. Gunther Sterba in his book first published in 1959 speaks of the quite remarkable and always astonishing sex-reversal in swordtails. He claims that in some strains as many as 30% of females later change into males. Yet in 1957 Myron Gordon, who had made a special study of the species, had already claimed that such changes were extremely rare, quoting a substantial report on swordtails by Friess, in 1933, in support of his claim.

Subjects for heredity study

If the supposedly remarkable sex-reversal is still in doubt there are other aspects of the breeding for which we have more reliable information. Swordtails have been almost domesticated and by selective breeding a wide range of colour varieties exist, usually named according to their colours, such as the green, the red, the red-eyed red, the red-wag, the black, the golden, and the albino. According to Dr Myron Gordon, quoted by William T. Innes, there are wild specimens comparable to all the selected varieties produced up to 1935 except the golden. There have, however, been others since then, including the one seen below.

Swordtails have been much used for the study of genetics, by crossing the colour varieties. In addition many hybrids with the platy (page 167) have been produced, increasing still further not only the range of colours but also the materials for further studies on heredity. These fishes are particularly suitable for laboratory work of this kind. The sexes can be readily recognized, which is always a help in such studies. The males not only differ from the females in having the 'sword', they also have a gonopodium for the insertion of milt, fertilisation being internal. They also breed rapidly. A brood may number up to 200, each ¼ in. long at birth. The newly-born must rise to the surface for air to fill the swimbladder after which they can swim well and start to feed almost immediately. They also grow quickly. At first the sexes look alike but soon the males start to grow a sword. Swordtails live 2–3 years, so there is a rapid turn over in populations. As a result swordtails, with their near relatives the platys, may be considered as a vertebrate equivalent of the fruit fly for genetical studies.

Hybridization

Probably the most remarkable feature of the sex life of the swordtail is the ease with which it hybridizes with platys in aquaria, yet although both species live virtually side by side in the fresh waters of Mexico and Guatemala no wild hybrids have been found. This is the more noteworthy since their breeding behaviour is so similar. There are, however, several small differences, hardly noticeable until close and critical study is made of them. To begin with, platys take about 5 minutes from the start of pre-mating behaviour to the actual mating, whereas swordtails take only one minute. The actual mating takes only half the time in platys that it does in swordtails and altogether the mating behaviour of platys is much the more vigorous. The differences are slight, and probably no one of them would be sufficient to form a barrier between the species, but taken as a whole they do. Under artificial conditions, as in an aquarium where the choice of mates is limited anyway, the barrier is readily overcome. In the wild, with a wide choice of mates, even small details count.

class	**Pisces**
order	Cypriniformes
family	Poeciliidae
genus & species	*Xiphophorus helleri*

▽ *Selective breeding results in a wide range of colour varieties: a recent breed is seen here.*

*Translucent trio: the reddish hues of these rosy tetra **Hyphessobrycon rosaceus** vary according to the angle at which the light strikes them.*

Tetra

*As with so many words that are bandied about with easy familiarity between the hundreds of thousands of aquarists throughout the world, the name 'tetra' — often shortened to 'tet' — has not yet found its way into dictionaries. It is, however, in commonplace use in books on freshwater fishes. In the early years of the present century, when keeping tropical fishes in home aquaria began to be popular, many favourite species were included in the genus **Tetragonopterus**, which soon became abbreviated to tetra. The generic name has now been almost abandoned, and today 'tetra' persists for at least 34 species, belonging to nine genera, although most of them are in the genus **Hyphessobrycon**.*

All these species have several things in common. They are all small, the majority being 2 in. or less maximum length. The giant among them is the glass

tetra, up to 10 in. long, taking its name from silvery flanks with a blue sheen. They all belong to the family Characidae, or characins (see page 53). They are all decorative fishes and this is reflected in their names: yellow tetra, lemon tetra, glowlight tetra, neon tetra, blue, platinum, silver, flame, cardinal and others. Some are named after their place of origin, such as Rio tetra and Buenos Aires tetra; others are named after the person who discovered or introduced them, such as Rodway's and Copeland's tetra. There is even one called the pretty tetra, a name which certainly has the force of understatement. Although they have such varying and descriptive names they are all similar in shape, with a high dorsal fin, a long anal fin, and a semi-forked tail.

The majority of tetras live in the rivers of the Amazon basin and adjoining regions, such as the Guianas, Peru, Paraguay and Uruguay, and two live as far north as Panama. The odd-man-out is the Congo tetra.

Every colour represented

To attempt to describe the colours of tetras would lead to a catalogue of the colours of the rainbow and the many combinations into which they can be grouped. The fishes live in loose shoals among water plants in standing or flowing water, from small watercourses to the standing water in bogs. They feed on small planktonic animals such as water fleas and insect larvae, also taking small insects that fall on the surface of the water as well as some plants.

Boisterous courtship

The males resemble the females except that they become slimmer as the breeding season approaches. Small internal differences can be detected in an aquarium against a strong light as their bodies are semi-transparent. The male's swimbladder, for example, is more tapered than the female's and there is a gap between the rear end of the swimbladder and the other internal organs, which is filled by the ovary in the female. Courtship is somewhat boisterous, the male chasing the female into and among water plants, but finally they come to lie side by

227

side, their bodies pressed close together and the male quivering. The female lays about a dozen small, transparent, slightly sticky eggs, which fall on to the leaves of plants. Most of them remain there but some fall to the bottom. When the male has fertilised these eggs, the female lays more. This continues until 100 or more have been laid. The eggs hatch in 2–3 days. The baby fishes feed on the microscopic plants and animals floating in the water. They are half-grown at 6 months, and tetras generally live 3–4 years, with a probable maximum of 5 years.

Little information
Little is known of the tetra's enemies in the wild. Indeed, we have so little information about them in the wild state that for some species we cannot be sure precisely where they come from. All we can say of their native home is that it is somewhere in northern South America. Because they breed well in captivity dealers have been able to rely on the extensive stocks that have been bred in aquaria. This reduces the need for collectors to go out to get them and it means that the only information we have for some species are the vague details given by those who first collected them. In aquaria, at least, the main enemies are the adult fishes themselves, which have a tendency to eat the spawn.

Brass mutants
Towards the end of the 1920's some new aquarium fishes made their appearance. They looked something like yellow tetras but had a bright metallic, almost brassy look. They were called brass tetras. Then others began to appear, not looking exactly like the original brass tetras although strongly reminiscent of them. Altogether four kinds appeared, puzzling even the expert aquarists. Eventually they came to the conclusion these did not represent new species but were individuals of different species that were alike in having a brassy look. The various species of tetras have very similar shapes and are distinguished as species largely by their colour, so shape did not help. The only thing to do was to breed the brass tetras to see what happened. Thousands were bred in aquaria but none of the offspring showed the pure brassy character. Added to this, observations in the field showed that 'brass' individuals occasionally showed up in different species of tetras. The only conclusion was that brass tetras are 'sports' or, as they are now known by a more scientific name, recurrent mutants.

A mutant is an individual that differs markedly in form, structure or colour beyond the normal variation for the species. Some mutants crop up time and time again, and therefore they are referred to as recurrent mutants.

class	**Pisces**
order	**Cypriniformes**
family	**Characidae**
genera & species	***Cheirodon axelrodi*** *cardinal tetra*
	Ctenobrycon spilurus *silver tetra*
	Geophyrocharax atracaudatus *platinum tetra*
	Hemigrammus caudovittatus *Buenos Aires tetra*
	H. erythrozonus *glowlight tetra*
	H. pulcher *pretty tetra*
	H. rodwayi *Rodway's tetra*
	Hyphessobrycon bifasciatus *yellow tetra*
	H. copelandi *Copeland's tetra*
	H. flammeus *Rio or flame tetra*
	H. pulchripinnis *lemon tetra*
	Micralestes interruptus *Congo tetra*
	Mimagoniates microlepis *blue tetra*
	Moenkhausia oligolepis *glass tetra*
	Paracheirodon innesi *neon tetra*

▽ *Bright spots: a group of neon tetras circle around a possible source of food. They are one of the most popular of aquarium fishes.*

Tilapia

*Tilapia is the name given to a hundred or so species of freshwater fishes which belong to the large family of cichlids. One species **Sarotherodon galilaea** was probably responsible for the miraculous draught of fishes mentioned in the Bible. Other species are also used as food fishes and have been spread around the world. Tilapias are also kept as aquarium fishes and their study has brought to light several unusual features of fish behaviour.*

They have large heads and deep bodies, strongly compressed from side to side. The long dorsal fin is spiny in front and soft-rayed in the hinder part, which usually rises to a point in the rear. The anal fin is larger and pointed behind. The tail fin is squarish along its rear edge. The pectoral fins are moderately large and the pelvic fins are more or less level with them. Most tilapias grow to a length of 8–12 in. and a few species may be 18–20 in. long. The colour varies from species to species and is often very variable within a species. The back may be yellowish to olive-brown, green, bronze, blue or violet, the flanks silvery and the belly even lighter. Usually there is a metallic sheen of bronze, golden or violet, and the body and fins are often marked with darker spots and bars.

Tilapias are widely distributed over Africa south of the Sahara, and from the Nile basin to Israel, Jordan and Syria.

Peripatetic tilapias

Tilapias live in lakes and the sluggish parts of rivers, estuaries and brackish lagoons, especially where there is shelter under banks, among water plants or among water-logged branches. Large numbers of *Tilapia grahami* live in the soda lake Magadi, in Kenya, in water of 28–45°C/80–112°F. Tilapias readily acclimatise and several species have been transported all over central and eastern Africa; so many have become established in local rivers to which they are not native. There are five species now in Lake Victoria, for example, two native and three introduced. The precise mechanics of these introductions are not always known, so it is usual to speak of the fishes as having 'escaped'. For example, *T. mossambica*, of East Africa, turned up in Java in 1939. By various means, some of which can only be guessed at, it is now found in Sumatra, Bali, Lombok, Celebes, the Philippines, Taiwan and South Korea, as well as Malaya, Thailand and Ceylon. In the west it is established on Trinidad, St Lucia and Haiti and, recently, in Texas.

△△▷ *Mouth brooder: a female **Paratilapia multicolor** with young fry showing through the cheeks of her brood pouch—the young are released as soon as they can swim.*
△ ▷ *Aggression not affection: male **T. variabilis** fight each other by pushing with their mouths.*
▷ *Small shoal of blue-grey tilapia in the clear water of the Mzima springs in Kenya.*

How they get there

In 1961 a press report told of tilapia 'turning up' in large areas of Florida. Apparently a biologist had suggested that they should be introduced into a pond to provide new sport for anglers, but that does not explain their being found in 16 lakes, 4 creeks and 2 rivers in southern Florida. The press report gives a clue when it continues, that although it is illegal to put tilapia into waters that are free of them, many tropical fish fanciers tire of having them in their aquaria and dump them in the nearest water. Since tilapia has 'an elephant's appetite and a rabbit's reproductive ability' it is not long before it cleans out a pond of food needed by other fish. This is a danger that has to be watched, and in some places native fishes have been wiped out after tilapias have been introduced. On the other hand, several of the larger species, including *T. mossambica*, are an important source of protein, and are often bred in special ponds.

Artificial ponds

In 1951 *T. melanopleura* was established in special fish ponds in Madagascar. These were so successful that more ponds were made. By 1958 there were 40 000, by 1960, 80 000. An adult could catch 11 lb of these fish a day, and even a child could catch 4 lb a day. In South Africa, where tilapias are called kurper or freshwater bream, they are used to clear sewage ponds of mosquito larvae, and at the same time they multiply and the young can be transferred to other ponds and rivers to provide food fishes. One problem that occurs when the tilapia multiply rapidly is that they eat up the vegetation and insect larvae, starve out or eat up the other fishes, and in the end the pond is

▽ *Playing safe: young **T. nilotica** stay close to their mother; when danger threatens they all rush back into her mouth.*

overstocked with undersized tilapias. A suggested cure is to use hatcheries and to separate the sexes, putting the females in one pond and the males in another. In one experiment *T. mossambica* were crossed with other species of *Tilapia* and the hybrids were all males—which could be grown to maturity for food without the problems of a population explosion.

Mainly plant eaters

Tilapias are basically vegetarian, some species sieving the plant plankton, others eating the small algae on stones, and a few doing both. Some seem to turn readily to animal food, such as water insects and their larvae, or fish fry—even tilapia fry.

Mouth nurseries

Some tilapias lay their sticky eggs on the surface of a stone which the male and female have carefully cleaned beforehand. Once the eggs are laid the male swims over them and sheds his milt to fertilise them. The parents aerate the eggs by fanning them with their fins, and when the fry have hatched the female keeps them together in a tiny shoal, shepherding them by signals until they are old enough to swim away on their own. Most tilapias are, however, mouth brooders. To start with the pair dig a pit an inch or two deep and 5—12 in. across in the sandy bottom, scooping up mouthfuls of sand or small pebbles and spitting them a little way from the nest. Then the male swims head downwards and mouths the bottom of the pit. Soon he starts to swim slowly over the nest, rubbing it with his belly. The female joins in and they take turns in swimming across it. Finally the female lays her eggs and the male sheds his milt over them. This is repeated several times and when all the eggs are laid either the male or the female, or both—the pattern varies with the species—suck the eggs into

the mouth. The eggs hatch in the mouth and 8—20 days later the fry leave it and swim away. In some species the female first sucks up the eggs and then the milt as the male sheds it, so that the eggs are fertilised in her mouth.

Careful tests made with one species showed that if the eggs are removed from the mouth of a mouth brooder they fail to hatch and become diseased. It was finally discovered why: the movement of the eggs in the throat makes them rub against each other and against the sides of the pouch, and this cleans them of any bacteria that might damage them.

Counts have shown that tilapia begin to spawn at 2—3 months, may spawn 6—11 times a year, and that some species multiply 1 000 times in 2—3 months.

Miraculous draught

Tilapias are today an important item of food in tropical countries. Paintings on Egyptian antiquities show they were fished thousands of years ago. The miraculous draught of fishes recorded in the Bible was almost certainly tilapias. Canon Tristam, writing over a century ago, told of seeing *Saratherodon galilaea* 'in shoals of over an acre in extent, so closely packed that it seemed impossible for them to move, and with their dorsal fins above the water. They are taken both in boats and from the shore by nets run deftly round, and enclosing what one may call a solid mass at one swoop, and very often the nets break'. A man was stationed at a high point on shore to spot the shoals.

class	Pisces
order	Perciformes
family	Cichlidae
genus	*Tilapia, Saratherodon*

Top minnows

The top minnows might almost have been designed to catch the eye and hold the attention of the aquarist while inflicting the maximum perplexity on those responsible for classifying them. Some experts put about 200 species into the top minnow family Cyprinodontidae, others divide the family up into half-a-dozen smaller families. A third group keeps the family as one unit and divides them into two halves, the egg-bearing top minnows and the live-bearing top minnows. The last of these contains several fishes we have already dealt with, such as guppies (page 97), mollies (page 33), platys (page 167) and swordtails. It is convenient therefore to deal now with the egg-bearing top minnows only.

These are all small carp-like fishes, but unlike carps they have many small comb-like teeth on the jaws and in the throat. Most top minnows are 2 in. long, the largest species reaching a maximum of 4 in. The upper surface of the head is flattened. The protrusible mouth is at the end of the snout and is directed slightly upwards. There are no barbels. The dorsal fin is prominent and lies behind the midline of the body; the anal fin is similar in shape and size but is located in a slightly more forward position.

They live in the rivers of North and South America, the Mediterranean region, much of tropical Africa, in southern and southeast Asia and in Japan.

Rainbow hues
Top minnows live in the smaller streams, especially those with clear water and a fair supply of water plants with finely divided leaves. They live in very loose formations

△ *This beautiful variety of* **Aphyosemion australe** *has only recently been developed. Fish of this genus are found in brackish pools around the river deltas of West Africa.*

▽ *A male American flagfish. One of the few species of top minnow that care for their brood — the male fans the eggs and looks after the fry in a similar way to the cichlids.*

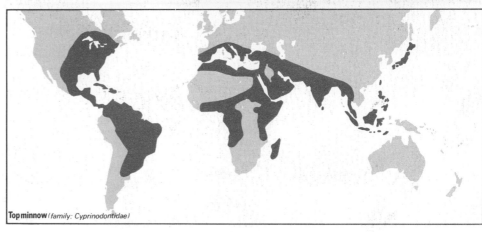

Top minnow *(family: Cyprinodontidae)*

or in small groups. Shoaling in the true sense is not possible because of the way many of them swim, alternately making rapid darts forward and then staying still for a few moments with beating fins. This method of swimming enables them to dash to cover among waterweeds, so concealing their bright colours. Between them, the top minnows show all the colours of the rainbow, with blues, reds and violet predominating. Their bodies are usually translucent or semi-translucent, and the males especially are brightly, even brilliantly coloured with spots, bars, or other markings in a variety of colours. The females, although less showy and with more subdued colours than the males, are nevertheless decorative. This is why so many of the species are popular aquarium fishes.

Good jumpers

Top minnows are used by anglers as bait in some places but they also have a value in helping to control insect pests such as mosquitoes. Their food is mainly midge and mosquito larvae, small crustaceans of the type commonly called water fleas, and small worms. Some of the larger species also take the young of other fishes. They eat a small amount of plant food. Some of the top minnows are described as 'good jumpers' and this to an aquarist means they are liable to leap out of an aquarium and land on the floor. Species of *Rivulus*, of tropical America, are very prone to do this. In the wild state they travel short distances over the ground in wet weather and will catch insects and worms while doing so.

High and low spawners

Apart from their less lively colours the females are usually slightly smaller than the males and have smaller fins. Top minnows may spawn among water plants or on the bottom. The plant spawners' courtship is often a lively affair. The male flutters around the female like a butterfly or nods and dances around her, with his fins spread and colours heightened. In the bottom spawners the male swims beside the female with spread fins and the two swim to the bottom to nestle side by side. The leaf spawners lay sticky eggs on water plants, the bottom spawners bury them in the mud with a powerful flick of the tail. The details vary considerably from species to species but generally it can be said they lay up to 200 eggs in batches of 8–12 and spawning may last 2–3 weeks. With leaf spawners the eggs hatch in 6–14 days, or as much as 36 days in some species. Eggs of bottom spawners develop more slowly and may take 3–9 weeks to hatch or as much as 6 months. The baby fishes feed on protistans and on the smallest larvae of crustaceans such as water fleas. Some top minnows have a life span of only one year, and are therefore, logically enough, known as annuals.

▽ *A pair of **Rivulus agilis**. These fish are pronounced surface feeders, often hanging motionless near the surface waiting for insect prey. They are good jumpers, and like to lie in the sun on the leaves of water plants. The spawning period may last several weeks—in the aquarium it is advisable to remove the parents after spawning as they tend to eat the eggs.*

Few eggs, few enemies

There is little recorded information on the enemies of top minnows and although a percentage of them almost inevitably must be taken by fish-eating birds and other such predators, this proportion cannot be high. The fact that a spawning produces the relatively small reproduction rate of no more than 200 eggs is a clear indication of this. So also is the small amount of parental care shown. One species that does show more parental care is the American flagfish, of Florida. The female lays her eggs in a depression in the mud and the male aerates and guards them.

Eggs buried in mud

In a sense all bottom spawners show some sort of parental care, if only by burying the eggs. In a few the female forces the eggs into the mud, using her pelvic fins cupped together as a kind of chute which guides each egg into the hole the fins make in the mud. In other species, living in streams liable to seasonal drying, the parents may be killed off by the loss of water but the eggs lying in the mud will hatch with the first rains, which may be weeks later. These are only a few of the many different ways in which the breeding habits of top minnows vary. Some lay their eggs one at a time, each being fertilised separately by the male. Others lay them in batches. The female ricefish, of Japan, carries her eggs around for a time in a mucus sheath which she later rubs off on a water plant. The Cuban killie female lays relatively large eggs which remain for a while in a bunch of half a dozen, hanging from her genital opening by a slender thread of mucus. Finally this catches in a water plant and sticks to it. Meanwhile the eggs have had some protection from being attached to the parent while undergoing the early stages of development. So spawning among top minnows is not such a haphazard process as it may seem at first sight.

Even the fertilisation is not as random as would appear. Fish eggs, in many species, including top minnows, are at first slightly flattened. Once laid, the egg's capsule, or outer covering, becomes spherical and sucks in, through a tiny opening called the micropyle, a small amount of the water which has just been charged with the male's milt.

class	**Pisces**
order	**Atheriniformes**
family	**Cyprinodontidae**
genera & species	**Cyprinodon variegatus** *sheepshead top minnow* **Cubanichthys cubensis** *Cuban killie* **Fundulus heteroclitus** *zebra killie* **F. diaphanus** *banded killifish* **Jordanella floridae** *American flagfish* **Oryzias latipes** *ricefish* **Rivulus cylindraceus** *green rivulus* *others*

Triggerfish

Triggerfishes have a spine on the back with an ingenious locking device, so that it remains erect until the spine behind it is depressed to release it. This is, however, only one of their many peculiarities.

The triggerfish's body is deep and compressed, and seen from the side it is almost diamond-shaped. The head occupies about a third of the length, the mouth is small, and the eyes fairly large. Just behind the eye is a short dorsal fin with spines, the first two making the locking device. The second dorsal fin is long and high; the anal fin is the same shape and lies exactly opposite it. The pectoral fins are small, while there are no pelvic fins to be found. The body, seldom more than 2 ft long, is covered with small rhomboidal bony plates, their outer surfaces bearing one or more small spines. As if artificially coloured, triggerfishes are often boldly marked with garish, sometimes almost grotesque patterns.

The filefishes, formerly placed in a separate family, are near relatives. They are similar in shape but usually up to only 1 ft long, and there is a single spine on the back, level with or in front of the eye. Although single it can still be locked in place. Its scales also carry more spines, so its surface looks velvety, yet is rough to touch — like a file. Moreover, the second dorsal and the anal fins are not so high. In place of pelvic fins there is a spine on the pelvic bone, which can move freely and is connected to the body by a wide flap of skin.

Both triggerfishes and filefishes live mainly in tropical coastal waters.

Dignified movement

The way in which triggerfishes and filefishes swim, is especially interesting. Although the two look alike and are now placed in the same family, an indication of how closely related they are, their swimming techniques are quite different. Both swim slowly with the body rigid, in what looks like a dignified manner. The triggerfishes swim by a simultaneous flapping of the dorsal and anal fins. In contrast, filefishes are driven through the water by waves passing backwards along these fins.

There is a second contrast, connected with their defence. The locking spine seems to be used when the triggerfish takes refuge in a crevice in rock or coral. It erects the spine and cannot be pulled out. It is impossible to press the spine down with the finger but the fish can lower it by dropping the second spine, which releases the large spine in front of it. The fish can be made to lower the first spine if the third one is pressed down. When a triggerfish is looked at from any but the side view its compressed body presents only a fairly thin edge. This is probably useful to a triggerfish for concealment, simply because as it turns it is transformed from an obvious large, solid rhomboidal object to something as incon-

△ *Abstract art: the strident, garish daubings on a Pacific triggerfish* **Rhinecanthus aculeatus** *—one of the two species called humahuma-nukanuka-a-puaa—have earned it the name of Picasso fish.*

△ *A spotted triggerfish* **Balistoides conspicillum** *near coral, into which it dives when frightened.*
▽ *Ladylike warpaint: the queen triggerfish* **Balistes vetula** *lives in the Atlantic and Indian Oceans.*

spicuous as a knife blade seen edge on. According to William Beebe, the celebrated American marine zoologist, at least one species of filefish *Alutera scriptus* goes one better. It stands on its head among clumps of eelgrass with its fins gently waving, and with its mottled green colour the fish is hard to tell from the eelgrass.

Unusual teeth
Both triggerfish and filefish have teeth implanted in sockets in the jaws, which is unusual for any fish. The triggerfishes have eight chisel-like teeth in each jaw which they use to hack holes in the shells of mussels, oysters and clams to eat the soft flesh inside, or to crack crabs and other crustaceans. They also eat carrion. Filefish are, as far as we know, vegetarian.

Curious pelvic spine
Little worth mentioning is known about the breeding habits or the enemies of triggerfishes. It is assumed that the spines might stick in the throat or damage the mouth of a predator. It could be argued that their striking colours are warning colours, so any predator taking a bite and suffering injury would leave the next triggerfish or filefish alone. It has also been suggested that the fishes may be poisonous, but so far the only evidence is that triggerfishes may sometimes be poisonous to eat when they themselves have eaten contaminated shellfish or carrion; any poison is of the ciguatera kind (page 27). There is still the curious pelvic spine to account for, especially in the filefishes, with its flap of skin. It has been suggested that this spine is used by the fish for fixing itself in crevices in rocks or coral, as a defensive measure, just as the triggerfish uses its spines.

People who have handled these fishes report that they can inflict deep bites with their strong sharp teeth. Triggerfishes and filefishes may not be as defenceless as their slow moving habits suggest. This seems to be supported by the fact that they make sounds—usually a sign of strong territorial instinct or an ability to defend themselves or both. Some triggerfishes grate their teeth together in the roof and floor of the throat. Other types, as well as the filefishes, rub together the bases of their fin spines. In all the fish, the sounds are amplified by resonance in the swimbladder. At least one species, the black durgon, of the West Indies, makes a rapid puttering sound by vibrating a membrane in front of its pectoral fins.

Why so colourful?
One species of triggerfish living in the tropical eastern Atlantic and the Mediterranean often wanders as far north as the British Isles in summer. It is grey-brown to green-brown with a violet tinge on the back and blue bands and yellow or black spots on the dorsal and anal fins. This is a sober colouring compared with most. The undulate triggerfish of the Indo-Pacific is purplish with small orange spots on the face, orange lines all over the body and golden orange fins. The humahuma-nuka-nuka-a-puaa of the southern Pacific has such a bizarre pattern it has been named the Picasso fish. Others are equally remarkable for their extraordinary colours and patterns. According to Craig Phillips, in *The Captive Sea*, triggerfishes are light-shy. He describes how those he had in an aquarium panicked when the light was suddenly switched on, and they put on an unusual facial expression, as if they were about to spit. All this suggests that triggerfishes must hide their splendid colours, which makes it even more puzzling why they should have them.

class	**Pisces**
order	**Tetraodontiformes**
family	**Balistidae**
genera & species	***Balistes carolinensis*** *eastern Atlantic* ***Melichthys radula*** *black durgon* ***Rhinecanthus aculeatus*** *Picasso fish* *others*

◁ *Submarine seascape. Nibbling from a honey-comb-like coral is an undulate triggerfish* ***Balistapus undulatus.*** *Solitary, slow and ponderous, the triggerfish is a tropical marine species. Adding to this underwater scene are two very spiny sea urchins tucked away in crevices in the mound of dead coral.*

Trout

The European trout, of very variable colour, is known by three names. The brown trout is small, dark and non-migratory. It can weigh up to 17 lb 12 oz and lives in the smaller rivers and pools. The lake trout is larger and paler. It lives in larger rivers and lakes and it may be migratory. The sea trout, large, silvery up to 4½ ft long and weighing up to 30 lb, is distinctly migratory. All three belong to the same species.

The European brown trout and lake trout are greenish brown, the flanks being lighter than the back, and the belly yellowish. They are covered with many red and black spots, the latter surrounded by pale rings. There are spots even on the gill covers. These two and the sea trout resemble the salmon in shape and appearance except that the angle of the jaw reaches to well behind the eye and the adipose fin is tinged with orange.

The North American species are similar. The cut-throat trout has two red marks across the throat. The Dolly Varden is named for its conspicuous red spots, coloured like the cherry ribbons worn by the Dickens character. In the brook trout the pattern is more mottled but it also has red spots on the flanks. The rainbow trout has a reddish band along the flanks. The lake or mackinau trout lives in deep water, down to 400 ft. The golden trout lives in water 8 000 ft or more above sea level.

▷ Like some figment of an angler's daydream, a big New Zealand rainbow trout jumps from its shoal for a flying titbit.
▽ Mixed bunch, with rainbow trout in front of brown. Because of aquarium glass, the red line on the rainbows' sides cannot be seen.

Temperature important

Trout grow best in clear, aerated waters and although they are sometimes found in turbid waters it is only when the surface layers are well supplied with oxygen. They are readily affected by silt; it may spoil their spawning sites, reduce their food supply or act directly on the fishes themselves. Laboratory experiments have shown that particles in suspension in the water, at a level as low as 270 parts per million, abrade the gills or cause them to thicken. The rate of growth of trout varies in other ways as well, often to a remarkable extent, with the conditions of their surroundings. Temperature, for instance, is highly important, and an example can be seen at the time when they resume feeding after the winter fast. Normally, trout stop feeding in autumn and resume in spring, in about March when the water reaches a temperature of $2°C/36°F$ or more. In a mild winter they may begin feeding in December and continue until the first cold snap of the following autumn.

The rate of growth also varies from one river to another, or from river to sea. Trout living in small streams grow more slowly than those in large rivers, and those in large bodies of fresh water grow more slowly than those living in the sea. A trout in a small river will grow $2\frac{1}{2}$, 5 and 8 in. in its first, second and third years respectively. Corresponding figures for a sea trout will be 3—5, 4—5 and 10—11 in.

Diet changes

The diet of trout varies with their age. Fry eat mainly aquatic larvae of insects, rarely the adults. Later they eat large numbers of winged insects, as well as water fleas and freshwater shrimps. When adult they eat mainly small fishes as well as shrimps, insect larvae and adults, especially the winged insects. Sea trout feed on sprats, young herring and sand eels and also on a large percentage of small crustaceans, including shrimps and prawns.

Correct place to spawn

Male trout begin to breed at two years, females at three, returning to do so to the place where they themselves were hatched. This homing has been verified experimentally, by transporting marked trout to other parts of a river system, then finding them later, back on their 'home ground'. Breeding usually takes place from October to February, the time varying from one locality to another. Spawning is normally in running water, trout living in lakes going into the feeder streams.

For spawning the female makes a 'redd' in gravelly shallows, digging a depression with flicks of her tail. As she lays her eggs, the male, in attendance on her, fertilises them, stationing himself beside her but slightly to the rear. It has been found that a successful redd is one with a current flowing downwards through the gravel. The eggs hatch in about 40 days. The fry are $\frac{1}{2}$—1 in. long at hatching, and the yolk sac is absorbed in 4—6 weeks.

Surrounded by enemies

WE Frost and ME Brown, in their book *The Trout*, state that 94% of fry are lost during the first 3—4 months of their lives. After this the mortality drops to 20%. Eels are often said to kill trout and especially to ravage the spawning grounds, but there is no evidence of this. The chief enemies of trout are water shrew, mink, the common rat, and to some extent otters and herons. Another enemy of trout is larger trout. Well grown ones have sometimes been found to have another trout, 5—6 in. long, in their stomachs. The record for the brown trout comes from New Zealand, where the fish were introduced. In 1967 a 20lb trout had a foot-long trout in its stomach. In their cannibalism, therefore, trout vie with pike, always regarded as a traditional enemy, which, with few exceptions, take only medium to large sized trout.

There are two other contributors to trout depletion—apart from man. Numbers of other animals compete with it for food, and of these, which include several water birds, the eel is probably one of the worst, more so in rivers than in lakes. The other natural 'enemy' is lack of oxygen, especially during the winter. When the pools and lakes are frozen over, trout must rely on oxygen trapped under ice. This is replenished by oxygen given out by water plants. When, however, the ice is blanketed by snow, light does not penetrate, plants cannot 'work', and trout are asphyxiated.

Many species

The wide variation in size and colour of the European trout is brought out by the history of its species. In 1758 Linnaeus named three species: the Swedish river trout, the sea trout and the lake trout. Dr Albert Gunther, leading authority on fishes, wrote in 1880: 'We know of no other group of fishes which offers so many difficulties . . . to the distinction of species'. He recognized 10 species in the British Isles alone—the sea trout, sewin, phinnock, Galway sea trout, Orkney sea trout, river trout, great lake trout, gillaroo, Welsh blackfinned trout and Loch Leven trout. Thirty years later, C Tate Regan, Günther's successor, put forward strong arguments for treating these and all species and races in continental Europe as one very variable species.

class	**Pisces**
order	**Salmoniformes**
family	**Salmonidae**
genera & species	***Salmo aguabonita*** *golden*
	S. clarki *cutthroat*
	S. gairdneri *rainbow*
	S. trutta *brown*
	Salvelinus fontinalis *brook*
	S. malma *Dolly Varden*
	S. namaycush *lake, others*

Young brown trout, easily identified by the red spots on the side of its body, swims in clear river water; the clearer the water, the faster it grows.

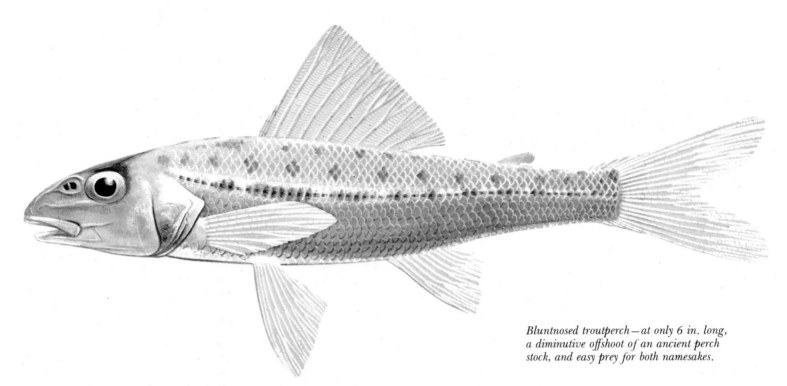

Bluntnosed troutperch—at only 6 in. long, a diminutive offshoot of an ancient perch stock, and easy prey for both namesakes.

Troutperch

When a fish looks like a trout yet in some ways resembles a perch, the obvious name to give it is troutperch. We now know, however, that it is related to neither. The only two species live in North America. The first, the bluntnosed troutperch or sandroller, is found in the freshwaters of most of Canada, from Quebec to Alaska and southwards to Virginia, Kentucky, Missouri and Kansas. The second, merely called a troutperch, is more localised, being found in the basin of the Columbia river, in western North America. Both are small, the first up to 6 in. long, the second up to 4 in. The body has much the same shape as a trout, yet it also recalls the appearance of a perch. There are the same number of fins as in a trout but they are spiny as in a perch, with one or more stout spines in the leading margin of the dorsal, anal and pelvic fins. There is, however, an adipose fin, as in trout. The body is covered with spiny scales and is spotted. The head is rather pointed, the mouth is small, the eye large, and when freshly caught troutperch have a peculiar translucent appearance.

Missing link

Troutperch are common in the larger streams and in deep clear lakes, especially those with sandy or gravel bottoms. These small shoaling fishes lead uneventful lives, feeding on aquatic insects and small freshwater crustaceans. They are important only as food for the various kinds of predatory fishes, such as trout and pike, or as livebait for fishermen. Lacking attractive colours or any special features of behaviour troutperch have not been closely studied. They have not even caught the fancy of aquarists. The only aspect of these two species that has caused any particular stir in zoological

circles is that they used to be regarded as a kind of missing link between the salmon family and the perch family. More recent studies have shown, however, that troutperch are an evolutionary offshoot of the perches that were probably once much more widespread, with many more species.

Running water spawners

In late May or early June in the southern parts of the range, slightly later in the north, troutperches move to sandbars in the lakes. They spawn in water not more than $3\frac{1}{2}$ ft deep and in lakes with no suitable shallow waters the shoals ascend the feeder streams. In the rivers they go upstream. There is much jostling among the members of the shoal as they sort themselves out, more or less into pairs, but more often with one female attended by two or more males. Fertilisation is external, and the eggs, $\frac{1}{18}$ in. diameter, sticky and heavier than water, sink to the bottom to adhere to the coarser gravel or rocks in the rapid waters of the streams.

Unsung but essential

Throughout the animal world there are some species, and troutperch seem to be one of them, whose only role seems to be to act as fodder for other species. It is an inglorious yet very essential part they play in the natural economy, converting either vegetation or small animal life into bulk protein —for the benefit of other fishes.

Pirateperch

There is, in fact, another species closely related to the troutperches which preys enough on other fishes to be called the pirateperch. Except that it has a deeper body and a more square-ended tail, the pirateperch looks very like the troutperch, but it has no adipose fin. It also is small, up to 5 in. long, and is olive green to brown with dark spots and blotches, usually in rows along the body, and yellowish brown on the underside. Pirateperch live in the eastern United States, from New York to Texas, in streams and standing waters. They are said

to be very quarrelsome, both with fishes of other species and with members of their own species. This is largely because they have a strong territorial drive. The pirateperch prefers waters with muddy beds, where there is debris and rotting leaves, under which it can hide, darting out to take a worm, insect larva or small fish, or to drive away an intruder.

Adipose fin

In the salmon, trout and other members of the salmon family the second dorsal fin has been modified to what is called an adipose fin. This is a small flap made up of fatty tissue covered by skin, which lacks fin rays or any other supporting skeleton. An adipose fin is also found in some of the large freshwater family of characins (page 53) and also in the majority of catfishes. In some species it is small, in others large. In the armoured catfishes (page 48) it has a strong spine in front. Conjecture surrounds the function of this small, fatty tag. We know the front dorsal fin of a salmon or trout prevents the fish from rolling and yawing as it moves forward. The pectoral fins, which prevent pitching as well as rolling, are used in turning and, with the pelvic fins, are used for braking. The tail fin helps drive the fish through the water and is used as a rudder. According to some experts the adipose fin has no function. This is hard to believe, but to say what its function might be is even harder.

class	**Pisces**
order	**Percopsiformes**
family	**Percopsidae**
genera & species	***Columbia transmontana*** *Columbia troutperch* ***Percopsis omiscomaycus*** *bluntnosed troutperch*
family	**Aphredoderidae**
genus & species	***Aphredoderus sayanus*** *pirateperch*

Trunkfish

The trunkfishes are the nearest we have to fishes masquerading as turtles. They are also known as boxfishes and cofferfishes because their bodies are enclosed within bony boxes made up of 6-sided bony plates fitting closely into one another, leaving only the tail unarmoured. Inside, the backbone is short with only 14 vertebrae between the skull and the beginning of the tail, all joined in a compact manner.

A typical trunkfish has a more or less conical head, the face sloping down at a steep angle to the small mouth, which is armed with strong crushing teeth. The eyes are large and there is only a small opening from the gill chamber. The length of a trunkfish seldom exceeds 1 ft. The single dorsal fin and the anal fin are fairly large, as are the pectoral fins, but there are no pelvic fins. The fleshy, naked tail ending in a large fanlike tail fin projects backwards from the bony box and, except for the other fins, is the only part capable of movement. The box enclosing the body is flat on the undersurface and it may be 3-, 4- or 5-sided in cross section, and one or more of its edges may be armed with strong spines.

Trunkfishes live at or near the bottom of warm waters, especially in tropical seas, all round the world.

Geometrical fishes: a comparison between the fishes above and opposite will show the 3- and 4-faced arrangements of trunkfish armour. These arrangements vary according to species and serve as a rough means of classification.

△ Its transparent, fan-shaped fins beating rapidly, the cumbersome body of a smooth trunkfish moves slowly forwards. Unlike most fish, trunkfishes swim almost entirely by just a rapid beating of their fins.
◁ Passing beauty: **Ostracion meleagris** in the Hawaii reef. Like other trunkfishes, it can adopt a variety of colour schemes. The sexes and young of the same species are often quite differently patterned and coloured.
▷ Front elevation: also known as boxfishes or cofferfishes, trunkfishes such as this **Lactophrys tricornis** are indeed like bony boxes. The tiny mouth is deceptive; it is armed with teeth perfectly capable of biting off coral chunks.

Slow moving

Like tortoises on land, trunkfishes are slow moving, and for much the same reasons. The normal fish swims by strong side to side movements of the whole body and, more especially, by the muscular tail. A trunkfish can move its tail only to a small extent. Its swimming is like a small boat being propelled by a single oar sculling from the stern. The only difference is that the hydrodynamic principles are more complex in the fish because the tail is flexible. The main swimming force is produced by side to side movements of the dorsal and anal fins, aided by the pectoral fins. A trunkfish is the very opposite of being streamlined—in fact the flat faces must create considerable resistance to progress—and when swimming it moves its fins very rapidly, giving the impression of a great expenditure of energy with only a little gain in forward movement.

Confusion of colours

Rapid movement is not necessary for so heavily armoured a fish, which can also rely on its colour and colour changes for security, and on its ability to poison other fishes. A common trunkfish found in the seas on both sides of the tropical Atlantic is the cowfish, so named because it has two sharp, forward-pointing spines on the forehead, rather like the horns of a cow. It is pale green in colour, marked with blue spots and lines, but it can change this to yellow with blue spots or brown with a network of light blue markings, or even to pure white. The colours also differ between the sexes. The 4-sided blue trunkfish of the Indo-Pacific is an example. The females and the young fish are purplish blue with numerous small white spots scattered thickly and evenly over the whole body. The male is very different, being purplish blue with a pale blue network except for the flat upper surface, which is a brownish purple with small white dots with a brick-red border. Even the eyes differ: in the females and young fish they are blue, in the males they have a red border.

Emit poison

It has been suggested that the gaudy colours act as warning colours, advertising to possible enemies that trunkfishes do not depend entirely on their armour but have other undesirable qualities. We do not know yet exactly how it is used, but we do know that trunkfishes can give out a poison. When one of them is placed in an aquarium it is not long before the other fishes begin to show signs of distress, coming to the surface to gulp air, and dying soon afterwards. The only fishes not affected are tough characters such as moray eels, the large groupers, and other trunkfishes. The poison persists even after the trunkfish have been removed.

Search for food in corals

Trunkfishes live among the corals, which they search for food, biting off pieces of coral to digest the polyps. At the same time, in biting pieces from the coral, they expose worms and other small invertebrates sheltering in it. Some trunkfishes use their spout-like snouts to blow jets of water at the sandy bottom to uncover and dislodge worms, molluscs and small crustaceans, which they immediately snap up.

Dingleberries

The breeding habits of the cowfish of tropical American waters are probably typical of the whole family. It lays buoyant eggs, $\frac{1}{32}$ in. diameter, which hatch in 2–3 days. The larvae begin to develop the hard cover in about a week and they become somewhat rounded in shape, and it is only as the young fishes mature that the box-like edges to the body become sharply defined. During the early stages of life young trunkfishes shelter under clumps of floating seaweed. Their rounded shape has earned them, in the United States, the name of dingleberries. At this stage they seem to have rather cherubic faces, with their large eyes, small mouths and what look like puffed cheeks.

Regarded as delicacy

The heaviest mortality among trunkfishes is in the early stages, when eggs, larvae and young fishes are often eaten. Once they reach maturity their protective boxes, and in some species the poison they give out, deter predators. Also, being so slow, they lack the large muscles that make the flesh of other fishes attractive. Yet trunkfishes are eaten, even by human beings, and in some places are regarded as a delicacy. They are cooked in their own boxes, and some people of the South Pacific are said to 'roast them like chestnuts'. There are, nevertheless, other opinions, one of which is that what little flesh there is cannot be praised for its flavour, although the liver is proportionately quite large and oily.

class	**Pisces**
order	**Tetraodontiformes**
family	**Ostraciontidae**
genera & species	*Lactophrys bicaudalis* large spotted trunkfish **L. quadricornis** cowfish **Ostracion lentiginosus** blue trunkfish others

◁ *Always in shape, the complete covering of interlocking hexagonal plates of* **O. cornutus** *forms a rigid protective shield over the whole of the body except the flexible tail.*

Follow the leader: a shoal of bluefin tuna migrate northward through the Florida-Bermuda channel.

Tuna

Although the name 'tunny' was first used in England—from the Latin **thunnus** *—at least as early as the 15th century, and the Spanish word* tuna *did not come into general use until the beginning of this century, tuna is rapidly becoming the accepted name for this large fish.*

The tunny or bluefin tuna of the Atlantic is said to reach 14 ft long and weigh 1 800 lb, but few exceed 8 ft in length. It has a sleek streamlined shape with a large head and mouth, and large eyes. The first dorsal fin is spiny and close behind it is a smaller soft-rayed second dorsal fin. The anal fin is of similar shape and size as the second dorsal, and behind these two, reaching to the crescentically forked tail, are finlets, nine on the upper and eight on the lower surface of the tail. The pectoral fins are medium sized, as are the pelvic fins, which are level with the pectorals. The back is dark blue, the flanks white with silvery spots and the belly white. The fins are dark blue to black except for the reddish brown second dorsal and the yellowish anal fin and fin-lets. There are three keels on each side at the base of the tailfin.

The bluefin is found on both sides of the North Atlantic as far north as Iceland.

Segregated by size

Tuna are oceanic fishes that sometimes come inshore but apparently never enter rivers. They move about in shoals in which individual fishes are all about the same size. The smaller tuna make up the largest shoals; the larger the tuna the smaller the shoal, and the really large individuals are more or less solitary. They swim near the surface in summer but are found between 100 and 600 ft in winter. Tuna are strongly migratory, their movements being linked with those of the fishes on which they feed and also on the

temperature of the water. They are intolerant of temperatures below 10–12°C/50–54°F, so although they move into northern waters in summer they migrate back to warmer seas in autumn. A cold summer will limit the northward migrations. There also seem to be movements across the Atlantic. Tuna tagged off Martha's Vineyard, Massachusetts in July 1954 were caught in the Bay of Biscay five years later and occasionally individuals from American waters turn up off the coasts of Norway. Two tagged off Florida in September and October 1951 were caught off Bergen, Norway 120 days later, having travelled 4 500 miles.

Tuna, like their relative the mackerel, swim with the mouth slightly open so that their forward movement forces water across the gills. Their oxygen requirements are high because of their great muscular activity which depends on a correspondingly abundant supply of relatively warm blood. Because of this high oxygen requirement they swim more or less continuously. Tuna are believed to reach speeds of up to 50 mph.

Feeding frenzy

Very young tuna feed largely on crustaceans especially euphausians but later they eat mainly shoaling fishes such as herring, mackerel, sprats, whiting, flying fishes and sand eels. They also eat some squid and cuttlefish. When a tunny shoal meets a shoal of food fishes it is seized with what has been called a feeding frenzy. It charges through, the tunny twisting and turning, often breaking the surface, and sometimes leaping clear of the water. The commotion usually attracts flocks of seabirds to feed on the smaller fishes that are driven to the surface.

Soon put on weight

Spawning takes place in the Mediterranean and to the southwest of Spain in June and July and off Florida and the Bahamas in May and June. The eggs are small and float near the surface. They hatch in about 2 days, the newly hatched larvae being less than $\frac{1}{4}$ in. long. The baby fishes grow quickly reaching a weight of 1 lb in 3 months. At a year old

they weigh 10 lb, at 2 years 21 lb, 35 lb at 3 years and 56 lb at 4 years of age. At 13 years of age they reach a length of 8 ft and weigh 440 lb. The two tagged at Martha's Vineyard were 18 lb and nearly two years old, and they had reached 150 lb when captured later in the Bay of Biscay, at the age of 7 years.

Ancient fisheries

The many references to the tunny in classical literature show it to have been as important to the Mediterranean peoples as the herring was to the people of northwest Europe. The fisheries have continued through the centuries. Many methods have been used for catching the fish, such as harpoons, baited hooks and nets. The most spectacular are the net fisheries; very long nets are used to intercept migrating shoals and guide them into a final compartment or 'death chamber'. When this is filled with jostling fish the net floor is raised, the surrounding boats close in and the massed fish are clubbed, speared and dragged into the boats. Tuna fishing, or tunny fishing, according to whether it is carried out in American or British waters, has become a popular sport during the last half century. A large fish has been described as 'the tiger of the seas' and 'a living meteor' that strikes like a whirlwind and, played with a rod, will give a man the contest of his life, perhaps towing his boat for hours over a distance of several miles before becoming exhausted. The chief natural enemy is the killer whale.

Wide ranging tunas

There has long been some doubt whether the tuna of the American Atlantic is the same species as the tunny of the European side. They differ slightly in details of anatomy and in the time of the breeding season. Nevertheless, the tendency now is to treat them as separate populations of a single species. Other related species have similar wide distributions. A near relative, the Atlantic albacore, up to 4 ft long and 65 lb weight, with long scythe-like pectoral fins, has its counterpart in the Pacific albacore which ranges from the Pacific coast of North America to Japan and Hawaii. In the yellow-finned albacores or yellow-finned tunas, up to 9 ft long and 400 lb weight, the second dorsal and anal fins are also long and scythe-like. One species ranges across the tropical and subtropical Atlantic and another ranges across the Pacific and into the Indian Ocean. The actual identification of species is difficult because tuna, like many of the large fishes, seldom reach museums, where they can be effectively studied.

class	**Pisces**	
order	**Perciformes**	
family	**Scombridae**	
genus & species	***Thunnus alalunga*** *albacore*	
	T. albacares *yellowfin*	
	T. atlanticus *blackfin*	
	T. obesus *bigeye*	
	T. thynnus *bluefin*	
	T. tonggol *longtail*	

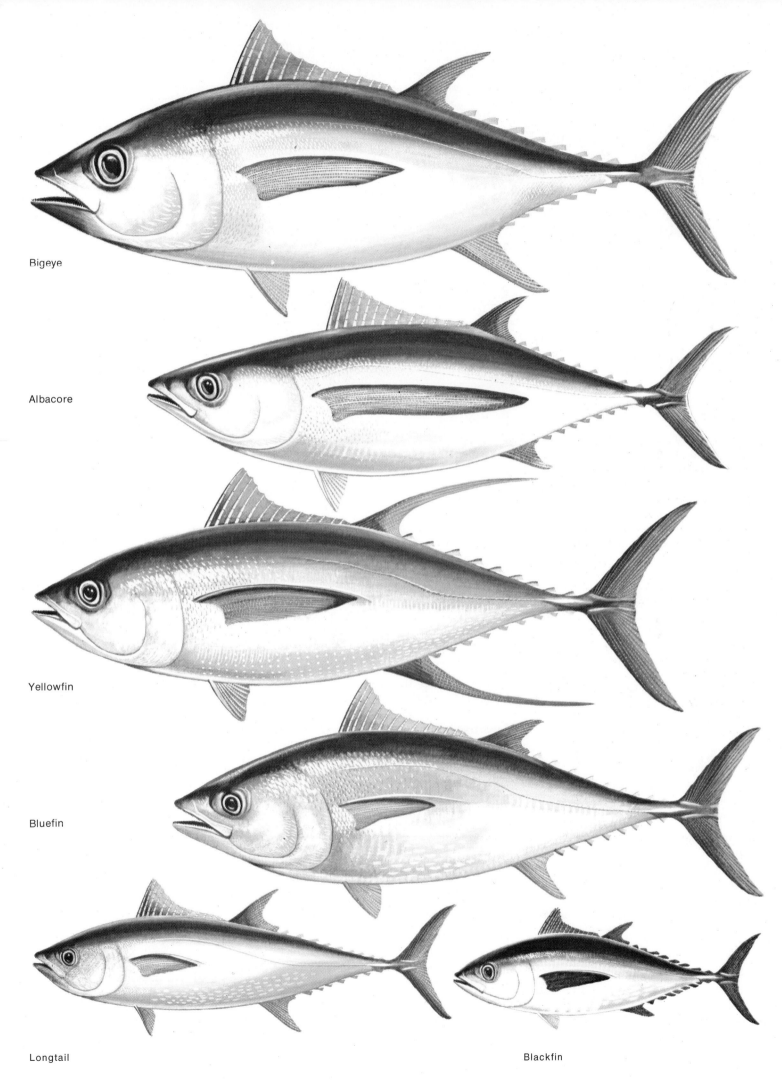

Bigeye

Albacore

Yellowfin

Bluefin

Longtail

Blackfin

243

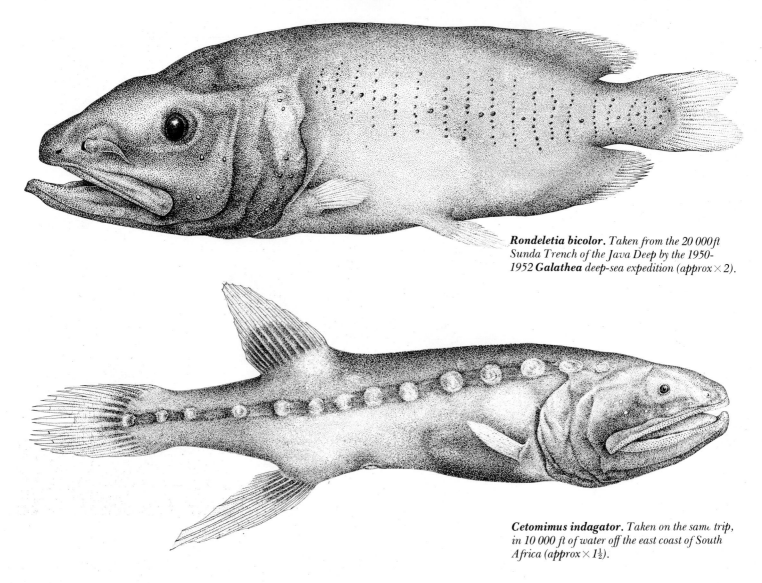

Rondeletia bicolor. *Taken from the 20 000 ft Sunda Trench of the Java Deep by the 1950-1952* **Galathea** *deep-sea expedition (approx × 2).*

Cetomimus indagator. *Taken on the same trip, in 10 000 ft of water off the east coast of South Africa (approx × 1½).*

Whalefish

Whalefishes are not named for their size. They are small deep-sea fishes, the largest being 6 in. long, and most of them are 4 in. or less. They resemble the leviathans of the sea in their shape, especially in the head and relatively huge mouth, which are also similar to the head and mouth of the large whalebone whales. Whalefishes are either blind or have degenerate eyes; when eyes are present they are only about $\frac{1}{25}$ in. diameter. Like so many deep-sea fishes whalefishes are black, but in contrast with other deep-sea fishes they have brilliant patches of orange and red around the mouth and fins. The body is plump but delicate and tapers in the rear third to a relatively small tail fin. The dorsal fin is fairly large and soft-rayed and so is the anal fin that lies opposite on the underside of the tail. Both these fins have luminous patches believed to be due to a secretion from glandular patches at the bases of the fins. There are no pelvic fins and the pectoral fins are small.

*The relationships of whalefishes are obscure. They were at one time placed in a separate order Cetunculi, then they were placed in a suborder near the squirrel-*fishes (page 207). Now they are placed in the order Cetomimiformes, near the salmon-like fishes, order Salmoniformes. The 30 species of whalefishes live at depths of 6–18 000 ft in tropical seas, from the Gulf of Mexico to West Africa and in the Indian Ocean to the western Pacific.*

Sensitive lateral line

Blind or poor sighted fishes in order to find their way about have a highly sensitive lateral line. Whalefishes have a lateral line made up of a relatively enormous hollow tube communicating with the exterior by a series of large pores, which suggests they have a highly developed distant touch and are able to detect the slightest vibrations in the water. They lack a swimbladder so the question arises as to how they maintain a position in mid-water without sinking. The answer probably lies in 'flotation appendages', typically cone-shaped, which lie between the pores of the lateral line.

Detect vibrations of prey

The stomach is highly distensible, so a whalefish is able to swallow fishes as large as itself. The position of the single dorsal and anal fins, set far back on the body, recalls the pikes, which capture their food by a quick dart forward. In view of what we know of the poor eyesight of whalefishes, we can only suppose they detect their prey from the vibrations the prey set up in the water. If a whalefish then darts at its prey its lateral line organs must detect the vibrations and give accurate direction-finding as well.

Going blind with age

Practically everything that is written about the way of life of deep-sea fishes must be based on speculation, on deduction from what can be studied of the structure in a dead specimen. Nothing is known of the life histories of whalefishes, yet there is reason to suppose that the larvae live in the surface layers of the ocean. This supposition springs from a detailed examination of the eyes of two species of whalefishes. In one, *Gyronomimus*, the tiny degenerate eye is covered by a small transparent area of pigmented skin. It has no remains of a lens, no iris and no eye muscles. The retina consists of a single instead of a double layer and little is left of the optic nerve. The other, *Ditropichthys storeri*, was previously thought to have lost its eye entirely but it was realized it has an optic nerve branching out to the region where the eye would normally lie. Close examination with the microscope has since shown that there are, in the adult of this species, the remains of a retina and lens, mere vestiges, as if the eye were slowly degenerating. All things considered it seems reasonable to suggest, therefore, that the larval whalefishes have eyes and live in the surface layers where light penetrates, and that the eyes degenerate as the fish grows up and sinks down to the depths of the ocean.

Dark depths

Daylight does not penetrate to more than 3 000 ft in the sea. The human eye can detect light down to 1 500 ft, and sensitive photographic plates lowered into the sea can register faint traces of light down to 3 000 ft. Beyond this all is in absolute darkness except for flashes and sparks from luminescent animals or from animals with light organs. In depths down to 3 000 ft fishes have more or less normal eyes. Below this depth they are blind or have degenerate eyes, or else they have extra large eyes. Those with large eyes are probably the fishes that come up into the surface layers at night. At other times they use their eyes either to recognize the signals from the light-organs of members of their own species or of the species they prey upon. All fishes so far examined that live permanently in the black depths of the ocean, and have degenerate eyes, have no light-organs. The luminous patches on the fins of whalefishes are not light-organs in the strict sense, and the only other fishes with luminescent glandular secretions of this kind are the deep-sea gulper eels. Their presence in whalefishes is something of a puzzle, and so are the red and orange patches on the fins and mouths of these nearly blind fishes.

class	**Pisces**
order	**Cetomimiformes**
family	**Cetomimidae**

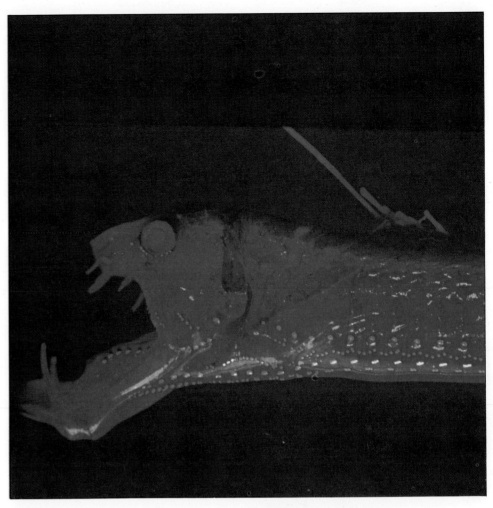

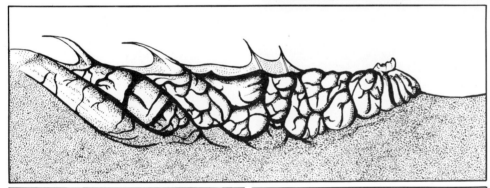

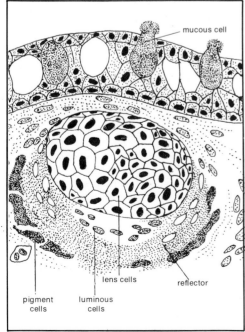

mucous cell

lens cells

reflector

pigment cells

luminous cells

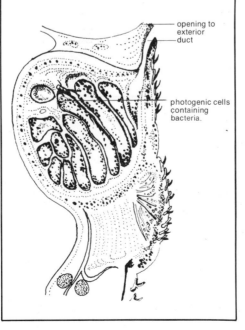

opening to exterior duct

photogenic cells containing bacteria.

Luminous organs

No sunlight penetrates the sea to more than 3 000 ft; only sparks and flashes from the luminous organs of fish interrupt the darkness. Whether these serve as sex- or species-recognition signals, shock predator deterrents or baits to attract smaller fishes is not known completely, but the fact remains that 95% of fishes caught from depths of 600 or more feet possess luminous organs.

There is an almost infinite variety of form, quantity and situation of these organs on the fishes' bodies, but most have them on the sides and belly — putting some whalefishes, with their dorsal glands, in the minority.

*Any classification of luminous fishes must have a primary division between those which glow directly and those which have glands containing symbiotic luminous bacteria. The spectacular viperfish **Chauliodus sloani** (above) produces its own light, through organs similar to the one illustrated at bottom left, which is from the toadfish **Porichthys notatus**. It is, in fact, a highly elaborated mucous gland.*

*In the other form of light production luminous bacteria are squeezed from a cell specialised to store them. This is illustrated at bottom right by the pre-anal gland of the rat-tail **Malacocephalus laevis** a deep sea fish with a large head.*

*Whether or not whalefishes have symbiotic bacteria is unknown, but their light is produced by the secretion of a luminous mucus into the cavernous tissue at the fin bases. The gland of **Cetomimus gillii** is illustrated at centre: mucus from the glands of this whalefish may spread over large portions of the head and body.*

245

Whale shark

The largest of all sharks, yet perfectly harmless, the whale shark grows to a length of 50 ft, although large specimens of 65 ft and even 70 ft have been recorded. Exact weights are not known but it has been estimated that a 70ft whale shark would weigh about 70 tons. It is readily distinguished from any other fish by its striking colour pattern, very dark grey or brownish with white underparts, the head and body covered in white or yellow spots which are smaller and closer together on the head. The spots on the back are separated by white vertical lines. The whale shark has a long cylindrical

fins are very wide and internally they are covered within the throat by closely-set rows of sieve-like gill-rakers, each 4—5 in. long, growing out from the gill-arches. They look like miniatures of the baleen plates of the whalebone whales and have the same function of straining off plankton and small fishes. This may be one reason for their common name of whale shark.

Whale sharks are found in all the tropical waters of the world. Occasionally individuals have been reported as far north as New York and as far south as Brazil and in Australian waters.

▽ *A 35ft whale shark gives a ride to small remoras clustered on the underside of its jaw.*
▷ *The same whale shark with an extra load.*

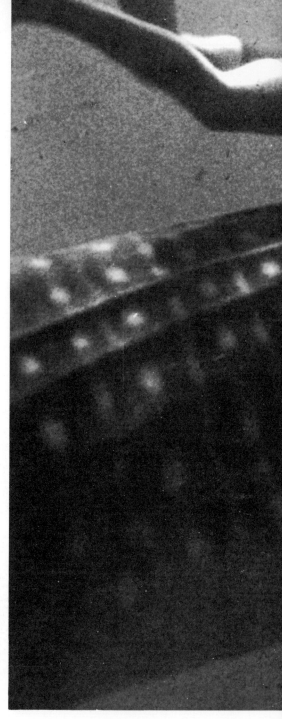

body with longitudinal ridges along its back, one down the middle and two or three on each side. Like all sharks it has a very tough skin, that of a 60ft whale shark being 6 in. thick. The powerful tail is keeled and has an almost symmetrical fin. The head is broad and blunt and the huge terminal mouth contains hundreds of very small teeth which form a sort of rasp. The gape of the mouth is so large, 5 ft across in even a medium-sized specimen, that it is said to be wide enough to allow two men to crouch inside. The eyes are small with small spiracles placed just behind them. The pectoral fins are large and sickle-shaped and there are two dorsal fins, the second one lying above the anal fin.

An unusual feature of the whale shark, which is shared by only one other shark, the basking shark (page 28), is the presence of gill-rakers. The external gill-openings above the base of the pectoral

Docile and sluggish

The whale shark lives near the surface of the open sea, swimming sluggishly at a leisurely pace of 2–3 knots. It is very docile and one underwater photographer has described how he swam holding onto a whale shark's tail without it taking any apparent notice. It is quite harmless, the only danger from it would be from its bumping against the side of a small boat and perhaps capsizing it. Whale sharks are known to rub themselves deliberately against boats, possibly to get rid of external parasites. This has been observed by the tunny fishermen of California and Thor Heyerdahl on the *Kon-Tiki* also describes one that rubbed itself on the raft, swimming around for about an hour.

Very few whale sharks have been caught and they are not often seen except perhaps when basking at the surface. When wounded by a harpoon the shark will dive straight down or streak away at speed, dragging the boat with it. It has very great powers of endurance and does not give in easily. It

is said that if harpooned the whale shark can contract the muscles of its back to prevent the entrance of another spear. While swimming the whale shark gives out a sort of croaking sound which is possibly a form of echo-location used in navigation.

Plankton feeder

The whale shark, like the basking shark, feeds on plankton and small schooling fishes such as sardines and anchovies, by opening its huge mouth. Water rushes out over the gills leaving the fish sticking to the inner walls of the throat and to the gill-rakers. Because of this type of diet one might expect the whale shark to be lacking in teeth. Its numerous small teeth are arranged in some 310 rows in each jaw, but only about 10 or 15 rows can function at any one time. Sometimes much larger articles, such as shoes, leather belts and even large poles, are taken into the mouth.

Stewart Springer of the US Fishery Vessel *Oregon* has described seeing 30 or 40 sharks standing vertically, head up and tail down,

during a spell of calm weather in the Gulf of Mexico. They were pumping up and down in the water feeding on small fishes and accompanied by small black-fin tuna that had stirred up the sea all around with their darting and leaping. 'The whale sharks looked like black oil drums slowly rising and sinking in a long swell; only there was no swell, just a choppy sea to a hundred yards in diameter, stirred up by the tuna.'

Breeding unknown
Nothing is known of the breeding habits of the whale shark but unlike the basking shark it is thought to be oviparous. In a Ceylon specimen 16 eggs were found.

No economic value
The whale shark has few natural enemies. Owing to its large size only the sea's largest carnivores would attempt to attack it and a blow from its powerful tail would probably be enough to drive even the largest enemy away. It is not hunted commercially—even its liver oil does not contain vitamin A.

Gentle giant
The whale shark could truly be called a giant that does not know its own strength, and this is illustrated more specially by three incidents that took place in the last half century. In 1919 one of these sharks became wedged in a bamboo stake-trap set in water 50 ft deep in the Gulf of Siam. It appeared to have made no attempt to break its way out. In the same area, in 1950, another one was captured and beached by the local fishermen, and while details of its capture are not to hand, it would seem that the giant fish offered little or no resistance. Prince Chumbhot, reporting this incident, says it was 'towed out to deep water and released by fishermen as a matter of luck, with a piece of red rag tied round its tail'.

In 1935 a 35ft whale shark was caught almost on the doorstep of New York City, having blundered into a huge fish trap on the southern shore of Long Island. Fishermen passed ropes around the fish's tail and pectoral fins, and hoisted it aboard a lighter with the aid of a petrol engine. Dr EW Gudger described the sight of the whale shark when landed, in the following words: 'The huge body, as large as a great oak in a primeval forest, stretched back and back to a vast tail within the spread of which a tall man could stand with room to spare. The whole thing was unbelievably enormous. For the first time in my life I beheld a whale shark in the flesh, the hugest thing that I ever saw come out of the sea. I looked at it head on, I walked around it, I climbed on its broad head, and I walked down its great back. It was the most enormous, the most colossal, the most gigantic sea animal I had or have ever seen.'

class	**Selachii**
order	**Pleurotremata**
family	**Rhincodontidae**
genus & species	***Rhincodon typus***

seaweed. Its heavy body is not built for speed like most other sharks that hunt their prey, but its perfect camouflage gives it an equally effective means of obtaining food. Wobbegongs do not need to keep moving, as do typical sharks, in order to breathe. They draw water into the gill chamber through the spiracles, in much the same way as skates and rays.

Wobbegongs are not aggressive and under normal circumstances are not considered very dangerous to humans. Nevertheless, cases have been known of their attacking people wading in shallow water. Their long pointed teeth are said to be perfectly capable of biting off a man's foot but they very seldom attack unless stepped on or provoked in some other way.

The wobbegong has little or no value as food but its colourful variegated skin makes it valuable in the shark-leather industry.

Snapping up fish

The wobbegong feeds on any fish or crustacean which comes within reach of its jaws as it lies hidden on the sea bottom. It has even been known to snap fish from the spears of underwater fishermen.

Little-known breeding

Very little is known about the breeding habits of the wobbegong. Like the nurse sharks it is ovoviviparous and produces large numbers of young at each birth.

A fisherman attacked

Despite the fact that the wobbegong is not considered a very dangerous shark an instance has been recorded in New South Wales, Australia, of one attacking a spear-fisherman who was fishing in Shellharbour in 1953. He was using a snorkel and wearing an underwater mask with a bright metal band. He was trying to spear a dying grouper and running out of shafts he surfaced and borrowed another gun. As he shot a spear into the fish it came out of its cave followed by a large, brown wobbegong shark with three or four tentacles hanging from its lip. The spear-fisherman swam quickly for about 15 yards but the shark rushed at him to attack. It is well known that bright objects and metal attract sharks and the wobbegong was obviously going for the mask with its bright metal band. It tore away the face piece and snapped off the snorkel. The rush of the attack was so great that both the shark and the fisherman were hurled from the water, enabling the fisherman to escape with injuries only under his chin and to his face and nose.

Wobbegong

Wobbegongs, or carpet sharks, are most unusual sharks. Unlike most sharks the wobbegong uses cunning instead of speed to obtain its food. Resting on the sea bottom it looks like a rock overgrown with seaweed, a perfect camouflage to enable it to pounce on unsuspecting victims. Most wobbegongs are small but some of the larger species grow to a length of 6—8 ft; the largest of all is **Orectolobus maculatus***, which ranges from Queensland to South and West Australia and Tasmania, reaching 10½ ft.*

The wobbegong is quite unlike the usual shark in shape. It has a stout, thick-set, flattened body with a very broad head and a blunt rounded snout ending in a wide straight mouth. Its teeth are slender and pointed, those in the centre of the mouth being the largest. Its eyes are small with folds of skin below them, and the wide, oblique slits of the spiracles are situated behind the eyes and lower down on the head. The last three or four external gill-clefts on each side open above the bases of the pectoral fins, which are broad

and sometimes rounded. The two dorsal fins are comparatively small. The anal fin either reaches to or is actually joined at its base to the lower lobe of the tailfin which is long and asymmetrical with a notch in the end. The skin is covered with small rough denticles. The colour of wobbegongs varies with different species and individuals but the ground colour is usually brown, yellowish or grey with distinctive mottled or striped markings of a lighter or darker colour. What distinguishes the wobbegong from any other shark is the fringe of fleshy lobes or flaps of skin around the sides of the head and mouth which resemble fronds of seaweed when the shark is at rest.

There are about five species of wobbegong which are known to live in the seas around China, Japan and east and south Australia.

Sluggish existence

The wobbegong lives an inactive life spending most of its time lying hidden on the sea bottom among the rocks and weeds, only coming to life when a fish passes by for it to snap up. It is further concealed by waving its flaps of skin so they look even more like

class	**Selachii**
order	**Pleurotremata**
family	**Orectolobidae**
genus & species	*Orectolobus maculatus others*

Zebra fish

There are several fishes with a common name that includes the word 'zebra'. The most noticeable of these is a small fresh-water fish of Bengal and eastern India. Less than 2 in. long, it is called the zebra fish or zebra danio and is a member of the large carp family. It is an extremely popular fish with aquarists.

It is a slim fish with the body only slightly compressed. The single dorsal fin and the anal fins are fairly large, and it has a relatively large tailfin and small pelvic and pectoral fins. There are two pairs of barbels. The back is brownish-olive, the belly yellowish-white and the flanks are Prussian blue with four golden stripes from the gill cover to the base of the tail. The dorsal fin is also blue with yellow at its base and a white tip. The anal fin is again blue-gold barred, and so is the tailfin. The effect of the stripes is to make the fish look even more streamlined than it is, and to give an impression of movement even when the fish is stationary.

Beauty in repetition

As so often happens with a fish of outstanding colour, subsequently popular with aquarists, there is little that is zoologically striking in zebra fishes. They swim among water plants or in schools—it is when they are all aligned, swimming in formation, evenly spaced, and all travelling in the same direction that they most catch the eye. Almost certainly their attraction owes much to the repetition of their stripes—termed the 'beauty in repetition' by Dr Dilwyn John in 1947. In 1935, William T Innes came very near to saying this in his comprehensive book *Exotic Aquarium Fishes* when he described it as a fish 'to show to advantage moving in schools, it scarcely has an equal, for its beautiful horizontal stripes, repeated in each fish, give a streamline effect that might well be the envy of our best automobile designers'.

Special precautions

Zebra fishes are carnivorous, feeding on any small animals they can swallow, which usually means small insect larvae, crustaceans and worms. After their colour, their strongly carnivorous tendencies provide one of their more interesting features. They are egg-eaters, and those who breed zebra fish in aquaria need to take special precautions to achieve success.

There is little difference between the sexes except that the female, especially just before spawning, is more plump than the male, and her stripes are more silver and yellow than the golden stripes of the male. In the pre-spawning behaviour the male leads the female in among the water plants and the two take up position side by side, she to shed her ova, he to shed his milt over them to fertilise them. As the eggs slowly sink there is a tendency for the two to snap up the eggs. The first precaution for the aquarist is therefore to provide a breeding aquarium with water so shallow that the fish have no chance to catch the eggs before they sink to safety in the spaces between the gravel on the bottom. The correct size of gravel pebbles must be used or the adults may become trapped between them. Marbles have been used, or else some sort of trap. An early trap used was a series of slender glass rods held together at the ends with soft wire and raised just off the bottom of the aquarium. This was later superseded by fine metal mesh or nylon.

Each female lays about 200 eggs which hatch in two days. The larvae are at first fairly helpless and inactive, but two days later they can swim and start to feed on microscopic plankton animals. They begin to breed at a year old. At two years they are old-aged, and a zebra fish of three or more years old is an extreme rarity.

Question of stripes

The name 'zebra' is from an Amharic or Ethiopian word and first gained currency in Europe in 1600. By the early years of the 19th century its use had been extended not only to cover all manner of striped animals but also materials showing stripes, and especially to striped shawls and scarves. In the world of fishes there is the zebra shark of the Indian Ocean, with black or brown bars on the body, more like the stripes of a tiger. So we have the anomaly of the common name being zebra shark and the scientific name *Stegostoma tigrinum*. In the extreme south of South America is the zebra salmon *Haplochiton zebra*. In pisciculture there is a hybrid of the trout *Salmo trutta* and the American brook trout *Salvelinus fontinalis*, which is called the zebra hybrid. A foot-long marine fish of the Indo-Pacific *Therapon jarbua* is sometimes called the zebra or tiger fish. It is, however, among the aquarium fishes that the name is most used —the striped or zebra barb *Barbus fasciatus* of Malaya and the East Indies is an example. The common killifish *Fundulus heteroclitus*, of North America, is also called the zebra killie, while the zebra cichlid *Cichlasoma nigrofasciatum* is also—and more appropriately—called the convict fish. Some of these fish have horizontal stripes and others vertical, and there has been some disagreement over which are more correctly termed 'zebra'. However, since a glance at a photograph of a zebra shows that the stripes run in different directions on the different areas of the body, there seems no reason why the name should not be applied to all.

class	**Pisces**
order	**Atheriniformes**
family	**Cyprinodontidae**
genus & species	***Brachydanio rerio***

▽ *On the right lines: the popular zebra fish proves that parallel stripes never meet.*

Acknowledgements

This book is adapted from 'Purnell's Encyclopedia of Animal Life', published in the United States under the title of 'International Wild Life'.
Photo sources:

A.F.A. (A.C. Wheeler, Geoffrey Kinns); Heather Angel; Toni Angermayer; R. Apfelbach; Aquatics; Ardea (Valerie Wright); Alan T. Band; Barnaby's Picture Library; Bavaria (A. Niestle, A. Sycholt); A. Baverstock; Carlo Bevilacqua; R. Boardman; Alice Brown; Camera Press; J. Allan Cash; Centre de Documentation du CNRS; Marcel Cognac; Bruce Coleman Ltd (Allan Power, Jane Burton); Dolly Connelly; Ben Cropp; Gerald Cubitt; Stephen Dalton; Treat Davidson; W.T. Davidson; T. Dennett; Colin Doeg; Barry Driscoll; Heinz Eder; Douglas Faulkner; Harry & Claudy Frauca; G.S. Giacomelli; Peter J. Green; Hilmar Hansen; Lilo Hess; Stan Hess & B.A. Woodling; Thor Heyerdhal; Peter Hill; Edmund Hobson; E.S. Hobson; Chris Howell-Jones; Hulton Picture Library; Jacana (J.M. Bossot, H. Noailles, P. Summ, J.P. Vanin, J. Vasserot, Albert Visage); Michael Johns; Denys A. Kempson; Keystone; G. Kinns; D.B. Lewis; E. Lindsey; T.H. Lineaweaver; H.W. Lissmann; Wolfgang Lummer; Kendall McDonald; Malcolm McGregor; Mansell Collection; Aldo Margiocco; Marineland, Florida, USA; P. Morris; G. Mundey; New York Zoological Society; NHPA (Anthony Bannister, M. Clayton); Ókapia (A. Root); Klaus Paysan; Barry Pengilley; Laurence Perkins; Photo Library Inc. (Roy Pinney); Photo Res (Jane Burton, Leslie Jackman, Russ Kinne, Graham Pizzey); Photographic Library of Australia; Popperfoto; Galatheo Report; Royal Norwegian Embassy; Philippa Scott; Seaphot (John Lythgoe); Fritz Siedel; Ludwig Sillner; Ol Sprungman; Helmut Stellrecht; William M. Stephens; Deryk Story; John Tashjian; Ron Taylor; Ronald Thompson; Time Life Inc.; Birgit Webb; D.P. Wilson; Gene Wolfsheimer; John Norris Wood; B.A. Woodling & Stan Hess; F.H. Wylie; Zoological Society, London.

The authors and publishers would like to thank Alwyne Wheeler for reading the text and giving valuable criticism.